D1126218

Contract Law Fundamentals

Adam Epstein
Central Michigan University

Upper Saddle River, New Jersey
Columbus, Ohio

Library of Congress Cataloging in Publication Data

Epstein, Adam.
Contract law fundamentals / Adam Epstein.
p. cm.
ISBN-13: 978-0-13-114748-5
ISBN-10: 0-13-114748-X
1. Contracts—United States—Outlines, syllabi, etc. 2. Contracts—United States—Cases. I. Title.
KF801.Z9E67 2008
346.7302—dc22

2007029566

Editor in Chief: Vernon R. Anthony
Senior Acquisitions Editor: Gary Bauer
Associate Editor: Linda Cupp
Editorial Assistant: Kathleen Rowland
Production Editor: Louise N. Sette
Production Supervision: Katie Boilard, Pine Tree Composition, Inc.
Design Coordinator: Diane Ernsberger
Cover Designer: Ali Mohrman
Production Manager: Deidra M. Schwartz
Director of Marketing: David Gesell
Marketing Manager: Jimmy Stephens
Marketing Coordinator: Alicia Dysert

This book was set in Meridien by Laserwords Private Limited, Chennai. It was printed and bound by Edwards Brothers, Inc. The cover was printed by Phoenix Color Corp.

Pearson Education Ltd.
Pearson Education Singapore Pte. Ltd.
Pearson Education Canada, Ltd.
Pearson Education—Japan
Pearson Education Australia Pty. Limited
Pearson Education North Asia Ltd.
Pearson Educación de Mexico, S.A. de C.V.
Pearson Education Malaysia Pte. Ltd.

10 9 8 7 6 5 4 3 2 1
ISBN-10: 0-13-114748-X
ISBN-13: 978-0-13-114748-5

This book is dedicated to my
grandmother, Goldie.

CONTENTS

Cases

PREFACE

This production is both a textbook and a case book written to reflect the basics of the black-letter law of contracts. It is designed for the undergraduate paralegal, legal studies and the business law student. It may be used as a stand-alone text or utilized as a supplemental resource when studying contract law generally. The book is intended to be used for a one semester (or quarter) course, and the approach is no frills and straightforward. It is not meant to be an academic authority or reference on the study of contract law, but it is meant to break down this very broad category of the law into its most basic foundation. Internet references are provided as a springboard and for guidance. Cases (edited) are provided to further enhance the study of that chapter's focus. Some chapters are much longer than others by design. Slightly greater emphasis is given to the first section of the book on common law contracts as opposed to the second section involving the UCC. In the end the instructor carries the burden of explaining how contract law relates to other areas of the law and the study of legal principles as the opportunities present themselves throughout the course.

Contract law, unlike other areas of the law, is one of often distinct categorization and classification. Contract law is mostly a creature of state law, and it is as consistent and predictable as any other area of the law. Courts often remind litigants that at most the role of the courts is to put the parties in the position they would have been in had the parties performed as mutually agreed or promised. However, the study of contract law cannot be appreciated in a vacuum. It is important to understand that contract law often overlaps with tort law (personal injury) in addition to many other separate areas of legal theory and practice. For example, these categories often overlap when there is a fraudulent sale of goods or services or when a defective product causes an injury.

For instructors, this text provides a solid, functional outline for the presentation of the study of contract law. PowerPoint™ slides are offered to enhance the learning experience and are designed to be used in conjunction with the book. Chapter objectives are offered, as are discussion and review questions. Key terms are bolded and provided for pedagogical enhancement.

Cases were edited but were intended to be as complete as plausible to help both instructor and student gain the most broad perspective on the case and to allow students to read (and possibly brief) cases rather than just offer highly truncated excerpts. This is especially helpful for students who might desire to pursue the study of law at a higher level. Some of the cases are considered classic contract law cases in the study of law while others are quite contemporary. Finally, Internet related exercises and contract forms might serve as a useful reference for class discussion, comparison, and analysis.

For students, this book is divided into major sections: one on common law contracts, and the other on Article 2 of the Uniform Commercial Code (UCC). A third section contains a short chapter on contract drafting that offers some practical considerations when drafting contracts. This must not be considered legal advice. Regardless of the level of this course, understanding common law contracts and the UCC should provide anyone with the basic tools to use and appreciate the role of contracts in business and in law.

I believe that after reading this text students and instructors will feel more comfortable conversing in the language of contracts and appreciating the legal issues surrounding them as well. In the end, I hope that students and instructors will appreciate how contracts (and their enforcement) are the mesh that binds our society and provides stability in personal and business relationships.

Acknowledgments

Many individuals assisted in the production of this textbook. I would like to thank my family, the faculty and administrative staff in the Finance and Law Department at Central Michigan University, Ryan Runella at LexisNexis, and all the students, clients, and lawyers throughout the years who have provided their perspectives on contract-related issues. I want to thank all my friends, and I would also like to thank all the members of Prentice Hall's team for their patience during the numerous and considerable revisions.

I would also like to acknowledge the reviewers of this book: Heidi Getchell-Bastien, Northern Essex Community College and Middlesex Community College; Preston Mighdoll, Kaplan University; Kent D. Kauffman, Ivy Tech Community College—Northeast; and S. Joseph Schramm, Everest Institute.

Part I

Common Law Contracts

Chapter 1

The Basics

After reading this chapter you will be able to:

1. Define the term contract.
2. Explain the contract formula and its elements.
3. Explain why the phrases "freedom of contract" and "sanctity of a contract" are important in the study of contract law.
4. Describe what the phrase "meeting of the minds" means.
5. Differentiate between a bilateral and a unilateral contract.
6. Discuss the basic difference between common law contracts and those which fall under the Uniform Commercial Code (UCC).
7. Explain the objective theory of contracts.
8. Discuss the important differences between oral and written contracts.
9. Describe what a personal services contract is and why it is special in contract law.
10. Discuss the differences between express and implied contracts.

Key Terms

Benefit of the bargain
Bilateral contract
Black-letter law
Breach
Collective bargaining agreement
Common law
Contract
De Havilland law
Detrimental reliance
Executed
Executory
Express contract
Formal
Four corners rule
Freedom of contract
Implied contract
Implied-in-fact
Implied-in-law
Informal
Meeting of the minds
Negligence
Nudum pactum
Objective theory of contracts
Oral contracts
Pacta sunt servanda
Parol evidence rule
Personal service contracts
Plain meaning rule
Promissory estoppel
Quantum meruit
Quasi contract
Rider
Statute of Frauds
Uniform Commercial Code
Unilateral contract
Unjust enrichment
Valid
Void
Voidable
Waiver

The purpose of this chapter is to explore the basics related to the study of contract law. Before advancing further in this text, one should master these concepts. Understanding the language of contract law and appreciating the fundamental principles are essential. Contracts permeate our lives and in one way or another are involved in all business transactions. Car loans, student loans, and mortgages are common examples of contractual relationships that involve promising to pay back a certain sum of money. Landlords and tenants usually reduce their relationship to a contract called a lease. The relationship between an employer and employee is an example of a contract even though that is not always reduced to writing, and the list goes on.[1] It is worthwhile to note that contract law is divided into various classifications and categories.

The study of contracts is special and unique in the law. The study of contract law also demonstrates one of the most consistent areas of law. Unlike constitutional, tort, or criminal law, contract law principles have changed relatively little over time. If anything, contract law has merely evolved in response to changes in technology more than anything else. Contract law provides stability and predictability in business and personal relationships in which promises are made and able to be enforced.

Often characterized as a study of promises and agreements, the study of contract law differentiates between enforceable promises and those which cannot be enforced. However, the distinguishing factor is unclear. One aspect of contract law that is clear is that courts or arbitrators will have the final say when it comes to contract interpretation and enforcement. One must also recognize that contract law applies to legal obligations, not necessarily moral obligations. Additionally, there are times when courts are asked to interpret and apply contract law principles to curious situations. In this regard, contract law is about what is "fair" or "equitable." This is remarkably different than the criminal law in which the focus is on what is "right" or "just." In many situations, tort law and its consideration of "fault" might be joined as a separate legal claim in a lawsuit though consideration of fault, *per se*, is not normally utilized in the study of contract law or applied by courts in this context alone.

CONTRACT

While definitions and descriptions of the definition of contract may vary, ultimately a **contract** represents a legally binding agreement between two or more persons (or entities such as a business). The parties to a contract must either act or refrain from acting, depending on the circumstances of the agreement. A contract may be represented by the following "formula":

$$K = O + A + C + (\text{Legality} + \text{Capacity})$$

Though not a formula in the mathematical or scientific sense, this formula represents the five required elements of a contractual agreement. A contract (K) represents an offer (O) plus an acceptance of the offer (A) plus consideration (C) and, too, the contract must be for a legal purpose (Legality) and the parties to the agreement must have the legal capacity (Capacity) to enter into that contract in the first place. Each of these contractual elements are discussed in further detail in the subsequent chapters.

Freedom of Contract

One of the significant aspects of contract law (and the study of contract law) is that two or more persons may agree on almost anything and can pursue legal action if that agreement is not met. The concept that parties can agree to almost anything is the essence of the phrase **freedom of contract**.

[1]There is considerable debate as to whether employment handbooks are considered contracts when an employee is classified as an at-will employee, or, for example, an employee is given the handbook after he or she has already worked at the employer's place of business and is then given the choice to take-it-or-leave-it. The legality and effect of employment handbooks are a matter of individual state law.

Sanctity of a Contract

At the same time, one of the most important roles that the courts play is to uphold the sanctity of that contractual agreement. This concept is represented by the Latin phrase, ***Pacta sunt servanda***. Translated literally, this means "agreements must be served." In other words, contracts are sacred (so to speak), and courts generally will uphold them. Courts are not in the business of undoing contracts, however. In fact, the judicial branch of government plays a major role in the enforcement mechanism of contract law, and the judicial system provides stability and certainty to contracts by providing interpretation and enforcement mechanisms (such as an injunction) when necessary. Without the courts, parties to a contract could make empty promises (***nudum pactum***) without fear of any enforcement or penalty whatsoever. This could stymie commerce especially when the sale of goods is involved.

MEETING OF THE MINDS

Courts often must ascertain what the parties to the contract actually agreed to or, in the worst case scenario, whether there was a **meeting of the minds** at all, especially if the terms of a contract are somewhat ambiguous.[2] Sometimes courts are forced to deal with these ambiguities and are called upon to determine the original intent of the parties. Still, when the parties to a contract are unclear, are not in writing, or the parties are not totally truthful during litigation, courts (or in some cases, juries) may have to be creative to determine what the remedy for a breach should be or how to resolve this contractual dispute. This proactive method by judges when it comes to contract enforcement and interpretation is vital when the parties have to resort to a court to decide contractual issues.

BILATERAL AND UNILATERAL CONTRACTS

Simply put, a promise for a return promise represents a **bilateral contract.** This is an exchange of promises. A promise for an act (in return), however, represents a **unilateral contract.** For example, if I promise to pay you $100 if you promise to walk across the bridge that represents a bilateral contract because it represents a promise for a promise. My obligation to pay you would begin once you agree (i.e., promise) that you will cross the bridge. On the other hand, if I promise to pay you $100 if you walk across the bridge, then this represents a unilateral contract because my duty to pay does not begin until you actually cross the bridge. In other words, you accept by performance. If one does not perform the return promise of a bilateral contract, then one may possibly sue for a breach of contract.

[2]The phrase "meeting of the minds" is often referred to as "mutual assent." A classic example is the case involving two ships having the same name—*Peerless*. In this English case, a contract to buy cotton scheduled to arrive from Bombay, India, on the ship *Peerless* appeared plain on its face. The evidence showed, however, that there were actually two ships by the same name in the same harbor. Thus, it became unclear which ship the goods would arrive on and extrinsic evidence was appropriate to aid in the resolution of the ambiguity. *Raffles v. Wichelhaus*, 2 H. & C. 906, 159 Eng. Rep. 375 (Ex. 1864). Ultimately, the court held that there was no meeting of the minds.

CONTRACT DRAFTING

An important aspect of drafting a contract is that there is never a sole perfect way to create one.[3] Parties to a contract can be as simple or as creative as they want to be in its form. At the end of this text, keys to successful contract drafting are offered. Good contract drafters know that if there is a future disagreement over their respective promises, the contract can and should be able to deal with the issue. When drafting contracts, one should consider the three "P's" of contract drafting: predict, provide, and protect.[4] *Predict* what might happen during the course of the contractual arrangement. *Provide* for it in the contract. *Protect* yourself in the event of a breach. The best contract drafters tend to be pessimists (possibly another "P") rather than optimists because it is often wiser at the beginning to consider what could go wrong in a contractual relationship (and provide for it in the contract) than remain naïve that the best of intentions will never lead to a contractual breach or interpretation or other conflict. As long as one is not giving legal advice (unless he or she is a licensed attorney), almost anyone can draft a contract. Giving legal advice without a license would constitute the unauthorized practice of law (UPL).[5]

OBJECTIVE THEORY OF CONTRACTS

When determining either the existence of a contract or its interpretation, courts use a legal principle referred to as the **objective theory of contracts.** This theory is quite rigid in the sense that courts do not favor trying to consider what the parties to a contract were actually thinking when they entered into the agreement. Otherwise, this theory would be referred to as the subjective theory of contracts. Courts consider what the reasonable person would have thought under the same or similar circumstances. This standard is similar to the reasonable person standard often studied in tort (personal injury) law involving negligence. The general rule is that if the parties to an agreement wanted a peculiar or special meaning to a term, then they should have defined that term somewhere in the agreement.

COMMON LAW v. UCC (UNIFORM COMMERCIAL CODE)

The study of contract law is generally divided into two major parts: **common law** contracts and the **Uniform Commercial Code.** The common law includes all the judge-made legal principles involving contract interpretation. American legal principles developed from the English system which can be traced back to ancient Roman law. On the other hand, the UCC is a relatively recent statutory

[3]Discussed further in Chapter 16.

[4]*See* Scott J. Burnham, Drafting Contracts (the Michie Company, 1987).

[5]UPL is one of many examples of consumer protection statutes at both state and federal levels. Consumer protection is a theme that also flows throughout the study of contract law and is discussed in greater detail in the later chapters of this text.

phenomenon which was developed to address the increased and fast-paced buying and selling of goods and their delivery throughout the United States. The UCC is a model act that all states have now adopted in its entirety or to some degree particularly with regard to the sale or lease of goods. The textbook discusses the UCC in more detail in the second half of the book.

RESTATEMENT OF CONTRACTS

The American Law Institute (ALI) composed the Restatement of Contracts in 1932 and revised it with the Restatement (Second) of Contracts in 1979. While not law *per se*, students of contract law should be aware that the Restatement (Second) of Contracts represents what is also known as the **black-letter law**. Many of the principles discussed in this text represent black-letter law. The ALI is a private organization founded in 1923 to improve the law by examining and bringing together the common law of all the states. It has also promulgated Restatements of the law on Property, Torts, and Agency, for example.

VALID, VOID, VOIDABLE

All contracts are described as being valid, void, or voidable. A **valid** contract is an agreement that is legal binding and enforceable. A **void** contract is one that is not binding and not enforceable. This may be due to an agreement made for an illegal purpose. A **voidable** contract is binding and enforceable, but one of the parties to the agreement may exercise an option to reject the agreement later upon the occurrence of a particular condition.

EXPRESS OR IMPLIED

An **express contract** is the most common type of contract because the parties have explicit (clear) terms. This can be written or oral. **Implied contracts**, however, focus on the words or conduct between the parties as opposed to whether there was a clear intent to form a contract. Courts are usually asked to imply a contract to prevent **unjust enrichment** by a party to another "as if" there was a contract, when in fact there really was not an express agreement between the parties at all. Implied contracts are considered in two ways: implied-in-fact and implied-in-law (sometimes referred to as *Quasi* contracts).

IMPLIED CONTRACTS

Regardless of their characterization, an implied contract is one in which a court decides that the parties acted if they had one. An **implied-in-fact** contract is where the agreement of the parties is indicated by their conduct rather than an explicit agreement. This can happen in several ways as exemplified by the following examples:

1. Plaintiff (P) furnished a service or property, thereby providing a benefit to the defendant (D).

2. P *expected* to be paid for the service or property, *and* D knew or should have known that payment was expected.
3. D had a chance to reject the services or property that was received and did not, and therefore would be unjustly enriched if the D did not pay something.

An **implied-in-law** contract is one in which an obligation is imposed by a court to avoid injustice or to prevent unjust enrichment. An implied contract is not one that exists, *per se*, but courts essentially impose a contract on the parties themselves. No promise was actually made in an implied-in-law contract. The doctrine of **promissory estoppel** is used by courts in extraordinary cases only and to avoid unjust results where an injustice can be avoided only by enforcing the promise. Under the doctrine of promissory estoppel (sometimes referred to as **detrimental reliance**), a party who has reasonably relied to his or her detriment based upon another's promise may still be able to enforce that promise (or part of the promise) to the extent of the reliance (e.g., out-of-pocket costs incurred in order to start a project). The plaintiff must demonstrate that the promise was made, however, and this can be extremely difficult.

QUANTUM MERUIT/QUASI CONTRACT

Even if successful, a plaintiff may still not recover the full **benefit of the bargain** of an alleged contract, but it still might be worth pursuing a claim under this legal doctrine if there are witnesses and other types of proof of the existence of an agreement. Courts often use the principle of ***quantum meruit*** ("as much as he or she deserved") to determine how much a plaintiff should receive in an implied or ***quasi* contract** situation. This usually means the reasonable value of the services provided and the market value of the materials furnished.

For example, let's say a local lawn mower man made a mistake by mowing your lawn instead of your next-door neighbor's yard. You noticed your lawn was being mowed, but you did not object. A court might later opine that you had to pay the lawn mower man some reasonable amount of compensation for the error since you noticed the mistake yet took no action to notify the lawn mower man of the error. On the other hand, a different court might hold that you had no legal duty to tell the lawn mower man of this error in the first place and that you should receive the benefit of the error as a matter of public policy.[6] This would send a message, then, to the lawn mower man that customers should not be "punished" for errors made by those in business. Of course, a court might rule in your favor, especially if you were not home and had no opportunity to object at all. Still this does not mean that individuals have to always pay for benefits that were "thrust" upon them. Courts must look at the facts and circumstances surrounding each case on a case-by-case basis.

[6]The term "public policy" is one of the more ambiguous phrases found in contract law. While this phrase cannot be precisely defined, it generally means that courts may invalidate (or enforce) a contract in order to protect consumers or to send a moral message to the community-at-large.

In another example, suppose you graduate from college and are offered a job several hundred miles away in another state. You accept the job, set up an apartment there, and the day before you start the job you are told, "Well, we think the world of you, but we cannot let you start here because our company has fallen on hard times." Certainly, the doctrine of promissory estoppel would be relevant in this instance. So, there are four legal theories by which a plaintiff may allege that there should be a recovery of damages in the event there is a contractual dispute whether the dispute is the result of an oral or written disagreement or breach:

1. Express contract.
2. Implied contract.
3. *Quasi* contract (P gives something to D and P expects something in return).
4. Promissory estoppel (D makes a promise to P and P relied to his/her detriment on the promise).

ORAL CONTRACTS

There are certain types of contracts that must be in writing in order to be enforced by a court. This principle is referred to as the **Statute of Frauds** and is discussed further in Chapter 6. On the other hand, numerous contracts emanate from business agreements involving **oral contracts**. Some persons take great pride in proclaiming that the rigid rules of written contracts do not apply to them. However, today it is quite common (and almost expected) that individuals reduce their agreement to writing. Though oral contracts often prove effective in close-knit industries or local communities, when the contractual relationship turns sour (e.g., one party breaches their promise to another), most wish that the contract had been reduced to writing from the beginning so as to establish a better position in litigation or for a settlement to avoid a lawsuit.

PLAIN MEANING RULE

As a general rule, courts do not get involved in the interpretation of words that have ordinary and unambiguous meanings. Courts generally hold that if a word had a special meaning in that contract, then the parties are better served if they had defined that in the contract itself. Most jurisdictions in the United States still utilize this **plain meaning rule** principle to some degree. Similarly courts try to not look beyond the pages of a written contract unless absolutely necessary. Courts often employ the **parol evidence rule** (Chapter 6) which excludes explanations as to what a word meant if it contradicts the plain, ordinary meaning of a word in a written contract. Looking beyond the four corners of a contract is not really the place for courts, and good contract drafters can utilize their skills by adding a merger clause that attempts to limit the consideration of extrinsic evidence of what the parties meant by their contract or by their specific words.[7] Also, this is referred to as the **four corners rule**.

[7]Specific contract drafting clauses including a merger clause are addressed in the final chapter of this text.

EXECUTORY v. EXECUTED

Executory contracts are not yet fully completed. In other words one or more of the parties still has an obligation remaining as part of the original agreement. **Executed** contracts (or "fully executed contracts") are completed ones, or ones in which are substantially completed. In some industries, the term "executed" might mean simply the signed contract (by both parties) even if performance has yet to begin at all.

FORMAL AND INFORMAL CONTRACTS

There are few **formal** contracts anymore today. Most contracts are, then, considered informal in the sense that their existence is based more on substance than formalities. **Informal** contracts are sometimes referred to as simple contracts; formal contracts required a special process or even a seal (maybe a notary public). In a rare instance, students might see the abbreviation *L.S.* at the end of a contract or other legal document today. This abbreviation actually stands for *locus sigilli* which means the "place for the seal" in Latin. Such formalities today have virtually been abolished by the states other than (possibly) in the formal process of buying or selling real estate.[8]

COLLECTIVE BARGAINING AGREEMENTS

A **collective bargaining agreement** (CBA) is a contract that spells out the terms of employment between a labor union and management (i.e., the employer). This negotiated contract concerns wages, hours of work, and other terms and conditions of employment. This also includes provisions for grievance and alternative forms of dispute resolution (arbitration or mediation or both) if there are disputes over the contract. Collective bargaining agreements are often the by-product of serious negotiations in almost all industries.[9] Examples of labor unions and organizations include the United Auto Workers (UAW) and the various professional sports players' associations (unions) such as the National Football League Players Association (NFLPA).

PERSONAL SERVICES CONTRACTS

Contracts to secure special or peculiar human talent are usually referred to as **personal service contracts**. A personal service contract is one in which the parties (or the party to perform) must possess special knowledge or a unique skill such that no performance except that of the contracting party could meet the obligations of the contract. A celebrity actor, musician, band, author, and so on are examples

[8]UCC §2-203 has abolished contracts under seal.

[9]http://www.detroitnews.com/apps/pbcs.dll/article?AID=/20061129/AUTO01/611290416.

of personal service contracts. California views personal services contracts differently than other states. California's Labor Code §2855 (also known as the Seven Year Statute) limits the amount of time anyone can be held to a contract for personal services to a maximum of seven years. This seven-year limitation law is known as the **De Havilland law**.[10] One cannot force someone to perform a personal services contract as this would be similar to a form of slavery. Additionally, personal services contracts cannot be assigned by the talent or uniquely skilled individual(s) to another as a matter of contract law since the very nature of the contract is based upon the uniqueness of their skills.

CONTRACT RIDERS

Sometimes called **riders**, technical riders, or merely an addendum to a contract, contract riders include the unique and particular aspects of a deal. Riders are found in all industries and especially common in the insurance industry. Some of the more interesting contract riders are found in the entertainment industry in which comedians, artists, musicians, and others have quite interesting demands as part of their contract to appear and peform. This includes food, beverage, and lodging accommodations; other individual requests by talent; stage specifications; light and sound requirements; electrical power requirements; set designers; and so on. Some riders can include very thorough (yet often ridiculous) requests though they are usually legal. One of the more famous (or infamous) examples of a contract rider's demands included the rock band Van Halen's stipulation that they be provided a bowl of M&Ms backstage, but that the bowl must not contain any brown M&Ms.[11]

WAIVERS

A **waiver** is the voluntary relinquishment of a privilege or a right. Good contract drafters often include waivers in any express agreement. Waivers (or release of liability) is a clause in a contract or its own document designed to protect a party from liability for personal injuries that may occur to others. Waivers may be used as protection from liability for accidents, activities carrying certain inherent risks, and even ordinary **negligence** or other unintentional conduct in certain circumstances. Waivers are sometimes referred to as disclaimers, releases, or exculpatory clauses as well.

TERMINATION OF A CONTRACT

A contract usually ends where each party to the contract simply does what they promised to do. Another way to terminate an agreement is by contract, where each party agrees to end the contract prematurely. Maybe the parties just did not

[10]This was the result of the favorable ruling handed down by California courts in Olivia de Havilland's lawsuit against the Warner Bros. Studios in 1945 in which her studio contract could not be extended beyond seven years. Still recording artists are now the only class of personal service workers in California who cannot take advantage of Labor Code §2855.

[11]*See* http://www.snopes2.com/music/artists/vanhalen.htm.

want to work with each other anymore. In the event one party **breaches** (i.e., breaks) the contract or unilaterally cancels the contract, litigation or other form of dispute resolution such as mediation or arbitration may be necessary to enforce the agreement. In many employment contracts today, termination clauses provide interesting challenges for contract drafters depending upon whether they wish to terminate an agreement with or without cause.

CONTRACT DEFENSES

Contract defenses are means in which a party to a contract can attempt to demonstrate to a court that the contract should end, the party should be excused from performance, or the agreement should be considered invalid. The strongest defense to any contract is that one party actually lied to the other. This defense is referred to as fraud, fraudulent inducement, or misrepresentation. It may be difficult to prove, but if provable it would likely result in the undoing of a contract.[12] Though courts generally mandate that parties to an agreement should read the terms of the agreement before signing the contract, failure to read the agreement would not normally prevent someone from still utilizing the defense of fraud. This is consistent with consumer protection statutes discussed later in the text. Other defenses to a contract include duress and bilateral (mutual) mistake.[13]

CHAPTER SUMMARY

This chapter explored the basic terms and fundamental principles of the study of contract law. Whether understanding the difference between common law contracts and the UCC, or the difference between express and implied contracts, it is very important to appreciate the different terminology used to characterize and classify contracts. Contracts may be oral or written. In business, the formation of a contract often represents a positive agreement between two or more parties and usually a buyer or seller. However, when something goes wrong or when someone breaks (breaches) a contract, the first thing most people will do is run to see what the contract says. This is important as courts are often called into play as referees to enforce these agreements. Contracts come in all shapes and sizes: from waivers to collective bargaining agreements to contract riders to contracts for an individual's unique talents, abilities, and skills (personal services). In the end, contracts are supposed to represent the agreed upon relationship between parties, and courts must decide how to enforce these agreements if the parties cannot otherwise come to a compromise.

[12]*See* Park 100 Investors, Inc. v. Kartes, 650 N.E.2d 347 (Ind. Ct. App. 1995) (where one employs misrepresentation to induce a party's obligation under a contract, one cannot bind that party to the terms of the agreement).

[13]Contract defenses are discussed further in Chapter 5.

Discussion and Review Questions

1. What is the "plain meaning rule" and why is it important?
2. Why do courts analyze contracts using the objective theory of contract interpretation rather than a subjective theory?
3. What is the difference between a bilateral and unilateral contract, and why is this difference important?
4. Why is it important to put contracts in writing?
5. Do you feel that the best contract drafters are pessimists? Why or why not?
6. What is a personal services contract, and why is this special in contract law?

Critical Thinking Exercises

1. John and Mary are all set to be married. They have all the necessary caterers and made all the deposits related to their rehearsal dinner, reception, and hotel. However, the 1980s rock band that was hired to perform music during the reception has called in sick and is unable to perform as promised. The band's manager called Mary to inform her of this a day before the wedding was set to take place. The manager suggested that a replacement (cover) band play instead on this special occasion, and the manager can "make it happen" under the same terms and conditions of the already existing performance contract. Mary and John were very disappointed since the rock band had a special ballad that they wanted played during their ceremony. Mary threatens to file a lawsuit forcing the band to perform. Do you think she will be successful if she brings a lawsuit? Could the original rock band assign their contract to the cover band? How might have this been resolved in the contract itself?
2. Gerry, a fine student, is unhappy about his grade in a course last semester at state college. He feels that the professor was biased against him and that the participation grade, which counted 10 percent, was unreasonably low. Do you feel that Gerry could have a claim for breach of contract? Is a syllabus a contract? Why or why not?
3. Kari has just graduated from her college. She is excited to begin her new job in Texas. She interviewed for this job on campus during career day. She accepted this job over the three other offers she received from the same career day interviews. There was no formal agreement and there is no employee handbook, but Kari still had the letter from her manager telling her what her salary and benefits would be when she showed up for the first day. Moving from Michigan has required a great amount of effort, a lot of money, and her new six-month lease in Texas is quite reasonable. After her very first week of employment, her new manager (the manager that hired her left for another job) informed her that she would have to be let go due to cost reductions. Since Kari had the least seniority, she was terminated from her position. Do you feel that Kari might have a legal claim? What fundamental contract law principles might apply (if at all) in this situation?

Online Research Exercises

1. The rock group Van Halen used to require the exclusion of brown M&M candies, though that requirement seems to have been deleted from their rider. http://www.thesmokinggun.com/backstagetour/vanhalen/vanhalen1.html
2. For a discussion of how the state of Wyoming has addressed employment contracts, visit http://caselaw.lp.findlaw.com/scripts/getcase.pl?court=wy&vol=/1997/&invol=96-151.

3. For a general discussion of contract law from a law professor's perspective, visit the regularly updated ContractsProf Blog at http://lawprofessors.typepad.com/contractsprof_blog/.
4. For examples of contracts found online for free, visit http://www.onecle.com/.
5. Consider how a student athlete is responsible for maintaining his or her eligibility by avoiding situations that could terminate their annual scholarship contract with a college or university under the complex set of rules found in the NCAA manual: http://www.ncaa.org/library/membership/division_i_manual/2006-07/2006-07_d1_manual.pdf.
6. Explore a collective bargaining agreement online. For starters, try the CBA between the players in the National Football League and the owners: http://www.nflpa.org/CBA/CBA.aspx.
7. Some people say that the role of contracts is that good fences make good neighbors. *See* http://www.bizinformer.com/50226711/why_clear_contracts_are_so_important_for_your_business.php.

CASE APPLICATIONS

Case 1

In the following case, consider whether you agree with the Supreme Court of South Dakota's decision that the car dealership breached its contract with the general public. What might the car dealership and golf course have done to avoid this situation altogether?

HARMS v. NORTHLAND FORD DEALERS

602 N.W.2D 58 (S.D. 1999)

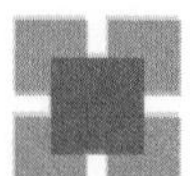

KONENKAMP, Justice

As a promotion during a golf tournament at Moccasin Creek Country Club, Northland Ford Dealers offered a new Ford Explorer to the first golfer to hit a hole-in-one at the eighth hole. Jennifer Harms scored a hole-in-one with a shot from the amateur women's tee box. Yet she was denied the prize. To be eligible to win, Northland revealed, all amateurs, male and female, had to tee off from the amateur men's tee box. This requirement was not made known to the players beforehand. Northland and Moccasin Creek blamed each other for the mix-up. When she sued, the circuit court granted Harms summary judgment against both Northland and Moccasin Creek. We affirm that decision. As the contest sponsor, Northland breached its contract to award the prize in accord with the announced rules. The court also granted summary judgment to Moccasin Creek on its cross-claim against Northland. We reverse that ruling because genuine issues of material fact remain on whether Moccasin Creek breached its agreement with Northland in setting up the hole-in-one contest to Northland's specifications.

FACTS

The Dakota Tour is a series of four golf tournaments played each summer in South Dakota. Participation is open to both men and women, professional and amateur. Moccasin Creek Country Club in Aberdeen is one of the Tour hosts. In 1995, Northland Ford Dealers, an association of dealerships, offered to sponsor a "hole-in-one" contest at Moccasin Creek during the Tour. To the first golfer to "ace" a specified contest hole, Northland would award a new Ford Explorer. Moccasin Creek agreed to include the contest as part of its tournament. Northland paid a $4,602 premium to Continental Hole-in-One, Inc. to insure the award of the contest prize. The insurance application stated in capital letters: "ALL AMATEUR MEN & WOMEN WILL UTILIZE THE SAME TEE."

A day before the Tour reached Moccasin Creek, its head golf pro, Ted Zahn, received a telephone call from Continental. Zahn told the caller that he was concerned about the lack of information and planning surrounding the hole-in-one contest. Continental's representative replied that there was no reason for concern because "[Continental] ran the deal." Continental faxed Zahn instructions for the minimum yardage distances for the contest hole. The distances varied for each day, but for the third day, the one under inquiry here, the fax message stated: "Pros-Minimum of 193 Yards; Ams-Minimum of 170 Yards." The instructions warned: "It is imperative that these yardages are correct each day to keep [Northland's] hole-in-one coverage valid." Zahn turned Continental's instructions over to his staff "to set up the hole according to the fax. . . ." Nothing in Continental's instructions suggested that any different yardages were to be used for the women contestants. But as Moccasin Creek's course superintendent later reflected, "I assumed it was a men's prize and was not informed either way, that women were also competing with it. . . ."

Continental asked Moccasin Creek to find someone to sit at the green and act as a "spotter" to verify claims of a hole-in-one. Continental paid the spotter $50 per day. The local Ford dealership hired another spotter for the same purpose. Continental supplied a banner and Moccasin Creek posted it on the course to advertise the contest. It announced that a hole-in-one would win the car, but it gave no other details. The local Ford dealership parked a Ford Explorer near the banner.

No explanation of the hole-in-one contest was given to the registered golfers in the tournament information sheet. The sheet did, however, stipulate that "USGA Rules govern all play except where modified by the Local Rules. . . ." For this tournament, the rules directed: "Professionals will play from the blue tees. Male amateurs will play from the yellow tees, female amateurs will play from the red tees." Amateur female participants were not told that to qualify for the hole-in-one contest, they would have to tee off from the amateur men's tee box. With no gender distinction announced for the hole-in-one contest, female contestants could infer that the rules for teeing applied to the eighth hole the same as every other.

On the last day of the tournament, Jennifer Harms, an amateur golfer, "aced" the contest hole, shooting from the red, amateur women's tee. After the distance between the red tee box and the hole was measured, however, it was decided that the required minimum distance had not been met. When Harms returned to the clubhouse on completing her round, she learned from her parents that her shot was pending disqualification. Northland later refused to award her the new vehicle.

Harms was a collegiate golfer at Concordia College in Moorhead, Minnesota. She returned to Concordia that fall to complete her last year of athletic eligibility. Then, in June 1996, she sued Northland and Moccasin Creek for breach of contract. Both defendants cross-claimed against the other. The circuit court granted summary judgment to Harms against Northland and Moccasin Creek, and also granted summary judgment to Moccasin Creek on its cross-claim against Northland. The court awarded Harms $25,125, with interest and costs. Northland appeals, contending that unresolved legal questions and genuine issues of material fact exist on Harms' breach of contract claim and Moccasin Creek's cross-claim. Moccasin Creek does not request our review of Harms' summary judgment against it; instead, it seeks only to uphold its cross-claim against Northland.

No one can seriously dispute that, based on the promulgated contest rules, Harms earned the prize when she sank her winning shot. She registered for the tournament and paid her $160 entrance fee. During play at the contest hole, she teed off from the amateur women's red marker, as she had done on all the other holes that day and the two previous days of the tournament. Concededly, she hit from a point under the minimum distance dictated by Northland's insurer, but she was following the tournament rule that required amateur women to tee from the red markers, not the yellow or the blue, as with the amateur men and the professionals. None of the participants knew of the minimum yardage requirement. Yet only amateur women stood ineligible to win the car if they followed the tournament rules.

We ascribe to contract terms "their plain and ordinary meaning." *Economic Aero Club, Inc. v. Avemco Ins. Co., 540 N.W.2d 644, 645 (SD 1995).* Northland must abide by the rules it announced, not by the ones it left unannounced. This was a vintage unilateral contract with performance by the offeree as acceptance. E. Allan Farnsworth, Contracts §3.4 (2d ed 1990). Accepting a sponsor's offer to participate in a contest creates an enforceable contract; awarding a prize to a contest winner is a contractual duty. *See Robertson v. United States, 343 U.S. 711, 713–14, 72 S. Ct. 994, 996, 96 L. Ed. 1237, 1240 (1952).* The circuit court rightly concluded that there were no issues of material fact on the breach of contract claim against Northland. What facts may support Harms' summary judgment against Moccasin Creek we need not consider, as it sought no review of that ruling.

Two similar cases from other jurisdictions support our decision. In *Las Vegas Hacienda, Inc. v. Gibson, 77 Nev.*

25, 359 P.2d 85 (Nev 1961), a golf course offered to pay $5,000 to any person scoring a hole-in-one. *359 P.2d at 86.* Gibson paid fifty cents for the chance and succeeded. The golf course refused to award the prize. Concluding that a valid contract existed between the golf course and Gibson, the court ruled that he had accepted the terms of the course's offer by paying the entry fee. His consideration was shooting the hole-in-one. *359 P.2d at 86.*

In *Grove v. Charbonneau Buick-Pontiac, Inc., 240 N.W.2d 853 (ND 1976)*, the court ruled for the golfer in an action to recover the prize in a hole-in-one contest. The contest offered a new car to the first participant who "shoots a hole-in-one on Hole No. 8." *240 N.W.2d at 855.* Every golfer was to play eighteen holes. The course, however, only had nine. To make eighteen holes, participants played the course twice. For the first nine, they used the blue tees; for the second, the red tees. The blue tees were marked one through nine (which matched the hole numbers); the red tees were marked ten through eighteen. Grove shot his hole-in-one while playing from the seventeenth tee and shooting at the green marked number eight. When the car dealership refused to award Grove the car because he did not make the ace on the eighth hole, he brought suit.

The North Dakota Supreme Court found that an enforceable contract existed between Grove and the dealership, though with ambiguous terms. *240 N.W.2d at 861-862.* The court resolved the ambiguities in the contestant's favor. *Id. at 862.* "We are not suggesting," the court wrote, "that [the dealership] intended to trifle with the public, but if we do not apply the rule of law on ambiguous contracts . . . to this situation we would permit promoters to trifle with the public, which we do not believe the law should permit, and in fact, does not permit." *Id.* Similarly, Northland's banner declared that a hole-in-one would win the car. Whatever ambiguity that announcement contained should not be resolved against a contestant.

Northland contends that Harms renounced the prize by returning to college to compete in the National Collegiate Athletic Association (NCAA). Under NCAA rules, accepting this prize, or agreeing to accept it at some later time, would have disqualified Harms from her final year of eligibility. After learning she could not accept the car, Northland insists, continuing her NCAA competition evinced unambiguous intent to waive acceptance and she should now be estopped from proceeding with it. At least, Northland asserts, there are genuine questions of fact on this issue.

Harms could not disclaim the prize; it was not hers to refuse. She was told her shot from the wrong tee disqualified her. One can hardly relinquish what was never conferred. Northland repudiated any duty to perform under its contract. Likewise, to suggest that she should be estopped from claiming the car because she returned to compete in collegiate sports is argument by diversion. For our analysis, Harms' NCAA eligibility is irrelevant. Even if she had foregone collegiate golf in hope of receiving the prize, Northland still maintained that she scored from the wrong tee. By its reckoning, whether she played college golf or not, she would never have the car. Under the elements of estoppel, then, how was Northland detrimentally misled by Harms' decision to play her last year? We find no waiver and no estoppel, and, thus, Harms cannot be denied the prize.

Affirmed in part, reversed in part, and remanded.

Case Questions

1. What is summary judgment?
2. Who insured this golfing event and what was the insurance premium?
3. How much money was the plaintiff awarded at trial?
4. Where did she play college golf and was this relevant to the court's decision?
5. What was the statutory authority or case precedent for this decision?

Case 2

In the following case, do you agree that there was a lack of mutual assent involving the sale of this Arizona real estate?

HILL-SHAFER PARTNERSHIP v. THE CHILSON FAMILY TRUST

799 P.2D 810 (ARIZ. 1990)

MOELLER, J.

JURISDICTION

A buyer sued for specific performance of a contract for the sale of land. The seller counterclaimed, seeking rescission of the contract. The trial court held there was a lack of mutual assent and granted summary judgment to the seller. The court of appeals reversed, holding that the facts did not present an issue of lack of mutual assent, but remanded for further proceedings on a theory of unilateral mistake. We granted seller's petition for review and have jurisdiction pursuant to *A.R.S.* §*12-120.24* and Ariz. Const. art. 6, §5(3).

ISSUES

1. Whether, under the facts of this case, rescission of a real estate purchase contract on grounds of lack of mutual assent is precluded because the misunderstanding relates to a legal description of land.
2. Whether the trial court, on the particular facts before it, correctly granted summary judgment rescinding the real estate purchase contract on the grounds of lack of mutual assent.

FACTS

Ernest Chilson and Evelyn Chilson, trustees of the Chilson Family Trust, own approximately twenty acres of land south of Flagstaff on Butler Avenue. The tract, although contiguous, can be divided into three distinct units. . . . The large parcel, containing about 17.3 acres, is bisected by Butler Avenue into "Butler North" and "Butler South." The smaller parcel, called the "Triangle," is a 2.4 acre triangular piece of land north of the larger parcel.

The Chilsons originally acquired the property in two separate transactions. Later, they directed a title agency to prepare one deed to include the property north of Butler and another deed to include the property south of Butler. The Chilsons used these two deeds to convey the property to themselves as trustees of a family trust.

In December 1984, the Chilsons listed the Triangle and Butler North with a broker, seeking a tenant for a long-term lease. Daniel Hill and Craig Shafer, general partners in the Hill-Shafer Partnership (buyer), saw a sign posted on the north side of Butler Avenue and became interested. Buyer contacted seller's broker and obtained a copy of the appraisal which listed the property as "15 acres of vacant land on the north side of Butler Avenue, one-quarter mile west of the Butler Interstate 40 interchange." The appraisal valued the property at $620,500.

Buyer inspected the land, and submitted a letter of intent proposing terms to purchase the listed property for the appraised value of $620,500. Buyer's letter of intent described the Triangle and Butler North plots of land, as had the listing and the appraisal. Buyer proposed that the final price of $620,500 be subject to an adjustment, depending on the actual acreage to be determined by a survey. The offer also contained certain proposed representations and warranties by seller as to location and size.

Seller rejected the proposal and, instead, directed its attorney to prepare a "take it or leave it" counteroffer at the same purchase price. Seller refused throughout negotiations to include a map as a part of the contract, and also refused to indicate the size of the parcel of land or to describe its location in lay terms or by reference to nearby landmarks. Seller also refused to agree to a price-per-acre adjustment mechanism or to make price in any way contingent upon an acreage figure to be determined by survey. Instead, seller insisted that the price be fixed at $620,500, and that the land be identified by legal description alone. Seller also proposed to make close of escrow contingent upon buyer's satisfaction with an economic and feasibility study that buyer would perform at its expense after receipt of a survey from seller.

The legal description contained in seller's counteroffer did not, in fact, describe the Triangle and Butler North. Rather, it described Butler North and Butler South. Buyer "accepted" seller's counteroffer and the parties entered into a contract. Escrow instructions were signed on July 5, 1985. When seller reviewed the escrow instructions in mid-July, he discovered the error in the legal description. Seller has consistently contended it always intended to sell Butler North and the Triangle, and that the use of the legal description which instead described Butler North and Butler South was due to an error. Seller contends the error originated in one of the two earlier deeds prepared by the title company by which the Chilsons transferred the property to the trust. Seller borrowed the description from one of the earlier deeds on the mistaken assumption that it described the Triangle and Butler North.

Upon discovery of the error, seller prepared an amendment to correct the legal description. Buyer refused to accept the amendment and contended it was entitled to a conveyance of the property included in the legal description. As a result of the dispute, seller cancelled the escrow, and buyer sued for specific performance. Seller counterclaimed, alleging fraudulent concealment and racketeering, and also sought rescission and a decree quieting title in it. The trial court granted summary judgment against seller on the fraud and racketeering claims, which are not involved in this appeal. The trial court also granted summary judgment against buyer on the specific performance claim and for seller on the quiet title claim, rescinding the contract for lack of mutual assent.

We granted seller's petition for review. We conclude the trial court properly granted summary judgment on a theory of lack of mutual assent.

Discussion

In the case before us, assuming all inferences in favor of buyer, we are convinced, as was the trial judge, that reasonable minds could only conclude that there was no mutual assent by the parties. All parties agree that initially all negotiations were directed towards Butler North and the Triangle. Both the appraisal and the letter of intent described and set a price only for the property north of Butler. Buyer's essential contention is that once seller made a counteroffer, the entire posture of the deal changed. Buyer argues that, although it offered to buy only the property north of Butler, once the seller insisted the property be identified by legal description alone, buyer's intent shifted (although uncommunicated to seller) and it thereafter intended to purchase whatever was contained in the legal description, regardless of what it was or where it was.

Generally, if a seller intends to sell and a buyer intends to buy land other than that described in a deed, a case of mutual *mistake* is presented. A mutual *mistake* exists where there has been a meeting of the minds of the parties, and an agreement is actually entered into, but the agreement in its written form does not express what was really intended by the parties.

Because we view the evidence in the light most favorable to buyer, we accept its contention that it intended to purchase whatever the legal description identified, regardless of size or location. Because seller did not have a similar intent and did not intend to convey whatever was included within the legal description, this case does not present a problem of mutual *mistake* but, rather, a problem of lack of mutual *assent*.

It is well-established that before a binding contract is formed, the parties must mutually consent to all material terms. A distinct intent common to both parties must exist without doubt or difference, and until all understand alike there can be no assent. If one party thinks he is buying one thing and the other party thinks he is selling another thing, no meeting of the minds occurs, and no contract is formed. *Fleischer v. McGehee, 111 Ark. 626, 163 S.W. 169, 171 (1914); see McCarty v. Anderson, 58 So.2d 255, 259 (La.App.1952)* (contracts are founded on the agreements, not on the disagreements, of the parties. Where they misunderstand each other, there is no contract).

The most famous statement of this point of law arose in the case of *Raffles v. Wichelhaus*, 2 Hurl. 906, *159 Eng.Rep. 375 (1864)*. In *Raffles*, the parties agreed on a sale of goods which was to be delivered from Bombay by the ship "Peerless." In fact, two ships named "Peerless" were sailing from Bombay at different times, and each party had a different ship in mind. The arrival time of the merchandise was of the essence to the contract. Because the understandings of the parties were different as to a material term, no binding contract was formed.

As long as the misunderstandings of the parties are reasonable under the specific circumstances of the case, a court may properly find a lack of mutual assent. We do not believe that the fact that a legal description is the source of the misunderstanding precludes relief.

The legal description in this case reads as follows:

> The following described real property situated in Coconino County, Arizona:
>
> The East half of the Northeast quarter of the Northeast quarter of Section 23, Township 21 North, Range 7 East;

EXCEPT the Southwest quarter of the Southeast quarter of the Northeast quarter of the Northeast quarter; and

EXCEPT a strip of land 88.00 feet in width, the centerline of which is described as follows:

BEGINNING at a point from which the Northeast corner of Section 23, Township 21 North, Range 7 East, Gila and Salt River Base and Meridian is North 0 degrees 44 minutes 59 seconds west a distance of 753.26 feet; Thence South 70 degrees 09 minutes 11 seconds West a distance of 32.67 feet to the point of curvature of the curve to the left having a radius of 600.000 feet and a central angle of 12 degrees 48 minutes 25 seconds; Thence along a side curve a distance of 134.11 feet to a point of tangency; Thence South 57 degrees 20 minutes 46 seconds West a distance of 340.23 feet to the North line of the Southwest quarter of the Southeast quarter of the Northeast quarter of said Section 23.

The seller believed the description covered only the property north of Butler. It did not. To an untrained person, the language of a legal description is susceptible of different interpretations. In fact, the parties in this case testified they could not understand the technical terminology of the legal description. Shafer, the buyer, testified the description looked "like Greek" to him. Chilson, the seller, testified that: "I just had to assume that it was correct of what we intended to do, and found out later it wasn't, however." Deposition of Chilson, Jan. 17, 1986, at p. 20. As stated earlier, the price of $620,500 was determined after an appraisal of the Triangle and Butler North. Buyer submitted a letter of intent only on the property north of Butler. The property south of Butler was never discussed. Seller believed the description contained in the offer described the property that had been listed and discussed. Had buyer accepted the offer on that basis and with the same intent, a binding contract (subject to reformation) might well have been formed for the sale of the land north of Butler. However, buyer's intent varied from seller's. Buyer's understanding was that it would acquire whatever was included in the legal description, regardless of size or location. We disagree with the court of appeals' conclusion that the preciseness of a legal description, as a matter of law, prevented a rescission based on a misunderstanding. Any reasonable view of the evidence inevitably leads to the conclusion that there was no meeting of the minds and no enforceable contract was formed. We conclude that the trial court properly granted summary judgment in favor of the seller.

DISPOSITION

The evidence supports the trial court's conclusion that, as a matter of law, there was no mutual assent. Therefore, the trial court's grant of summary judgment in favor of the seller is affirmed. The court of appeals' decision is vacated.

Case Questions

1. What is specific performance?
2. What was the famous English case involving the lack of mutual assent that was cited by the court?
3. Is a letter of intent (LOI) an offer or is it a summary of the preliminary discussions?
4. Do you feel that either of the parties acted in bad faith? Why or why not?
5. Do you feel that the parties in this case would have been better served to have had lawyers review the real estate contract first?
6. Do you feel that this dispute might have been better resolved by alternative forms of dispute resolution such as mediation or arbitration?

Exercise

Review the following contract rider for a musical performance. Notice the technical issues related to production and explore the unique demands by the artist involving food and drink found at the end of the agreement. Prepare a similar (yet less complex) rider for a musician or other artist who might perform at your school on the invitation of the university campus entertainment board this year. Consider other unique needs that might be found at the end of the agreement.

CONTRACT RIDER FOR MUSICAL ARTIST

This rider, a legal document, is hereby attached to and made part of the original contract dated ________________, between ______________________(“Artist”) and ____________________ (“Purchaser”) for Artist’s engagement located at __________________________ on this date ________________________.

Purchaser understands that the items required below are reasonable and necessary in order for the Artist to provide the best possible show for the Purchaser and his or her customers. Purchaser also understands that Artist cannot perform without all of the following paragraphs, and that the failure to provide any of the items could result in the Purchaser being held in default of this contract rider. While flexible, any additions or deletions to this agreement must be signed and dated by both parties to be binding.

1. **Production**. Purchaser agrees to furnish, at his or her sole cost, the following: a raised performance area (stage) which is at least four (4′) feet above the floor of the arena floor or main seating level. This stage is to be not less than forty (40′) feet deep and fifty-six (56′) feet wide. It is to be free of all obstructions and of a sound physical construction. Should the facility not be riggable, the following additional stage pieces will be required: Two (20 sound wings, each sixteen (16′) feet wide and sixteen (16′) feet deep. One is to be placed on each side of the stage, attached to the stage at the front (downstage) most edge. Stair units are required for both sides of the stage. Small light units are requested for these stair units. A Stage Diagram shall be attached to this agreement to visually demonstrate all terms contained within this Rider.
2. **Consoles**. An area not less than twenty-four (24′) feet wide by ten (10′) feet deep is to be reserved, with tickets pulled before going on sale, for lighting and sound consoles. This area is to be at the house center, not less than thirty (30′) feet from the stage. Furthermore, it shall not exceed one-half ($\frac{1}{2}$) the length of the arena floor, under any circumstances.
3. **Personnel Requirements**. The assistance of not less than 12 stagehands, 3 riggers, 4 truck loaders, 1 qualified licensed electrician, 1 forklift operator, and 2 additional stagehands are required for load-in and load-out. All personnel related to the production shall NOT be drinking alcoholic beverages. Any Runner and others involved in transporting Artist must have a valid driver’s license. All machinery should be in the best possible mechanical/working condition. Plenty of fuel should be on hand. All precautions should be taken to insure that the machinery is as safe as possible. Fork is to have minimum lift

capacity of 6,000 pounds and a lift range of 14 feet. Electrician is to be qualified and licensed and familiar with the venue. He or she must be on hand at all times, and an emergency number should be available. All of the personnel involved in the production are to be able bodied, English speaking adults. No minors are allowed. A runner is required for the first call time until the end of the show. The runner must be able to provide a vehicle that can comfortably fit six people. Runner is to report to Artist's stage manager before and after each run is made. Purchaser or his or her representative must be present and available from load-in through load-out and must have copies of this entire contract and rider during this engagement.

4. **Venue**. Purchaser agrees that the venue (auditorium, coliseum, theatre or club) shall be available to Artist's production staff and set-up, at least 12 hours prior to show time. Said venue shall not be open to the public until 1 hour before show time. Loading areas and backstage areas should be cleared of all vehicles and equipment prior to the arrival of Artist's entourage. Two clean separate dressing rooms with mirrors, soap, sinks and 36 towels is a must. A shower with hot water and toilet facilities are also to be provided (portable toilet facilities are unacceptable). These facilities must be located backstage and away from public access and sightlines. A production office must be provided for Artist's staff with a direct phone line, long distance privileges, and cell phones if better served. Parking for three buses and two trucks with at least one security guard will be offered during the performance. If parking is available only on the street, spaces must be blocked off by 5:00 AM of the day of the show.
5. **Lights & Sound**. Four spotlights and eight experienced operators will be available during the performance to assist in Artist's own sound equipment. Additionally, 1 400 amp per leg, 208 volt, three-phase service will be provided within 50 feet of stage left. 1 100 amp, 100 volt, single-phase service will be provided within 100 feet of stage right. Artist's own sound engineer shall operate the house mixing console. Additionally, colored fill lighting (red, blue, amber) and dimmer controls must be functional on all stage lighting.
6. **Security**. Purchaser shall provide an adequate security staff of experienced, properly trained, unarmed, easily identifiable and non-uniformed personnel who will work in connection with the Artist's security requests. The security must be stationed at the backstage and dressing room 3 hours prior to show time. Four security guards must be available to Artist before, during and after each performance. Artist will provide all stage passes, which will be the only passes honored in the backstage area. Purchaser agrees that any passes issued by Artist will be recognized by his or her security personnel. No person without the proper pass is to be admitted to any non-public areas. Should the performance span multiple days, security must be provided for the equipment on a 24 hour basis. Artist retains the right to demand substitution of any security guard who, in the Artist's sole judgment, is not physically, mentally or emotionally capable of performing their assigned duties. Purchaser will provide a list of guests to Artist prior to house opening.
7. **Advertising and Promotion**. Artist requires only the trademarked, custom-produced advertising materials be used in their entirety. For radio, Artist will provide at its own cost one 60 second or 30 second "pre-sale" commercial, one 60 second or 30 second "week of show" commercial, one 60 second or 30 second "day of show" commercial, and, if appropriate, one 60 second or 30 second "welcoming station" commercial. For television, one 30 second commercial. For newspaper, one 3" by 6" ad slick. Plus, 100 four-color posters,

21" by 14" in size. Purchaser agrees not to commit Artist to any personal appearances, interviews or photos or any other type of promotional purpose without prior approval. Purchaser shall also not represent that this engagement is co-promoted or co-sponsored by any third party without written permission of Artist. Artist is to receive 100% Star Billing in all advertisement and publicity.

8. **Other**. Purchaser agrees that there shall be no signs, placards, banners or other advertising materials on or near the stage at any time when the audience is in the building. During the performance, vending is not permitted in the audience. Purchaser agrees to make building and concessions management aware of these requirements. Additionally, the recording, broadcasting or filming of the live performance will not be permitted unless previously authorized in writing, including the working press back stage. This prohibition applies to patrons as well. Artist does not perform in the round. There shall be no intermission and Artist will play between 60 and 90 minutes.
9. **Merchandise**. Artist shall have the right to sell merchandise at the show site on the day of the show. No other sales or distribution of material pertaining to Artist will be allowed without prior written consent. Buyer agrees to provide adequate space for Artist or designee to vend such material.
10. **Master of Ceremonies**. No announcer or Master of Ceremonies (Emcee) shall appear without prior approval by Artist or stage manager.
11. **Tickets**. Purchaser is to use no more than 50 complimentary tickets for advertising or working press. All (any) unused tickets shall be returned for sale to the public no later than 2 hours before the performance. Artist requires 40 complimentary tickets per performance (2 performances would require a total of 40 tickets).
12. **Force Majeure/Inclement Weather**. Artist's obligation to perform is specifically subject to (i.e., conditional upon) cancellation due to sickness, physical injury (or other inability to perform), accident, and considerable delay in transportation to venue, fire, riot, strikes, or any other unexpected interference with the performance of the show. Purchaser shall not be responsible for payment to Artist for any other fee other than the relinquishment of the down payment (previously paid) in the event of such occurrence characterized by Artist as a force majeure or Act of God are raised. However, in the unfortunate event that the show cannot be presented due to weather, Artist must still be paid in full. Determination of whether any weather conditions shall render the performance(s) unsafe must be made in good faith but is at the sole discretion of the Artist.
13. **Times**. Show times may only be changed with Artist's written approval.
14. **Amendment**. This agreement may be modified up to 30 days prior to the show. Any modifications must be in writing, signed by both parties.
15. **Cancellation**. Artist shall have the right to cancel the performance, without any liability, upon written notice to the Purchaser, not less than 30 days prior to the date of performance.

16. **Payments**. All payments must be made in the form of a cashier's check made payable to: ____________. Down payments must be received by ____________ in accordance with the agreement that this contract rider amends.
17. **Gross Receipts**. The term "gross receipts" shall mean box office receipts less federal, state or local admission taxes; commissions and discounts in connection with season ticket sales, credit card charges, remote box offices, parking fees, food, merchandise or other concession income.
18. **Insurance**. Purchaser agrees to provide public liability insurance coverage to protect against injuries to persons or property prior to, during, and subsequent to the performance. This comprehensive policy must cover not less than Two Million Dollars ($2,000,000) per occurrence. Artist shall be individually covered under this policy as well and paid for by Purchaser. Purchaser also agrees to maintain worker's compensation insurance for all of its employees. Insurance for Force Majeure and "Act of God" is highly recommended as Purchaser risks cancellation due to the aforementioned acts but only in good faith.
19. **Hospitality Meals**. Purchaser shall provide the following special needs for the Artist as noted in their standard rider:

Special Needs

Please place all perishable items on ice or keep refrigerated.

Six Hours Prior to Performance

Ten (10) bottles of room temperature bottled water (non-carbonated only)
Full roasted coffee and tea set to include real ceramic coffee mugs
Honey
Variety of teas/herbal
Sugar
Spoons
One (1) 6 pack of Coke or Pepsi (not diet)
One (1) pint of whole milk
One (1) gallon of skim milk
One (1) box of Honey Smacks cereal
One (1) package of mozzarella or cheddar cheese
One (1) bottle of Echinacea capsules
One (1) small fruit platter of raspberries, blueberries, strawberries, plums and whole bananas
One (1) small tray of fresh roasted turkey, chicken & roast beef deli only (No pressed or processed meats)
One (1) small veggie tray with carrots, cherry tomatoes, red peppers, cauliflower, celery, and blue cheese dip

Assorted raw almonds, banana chips, dried cranberries
Assortment of energy bars of various brand names
One (1) small bottle of multi-vitamins
One (1) small bottle of chewable Flintstones vitamin "C" tablets
One (1) small cheese platter with Cheddar, Jack, Gouda and Swiss
Platter assortment of gums and mints
One (1) roll of film/200 speed exposure
Six (6) clean, large bath towels
Display of fork, knives, spoons, plates (Not plastic)
One (1) 1/2 pint of fat free small curd cottage cheese
One (1) container of "Coffee Mate" non-dairy creamer
Twelve (12) Solo cups
Four (4) votive candles with matches
Two (2) chicken or turkey club sandwiches (white bread with bacon, lettuce and tomato)
No less than six (6) bottles of water
Chocolate chip or Oreo cookies

After Performance

Twelve (12) bottles of very cold water
Eight (8) bottles ice coffee
Eight (8) cans of diet cola
Two (2) six packs of other assorted soda and ice teas
Fresh made deli sandwiches: assorted turkey, roast beef or chicken
Fresh fruit
Cookies

Signatures:

AGREED (sign and date):

____

Purchaser

____

Artist

References

Astorino, S.J., *Roman Law in American Law: Twentieth Century Cases of the Supreme Court,* 40 Duq. L. Rev. 627 (2002).

Farnsworth, E.A., *Promises and Paternalism,* 41 Wm. Mary L. Rev. 385 (2000).

Hillman, R.A., PRINCIPLES OF CONTRACT LAW (Thomson/West 2004).

Jentz, G.A., R.L. Miller & F.B. Cross, WEST'S BUSINESS LAW ALTERNATE EDITION (Thomson/West, 10th ed. 2007).

Kelley, P.J., *A Critical Analsyis of Holmes's Theory of Contract,* 75 Notre Dame L. Rev. 1681 (2000).

Kidwell, J., *Teaching Important Contracts Concepts: Ruminations on Teaching the Statute of Frauds,* 44 St. Louis L.J. 1427 (2000).

Kohn, B.T., *Contracts of Convenience: Preventing Employers from Unilaterally Modifying Promises Made in Employee Handbooks,* 24 Cardozo L. Rev. 799 (2003).

Perillo, J.M., *The Origins of the Objective Theory of Contract Formation and Interpretation,* 69 Fordham L. Rev. 427 (2000).

Tollen, D.W., *Three Lessons About Entertainment & Sports Technology Contracting,* 24 Ent. & Sports Law. 4, 6-7 (2007).

Twomey, D.P. & Jennings, M.M., BUSINESS LAW: PRINCIPLES FOR TODAY'S COMMERCIAL ENVIRONMENT (Thomson/West, 2e, 2008).

Walters, J.A., *The Brooklyn Bridge Is Falling Down: Unilateral Contract Modification and the Sole Requirement of the Offeree's Assent,* 32 Cumb. L. Rev. 375 (2001).

Wright, M., *A Comparative Analysis of Selected North Carolina Contractual Provisions,* 27 N.C. Cent. L.J. 23 (2004).

Chapter 2

The Agreement

After reading this chapter you will be able to:

1. Explain the difference between an offer and acceptance in the contract formula.
2. Provide examples of the differences between legitimate offers as opposed to unenforceable statements.
3. Describe what the phrase "void for vagueness" means.
4. Define and discuss the mailbox rule in contract law.
5. Differentiate between auctions with reserve and auctions without reserve.
6. Explain why offers must be definite.
7. Identify how one may accept an offer.
8. Describe how reward offers fit in contract law.

Key Terms

Acceptance	Offer	Reward offer
Advertisements	Offeree	Silent auction
Agreements to agree	Offeror	Statement of intention
Auction	Option contract	Statement of opinion
Charitable subscription	Output contract	Termination by operation of law
Counteroffer	Pledge	Void for vagueness
Dutch auction	Prelimary negotiation	With reserve
Estimates	Reject	Without reserve
Letter of intent	Requirements contract	
Mailbox rule	Revocation	

K = **O** + **A** + C + (Legality + Capacity)

This chapter focuses on the contractual agreement, primarily the *offer* and *acceptance* elements of the contract formula. Any contract begins with the offer, and offers are the driving force behind individual and business transactions and other agreements. The parties to a contract must also manifest their assent to be bound by a contract from an objective point of view. This can be done by either accepting by words or by accepting by conduct. Courts look to see whether there was a mutual assent and whether the parties were serious about entering into the contract. Questions often considered by courts include whether there was a meeting of the minds (i.e., mutual assent), whether the parties understood each other to be entering a contract, and in whether an enforceable agreement was being formed with serious intent. Special offer and acceptance relationships such as those found at auctions are explained, as well as the manner in which courts view reward offers.

THE OFFER

An **offer** is a promise to do (or not to do) something in the future. An offer indicates the willingness or intent to be bound by an agreement. Offers must be definite in that the terms of the agreement have to be reasonably certain when presented from the **offeror** to the **offeree**. Otherwise, a court could later hold that an offer was void for being too vague to be enforced (i.e., it is **void for vagueness**) if the offer was too indefinite. Those who make offers are known synonymously and interchangeably as offerors, promisors or obligors. Those who receive the offer are known as offerees, promisees, and sometimes obligees.[1] Offerees have the power of acceptance.

One of the important aspects of being the offeror is the control that the offeror has at the outset of the contract formation process. In other words, the offeror is the master of the offer. The offeror can create all terms and conditions of the offer. The offeror may even dictate how acceptance can be communicated back to the offeror. For example, the offeror might establish that acceptance of the offer is effective only when *received* in return to the offeror rather than the moment it was sent by the offeree. The offeror might even stipulate that acceptance can be made by fax, e-mail, and so on. Offers must meet the following requirements in order to be valid:

1. Serious intent to be bound to an agreement (as opposed to joke or jest) must be demonstrated. This is sometimes unclear for a court, but again courts will utilize the objective theory of contracts to determine whether a reasonable person would have believed a serious offer was being made.
2. Contract terms must be reasonably certain and not too vague. In other words, the words and phrases used must be definite and not ambiguous. The words do not have to be precise, however, for a court to affirm that an offer was made. On the other hand, overly vague offers might prompt a court to invalidate the agreement altogether for being void for vagueness.
3. The offer must be communicated to offeree or the offeree's agent, if applicable.

NONOFFERS

Throughout the study of and development of contract law courts have determined that certain communications do not rise to the level of an actual offer. Courts often have to deliberate over the use of language and apply it in its appropriate context. The following examples have been held by courts as nonoffers.

1. **Statements of opinion** (a doctor says that an ailment would "probably heal" and later does not).[2]
2. **Statements of intention** ("I plan on doing this" . . .).
3. Statements considered merely **preliminary negotiations.** Be careful, though, because there is an emerging trend to hold preliminary negotiations to the level of enforceable contracts depending on the facts, seriousness, terms, whether performance has begun, and so on. Just because a written agreement has not been drafted does not necessarily preclude the finding of a contract especially if the doctrine of promissory estoppel is invoked by a court.[3]

---

[1]The words offeror and offeree might take a different shape depending on the context of the relationships. Examples include landlords (lessors) and tenants (lessees), employers and employees, and sellers (vendors) and buyers (vendees).

[2]Consider when lawyers might promise specific results as well.

[3]Some written correspondence might be referred to as letters of intent (LOI).

4. **Agreements to agree** (or agreements to disagree). Statements that "we will agree" or "we will agree to disagree" are not considered offers and have almost no legal effect whatsoever. The only exception would be that everything was agreed upon by the parties except a minor contract term. However, this would have to be determined by a court.[4]
5. **Advertisements** are generally not offers, but rather invitations to negotiate.[5] Under contract law principles, advertisements technically solicit offers from customers. This is expected in automobile sales, for example, in which the price listed on the car is merely an invitation to negotiate. However, consider if the ad read, "To the first five customers."[6]
6. **Estimates** for services.[7]

DEFINITENESS

Offers should be clear; offers should not be vague. Courts consider the following elements when determining whether an offer was clear enough to be enforced:

1. The parties
2. The subject matter at hand
3. The consideration (price)
4. The time of payment/delivery/performance

All of the above are important in order for a court to provide a remedy in the event of a breach of contract claim. Sometimes, a contract might require a series of performances by both parties. This type of contract may be referred to as a divisible, installment, or several contract.[8] In this instance, the overall agreement represents a series of offers and acceptances by both parties. This often occurs in shipment contracts in which deliveries are made periodically from a seller to a buyer. The UCC allows for **requirements** and **output contracts,** too.[9] These types of contracts lack definiteness in terms of the quantity element, but the UCC still allows the indefiniteness to exist in order to promote commerce. Good contract drafters might want to include minimum (floors) or maximum (ceilings) purchase amounts to provide some measure of certainty for the parties as well.

---

[4]*See* Walker v. Keith, 382 S.W.2d 198 (Ky. 1964).

[5]*See* Leonard v. Pepsico, Inc., 88 F.Supp.2d 116 (S.D.N.Y. 1996) (discussed later in Chapter 6). *But See* Carlill v. Carbolic Smoke Ball Co., 1 QB 256 (1893) in which the defendants advertised that they would pay anyone who used their product and still caught the flu 100 pounds and the court held that this was an offer.

[6]Consider, too, if an advertisement named a price, but then qualified it with "or best offer" (obo). Is that a valid offer? Is it definite enough?

[7]Unless the estimates and quotations for services are characterized as a firm offer, a special phrase used by merchants under the UCC discussed in the second half of the book, estimates are just that. However, it would be bad business practice to make poor estimates, and, of course, one might also pursue a tort law claim for fraud or misrepresentation.

[8]Several is also referred to as "separate."

[9]Requirements contract: "I will buy all that I need." Output contracts: "I will buy all that you produce." *See* UCC §2-306.

COMMUNICATION OF THE OFFER

An offer must be communicated to the offeree or the offeree's agent. Before acceptance, the offer could actually be revoked by the offeror, but that, too, would have to be communicated to the offeree prior to receiving acceptance. The act of revoking an offer (i.e., **revocation**) means that the offeror, as the master of the offer, has decided to terminate the power of the offeree to accept for whatever reason. Only firm offers are considered irrevocable (Chapter 11).

AUTOMATIC TERMINATION OF AN OFFER

Sometimes, offers will automatically end. Automatic termination is sometimes referred to as **termination by operation of law**. The following represent situations in which an offer will automatically end:

1. Lapse of time (a reasonable amount of time)
2. If subject matter is destroyed *before* acceptance is made
3. Death of offeror or offeree *before* the offer is accepted
4. Supervening (or subsequent) illegality. That is, the law changes *before* acceptance was made

AUCTIONS

In **auctions**, those who make bids (i.e., the bidders) are the offerors. Also, the auctioneers are agents for the seller (the offeree) and are usually paid a percentage of the sale.[10] The striking of the hammer constitutes the acceptance of the offer. Sometimes bidders may revoke an offer before the hammer falls. It depends upon that auction's rules. There are two popular types of auctions:

1. **With reserve** (seller may choose NOT to sell to highest bidder). In auctions with reserve, the seller does not have to sell if the bidder does not meet the reserve (i.e., minimum) price.
2. **Without reserve** (seller must sell to highest bidder). This is sometimes referred to as an absolute auction.

Other Auctions

There are various other auctions than those with or without reserve. For example, in a **Dutch auction**, the auctioneer begins with a high asking price and works his way down until a bidder agrees to the auctioneer's price.[11] In a **silent auction**, many items are sold at one time in which the bidders write their bid offer on paper posted near the item itself. The one with the highest bid wins the prize, so to speak.

[10]Under the UCC, auctions are addressed in §2-328.

[11]Some may refer to a Dutch auction as a reverse auction.

The auction is considered "silent" since no one really speaks—they simply record their bids. In other silent auctions, the bidders may (or may not) actually know what the other bids are if the bids are secret and required to be dropped into a bowl in which no one knows what the highest bid is until all the bids are compared with each other when the bidding process is over.

Consider the following challenges for courts and parties to the contract as to whether there was actually a legally binding agreement. Always looming in any potential contract dispute is the role of promissory estoppel which allows a court to enforce an agreement in which a promise is made leading to reasonable detrimental reliance (i.e., inducement) by one of the parties and resulting in a possible implied or *quasi* contract.[12]

MAILBOX RULE

The **mailbox rule** principle in contract law is almost extinct today though it is still a valid concept.[13] Traditionally, the mailbox rule (sometimes referred to as the postal acceptance rule) applies when a contract has been negotiated and the parties have been communicating via the U.S. mail in order to obtain the appropriate signatures for the binding agreement. Under this rule, when an offer was made, as soon as the offeree dropped acceptance of the offer into the mailbox (or possession to the postal service), then a legally binding agreement had been formed and the offer was irrevocable by the offeror. The mailbox rule was instituted to avoid the situation where the acceptance by the offeree was made (by dropping it in the mailbox) and then the offeror attempted to revoke the offer prior to receiving the acceptance. Interestingly, if the offeree first says "no" and then changes his or her mind, whichever communication the first one to be received by the offeror should prevail. Good contract drafters can avoid the mailbox rule altogether by establishing that acceptance of an offer is effective when *received* rather than when *mailed* and this rule can be applied to a fax or e-mail as well. This concern has been addressed by so many good contract drafters in standard agreements that the mailbox rule is not often an issue for courts.

REWARD OFFERS

When someone loses an item and posts a **reward offer** for those who find and return it, do rewards constitute offers? This happens frequently with lost animals such as dogs and cats. Certainly, if the one who found the animal knew of the existence of the reward, then there is usually not a concern as courts hold that there

[12]The terms promissory estoppel and detrimental reliance are often used interchangeably and are principles that reflect how contract law takes into consideration equitable principles. In fact, those who rely on promises to their legal detriment have even been characterized as "victims" by some English decisions though that term is normally used in criminal or tort law. *See* Katz v. Danny Dare, Inc., 610 S.W.2d 121 (Mo. Ct. App. 1980) (failure to provide a pension to a retired employee after a promise was made by the company president).

[13]*See also* the Federal Postal Reorganization Act (39 U.S.C. §3009 (a)) which actually authorizes the Federal Trade Commission (FTC) to prosecute as an unfair or deceptive practice any use of the mails to send unordered merchandise.

certainly was an offer and an acceptance. However, what if the one who returned the animal did not originally know of the existence of the reward, but then discovers its existence after the fact? It really depends on that court on that given day. Under black-letter general contract law principles, there was no real offer and acceptance. There was no meeting of the minds if the one who found (and returned) the animal was actually unaware of the reward offer itself. On the other hand, many courts imply that a contract existed as a matter of public policy to encourage individuals to help others and to provide stability in community relationships.[14]

OPTION CONTRACTS

Sometimes referred to as voidable contracts, **option contracts** play a special role. Option contracts allow the parties to agree on a contract as long as certain conditions occur or, alternatively, do not occur at all. An option contract is defined as "a promise which meets the requirements for the formation of a contract and limits the promisor's power to revoke an offer."[15] An option contract is a type of contract that protects an offeree from an offeror's ability to revoke the contract. Option contracts are very common in entertainment and sport industry agreements since an artist's or athlete's market value can go up (or down) frequently during the course of a career. A professional team might therefore place an option contract provision in their agreement which allows them to keep a player for an extra year (or terminate them early) depending upon their recent performances. Options can also allow the parties to even restructure a sports contract to rework the agreement to remain under a team salary cap, for example.[16] Consider, too, real estate transactions and the concept of "earnest money" which holds open the offer on the condition that one is able to obtain financing (i.e., a loan) to purchase the real estate. Option contracts can be found in any industry in order to hold open the right to purchase something for a period of time.[17]

CHARITABLE SUBSCRIPTIONS

Sometimes referred to as **pledges**, **charitable subscriptions** are enforceable offers.[18] Those who do not fulfill their pledges, however, rarely go to court because enough money is not often involved or it would be very unpopular to litigate.[19] However, these charitable subscriptions will be enforced, especially if reliance on

[14]Consider, too, rewards "leading to the arrest" that are published or otherwise broadcast to the public at large? What does the phrase "leading to the arrest" actually mean? What about "leading to the arrest and conviction"? Does the latter require both or just one or the other?

[15]Restatement (Second) of Contracts §25 (1981).

[16]*See, e.g.*, the salary cap history in the National Basketball Association (NBA), http://sports.espn.go.com/nba/news/story?id=2516704. *See also*, http://en.wikipedia.org/wiki/Salary_cap for a most general look at salary caps for teams and leagues.

[17]Consider the irrevocable merchant's firm offer of UCC §2-205.

[18]Consider issues involving revocation of pledges involving Harvard University and others, prompting some institutions to consider requiring donors to pay a penalty if they change their mind, similar to a prenuptial agreement between spouses. http://www.insidehighered.com/news/2006/06/29/ellison.

[19]*See* http://www.miami.com/mld/miamiherald/news/breaking_news/15975372.htm. *See also*, http://www.uh.edu/admin/media/topstories/2002/nytimes/200211/20021115case.html.

the pledge was reasonable. Charitable subscriptions are often seen on television during a telethon. One might argue that a pledge such as a charitable subscription or a promise made by a good samaritan lacks consideration (discussed further in Chapter 3), but courts address the issue on a case-by-case basis.[20]

ACCEPTANCE

So much time is spent on the offer element of the contract formula that one might overlook the other major part of the agreement: the **acceptance**. An acceptance of an offer occurs when the offeree assents to the terms of the offer and communicates that to the offeror by words or by performance. An offeree can do one of four things when he or she receives an offer: accept, **reject**, make a **counteroffer**, or do nothing. When either a rejection or counteroffer occur, the original offer is no longer valid. Still, when a counteroffer is made, the roles reverse, and the offeror is now the one who once was the offeree. This process may continue indefinitely. Acceptance of a contract must be:

1. Unequivocal and unconditional (referred to as the "mirror image rule" of common law contracts which requires that the acceptance must mirror the offer with no changes in terms whatsoever).
2. Timely (while the offeror can control the time frame, the law will imply a reasonable period of time if none is stated in the offer).
3. Communicated to the offeror (or the offeror's agent).[21]

SILENCE

Silence is not normally an acceptance of any offer. This includes when someone receives something in the mail (unsolicited) saying that you have to reject (i.e., return) the item or else you have accepted.[22] On the other hand, solicited or regular mailings (such as book or CD or DVD of the month club) usually require that the recipient affirmatively reject the shipment, otherwise a contract is created and the recipient must pay for the delivery accordingly. That, however, is established at the beginning of the contractual relationship.

LETTER OF INTENT

In business, a **letter of intent** is often a succinct summary of what the parties agreed upon. Letters of intent (sometimes abbreviated as LOI) are also referred to as a memorandum of understanding or a memorandum of agreement. These documents—no

[20]*See, e.g.,* the classic Massachusetts case of Mills v. Wyman, 3 Pick. 207 (Mass. 1825) in which an oral promise by a good samaritan to take care of a man's dying son was made then breached but was held to lack consideration in the first place. *See also,* Webb v. McGowin, 168 So. 196 (Ala. 1936).

[21]Agents, for example, might include lawyers, sports agents, real estate agents, and so on.

[22]http://www.usps.com/postalinspectors/fraud/merch.htm.

matter what they are called—are used to demonstrate that the parties are serious and that the basics of the contract have been negotiated after, usually, rounds of initial discussions. A question often asked in dispute resolution is whether the LOI was a contract or was merely a summary of the discussion between the parties. The answer is simply unclear.[23]

Quantum Meruit

As referenced in Chapter 1, the Latin phrase *quantum meruit* literally means "as much as he or she deserved." Today it could also mean "what a job or task is worth" or "what were the reasonable value of services already performed." *Quantum meruit* is used by courts to award money or damages to prevent someone from being unjustly enriched (i.e., unjust enrichment) by another's performance. This often occurs in construction contracts. As a general rule for unjust enrichment to apply, there must have been the conferring of benefit to another in which it simply would be unfair or unjust to allow the recipient to retain the benefit without paying some amount. *Quantum meruit* claims can occur as a direct result of a contractual agreement, a contract breach, or even if no contract existed between the parties but one was implied (*quasi* contract) by a court. There is no crystal-clear formula for providing *quantum meruit* awards, but courts must consider the specific facts of each individual case to provide the appropriate remedy. A way to avoid *quantum meruit* issues, of course, is not to begin work on a project until a contract is signed and, of course, to provide in the contract itself the remedy for a breach of contract. In many relationships, however, this is not always practicable.

CHAPTER SUMMARY

The offer and acceptance relationship is the heart of the contract formula. The offeror is the master of the offer and has all the power, at the outset, to create the terms of acceptance. Sometimes courts must determine whether there was actually an offer, especially if the terms of the offer were too vague. If it was too vague, then a court would likely hold that the offer was void for vagueness. Statements of opinion and statements of intention may sound like offers, but they usually are not enforceable due to the lack of definiteness. The concept of promissory estoppel allows a court to imply the existence of a contract if it can be proven that a statement was made or there was conduct that would reasonably induce the other party to perform. While the mailbox rule may seem antiquated today, the principle remains legitimate in the study of contract law. Good contract drafters can avoid the mailbox rule altogether by offering language in an agreement that effectively triggers acceptance when received in-hand by the offeror. Other interesting examples of offer scenarios include reward offers, option contracts, and auctions. How one may accept is normally controlled by the offeror at the beginning of the offer. Silence is not normally an acceptance of an offer. Letters of intent can present challenges for courts as to whether they reflect a legally binding agreement or are simply a summary of the preliminary negotiation phase up to that point.

---

[23]*See* Weigel Broad. Co. v. TV-49, Inc., 2006 U.S. Dist. LEXIS 87246 (N.D. Ill. Nov. 29, 2006).

Discussion and Review Questions

1. Why must an offer be definite in order to be enforced?
2. Who has more control over the heart of the contract, generally speaking: the offeror or the offeree, and why?
3. How do contract offers automatically terminate?
4. Discuss what the phrase *quantum meruit* means and why it is important.
5. Why are advertisements not considered offers?
6. Are rewards for a lost dog generally enforceable?
7. Are charitable subscriptions valid offers?
8. What is in option contract and why is it used?
9. What is the difference between an auction with reserve and one without reserve?
10. May someone accept a contract by doing nothing?

Critical Thinking Exercises

1. April enrolls in a DVD of the month club online. As part of the terms of the agreement, April agreed that the company would send her a DVD via the mail on the 15th of every month. In the event that she did not want the DVD, she had to send it back within 10 business days at no additional expense to her. If she did not, then the company would charge her credit card automatically on the 11th business day. During one month, April was on vacation and forgot about the DVD club. Her credit card was billed accordingly. Does April have a legitimate argument that she should not have to pay since she did not even know what DVD was sent to her while she was out of town? See if you can find automatic renewal provisions of a book, CD, or DVD of the month club online which might be characterized as a recurring charge.
2. During the holiday season, Jason received a package from a sender who is located out of state. The package included a variety of gifts, including small household items. Jason never asked for this product, never ordered it, and never even heard of the company. Does Jason have to pay for the received merchandise which stated that he either had to pay the sender money or had to return the goods at his own expense? *See* http://www.ftc.gov/bcp/conline/pubs/buspubs/mailorder.htm.
3. Jordan is looking to buy his girlfriend a gift. One day, while reading the local newspaper, he sees an advertisement involving a special sale of purses for the first 20 customers at a local women's specialty store. When Jordan shows up, he is turned down by the store which claims that the offer was intended for the first female customers only, not male. Do you feel that the store has a legimitate argument? Why or why not? Consider the classic Minnesota case of *Lefkowitz v. Great Minneapolis Surplus Store, Inc.*, 86 N.W.2d 689 (Minn. 1957).
4. Jill, a high school senior, applied to various colleges around the United States. Most of the colleges she applied to are very competitive in terms of the admissions process. Due to an error, the university where she applied sent her an e-mail admitting her to the school. This excited Jill as it was her number one choice! However, the next day the same university apologized and said that the e-mail was sent to all applicants by mistake. The e-mail also said that her application was still under consideration. Do you feel that Jill (if she was not later admitted) would have a successful claim for breach of contract? Why or why not? *See* http://www.cnn.com/2007/EDUCATION/01/26/admissions.mistake.ap/index.html.
5. James really enjoys the company of his bartender Jessica. For the last two years, James has been a regular at the bar on Friday nights and he and Jessica get along really

well. During the holiday season, James has been drinking a lot (as usual), but instead of the standard twenty percent tip he normally leaves her, he leaves her a tip in the amount of $1,500 on his credit card. She was beaming with happiness and did not object to the tip. She really did not know what to say, but she gave him a big hug and said, "Thank you so much, James!" The next day James could not believe that he left her such a high tip and said that as much as he likes Jessica, that such an amount was clearly in error and that he would never be serious about leaving her such an outrageous amount. Do you think James would have a successful argument if Jessica refuses to return the tip money? Why or why not? Explore http://abcnews.go.com/US/wireStory?id=2377773. *See also* http://www.msnbc.msn.com/id/11877571/.

Online Research Exercises

1. The National Letter of Intent program is what athletically talented high school seniors sign when they are offered a scholarship to a college or university. Review the following contract found at http://www.national-letter.org/.
2. What happens when a radio station (or an employer) during a radio or sales promotion causes embarrassment to a participant or the employee which was meant as a joke. For example, how would you feel if you were told that you won a Toyota when in fact you won a toy Yoda doll? http://www.usatoday.com/news/nation/2002/05/09/toy-yoda.htm. How about winning a toy Hummer: http://www.snopes.com/business/deals/hummer.asp. Unfortunately, radio station promotions can turn fun into serious danger or even death, http://cbs13.com/local/local_story_017225921.html. *See also* http://www.thesmokinggun.com/archive/years/2007/0125073wii1.html and http://news.findlaw.com/hdocs/docs/pi/strangekdnd12507cmp.html.
3. Should you have to pay for something that is sent to you via the mail but you did not order it? Consider: http://www.usps.com/postalinspectors/fraud/merch.htm.
4. Do you feel that Starbucks might reconsider future promotional opportunities (offers) sent via e-mail? http://www.snopes.com/inboxer/nothing/starbucks.asp. *See also* http://seattlepi.nwsource.com/business/284448_starbucks09.html.
5. Could someone sue for the breach of a promise to purchase an amount of Girl Scout cookies? http://abclocal.go.com/wls/story?section=News&id=3024786.
6. See if you can find an example of a reward offer online. Note that reward offers often occur for missing persons as well as in http://www.foxnews.com/story/0,2933,275438,00.html.
7. In 2007, the head basketball coach at the University of Florida men's team accepted a job with the NBA's Orlando Magic. Shortly thereafter, he changed his mind and wanted out of his contract. This proved to be an embarrassing situation for all involved. However, he was let out of his agreement with the NBA team though contractually they probably did not have to. This was not the first time that this has happened in the sports context, however. Similar scenarios have happened in recent years to college coaches who sign contracts then immediately change their minds. Maybe contract law should carve out a special "college coach contract exception" to all basic contract law principles? *See* http://www.msnbc.msn.com/id/19036994/. See also http://www.msnbc.msn.com/id/15020960/.

CASE APPLICATIONS

Case 1

Read the following classic contract case and consider why the court refused to accept the Zehmers' defense that they were simply intoxicated and had no serious intent to enter into the agreement. Why do you feel the court ruled the way it did, and what can we learn from this classic contract law case?

LUCY v. ZEHMER

84 S.E.2D 516 (VA. 1954)

BUCHANAN, J.

This suit was instituted by W. O. Lucy and J. C. Lucy, complainants, against A. H. Zehmer and Ida S. Zehmer, his wife, defendants, to have specific performance of a contract by which it was alleged the Zehmers had sold to W. O. Lucy a tract of land owned by A. H. Zehmer in Dinwiddie county containing 471.6 acres, more or less, known as the Ferguson farm, for $50,000. J. C. Lucy, the other complainant, is a brother of W. O. Lucy, to whom W. O. Lucy transferred a half interest in his alleged purchase.

The instrument sought to be enforced was written by A. H. Zehmer on December 20, 1952, in these words: "We hereby agree to sell to W. O. Lucy the Ferguson Farm complete for $50,000.00, title satisfactory to buyer," and signed by the defendants, A. H. Zehmer and Ida S. Zehmer.

The answer of A. H. Zehmer admitted that at the time mentioned W. O. Lucy offered him $50,000 cash for the farm, but that he, Zehmer, considered that the offer was made in jest; that so thinking, and both he and Lucy having had several drinks, he wrote out "the memorandum" quoted above and induced his wife to sign it; that he did not deliver the memorandum to Lucy, but that Lucy picked it up, read it, put it in his pocket, attempted to offer Zehmer $5 to bind the bargain, which Zehmer refused to accept, and realizing for the first time that Lucy was serious, Zehmer assured him that he had no intention of selling the farm and that the whole matter was a joke. Lucy left the premises insisting that he had purchased the farm.

W. O. Lucy, a lumberman and farmer, thus testified in substance: He had known Zehmer for fifteen or twenty years and had been familiar with the Ferguson farm for ten years. Seven or eight years ago he had offered Zehmer $20,000 for the farm which Zehmer had accepted, but the agreement was verbal and Zehmer backed out. On the night of December 20, 1952, around eight o'clock, he took an employee to McKenney, where Zehmer lived and operated a restaurant, filling station and motor court. While there he decided to see Zehmer and again try to buy the Ferguson farm. He entered the restaurant and talked to Mrs. Zehmer until Zehmer came in. He asked Zehmer if he had sold the Ferguson farm. Zehmer replied that he had not. Lucy said, "I bet you wouldn't take $50,000.00 for that place." Zehmer replied, "Yes, I would too; you wouldn't give fifty." Lucy said he would and told Zehmer to write up an agreement to that effect. Zehmer took a restaurant check and wrote on the back of it, "I do hereby agree to sell to W. O. Lucy the Ferguson Farm for $50,000 complete." Lucy told him he had better change it to "We" because Mrs. Zehmer would have to sign it too. Zehmer then tore up what he had written, wrote the agreement quoted above and asked Mrs. Zehmer, who was at the other end of the counter ten or twelve feet away, to sign it. Mrs. Zehmer said she would for $50,000 and signed it. Zehmer brought it back and gave it to Lucy, who offered him $5 which Zehmer refused, saying, "You don't need to give me any money, you got the agreement there signed by both of us."

The discussion leading to the signing of the agreement, said Lucy, lasted thirty or forty minutes, during which Zehmer seemed to doubt that Lucy could raise $50,000. Lucy suggested the provision for having the title examined and Zehmer made the suggestion that he would sell it "complete, everything there," and stated that all he had on the farm was three heifers.

Lucy took a partly filled bottle of whiskey into the restaurant with him for the purpose of giving Zehmer a drink if he wanted it. Zehmer did, and he and Lucy had one or two drinks together. Lucy said that while he felt the drinks he took he was not intoxicated, and from the way Zehmer handled the transaction he did not think he was either.

December 20 was on Saturday. Next day Lucy telephoned to J. C. Lucy and arranged with the latter to take a half interest in the purchase and pay half of the consideration. On Monday he engaged an attorney to examine the title. The attorney reported favorably on December 31 and on January 2 Lucy wrote Zehmer stating that the title was satisfactory, that he was ready to pay the purchase price in cash and asking when Zehmer would be ready to close the deal. Zehmer replied by letter, mailed on January 13, asserting that he had never agreed or intended to sell.

Mr. and Mrs. Zehmer were called by the complainants as adverse witnesses. Zehmer testified in substance as follows:

He bought this farm more than ten years ago for $11,000. He had had twenty-five offers, more or less, to buy it, including several from Lucy, who had never offered any specific sum of money. He had given them all the same answer, that he was not interested in selling it. On this Saturday night before Christmas it looked like everybody and his brother came by there to have a drink. He took a good many drinks during the afternoon and had a pint of his own. When he entered the restaurant around eight-thirty Lucy was there and he could see that he was "pretty high." He said to Lucy, "Boy, you got some good liquor, drinking, ain't you?" Lucy then offered him a drink. "I was already high as a Georgia pine, and didn't have any more better sense than to pour another great big slug out and gulp it down, and he took one too."

After they had talked a while Lucy asked whether he still had the Ferguson farm. He replied that he had not sold it and Lucy said, "I bet you wouldn't take $50,000.00 for it." Zehmer asked him if he would give $50,000 and Lucy said yes. Zehmer replied, "You haven't got $50,000 in cash." Lucy said he did and Zehmer replied that he did not believe it. They argued "pro and con for a long time," mainly about "whether he had $50,000 in cash that he could put up right then and buy that farm."

Finally, said Zehmer, Lucy told him if he didn't believe he had $50,000, "you sign that piece of paper here and say you will take $50,000.00 for the farm." He, Zehmer, "just grabbed the back off of a guest check there" and wrote on the back of it. At that point in his testimony Zehmer asked to see what he had written to "see if I recognize my own handwriting." He examined the paper and exclaimed, "Great balls of fire, I got 'Firgerson' for Ferguson. I have got satisfactory spelled wrong. I don't recognize that writing if I would see it, wouldn't know it was mine."

After Zehmer had, as he described it, "scribbled this thing off," Lucy said, "Get your wife to sign it." Zehmer walked over to where she was and she at first refused to sign but did so after he told her that he "was just needling him [Lucy], and didn't mean a thing in the world, that I was not selling the farm." Zehmer then "took it back over there * * * and I was still looking at the dern thing. I had the drink right there by my hand, and I reached over to get a drink, and he said, 'Let me see it.' He reached and picked it up, and when I looked back again he had it in his pocket and he dropped a five dollar bill over there, and he said, 'Here is five dollars payment on it.' * * * I said, 'Hell no, that is beer and liquor talking. I am not going to sell you the farm. I have told you that too many times before.'"

Mrs. Zehmer testified that when Lucy came into the restaurant he looked as if he had had a drink. When Zehmer came in he took a drink out of a bottle that Lucy handed him. She went back to help the waitress who was getting things ready for next day. Lucy and Zehmer were talking but she did not pay too much attention to what they were saying. She heard Lucy ask Zehmer if he had sold the Ferguson farm, and Zehmer replied that he had not and did not want to sell it. Lucy said, "I bet you wouldn't take $50,000 cash for that farm," and Zehmer replied, "You haven't got $50,000 cash." Lucy said, "I can get it." Zehmer said he might form a company and get it, "but you haven't got $50,000.00 cash to pay me tonight." Lucy asked him if he would put it in writing that he would sell him this farm. Zehmer then wrote on the back of a pad, "I agree to sell the Ferguson Place to W. O. Lucy for $50,000.00 cash." Lucy said, "All right, get your wife to sign it." Zehmer came back to where she was standing and said, "You want to put your name to this?" She said "No," but he said in an undertone, "It is nothing but a joke," and she signed it.

She said that only one paper was written and it said: "I hereby agree to sell," but the "I" had been changed to "We." However, she said she read what she signed and was then asked, "When you read 'We hereby agree to sell to W. O. Lucy,' what did you interpret that to mean, that particular phrase?" She said she thought that was a cash sale that night; but she also said that when she read that part about "title satisfactory to buyer" she understood that if the title was good Lucy would pay $50,000 but if the title was bad he would have a right to reject it, and that that was her understanding at the time she signed her name.

On examination by her own counsel she said that her husband laid this piece of paper down after it was signed; that Lucy said to let him see it, took it, folded it and put it in his wallet, then said to Zehmer, "Let me give you $5.00," but Zehmer said, "No, this is liquor talking. I don't want to sell the farm, I have told you that I want my son to have it. This is all a joke." Lucy then said at least twice, "Zehmer, you have sold your farm," wheeled around and started for the door. He paused at the door and said, "I will bring you $50,000.00 tomorrow. * * * No, tomorrow is Sunday. I will bring it to you Monday." She said you could tell definitely that he was drinking and she said to her husband, "You should have taken him home," but he said, "Well, I am just about as bad off as he is."

The waitress referred to by Mrs. Zehmer testified that when Lucy first came in "he was mouthy." When Zehmer came in they were laughing and joking and she thought they took a drink or two. She was sweeping and cleaning up for next day. She said she heard Lucy tell Zehmer, "I will give you so much for the farm," and Zehmer said, "You haven't got that much." Lucy answered, "Oh, yes, I will give you that much." Then "they jotted down something on paper * * * and Mr. Lucy reached over and took it, said let me see it." He looked at it, put it in his pocket and in about a minute he left. She was asked whether she saw Lucy offer Zehmer any money and replied, "He had five dollars laying up there, they didn't take it." She said Zehmer told Lucy he didn't want his money "because he didn't have enough money to pay for his property, and wasn't going to sell his farm." Both of them appeared to be drinking right much, she said.

She repeated on cross-examination that she was busy and paying no attention to what was going on. She was some distance away and did not see either of them sign the paper. She was asked whether she saw Zehmer put the agreement down on the table in front of Lucy, and her answer was this: "Time he got through writing whatever it was on the paper, Mr. Lucy reached over and said, 'Let's see it.' He took it and put it in his pocket," before showing it to Mrs. Zehmer. Her version was that Lucy kept raising his offer until it got to $50,000.

The defendants insist that the evidence was ample to support their contention that the writing sought to be enforced was prepared as a bluff or dare to force Lucy to admit that he did not have $50,000; that the whole matter was a joke; that the writing was not delivered to Lucy and no binding contract was ever made between the parties.

It is an unusual, if not bizarre, defense. When made to the writing admittedly prepared by one of the defendants and signed by both, clear evidence is required to sustain it.

In his testimony Zehmer claimed that he "was high as a Georgia pine," and that the transaction "was just a bunch of two doggoned drunks bluffing to see who could talk the biggest and say the most." That claim is inconsistent with his attempt to testify in great detail as to what was said and what was done. It is contradicted by other evidence as to the condition of both parties, and rendered of no weight by the testimony of his wife that when Lucy left the restaurant she suggested that Zehmer drive him home. The record is convincing that Zehmer was not intoxicated to the extent of being unable to comprehend the nature and consequences of the instrument he executed, and hence that instrument is not to be invalidated on that ground. 17 C.J.S., Contracts, §133 b., p. 483; *Taliaferro v. Emery, 124 Va. 674, 98 S.E. 627.* It was in fact conceded by defendants' counsel in oral argument that under the evidence Zehmer was not too drunk to make a valid contract.

The evidence is convincing also that Zehmer wrote two agreements, the first one beginning "I hereby agree to sell." Zehmer first said he could not remember about that, then that "I don't think I wrote but one out." Mrs. Zehmer said that what he wrote was "I hereby agree," but that the "I" was changed to "We" after that night. The agreement that was written and signed is in the record and indicates no such change. Neither are the mistakes in spelling that Zehmer sought to point out readily apparent.

The appearance of the contract, the fact that it was under discussion for forty minutes or more before it was signed; Lucy's objection to the first draft because it was written in the singular, and he wanted Mrs. Zehmer to sign it also; the rewriting to meet that objection and the signing by Mrs. Zehmer; the discussion of what was to be included in the sale, the provision for the examination of the title, the completeness of the instrument that was executed, the taking possession of it by Lucy with no request or suggestion by either of the defendants that he give it back, are facts which furnish persuasive evidence that the execution of the contract was a serious business transaction rather than a casual, jesting matter as defendants now contend.

On Sunday, the day after the instrument was signed on Saturday night, there was a social gathering in a home in the town of McKenney at which there were general comments that the sale had been made. Mrs. Zehmer testified that on that occasion as she passed by a group of people, including Lucy, who were talking about the transaction, $50,000 was mentioned, whereupon she stepped up and said, "Well, with the high-price whiskey you were drinking last night you should have paid more. That was cheap." Lucy testified that at that time Zehmer told him that he did not want to "stick" him or hold him to the agreement because he, Lucy, was too tight and didn't know what he was doing, to which Lucy replied that he was not too tight; that he had been stuck before and was going through with it. Zehmer's version was that he said to Lucy: "I am not trying to claim it wasn't a deal on account of the fact the price was too low. If I had wanted to sell $50,000.00 would be a good price, in fact I think you would get stuck at $50,000.00." A disinterested witness testified that what Zehmer said to Lucy was that "he was going to let him up off the deal, because he thought he was too tight, didn't know what he was doing. Lucy said something to the effect that 'I have been stuck before and I will go through with it.'"

If it be assumed, contrary to what we think the evidence shows, that Zehmer was jesting about selling his farm to Lucy and that the transaction was intended by him to be a joke, nevertheless the evidence shows that Lucy did not so understand it but considered it to be a serious business transaction and the contract to be binding on the Zehmers as well as on himself. The very next day he arranged with his brother to put up half the money and take a half interest in the land. The day after that he employed an attorney to examine the title. The next night, Tuesday, he was back at Zehmer's place and there Zehmer told him for the first time, Lucy said, that he wasn't going to sell and he told Zehmer, "You know you sold that place fair and square." After receiving the report from his attorney that the title was good he wrote to Zehmer that he was ready to close the deal.

Not only did Lucy actually believe, but the evidence shows he was warranted in believing, that the contract represented a serious business transaction and a good faith sale and purchase of the farm.

In the field of contracts, as generally elsewhere, "We must look to the outward expression of a person as manifesting his intention rather than to his secret and unexpressed intention. 'The law imputes to a person an intention corresponding to the reasonable meaning of his words and acts.'" *First Nat. Bank v. Roanoke Oil Co., 169 Va. 99, 114, 192 S.E. 764, 770.*

An agreement or mutual assent is of course essential to a valid contract but the law imputes to a person an intention corresponding to the reasonable meaning of his words and acts. If his words and acts, judged by a reasonable standard, manifest an intention to agree, it is immaterial what may be the real but unexpressed state of his mind. So a person cannot set up that he was merely jesting when his conduct and words would warrant a reasonable person in believing that he intended a real agreement, 17 C.J.S., Contracts, §47, p. 390; Clark on Contracts, 4 ed., §27, at p. 54.

Whether the writing signed by the defendants and now sought to be enforced by the complainants was the result of a serious offer by Lucy and a serious acceptance by the defendants, or was a serious offer by Lucy and an acceptance in secret jest by the defendants, in either event it constituted a binding contract of sale between the parties. Reversed and remanded.

Case Questions

1. How long had the parties to the lawsuit known each other prior to entering into this "agreement," and do you feel that this affected the decision of the Virigina court?
2. How much did Zehmer originally pay for the farm?
3. What night was the agreement signed?
4. What contract remedy did the court ultimately order?

Case 2

In this 2004 unpublished decision from New York state, consider the various legal theories involving contract and tort law that the plaintiff alleged the defendant breached.

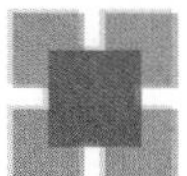

SEFTON v. HEWITT

2004 N.Y. Slip. Op. 50589 (u) (Kings 2004)

MEMDEZ, J.

Plaintiff brings this action in breach of contract and architectural malpractice to recover damages in the amount of $25,000. Defendant counterclaims to recover the amount of $46,800 in *quantum meruit*, conversion, unjust enrichment and in breach of contract. The matter was tried by the court April 20 through April 22, 2004. Plaintiff presented one witness, Curry Rinzler, an expert in the field of architecture, and also testified on his behalf. Defendant presented two witnesses, Dan Heyden, an expert in the field of architecture; Gretel Schwartzott, defendant's girlfriend; and also testified on his behalf.

Sometime before September 1999, plaintiff approached defendant to obtain his professional opinion and suggestions in the design and construction of a house which he wanted to build in Woodstock, New York. The parties' conversation culminated in an oral agreement which, according to plaintiff, provided for defendant to design the house, draw the necessary plans and supervise construction on site. For these services, defendant was to receive a flat fee of $14,400. However, according to defendant, the oral agreement provided only for defendant to design the house and draw the plans for a fee of twelve percent of the total cost of construction. No on-site construction supervision was required.

On September 2, 1999, defendant submitted to plaintiff a "cost estimate" for a house of approximately 1900 square feet. The estimate contained an estimated cost of construction of $122,455 and allocated an "architecture/engineering fee of 10–15% of construction cost." Defendant testified that at the time he submitted this estimate "it was a preliminary pricing just to establish an understanding of how we should proceed." The parties continued negotiations and in November 24, 1999, plaintiff tendered defendant the sum of $2,400 by check number 142. This check had written on it "Architectural services 1/6th total fee house on Violi road." On March 27, 2000, plaintiff tendered the sum of $2,400 by check number 147. This check had written on it "2nd of 6 payments for architectural services for house on Violi Road."

On March 27, 2001, plaintiff tendered the sum of $2,400 by check number 167. This check had written on it "3rd of 6 payments for architectural services for Violi Road." Defendant cashed these checks without protest.

A project schedule dated January 14, 2001, well over one year after the original cost estimate and the first payment by plaintiff, delineates the time at which every payment was to be made. The third payment was due in February 2001; the fourth payment in March 2001; the fifth payment in May 2001 and the sixth and final payment at substantial construction completion in February 2002. This project schedule did not state the amount to be paid or whether it was being calculated as a flat fee or a percentage of construction cost.

According to defendant, plaintiff was not satisfied with the design and drawings originally made and requested changes which increased the cost of construction. As a result of this, defendant requested immediate payment and an increase in fees. However, plaintiff refused to make additional payments until modified drawings were delivered and defendant refused to deliver these drawings before he received payment.

Subsequently, plaintiff retained the services of Curry Rinzler, an architect licensed in the field for over twenty years. Mr. Rinzler made a set of drawings which were to plaintiff's liking and acceptance. Plaintiff paid Mr. Rinzler a flat fee of $9,225 for these drawings.

Mr. Rinzler was qualified as an expert in the field of architecture and testified on plaintiff's behalf. His testimony regarding the quality of the drawings and the cost estimate was of great importance to this Court. In his expert opinion, the drawings made by defendant are "reasonable within the standards of the profession." "Mr. Rinzler is familiar with the means catalog (which was used by the defendant in estimating the cost of construction), has used it in the past and finds the estimate given by defendant to be close to the actual cost of construction for a house of this type, without interiors."

Defendant counters that the contract is void under the Statute of Frauds. Furthermore, in the event there was a contract, plaintiff breached it when he refused to make payment. Defendant also claims *quantum meruit* for the drawings and changes to the drawings for which plaintiff failed to pay.

The formation of a contract requires at least two parties with legal capacity to contract, mutual assent to the terms of the contract and consideration. Mutual assent is a meeting of the minds of the parties on all essential terms of the contract.

The manifestation of assent may take the form of written or spoken words (expressed contract) or of an act or failure to act (implied in fact contract).

A mere agreement to agree in which a material term is left for future negotiations is unenforceable. If the terms of the agreement are so vague and indefinite that there is no means by which such terms may be made certain, then there is no enforceable contract. If an agreement is not reasonably certain in its material terms, there can be no legally enforceable contract.

To establish a claim for breach of contract under New York law, a plaintiff must prove:

1. That an agreement existed between it and the defendant;
2. What the respective obligations of the parties were;
3. That plaintiff performed it's obligation under the agreement;
4. That the defendant breached the agreement by failing to perform its obligation;
5. That the plaintiff suffered damages as a result of the breach.

Where a contract does not have such essential terms as the time or manner of performance or price to be paid, the contract is unenforceable.

The facts demonstrate that the parties did not agree on the price or the manner of performance. While plaintiff believed the price to be $14,400 based on a flat fee, the defendant believed the price to be a percentage of the construction cost. While plaintiff believed the defendant was to supply the design sets and provide on-site supervision, defendant believed his only obligation was to provide the set of drawings. There was no agreement on material elements of the contract; therefore, there was no enforceable contract. Since there was no enforceable contract, a necessary element to be proven in a breach of contract claim, there was no breach of contract.

The Statute of Frauds provides that an agreement will not be recognized or enforced if it is not in writing and subscribed by the party to be charged when the agreement by its terms is not to be performed within one year from its making or is not completed before the end of a lifetime (*General Obligation Law §5-701(a)(1)*). An agreement for the design of a house does not fall within the Statute of Frauds as a contract for the sale of an interest in real property. If the oral agreement can be fully performed within one year, it will not be void under the Statute of Frauds. The defendant has the burden of establishing the defense of the Statute of Frauds.

Where the alleged oral agreement requires the balance of the contract price to be paid at a date beyond one year, the contract can not be performed within one year and is therefore void under the Statute of Frauds.

Under New York Law, the Statute of Frauds requires complete performance of the contract within one year and not just a part thereto. The Doctrine of Part Performance may be invoked to remove an oral agreement from the operation of the Statute of Frauds only where plaintiff's actions, viewed alone, can be characterized as unequivocally referable to the agreement alleged. The facts do not support plaintiff's position. It can not be said that his actions, when viewed alone, unequivocally refer to the agreement alleged. At most, his actions may be viewed as payment for services at the time they are rendered and not for the establishment of a contract for the design of a house with on-site construction supervision.

Plaintiff's evidence is insufficient to prove that defendant committed architectural malpractice. His own expert opined that the use of the means catalog was good and accepted practice. He also opined that the design drawings were reasonable within the standards of the profession. There was no expert testimony indicating defendant deviated from what is considered to be good and accepted practice in the profession.

In the absence of a contract, a party may recover in *quantum meruit* if the party provided services and materials under circumstances implying an understanding by both parties that the provider would be paid. *Quantum meruit* is an equitable doctrine that allows the party claiming it to recover on a partly performed contract only the reasonable value of the work performed and materials furnished.

To prevail on a cause of action in *quantum meruit*, the party claiming it must prove 1.) Performance of services in good faith, 2.) Acceptance of the services by the person for whom they are rendered, 3.) An expectation of compensation, and 4.) The reasonable value of the services performed. What is the reasonable value of the services rendered, in this situation, needs to be established through testimony of expert witnesses, not the self-serving assertions of the party claiming *quantum meruit*.

There was no testimony, expert or otherwise, as to what the "reasonable value" of defendant's services; or as to the reasonable number of hours required to make the changes requested by plaintiff. Mr. Rinzler testified that when he made changes to a design he wouldn't make a "new sketch." "Since he worked with a computer, he would alter the model that is in the computer." The conclusion to be reached from this testimony is that it is not required nowadays to spend hundreds or thousands of hours making a new sketch whenever a client is dissatisfied with the design. If the defendant saw it fit to spend his time in this manner he does so at his own peril. Furthermore, the fact that plaintiff requested these changes is an indication of his dissatisfaction. Moreover, it also shows he did not accept the services rendered by defendant. In addition, the defendant testified that he did not give plaintiff all the sets of drawing as they were not yet fully completed. The stonewall construction set which plaintiff obtained after a meeting with defendant in August was obtained after the third payment was made. After those plans were in plaintiff's possession no additional work was required from the defendant. As such, defendant failed to establish that he was entitled to recover on *quantum meruit*. He was paid for the work he performed for the plaintiff, therefore, plaintiff did not convert the stonewall construction set or unjustly enriched himself because he had paid for them in advance.

This Court finds that there was no enforceable contract. There was no agreement as to price, time, and manner of performance. As such, plaintiff failed to establish an essential element of a breach of contract claim and his claim for breach of contract is dismissed. There was no malpractice, plaintiff failed to establish that the use of the means catalog was not good and accepted architectural practice. Plaintiff also failed to establish that the design sets were defective and not within the reasonable standards of the architecture profession, therefore, plaintiff's claim for architectural malpractice is also dismissed.

The defendant did not prove that plaintiff was unjustly enriched or converted the stonewall constructions plans because plaintiff paid for the plans before he obtained them and only got what he paid for. The defendant did not prove that he is entitled to recover in *quantum meruit*. He failed to establish the reasonable value of his services. Furthermore, plaintiff did not accept his service. Therefore, defendant's counterclaims for *quantum meruit*, unjust enrichment, and conversion are respectively dismissed.

This constitutes the decision and judgment of this Court.

Case Questions

1. In which town did the plaintiff intend to build the house?
2. Who testified on behalf of the plaintiff as an "expert witness"?
3. How many elements must a plaintiff prove for a breach of contract under New York state law?
4. Did the court agree that the design of a house falls within the Statute of Frauds (i.e., certain contracts must be in writing to be enforced) requirement that it was a "sale" of an interest in real property?
5. Did the defendant prove the tort of architectural malpractice?

Exercise

Review the attached agreement to mediate. Draft a general cover letter on behalf of the mediator involved in the case to parties and their attorneys. Consider the following language when drafting the cover letter and attaching the agreement to mediate. Also consider other aspects of this basic mediation agreement which might not have been considered:

> The proposed Mediation Agreement reflects the mediation scheduled for ____________. The mediation will be in my ______________ office beginning at ________________ a.m./p.m. Assuming the agreement meets with your approval, I would appreciate your signing it on behalf of you or on behalf of your respective clients.

I am requesting that once you have signed your original, please forward it back to me for my file. If there are any changes that need to be made, please let me know. It would be helpful to me if, at least 24 hours prior to the mediation conference, that each of you would forward me a statement of the basic facts in the case along with a statement of the issues which need to be resolved and the position of your respective clients as to these issues.

If there is any unusual law applicable to these issues or any documents which you feel are relevant to the case and would be helpful for me to review prior to the mediation, please feel free to provide that information also. Otherwise, I will leave it to you as to what information you feel would be useful to me. If this is a court ordered mediation, please forward me a copy of the Order of Reference so I can file a report with the court following our mediation.

Agreement to Mediate

1. **Agreement to Mediation**. The undersigned parties hereby agree to submit to mediation their dispute, ________________________ pursuant to the following terms and conditions.
2. **Time, Place, and Location of Mediation**. The mediation in this case shall be held at __________ a.m./p.m. on _____________________ at the office of _______________________.
3. **Mediator**. The parties have agreed that __________ will act as mediator in this case. As mediator, he shall use his best efforts to help the parties reach a mutually satisfactory resolution of their dispute. He has no authority to resolve any issues for the parties, but may offer suggestions to the parties to help them resolve this matter. Although all persons will participate in good faith in the mediation process, the mediator does not warrant settlement will result from this process. It is the responsibility of the parties to reach a settlement that is acceptable to them. The mediator will not give legal advice or act as legal counsel to any party in this dispute.
4. **The Mediation**. At the outset of the mediation, the mediator will meet with both parties and their counsel. During the course of the mediation, the mediator will meet separately with each party and that party's counsel. The mediator also may meet separately with counsel outside the presence of the parties and party representatives if necessary to help facilitate settlement.
5. **Party Presence**. Each party or a party representative with full settlement authority shall be present during the entire mediation. If a party or party representative with full settlement authority will not be present at the mediation, the attorney for that party shall immediately notify all opposing counsel or parties of this fact. Any other persons necessary to a settlement also shall be present during the entire mediation. Persons other than the parties, their representatives, their counsel, and the mediator may attend the mediation only with the consent of the parties and the mediator.
6. **Confidentiality**. Statements made or documents offered by any person in connection with the mediation are confidential. However, with the consent of the person making a statement or offering a document, the mediator may reveal information to another person during the mediation in an effort to facilitate settlement.

   The mediation is considered by both parties to be a compromise negotiation within the meaning of Rule 408 of the _________________ (**name the state**) and Federal Rules of Evidence. No party shall attempt to introduce statements made or documents offered by any person in connection with the mediation in any judicial, arbitral, or other forum, except to the extent that the evidence is admissible under Rule 408 or other governing law. The parties will not attempt to subpoena the mediator or any documents considered or created in connection with the mediation in any other proceeding.
7. **Party Statements**. At least two days prior to the mediation, each party shall provide the mediator with a short statement describing their case and their individual position on the

issues to be resolved by the mediation. This statement should include any information which the parties believe may be helpful to the mediator to facilitate the mediation process. If the parties send information to the mediator which they wish to be kept confidential by the mediator from opposing parties, such information should be clearly designated as confidential. Each party may send a copy of their position statement to opposing parties.

8. **Fees**. The mediator shall be compensated for time expended in connection with the mediation process at the rate of $225.00 per hour. The mediator's time shall include time spent in the mediation, scheduling and preparation time for the mediation, and any communications with the attorneys and/or their clients. The mediator's fee shall be shared equally by the parties, unless the parties reach another agreement. The mediator's statement for services shall be sent directly to the parties' attorneys for payment. If the scheduled mediation is canceled by a party or parties, a cancellation fee will be charged in the amount of $250.00, unless a new mediation date is scheduled at the time of the cancellation.
9. **Exclusion of Liability**. The mediator shall not be liable for any act or omission in connection with this mediation and shall not be considered a necessary party to any other proceedings related to the mediation.
10. **Termination of the Mediation**. The mediation may be terminated by an agreement of the parties to settle thei\r dispute, a determination by the mediator that further mediation will not be productive, or a decision by either party that the mediation should be concluded.

______________________________	______________________________
Attorney for Plaintiff	Attorney for Defendant
______________________________	Party
Mediator	Other
Date: ____________________	(circle all the above which are relevant)

References

Bridgeman, C., *Allegheny College Revisited: Cardozo, Consideration, and Formalism in Context*, 39 U.C. Davis L. Rev. 149 (2005).

Chevlin, D., *Schemes and Scams: Auction Fraud and the Culpability of Host Auction Web Sites*, 18 Loy. Consumer L. Rev. 223 (2005).

Eisenberg, M.A., *The Revocation of Offers*, 2004 Wis. L. Rev. 271 (2004).

Fasciano, P., *Internet Electronic Mail: A Last Bastion for the Mailbox Rule*, 25 Hofstra L. Rev. 971 (1997).

McCarthy, M.R., *Revenue Sharing in Major League Baseball: Are Cuba's Political Managers on Their Way over Too?* 7 Vand. J. Ent. L. & Prac. 555 (2005).

Rowley, K.A., *You Asked for It, You Got It . . . Toy Yoda: Practical Jokes, Prizes, and Contract Law*, 3 Nev. L.J. 526 (2003).

Teeven, K.M., *A Legal History of Binding Gratuitous Promises at Common Law: Justifiable Reliance and Moral Obligation*, 43 Duq. L. Rev. 11 (2004).

Chapter 3

Consideration

After reading this chapter you will be able to:

1. Define the term consideration, the third element of the contract formula.
2. Discuss the role of the preexisting duty rule when determining whether there was valid consideration for a new contract.
3. Understand that past consideration is not considered consideration for a new contract.
4. Describe and give examples of illusory promises.
5. Explain the various ways in which a contract might be modified after it has been formed.

Key Terms

Accord and satisfaction	Disclaimer	Preexisting duty rule
Bargained-for exchange	Exculpatory clause	Rescission
Cancel at anytime	Illusory promise	Release
Consideration	Past consideration	

K = O + A + **C** + (Legality + Capacity)

Consideration is the third element of the contract formula and is a vital element in the law of contracts. It is often characterized as the "price" of a promise in a **bargained-for exchange**.[1] Consideration may also be described as a bargained-for exchange with legally sufficient value.[2] Consideration usually involves the payment of money for a product, service, option, or for the forbearance of an act. In other words, a party to a contract gives something of value to another party, and there was no previous obligation to do so. Consideration is the aspect of a contract that induces a party to enter into an agreement in the first place. Thus, consideration is that aspect of contract law which differentiates it from a gift, donation, or an off-the-cuff promise which normally involve no consideration whatsoever.[3] Courts generally do not question whether the consideration was (or was not) legally sufficient or genuine "enough" as an element of the contract formula unless it was designed to defraud or scam. Consideration does not have to be represented in monetary terms. Also promises that are purely moral in nature generally fail to rise to the level of consideration for the purposes of a contract.

[1] In essence, a bargained for exchange is a *quid pro quo*: this for that (something for something).
[2] *See* Fischer v. Union Trust Co., 101 N.W. 852 (Mich. 1904) ($1 as consideration for a deed on property).
[3] *Id.*

PREEXISTING DUTY RULE

If one already has an obligation to perform under a contract, using that already agreed-upon obligation as consideration for a subsequent contract is simply not valid to satisfy this third element. This is because there was no subsequent bargained-for exchange. There was no new offer, no new acceptance, and no new consideration. The **preexisting duty rule,** then, requires a new bargained-for exchange between the parties in order to prevent forms of extortion or the "holdup game" in which one party to an existing contract states that they will not perform (as already agreed) unless the other party agrees to this newer arrangement. Many courts are open to good faith adjustments to contracts, especially those involving the buying and selling of goods, as long as there are extraordinary circumstances involving unforeseen difficulties in performing the contract. However, this is something that the parties could have agreed to prior to entering into the agreement in the first place—the work of proficient contract drafters.

PAST CONSIDERATION

Similar to the preexisting duty rule, **past consideration** cannot count as future consideration. For example, if A makes a promise to B, "I will deliver your pizzas for you today" and A follows through, and then the next day B says, "In consideration for your efforts, I'll pay you $500," the second statement is not an enforceable promise because there is no consideration. In other words it is more akin to a gift (a gratuitous promise).

ILLUSORY PROMISES

An empty promise (*nudum pactum*) is not enforceable in a court of law. These empty promises are also known as **illusory promises**. An example of this might be when a sales manager says, "If we continue to have high sales this month, then I will give you all a bonus of 10 percent." This statement is not actually an enforceable promise, and therefore there is no consideration because it is so uncertain (what does "high" mean?) and sounds like a matter of opinion or discretion. Consider the statement, "I will give you a bonus if I am in a good mood." Is this an illusory statement? Most likely it is and is remarkably similar to a contract that lacks definiteness or is considered void for vagueness. Illusory promises are not valid, while enforceable promises are enforceable. However, as in many contract disputes, the line between an enforceable promise and an illusory promise is not always clear. A court might consider (as a substitute for consideration) detrimental reliance on a promise after a promise is made to another party to an agreement.[4]

[4]*See* Hoffman v. Red Owl Stores, 133 N.W.2d 267 (Wis. 1965) (Discussion of promissory estoppel).

POSTCONTRACT ISSUES

Issues may emerge from a contractual relationship following the execution of the legally binding agreement which might cause the parties to want to later modify or even terminate their agreement. In each instance, the concern is whether these subsequent actions can legally supersede the original (and still legally enforceable) agreement. The answer is "yes" unless there was fraud, duress, or mutual mistake, and there was no abuse of power in the contractual relationship (often referred to as adhesion). One must expect that once a contract has been formed, it is possible that a modification might be made later. The issue is whether further consideration is needed in that situation. It depends on whether the parties had agreed to it in their original agreement. If not, one could still modify an agreement later as long as both parties agreed to the change. The subsequent waiver or modification would be valid consideration to modify the agreement. The following sections involve postcontract issues.

ACCORD AND SATISFACTION

The phrase **accord and satisfaction** is often used to describe a final and binding settlement of an otherwise enforceable contract. A settlement of debts for less than what was owed would be an example of an accord and satisfaction. For example, A owes B some money. They eventually settle that debt for less than what was owed (or even waive the whole amount altogether). B has agreed to less than what was owed. That settlement then supersedes the original agreement and can be referred to as an accord and satisfaction; it is used to wrap up an obligation so that the parties can move on.[5]

RELEASE

Similar to an accord and satisfaction, a **release** (sometimes called a waiver, **disclaimer**, **exculpatory clause**) is used to avoid liability (financial or otherwise) in a contractual relationship. It might be signed after the contract has already been entered into. Whether it is valid, of course, is up to a court, but unless there was evidence of extortion, adhesion, gross negligence, or recklessness, releases will usually be upheld as valid.

FORBEARANCE

Consideration could be valid by refraining from doing an act in which a party actually had a legal right to perform in the first place based upon the original contract. Forbearance as a form of consideration was at the heart of the classic contract case *Hamer*

[5] *See* http://www.themorningsun.com/stories/062006/spo_waived001.shtml (university waived right to pursue damages from a former coach after the coach resigned).

v. Sidway, 124 N.Y. 538, 27 N.E. 256 (1891) in which a nephew gave up drinking, smoking, and playing cards and billiards for money in reliance on a promise made by his uncle to him that he would be paid $5,000 on his twenty-first birthday for doing so. The court made clear that it was irrelevant whether giving up those things was good or bad for the nephew. The fact remained that he did not have a duty to give up those choices otherwise, and refraining from these acts constituted valid consideration.

RESCISSION

Rescission is an act in which a party to the contract has the right to void the agreement. In essence, the contract is canceled by one of the parties. This could involve the entire contract or simply a part of it. This is usually agreed upon ahead of time by the parties. Rescission is an equitable remedy: it destroys the existing contract and restores the parties to their situation prior to entering into the agreement.[6] If money had been paid by one party to the other, it must be returned. Rescission might be used as a remedy to avoid a contract that was formed as a result of a misrepresentation, the lack of legal capacity by a party, impossibility of performance, or duress (undue influence). For example, assume you agreed to sell and the buyer agreed to buy some land that you *thought* you owned. Later it turns out that you did not have clear title to the property. Rescission, then, might be the appropriate legal remedy for the parties.

UCC

According to the UCC, consideration is not required for a merchant's written firm offer, written discharge of a claim for breach of contract, or for an agreement to modify a contract for the sale of goods.[7] This makes the UCC much more flexible than the principles found in common law contracts. The UCC is discussed in greater detail in the second half of this text.

CANCEL AT ANYTIME

When a buyer and seller contract for the sale of goods or services and there is a **cancel at anytime** clause, this clause is valid, but it can create challenges for courts. For example, if party A agrees "to give B $5,000 per month for B's services, but A can cancel at anytime," one could challenge the validity of that statement. Is that statement an enforceable promise at all since A could fire B before B even provided any services? If services are provided, must A give so many days notice prior to termination? Must goods be returned? The best way to deal with this issue might be to draft more specific contracts. Otherwise, courts will have to consider

[6]Often referred to as *status quo ante*.
[7]*See* UCC §2-209(1).

issues such as promissory estoppel (detrimental reliance), *quasi* contract issues, *quantum meruit*, and so on.

CHAPTER SUMMARY

Consideration is a curious yet very important part of the contract formula. Consideration is the price of the promise. Without consideration, promises would not be able to be enforced. The consideration element of a contract differentiates a contract from a gift. Important to the understanding of contract law, one must appreciate the differences between the preexisting duty rule and past consideration, neither of which provide for valid consideration for subsequent contract formation. One of the more interesting areas of contract law is differentiating between contracts that can be enforced and those that are merely illusory in nature. Once a contract is formed, issues might arise in the postcontract setting, including modifying the contract (by agreement) between the parties.

Discussion and Review Questions

1. What is consideration and why is it important in contract law?
2. Describe the similarities or differences between the preexisting duty rule and past consideration.
3. What does the phrase "bargained-for-exchange" mean?
4. What is an illusory promise? Is it enforceable?
5. What are various postcontract law issues, and how might they relate to consideration?

Critical Thinking Exercises

1. Rachel writes a check to Greg for less than the total amount that was owed to him. In the memo part of the check, Rachel writes "payment in full." Greg accepts the check and deposits it into his bank account. Do you believe that Greg's acceptance of Rachel's check constitutes an accord and satisfaction and therefore he is not entitled to the full amount? Consider California Civil Code §1526.
2. Ian gives Jennifer an engagement ring immediately after his football team scores the winning touchdown in overtime. He gets down on his knee and asks her to marry him in front of a national audience. All the cameras are on Jennifer and she says, "Yes." Unfortunately for the two, Jennifer breaks down several months later and says that she cannot go through with the marriage. Is Ian entitled to the ring back? Is the ring a conditional gift? Should engagement rings fit into a special category of contract law since they are gifts in consideration of ultimately establishing a marriage? *See* http://www.msnbc.msn.com/id/16434314/. *See also*, http://www.foxnews.com/story/0,2933,251498,00.html.
3. Heath, a junior in high school, has a bet with his father that if he gives up drinking soft drinks until the end of his senior year in high school that his father will give him $1,000. Heath successfully completes his challenge, and his father refuses to pay Heath. Could Heath sue his father for breach of contract even though giving up soft drinks was actually good for him?

Online Research Exercises

1. Explore the Internet to find various waivers and releases related to participation in youth sport activities.
2. Explore the Internet to see if you can find examples of cancel at anytime clauses involving the sale of products or services.

CASE APPLICATIONS

Case 1

Consider how this Ohio court dealt with the issue of whether an engagement ring should be treated differently than other gifts and whether the gift was given in consideration of marriage.

COOPER v. SMITH

800 N.E.2D 372 (OHIO 2003)

HARSHA, J.

Lester Cooper appeals a judgment of the Lawrence County Common Pleas Court dismissing his complaint, which sought reimbursement for gifts he had given to his ex-fiancee, Julie Smith, and her mother, Janet Smith. Cooper contends the gifts he gave to Julie were given in contemplation of marriage and should be returned to him now that the engagement has ended. In addition, he contends the gifts he gave to Janet should be returned to him under a theory of unjust enrichment. With the exception of the engagement ring, the gifts Cooper gave to Julie were irrevocable *inter vivos* gifts. Thus, he is not entitled to their return. Moreover, because enrichment of the donee is the intended purpose of a gift, there is nothing "unjust" about allowing Janet to retain the gifts she received from Cooper in the absence of fraud, overreaching or some other circumstance. Accordingly, the judgment of the trial court is affirmed.

In May 2001, Cooper suffered serious injury that caused him to be hospitalized for an extended period of time. While he was hospitalized, Julie, who Cooper had met the year before, and Janet made numerous trips to visit him. Although Julie was legally married to another man at the time, a romantic relationship developed between Cooper and Julie. While still in the hospital, Cooper proposed to Julie and she accepted, indicating that she would marry him after she divorced her husband. Although Julie obtained a divorce from her husband in October 2001, she and Cooper did not marry.

Cooper ultimately received an $180,000 settlement for his injuries. After being released from the hospital, Cooper moved in with Janet and Julie. Over the next couple of months, Cooper purchased a number of items for Julie, including a diamond engagement ring, a car, a computer, a tanning bed, and horses. Cooper also paid off Janet's car loan and made various improvements to her house, such as having a new furnace installed and having wood flooring laid in the kitchen. By December 2001, the settlement money had run out.

In June 2002, an incident occurred between Janet and Cooper and he moved out of the house. However, he and Julie continued their relationship. One month after moving out, Cooper informed Julie that he intended to sue Janet to recover the money he had invested in her house. Julie responded by telling Cooper that she could not be with him if he sued her mother. That same month, Cooper filed suit against both Julie and Janet.

In December 2002, Cooper's case proceeded to trial before the magistrate. At trial, Cooper testified that the gifts he gave to Julie were given in contemplation of marriage. He also attempted to show that the gifts he gave to Janet, including the improvements to her house, were conditional gifts. He indicated that he paid off Janet's car loan so that when the settlement money ran out, they could live on the money that was previously being used for the monthly car payment. He also indicated that he paid for the improvements to Janet's house because he believed he would be living there in the future.

At the conclusion of Cooper's case-in-chief, appellees moved to dismiss his complaint. The magistrate granted the motion, concluding that even if Cooper's evidence was viewed in the most favorable light, appellees were entitled to dismissal. The magistrate concluded that the gifts Cooper gave to Julie were not given in contemplation of marriage since Julie was legally married to another man at the time. The magistrate further found that even if the gifts were given in contemplation of marriage, Cooper was not entitled to their return because he unjustifiably broke the engagement. With respect to the gifts Cooper gave Janet, the magistrate found that there was no evidence that the gifts were given on any condition. Rather, the magistrate concluded that the gifts were final and could not be recovered since "a gift is an unearned enrichment that cannot be converted into an unjust enrichment."

The term "gifts in contemplation of marriage" refers to gifts made during the engagement period, following the couple's agreement to marry. Annotation, Rights in Respect of Engagement and Courtship Presents When Marriage Does Not Ensue (1996), 44 A.L.R.5th 1, 17. Gifts in contemplation of marriage become problematic when the marriage does not occur. If a donor gives gifts in contemplation of marriage and the marriage does not occur, is the donor entitled to recover the gifts? If the donor is entitled to recover the gifts, is that right absolute or is it subject to limitations?

The majority of cases addressing gifts in contemplation of marriage deal exclusively with engagement rings. However, our research has uncovered some cases, including two from Ohio, that address gifts other than engagement rings. After reviewing the cases from Ohio and elsewhere, we have identified five possible approaches to the present issue.

Under the first approach, the donor is denied recovery if the donee was legally married to someone else at the time the donor and donee became engaged. This approach recognizes that an agreement to marry where one party is already married is void as against public policy. *See* Lowe. Where the donor has sought equitable relief, courts adopting this approach have denied recovery based on the doctrine of "unclean hands." Lowe; Morgan. As the Supreme Court of Georgia stated: "The deliberate attempt to take another man's wife from him, and entering into an engagement with her to marry at a time when she could not lawfully marry, and giving a ring to further such an unlawful engagement is a defiance of public policy and constitutes the rankest sort of unclean hands. The doors of equity are closed to petitioner and deny him any relief whatsoever."

Although the trial court adopted this approach in denying Cooper recovery, we are not persuaded that this is the best approach. While this approach punishes the donor for his conduct, it rewards a party that is equally guilty. *Witkowski, supra.* Julie knew when she accepted Cooper's proposal that she could not lawfully marry him, yet she accepted the proposal anyway. We see no reason to adopt a rule that allows Julie to benefit from her conduct while punishing Cooper for his.

The second approach treats all gifts exchanged during the engagement period as irrevocable *inter vivos* gifts. A variation on this approach treats the gifts as irrevocable *inter vivos* gifts unless they are expressly conditioned on the subsequent marriage. This approach adheres to general gift law, which provides that an *inter vivos* gift is irrevocable once complete. *See* Albinger. Courts adopting this approach refuse to imply a condition on the gifts simply because they were given during the engagement period. *See* Id.

This approach is easy to apply and encourages a donor to think twice before giving extravagant gifts. Moreover it does not allow a donor to recover/revoke a gift simply because he or she later regrets having given it. However, without an exception for fraud, this approach works an injustice on unsuspecting donors who are deceived by wily donees. Moreover, the variation on this approach attempts to apply logical reasoning to an emotional situation. During the engagement period, the donor is focused upon the romantic nature of the relationship and is not likely to consider the possibility that the marriage may not occur. Thus, a donor only rarely thinks about putting a condition on the gifts he or she gives.

The third approach treats the engagement ring as a conditional gift but treats all other gifts as irrevocable *inter vivos* gifts unless they were expressly conditioned on the subsequent marriage. This approach recognizes that an engagement ring symbolizes the couple's promise to marry. *See* Albanese. Because of that symbolic significance, it implies a condition with respect to the engagement ring only. *See* Id. This approach also recognizes that "* * * in the natural course of events it would be unusual for the donor to give the engagement ring upon the expressed condition that marriage was to ensue." Thus, it implies a condition to the gift of the engagement ring. However, this approach recognizes that the other gifts lack the symbolic significance of the engagement ring. *See* Albanese. It recognizes that gifts other than the engagement ring are "only a token of the love and affection which [the donor] bore for the [donee]." It refuses to allow the donor to recover the gift simply because he or she later regrets having given it. Thus, it applies general gift law and treats the other gifts as irrevocable *inter vivos* gifts unless they were expressly conditioned on the subsequent marriage.

Like the second approach, this approach is easy to apply and would encourage donors to think twice before giving extravagant gifts. However, it suffers from the same disadvantages as the second approach. It, too, would require a fraud exception to avoid injustice. Moreover, it also assumes the donor will consider the possibility that the marriage might not occur.

Both the fourth (fault-based) and fifth (no-fault) approaches generally allow recovery based on a conditional gift theory, although the fault-based approach contains limitations on recovery. *See*, generally, Annotation, 44 A.L.R.5th at 18 ("A predominate theory used in ordering recovery of engagement gifts to the donor relies upon the theory of conditional gifts"). Under both approaches, courts will imply a condition on the gifts because of the nature of the engagement period or, in the case of engagement rings, the nature of the gift. Although the fault-based approach used to be the majority position, the modern trend leans toward a no-fault approach.

The fault-based approach permits the donor to recover the gifts unless he or she unjustifiably broke the engagement. This approach appeals to society's sense of justice, especially in those situations where the donor has truly "wronged" the donee. This approach also recognizes that if the donor had kept the promise, the gifts would belong to the donee. Thus, it attempts to prevent the donor from being rewarded for breaking a promise. *See* Id. In the engagement ring situation, this approach also recognizes that the donee has often expended money towards the wedding by the time the donor ends the engagement. Since the donee has no recourse for recovering the money, allowing the donee to keep the engagement ring may serve as compensation. However, as a discussion of the no-fault approach will show, the fault-based approach has its disadvantages.

Under the no-fault approach, gifts given in contemplation of marriage are returned to the donor if the marriage does not occur, regardless of who is at fault in ending the engagement. Courts adopting this approach have noted that legislatures and courts are moving away from a fault-based approach to divorce. *See* Vigil; Aronow. These courts conclude that "the policy statements that govern 'our approach to broken marriages [are] equally relevant to broken engagements.'" Courts adopting this approach also point to the difficulties involved in determining who is at fault and whether a person's reasons for ending an engagement are justifiable. Lyle; Patterson; Heiman. These courts express a concern that a fault-based approach will lead to acrimonious lawsuits, with each party attempting to blame the other for the termination of the engagement.

Having carefully considered the five different approaches, we conclude the third approach, which implies a condition on the gift of the engagement ring only, is the best approach. The engagement ring has a special significance because it symbolizes the couple's promise to marry. As a symbol of the promise to marry, what value does the ring have for the donee once the engagement is ended? Moreover, we realize that a donor proposing to his or her beloved is unlikely to expressly condition the gift of the engagement ring on the occurrence of the marriage. Not only do we realize how unlikely this is, we recognize how unromantic such a requirement would be. Thus, because of the engagement ring's symbolic significance, we are willing to imply a condition to the gift of the engagement ring. Unless the parties have agreed otherwise, the donor is entitled to recover the engagement ring (or its value) if the marriage does not occur, regardless of who ended the engagement.

While we are willing to imply a condition concerning the engagement ring, we are unwilling to do so for other gifts given during the engagement period. Unlike the engagement ring, the other gifts have no symbolic meaning. Rather, they are merely "tokens of the love and affection which [the donor] bore for the [donee]." *Albanese, supra.* As the Albanese Court noted: "Many gifts are made for reasons that sour with the passage of time." Unfortunately, gift law does not allow a donor to recover/revoke an *inter vivos* gift simply because his or her reasons for giving it have "soured".

Generally, a completed *inter vivos* gift is absolute and irrevocable. However, a donor may impose conditions on a gift so that if the conditions fail, the gift also fails. If we were to imply a condition on gifts given during the engagement period, then every gift the donor gave, no matter how small or insignificant, would be recoverable. Surely, the donor will give some gifts during the engagement period that are intended as absolute gifts. However, with an implied condition, the donor would have to expressly indicate he does not expect the gift back in order to make an absolute gift. Such a rule turns traditional gift law on its head. We believe the best approach is to treat gifts exchanged during the engagement period (excluding the engagement ring) as absolute and irrevocable *inter vivos* gifts unless the donor has expressed an intent that the gift be conditioned on the subsequent marriage.

Applying this approach to the present case, we affirm the trial court's ruling, although for different reasons. At trial, Cooper testified that Julie returned the diamond engagement ring to him before he filed the lawsuit. Therefore, Cooper could not prevail on a claim for return of the engagement ring because he already had possession of it. As for the other gifts, Cooper offered no evidence establishing that he gave the gifts on the express condition that they be returned to him if the engagement ended. Thus, the gifts are irrevocable *inter vivos* gifts and Cooper is not entitled to their return.

As we noted earlier, once an *inter vivos* gift is complete, it is generally absolute and irrevocable. However, a donor may impose conditions on a gift so that if the conditions fail, the gift fails. "Whether a gift is conditional or absolute is a question of the donor's intent, to be determined from any express declaration by the donor at the time of the making of the gift or from the circumstances." 38 American Jurisprudence 2d (1999) 767-68, Gifts, Section 72. In its entry, the trial court found that "there is simply no evidence that [the gifts] were given on any condition, but instead were absolute and irrevocable." Having reviewed the record, we conclude there is some competent, credible evidence to support the court's finding.

Cooper contends he only paid for the improvements to Janet's house because he believed he would be living there for the rest of his life. However, the record indicates that Cooper merely presumed he would be living there in the future. During the trial, he testified that he "figured [he] was going to be living there and [he] was going to be married to Julie." There is nothing in the record to indicate that Cooper told Janet he was giving her the gifts because he planned on living in her house in the future. In fact, when confronted with his deposition testimony, Cooper admitted that he never expressly told Janet he was giving her the gifts because he expected to live in her house.

Cooper also contends he paid off Janet's car loan because they agreed she would help support him when the settlement money ran out. However, a review of the record does not indicate such an explicit agreement. According to Cooper's testimony, Julie suggested it would be a good idea to pay off Janet's car loan so they could live on the money normally used to pay the monthly car payment when the settlement money ran out. Cooper testified that he thought it was a good idea because he was going to be living in the house. However, as stated above, Cooper simply presumed he would live in Janet's house in the future. Thus, he assumed he would benefit from having the extra money around each month. There is nothing in the record to indicate that Janet promised to support Cooper if he paid off her car payment. Nor is there evidence that Cooper expressed an intent that the gift be conditioned on her supporting him in the future.

Finally, Cooper contends he purchased a horse trailer and other related equipment for a business the parties were planning to start. He asserts that Janet has retained possession of the items even though she did not contribute to the purchase of them. During his testimony, Cooper testified that he gave Janet $10,000. He testified that he gave her the money "because nobody lives nowhere for free." According to Janet's testimony, she used $7,000 of the money to purchase a horse trailer. She testified that she attempted to return the remaining $3,000 to Cooper but he told her to keep it. Thus, some evidence supports the trial court's conclusion that the $10,000, which Janet used to purchase the horse trailer, was an absolute gift. As for the related equipment, Cooper does not indicate what "related equipment" he is referring to. However, Cooper's testimony contains no mention of the business the parties were planning to start or the horse trailer and related equipment. When questioned about the alleged business, Janet denied knowledge of it. The only witness that offered testimony related to the business was a neighbor of Janet's, and his testimony related solely to the horse trailer.

Accordingly, we conclude the court's finding declaring the gifts final and absolute was not against the manifest weight of the evidence. Because the gifts to Janet were final and absolute, no issue of unjust enrichment arises. As noted above, "enrichment of the donee is the intended purpose of a gift." JUDGMENT AFFIRMED.

Case Questions

1. How much of an insurance settlement did the plaintiff receive as a result of his personal injuries?
2. Did the trial court award the engagement ring back to Cooper? Why or why not?
3. What were some of the items that the plaintiff purchased for the defendant even though they never married?
4. What does the phrase *inter vivos* mean?
5. According to this appellate court, is the donor of an engagement ring in Ohio entitled to a return of the ring if the marriage never occurs?

Case 2

Consider this classic case from New York state. This case is frequently cited as a seminal case in contract law. Ultimately, it demonstrates that whether consideration is "good" or "bad" is not relevant.

HAMER v. SIDWAY

27 N.E. 256 (N.Y. 1891)

PARKER, J.

The question which provoked the most discussion by counsel on this appeal, and which lies at the foundation of plaintiff's asserted right of recovery, is whether by virtue of a contract defendant's testator William E. Story became indebted to his nephew William E. Story, 2d, on his twenty-first birthday in the sum of five thousand dollars. The trial court found as a fact that "on the 20th day of March, 1869, * * * William E. Story agreed to and with William E. Story, 2d, that if he would refrain from drinking liquor, using tobacco, swearing, and playing cards or billiards for money until he should become 21 years of age then he, the said William E. Story, would at that time pay him, the said William E. Story, 2d, the sum of $5,000 for such refraining, to which the said William E. Story, 2d, agreed," and that he "in all things fully performed his part of said agreement."

The defendant contends that the contract was without consideration to support it, and, therefore, invalid. He asserts that the promisee by refraining from the use of liquor and tobacco was not harmed but benefited; that that which he did was best for him to do independently of his uncle's promise, and insists that it follows that unless the promisor was benefited, the contract was without consideration. A contention, which if well founded, would seem to leave open for controversy in many cases whether that which the promisee did or omitted to do was, in fact, of such benefit to him as to leave no consideration to support the enforcement of the promisor's agreement. Such a rule could not be tolerated, and is without foundation in the law. The Exchequer Chamber, in 1875, defined consideration as follows: "A valuable consideration in the sense of the law may consist either in some right, interest, profit or benefit accruing to the one party, or some forbearance, detriment, loss or responsibility given, suffered or undertaken by the other." Courts "will not ask whether the thing which forms the consideration does in fact benefit the promisee or a third party, or is of any substantial value to anyone. It is enough that something is promised, done, forborne or suffered by the party to whom the promise is made as consideration for the promise made to him." (Anson's Prin. of Con. 63.)

"In general a waiver of any legal right at the request of another party is a sufficient consideration for a promise." (Parsons on Contracts, 444.)

"Any damage, or suspension, or forbearance of a right will be sufficient to sustain a promise." (Kent, vol. 2, 465, 12th ed.)

Pollock, in his work on contracts, page 166, after citing the definition given by the Exchequer Chamber already quoted, says: "The second branch of this judicial description is really the most important one. Consideration means not so much that one party is profiting as that the other abandons some legal right in the present or limits his legal freedom of action in the future as an inducement for the promise of the first."

Now, applying this rule to the facts before us, the promisee used tobacco, occasionally drank liquor, and he had a legal right to do so. That right he abandoned for a period of years upon the strength of the promise of the testator that for such forbearance he would give him $5,000. We need not speculate on the effort which may have been required to give up the use of those stimulants. It is sufficient that he restricted his lawful freedom of action within certain prescribed limits upon the faith of his uncle's agreement, and now having fully performed the conditions imposed, it is of no moment whether such performance actually proved a benefit to the promisor, and the court will not inquire into it, but were it a proper subject of inquiry, we see nothing in this record that would permit a determination that the uncle was not benefited in a legal sense. Few cases have been found which may be said to be precisely in point, but such as have been support the position we have taken.

In *Shadwell v. Shadwell* (9 C. B. [N. S.] 159), an uncle wrote to his nephew as follows:

> "My Dear Lancey—I am so glad to hear of your intended marriage with Ellen Nicholl, and as I promised to assist you at starting, I am happy to tell you that I will pay to you 150 pounds yearly during my life and until your annual income derived from your profession of a chancery barrister shall amount to 600 guineas, of which your own admission will be the only evidence that I shall require.
>
> "Your affectionate uncle,
>
> "CHARLES SHADWELL."

It was held that the promise was binding and made upon good consideration.

In *Lakota v. Newton*, an unreported case in the Superior Court of Worcester, Mass., the complaint averred defendant's promise that "if you (meaning plaintiff) will leave off drinking for a year I will give you $100," plaintiff's assent thereto, performance of the condition by him, and demanded judment therefor. Defendant demurred on the ground, among others, that the plaintiff's declaration did not allege a valid and sufficient consideration for the agreement of the defendant. The demurrer was overruled.

In *Talbott v. Stemmons* (a Kentucky case not yet reported), the step-grandmother of the plaintiff made with him the following agreement: "I do promise and bind myself to give my grandson, Albert R. Talbott, $500 at my death, if he will never take another chew of tobacco or smoke another cigar during my life from this date up to my death, and if he breaks this pledge he is to refund double the amount to his mother." The executor of Mrs. Stemmons demurred to the complaint on the ground that the agreement was not based on a sufficient consideration. The demurrer was sustained and an appeal taken therefrom to the Court of Appeals, where the decision of the court below was reversed. In the opinion of the court it is said that "the right to use and enjoy the use of tobacco was a right that belonged to the plaintiff and not forbidden by law. The abandonment of its use may have saved him money or contributed to his health, nevertheless, the surrender of that right caused the promise, and having the right to contract with reference to the subject-matter, the abandonment of the use was a sufficient consideration to uphold the promise." Abstinence from the use of intoxicating liquors was held to furnish a good consideration for a promissory note in *Lindell v. Rokes (60 Mo. 249).*

The cases cited by the defendant on this question are not in point. In *Mallory v. Gillett (21 N.Y. 412); Belknap v. Bender (75 id. 446),* and *Berry* v. *Brown (107 id. 659)*, the promise was in contravention of that provision of the Statute of Frauds, which declares void all promises to answer for the debts of third persons unless reduced to writing. In *Beaumont v. Reeve (Shirley's L. C. 6), and Porterfield v. Butler (47 Miss. 165),* the question was whether a moral obligation furnishes sufficient consideration to uphold a subsequent express promise. In *Duvoll v. Wilson (9 Barb. 487),* and *In re Wilber v. Warren (104 N.Y. 192),* the proposition involved was whether an executory covenant against incumbrances in a deed given in consideration of natural love and affection could be enforced. In *Vanderbilt v. Schreyer (91 N.Y. 392),* the plaintiff contracted with defendant to build a house, agreeing to accept in part payment therefor a specific bond and mortgage. Afterwards he refused to finish his contract unless the defendant would guarantee its payment, which was done. It was held that the guarantee could not be enforced for want of consideration. For in building the house the plaintiff only did that which he had contracted to do. And in *Robinson v. Jewett (116 N.Y. 40),* the court simply held that "The performance of an act which the party is under a legal obligation to perform cannot constitute a consideration for a new contract." It will be observed that the agreement which we have been considering was within the condemnation of the Statute of Frauds, because not to be performed within a year, and not in writing. But this defense the promisor could waive, and his letter and oral statements subsequent to the date of final performance on the part of the promisee must be held to amount to a waiver. Were it otherwise, the statute could not now be invoked in aid of the defendant. It does not appear on the face of the complaint that the agreement is one prohibited by the Statute of Frauds, and, therefore, such defense could not be made available unless set up in the answer. (*Porter v. Wormser, 94 N.Y. 431, 450.*) This was not done.

In further consideration of the questions presented, then, it must be deemed established for the purposes of this appeal, that on the 31st day of January, 1875, defendant's testator was indebted to William E. Story, 2d, in the sum of $5,000, and if this action were founded on that contract it would be barred by the Statute of Limitations which has been pleaded, but on that date the nephew wrote to his uncle as follows:

> "Dear Uncle—I am now 21 years old to-day, and I am now my own boss, and I believe, according to agreement, that there is due me $5,000. I have lived up to the contract to the letter in every sense of the word."

A few days later, and on February sixth, the uncle replied, and, so far as it is material to this controversy, the reply is as follows:

> "Dear Nephew—Your letter of the 31st ult. came to hand all right saying that you had lived up to the promise

made to me several years ago. I have no doubt but you have, for which you shall have $5,000 as I promised you. I had the money in the bank the day you was 21 years old that I intended for you, and you shall have the money certain. Now, Willie, I don't intend to interfere with this money in any way until I think you are capable of taking care of it, and the sooner that time comes the better it will please me. I would hate very much to have you start out in some adventure that you thought all right and lose this money in one year. * * * This money you have earned much easier than I did, besides acquiring good habits at the same time, and you are quite welcome to the money. Hope you will make good use of it. * * *

W. E. STORY.

"P. S.—You can consider this money on interest."

The trial court found as a fact that "said letter was received by said William E. Story, 2d, who thereafter consented that said money should remain with the said William E. Story in accordance with the terms and conditions of said letter." And further, "That afterwards, on the first day of March, 1877, with the knowledge and consent of his said uncle, he duly sold, transferred and assigned all his right, title and interest in and to said sum of $5,000 to his wife Libbie H. Story, who thereafter duly sold, transferred and assigned the same to the plaintiff in this action."

It is essential that the letter interpreted in the light of surrounding circumstances must show an intention on the part of the uncle to become a trustee before he will be held to have become such; but in an effort to ascertain the construction which should be given to it, we are also to observe the rule that the language of the promisor is to be interpreted in the sense in which he had reason to suppose it was understood by the promisee. (*White v. Hoyt, 73 N.Y. 505, 511.*) At the time the uncle wrote the letter he was indebted to his nephew in the sum of $5,000, and payment had been requested. The uncle recognizing the indebtedness, wrote the nephew that he would keep the money until he deemed him capable of taking care of it. He did not say "I will pay you at some other time," or use language that would indicate that the relation of debtor and creditor would continue. On the contrary, his language indicated that he had set apart the money the nephew had "earned" for him so that when he should be capable of taking care of it he should receive it with interest. He said: "I had the money in the bank the day you were 21 years old that I intended for you and you shall have the money certain." That he had set apart the money is further evidenced by the next sentence: "Now, Willie, I don't intend to interfere with this money in any way until I think you are capable of taking care of it." Certainly, the uncle must have intended that his nephew should understand that the promise not "to interfere with this money" referred to the money in the bank which he declared was not only there when the nephew became 21 years old, but was intended for him. True, he did not use the word "trust," or state that the money was deposited in the name of William E. Story, 2d, or in his own name in trust for him, but the language used must have been intended to assure the nephew that his money had been set apart for him, to be kept without interference until he should be capable of taking care of it, for the uncle said in substance and in effect: "This money you have earned much easier than I did * * * you are quite welcome to. I had it in the bank the day you were 21 years old and don't intend to interfere with it in any way until I think you are capable of taking care of it and the sooner that time comes the better it will please me." In this declaration there is not lacking a single element necessary for the creation of a valid trust, and to that declaration the nephew assented.

The learned judge who wrote the opinion of the General Term, seems to have taken the view that the trust was executed during the life-time of defendant's testator by payment to the nephew, but as it does not appear from the order that the judgment was reversed on the facts, we must assume the facts to be as found by the trial court, and those facts support its judgment.

The order appealed from should be reversed and the judgment of the Special Term affirmed, with costs payable out of the estate.

Case Questions

1. Who is a testator?
2. How much money did the uncle promise his nephew when he turned 21 if he complied with all the conditions of their agreement?
3. Did the nephew have the legal right to use tobacco and drink liquor even though he was under the age of 21 at the time?

Exercise

Review the following sponsorship agreement in the sport of triathlon (swimming, biking, and then running). Note the obligations between the sponsor and the Triathlete as part of the consideration of the contract. Accordingly, prepare a sponsorship agreement between a local cyclist (someone who is a competitive bicycle rider) and a local clothing store. The store will outfit the cyclist with clothing and provide a small stipend as part of a weeklong ride across the state to draw awareness for breast cancer and breast cancer research. The store is willing to pay the cyclist more if the name and/or logo are mentioned on local radio and television broadcasts or even in newspaper and magazines as well. Consider location, dates and times, and product support for this one-time event.

Sponsorship Agreement between ACE Sport, Inc. and Victoria Preneveaux

A. Assumptions

1. Agreement/Term. All points and financial specifications outlined below are based on a one-year performance apparel sponsorship agreement between Victoria Preneveaux ("Preneveaux") and ACE Sport, Inc. ("ACE") of 15391 Winterhaven Ave, Huntington Beach, CA 92649 beginning March 1, 2007 and continuing through February 28, 2008. ACE reserves the first right of refusal for two (2) additional one-year contracts, the specifics of which would be mutually agreed upon.

2. Primary Performance Apparel Sponsorship. The contract names ACE as Preneveaux's Primary Apparel Sponsor with an exclusive sponsorship agreement covering professional triathlon competition and training apparel as specified in the annual U.S. ACE Catalog (the "Product"). Preneveaux shall provide ACE reasonable notice for ACE to supply requested products. In the event that Preneveaux requests products which ACE does not supply, Preneveaux may purchase such products provided he does not directly purchase from ACE competitors. Preneveaux may not wear non-ACE apparel without prior approval from a ACE representative.

As Primary sponsor, ACE will be entitled to the premier logo placement on the Product, including the competition suit front and rear. Preneveaux agrees to wear the Product and display the screened promotional ACE logo, as defined above, while engaged in athletic activities, including, but not limited to, competitions, awards ceremonies, pre- and post-race functions, clinics, training sessions, sport camps, meetings and promotional events, photo shoots, travel, etc., where deemed appropriate by ACE. In addition, while competing Preneveaux shall wear two ACE temporary tattoos as follows: (1) one logo on both upper arms immediately below the shoulder area.

3. Logo Space. It is understood that ACE shall be Preneveaux's exclusive Primary Performance Apparel Sponsor. Placement of logos on Preneveaux's competition suits will include a single horizontal ACE promotional logo (approx. 21 cm × 5 cm) on the front center of the race top; a single horizontal ACE logo (approx. 21 cm × 5 cm) on the back center of the suit bottom; and a smaller (approx. 8 cm × 4 cm) ACE logo on the back of the race top in the shoulder area. ACE temporary tattoos will remain as specified above (*see* A-2). Preneveaux also agrees to wear a ACE hat (when appropriate) during competition. ACE reserves the right to deduct from Preneveaux's bonus compensation on a pro-rated basis for any logo size or placement non-compliance.

4. Competition. ACE will be provided with a tentative competition schedule by March 1, 2007. ACE also requests to be provided with monthly updates to race schedules in order to coordinate regional marketing and promotional opportunities. ACE also requests race results to be electronically transmitted directly to ACE (pzk@ACESport.com) no more than one week post competition.

5. Rights. ACE is granted the rights to use Preneveaux's name, likeness and endorsement in all aspects of the company's marketing, advertising and promotion; including, but not limited to print and electronic advertising, POP material, personal appearances, press releases, catalogs, etc.

6. Marketing/Promotional Programs. ACE may incorporate Preneveaux into the company's national marketing/promotional/advertising programs as deemed appropriate by ACE. Such involvement may include the creation of advertising materials featuring Preneveaux, appropriate placement in national publications, use of Preneveaux as a spokesperson at clinics and trade shows, etc. ACE reserves the right to specify the nature and extent of the advertising and promotional programs it produces.

7. Appearances. This sponsorship proposal as outlined entitles ACE to a total of three (3) annual appearances from Preneveaux. The appearances can be used at ACE's discretion and may include personal appearance, photo shoots, press conferences, clinics, employee meetings, commercial production, customer relations, etc. For every day in addition to the three (3) contracted days, ACE will compensate Preneveaux a fee of $1,000.00 per day. Travel days will not be included against these three annual appearance days. ACE will provide for reasonable travel expenses for requested appearance days.

8. Ethical Conduct/Early Termination. Preneveaux agrees to uphold the highest standards of ethical conduct so as not to do anything detrimental to the reputation, goodwill, name or logo of ACE. Preneveaux agrees to follow all competition rules and regulations, speak favorably of ACE and conducting himself in a manner exemplifying professional sportsmanship. Preneveaux shall not take any action inconsistent with the endorsement of ACE products and shall not discourage the use of ACE products in any manner whatsoever.

ACE reserves the right to terminate the agreement upon any of the following: (a) If Preneveaux retires from triathlon or becomes seriously ill or injured so as not to compete for an extended period of time; (b) If Preneveaux's conduct becomes detrimental to the sale of it's Products; or (c) If Preneveaux is sanctioned by USA Triathlon during the term of this Agreement for violation of applicable doping control rules and regulations.

9. Indemnity. Each party agrees to indemnify and hold harmless the other against any and all expenses, damages, claims, suits, actions and costs whosoever arising out of, or in any way connected with, the actions, omissions or negligence of the other in the execution of this Agreement.

B. Investment

1. Incentive Program. All incentives to be paid within 21 business days upon receipt of valid invoice(s).

a. Performance Bonus. ACE will offer Preneveaux a competition bonus package totaling up to $3,000 per year for finishes in up to seven (7) mutually agreed upon events. The bonus award breakdown is as follows:

1. First out of Water	$200
2. First Place	$500
3. Top 5 Finish	$250
4. Top 10 Finish	$125

The following is understood:

1) ACE must be notified of and agree on seven races for consideration of Performance Bonus Awards by February 15 of each year of the contract.
2) The seven (7) tentatively agreed upon triathlon races in 2007 shall be: St. Anthony's, St. Croix, Accenture, Escape from Alcatraz, U.S. Nationals and Memphis in May.
3) It is the responsibility of Preneveaux to obtain videotape copies of the relevant TV coverage if applicable.
4) ACE will accept a maximum of seven (7) races for performance bonuses.

b. Television Exposure. ACE will offer Preneveaux a television bonus package totaling up to $5,000.00 per year for exposure of Preneveaux during competition or an interview with the ACE logo clearly displayed.

Following is a breakdown of bonuses:

1. $500 for 10 or more continuous seconds of domestic cable TV exposure.
2. $1000 for 10 or more continuous seconds of network TV exposure.

The following is understood:

1) One bonus will be awarded for all airings of an interview/competition on a single TV station (i.e., multiple time slots)
2) One bonus will be awarded for all aired exposure of competition/interviews given during a single TV show.
3) Network tevevision shall be defined as: ABC, NBC, CBS, FOX.
4) Domestic cable shall be defined as: FOX Sports, ESPN, Sports Channel, ESPN2, CNN.
5) It is the responsibility of Preneveaux to obtain videotape copies of the relevant TV coverage. ACE will award Preneveaux the above mentioned TV exposure bonuses upon receipt of such documentation.
6) Preneveaux is eligible to receive bonuses as defined above for any exposure gained through the direct efforts of ACE.
7) Television bonuses apply only to airings on domestic stations.

c. Print Exposure. ACE will offer Preneveaux a print bonus package totaling up to $2,000.00 per year for photo exposure of Preneveaux (min. dimensions: 9 square inches) with the ACE logo clearly displayed through editorial materials or. To qualify for a print exposure bonus, Preneveaux must be wearing the ACE product with the ACE logo clearly displayed. For each issue of a publication which Preneveaux receives photo exposure through editorial materials or ads. ACE will award the following bonuses for domestic exposure:

- Magazines with 10,000 – 49,999 circulation = $50.00 ea.
- Magazines with 50,000 – 99,999 circulation = $100.00 ea.

- Magazines with 100,000 – 499,000 circulation = $150.00 ea.
- Magazines with 500,000 – 999,000 circulation = $200.00 ea.
- Magazines with 1 Million + circulation = $400.00 ea.
- Newspapers with 1 Million + circulation = $200.00 ea.

The following is understood:

1) It is the responsibility of Preneveaux to obtain originals of the relevant print coverage/clippings. Clippings must accompany invoices and ACE will award Preneveaux the above mentioned print bonuses upon receipt of such documentation.
2) Multiple exposures on a single page qualify for one bonus; however, Preneveaux is eligible to receive more than one bonus for multiple exposures within a publication, given the size specifications outlined above.
3) Ads placed by another sponsor that feature Preneveaux wearing a clearly visible ACE logo are eligible for bonus but can account for no more than $500 of the $2,000.00 maximum.
4) Preneveaux is eligible to receive bonuses as defined above for any exposure gained through the direct efforts of ACE.
5) To qualify for the print bonus, the minimum size of the photo may be no less than nine (9) square inches.

2. Product Support. ACE will provide Preneveaux with an apparel package valued at approximately $2,000.00 retail on an annual basis designed for use at competitions and during daily workouts. While flexibility is available in apparel quality and selection, ACE reserves the right to designate the specific apparel worn to triathlon functions where deemed appropriate. Preneveaux agrees to use the Product consistently and on a regular basis, and to provide feedback to ACE as required. Additional product for family and friends is not included within this package but can be offered at wholesale cost. Additional product requests of this nature are subject to ACE's discretion.

C. Total Package Value

1. Year 1

ITEM	VALUE
Performance Bonus (max.)	$ 3,000
TV Exposure (max.)	$ 5,000
Print Exposure (max.)	$ 2,000
Product Support	$ 2,000
TOTAL	**$12,000**

Dated: ______________ By: ______________________________
P. Z. Kessler, Team & Promotions Director

Dated: ______________ By: ______________________________
Victoria Preneveaux

References

Barnes, R.L., *Rediscovering Subjectivity in Contracts: Adhesion and Unconscionability,* 66 La. L. Rev. 123 (2005).

Siprut, J., *The Peppercorn Reconsidered: Why a Promise to Sell Blackacre for Nominal Consideration Is Not Binding but Should Be,* 97 Nw. U.L. Rev. 1809 (2003).

Staidl, T.L., *The Enforceability of Noncompetition Agreements When Employment Is At-Will: Reformulating the Analysis,* 2 Empl. Rts. & Employ. Pol'y J. 95 (1998).

Chapter 4

Legality and Capacity

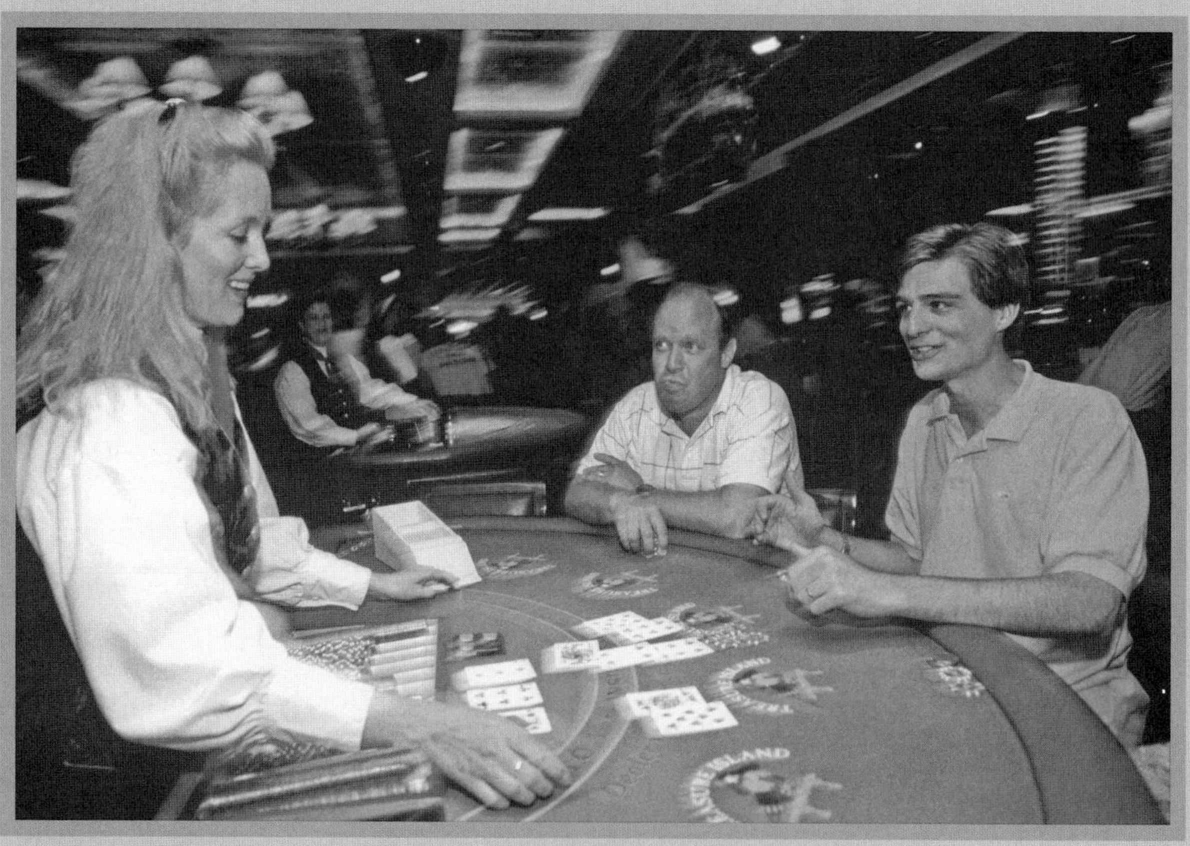

After reading this chapter you will be able to:

1. Compare and contrast the legality and capacity elements of the contract formula.
2. Define the term usury and how it applies to contract law.
3. Explain how (and why) gambling and Sabbath laws differ among states.
4. Describe adhesion and unconscionable contracts.
5. Discuss why the law protects minors when it comes to contractual agreements.
6. Define the term ratification in the context of contract law.
7. Discuss how courts address legal competence, including whether intoxication is a defense.
8. Explain the term necessaries and why it might be important in contracts.
9. Understand what an exculpatory clause is.

Key Terms

Adhesion	Lucid interval	Ratification
Antitrust laws	Malpractice	Restitution
Capacity	*Malum in se*	Sabbath laws
Disaffirmance	*Malum prohibitum*	Unconscionable
Emancipated	Minors	Usury laws
Exculpatory clause	Necessaries	Void
Legality	No compete clauses	Voidable
Licensing	Price fixing	

K = O + A + C + (**Legality** + **Capacity**)

Legality and capacity represent the final elements of the contract formula though they are quite different concepts. While there may be an otherwise valid offer, an acceptance, and consideration, if either of these last two elements of the contract formula is missing, then a court would likely declare the agreement to be void (or **voidable**). Courts will not enforce illegal contracts, contracts that are contrary to public policy or those agreements that are too one-sided to be enforced (i.e., contracts of adhesion).

LEGALITY

A contract must be **legal** in order to be valid. If a contract is considered illegal (i.e., it is for an illegal purpose or violates the law) then it is **void** from its inception. Contracts that violate local, state, or federal law are sometimes referred to as ***malum prohibitum*** (a prohibited wrong or evil). This means that a statute was created or legislation was enacted to prohibit this type of conduct or to prevent a certain activity from occurring. For example, state laws designed to limit the maximum amount of interest that can be charged to a borrower could be characterized as *malum prohibitum*. A contract is considered ***malum in se*** (evil in itself) if the agreement or conduct in the agreement is morally wrong in any sense. For example, murder, bribery, and perjury are considered evils *per se*, and, therefore, regardless of whether there is a statute addressing these deeds, a court would not enforce such misconduct. While parties to a contract might not even know that what they have agreed upon is illegal, that is not the concern of courts. Certainly the study of criminal law provides ample amounts of opportunites to explore not only prohibited conduct in society by law, but also conduct that is wrong in any moral sense as well. The following examples demonstrate situations in which a court could declare that an otherwise valid contract is illegal.

COMMISSION OF A CRIME

If the terms of the contract are illegal (such as committing a crime), then the contract is simply not enforceable. If A hires B to commit physical harm to a third party, C, that agreement would not be enforceable. Contracts to commit crimes are therefore void from the beginning.

USURY

Usury laws are designed to protect against the charging of excessive rates of interest in credit cards and certain types of loans, including "payday loans."[1] The maximum rates of interest are promulgated by individual states.[2] These limits vary from state to state and often depend on what type of loan is involved (mortgage, car, furniture, and so on). Of recent interest, however, is a concern not over the rate of interest being charged, but rather the hidden fees associated with the interest rate such as a one-time fee, late fees, and other service charges.[3]

GAMBLING

Generally, gambling (sometimes referred to as wagering) is illegal unless a state statute says otherwise. Most states do allow some form of gambling (including casino gambling) such as Nevada, New Jersey, and Louisiana, though it is highly regulated. Until a few years ago, all forms of gambling (even Bingo) were illegal in Tennessee. Now that state has joined the majority of the states and allows for participation in a lottery run by the state government. In fact, in Tennessee at one time rubber duck races for charity in Tennessee were illegal, since they involved a game of chance. One had to pay in order to play, and it was held that the race was

[1]One might characterize the loaning of money in this context as predatory lending though not necessarily true. *See* http://www.buffalonews.com/editorial/20060620/1025214.asp.

[2]For a summary of state usury laws explore http://www.lectlaw.com/files/ban02.htm. Michigan usury laws, e.g., can be summarized at http://www.michigan.gov/documents/cis_ofis_ceilings_24956_7.pdf.

[3]*See, e.g.*, http://www.bankrate.com/brm/green/cc/basics3-3a.asp?caret=18.

an illegal lottery. This ruling, however, has since been abolished by an amended state constitution.[4] Tennessee has also become infamous for staging illegal cock-fighting gambling rings in recent years.[5]

SABBATH (SUNDAY) LAWS

Some states (or cities, counties) prohibit certain types of sales on Sunday. For example, towns, cities, and counties are found throughout the country in which no one may sell alcohol at all let alone before or after a certain time of day. **Dry counties** prohibit the sale of alcohol altogether within the county. Shopping on Sundays is, of course, acceptable everywhere, but some jurisdictions restrict the types of sales of certain products before or after a certain time of day.[6]

LICENSING

If one contracts with someone who was supposed to be licensed by the state for that activity or purpose but was not, the contract may or may not be enforceable. **Licensing** is the process by which a state or government grants an individual or business the right to do something for a fee. There are all kinds of licenses: lawyers, accountants, dentists, cosmetologists, and so on. Courts will consider the facts of each case and the type of licensure involved. If the license is to protect the public from **malpractice** or other harm, then it is likely to be unenforceable. If the license is purely to raise revenue for the state and no special training is needed to maintain that profession, then the contract might be enforceable. Consider the various contract issues that could present themselves related to operators of machinery, doctors and lawyers, door-to-door salespersons, and others who were supposed to obtain or maintain a license and did not.

EXCULPATORY CLAUSES

When one participates in an activity that requires some element of danger, often a contract is signed known as an **exculpatory clause**. These clauses (waivers, disclaimers, releases) are upheld as legal as long as they are reasonable in the court's eyes. Courts do not favor but will allow waivers that release a party from ordinary negligence. Most courts, however, will not enforce the waiver of a suit or liability for gross negligence or recklessness as this is against public policy and might even encourage grossly negligent activity.

[4]http://www.tennessean.com/local/archives/04/09/59803410.shtml?Element_ID=59803410. Consider that national scratch-and-win competitions of all sorts often contain the disclaimer "no purchase necessary" in order to avoid claims that a purchase was required and, therefore, it involved a game of chance. *See also*, http://en.wikipedia.org/wiki/Rubber_Duckie.

[5]http://www.wate.com/Global/story.asp?S=6526652.

[6]Also referred to as "blue laws" and some states disallow the sales of automobiles on Sundays. *See* http://www.snopes.com/language/colors/bluelaws.htm. *See also*, http://en.wikipedia.org/wiki/Blue_law.

NO COMPETE CLAUSES

No compete clauses are generally and legally enforceable in agreements as long as they are reasonable in scope (time, manner, place).[7] For example, a business might hire and train new employees and spend a lot of money in doing so. Having these employees sign such agreements provides an enforceable deterrent to leave. It could force a former employee to pay a fee or prevent them from working with a competitor. If the employee did not comply with this clause, an appropriate remedy for a court would be an injunction. Still, many judges and courts do not like to enforce such agreements if they are unreasonable. Each instance must be judged on its own merits on a case-by-case basis, and states might have different interpretations and applications of this rule.[8]

RESTRAINTS OF TRADE

Contracts which restrain trade violate federal **antitrust laws** and are generally voidable if the restraint is unreasonable.[9] For example, **price fixing** is a violative of federal antitrust laws. Of course, a court would have to make the determination that two or more companies conspired to fix prices.

ADHESION

Some contracts are so one-sided that courts say they are unenforceable. These are often referred to as contracts of **adhesion** or **unconscionable** contracts. They are one-sided, lack consideration, or are so shocking and unfair that they rival illegality.[10] For example, a contract that is offered on a take-it-or-leave-it basis might be considered an adhesion contract if the offeree had no other realistic choice but to accept.

CAPACITY

Capacity is the final element of the contract formula. It also protects those individuals who are minors (i.e., those who are under the age of 18) in the context of contract law. Courts also consider capacity as a matter to nullify a contract if one could not appreciate that a contract was being formed or one has been adjudged to be mentally incompetent.

---

[7]Sometimes no compete clauses are referred to as "covenants not to compete."

[8]Similarly, covenants not to sue are valid unless a court believes there was fraud, duress, undue influence, or simply unequal bargaining power between the parties. The modern contract drafting trend is to not include covenants not to sue, but rather provide alternatives to litigation such as mediation and arbitration.

[9]Federal antitrust acts include the Sherman Antitrust Act (1890), the Clayton Antitrust Act (1914), the Robinson-Patman Act (the Ant-Price Discrimination Act) (1936), and the Hart-Scoss-Rodino Antitrust Improvements Act (1976), also known as the HSR Act.

[10]The UCC addresses unconscionability in §2-302.

MINORS

Minors (also known in some jurisdictions as "infants") are those individuals under the age of 18 years old or those who are not yet **emancipated** from their parental or guardian supervision.[11] Minors (as opposed to adults) *do* have the ability to enter into contracts, but minors also have a voidable right to rescind that contractual relationship as well. This right to rescind by minors is sometimes referred to as **disaffirmance**. Still, minors who disaffirm a contract must then put the other party back in the financial position they would have been in had the contract not been agreed to in the first place, or in at least no worse position.[12] This is referred to as **restitution**. Some contracts cannot be disaffirmed by minors as a matter of public policy: student loans and enlisting in the military are frequent examples. In the entertainment industry, certain laws have been specifically designed to protect minors to some degree with regard to contracts.[13] While laws vary from state to state, if a minor intentionally misrepresents his or her age, that particular state law might (or might not) uphold the contract and not allow a disaffirmance of the agreement. A state law might also say that the contract is voidable, but that the non-breaching party may then sue for misrepresentation in tort law.

RATIFICATION

Ratification is an expression in words or actions, on or after reaching the age of the majority, which indicates an intention to remain bound by an agreement. If a minor enters into a contract and then subsequently turns 18 years old, the issue often faced by courts is whether the minor ratified the contract. Most jurisdictions hold that if a minor turns 18 and does not affirmatively disaffirm the contract, then the contract is ratified. Some jurisdictions give a reasonable amount of time to disaffirm after the minor turns 18.

COMPETENCE

A contract is actually void if a party to the contract is adjudged (by a court) to be mentally incompetent or mentally impaired. For example, an individual with an unfortunate illness such as Alzheimer's disease might be adjudged to be legally incompetent. Still, even those with mental illness might, depending on the facts of the case, have a **lucid interval**: a moment in which he or she is actually competent. Again, however, this would depend on the facts of each case, and this determination can present very interesting challenges for courts. Courts do not favor (and often reject) claims of voluntary intoxication as an attempt to void an otherwise valid agreement.

---

[11]*See, e.g.*, Goodfellow, S., *Who Gets the Better Deal?: A Comparison of the U.S. and English Infancy Doctrines*, 29 Hastings Int'l & Comp. L. Rev. 135 (2005).

[12]Often referred to as *status quo ante*.

[13]*See* Jessica Krieg, *There's No Business Like Show Business: Child Entertainers and the Law*, 6 U. PA. J. LAB. & EMP. L. 429(2004).

NECESSARIES

The term **necessaries** is an ambiguous term, but generally food, clothing, medicine and medical care, and shelter have been considered necessaries (of life). It really means the necessities for survival. As a general rule, minors are liable for the reasonable value of necessaries even if they claim they should not have to pay for them due to their protected status. Necessaries does not mean $150 basketball shoes, cell phones, cable television, or video game systems, however.

CHAPTER SUMMARY

Legality and capacity represent the final two elements of the contract formula. They are as essential as the other elements. Contracts considered invalid from their inception are considered void. Agreeing to commit a crime would be an example of a void contract regardless if there was an offer, acceptance, and so on. Since what is and is not legal varies from state to state, being aware of individual state laws is vital, especially with regard to usury laws, gambling and licensing issues, blue laws, and so on. Contracts that are considered too one-sided to be enforced are known as unconscionable (adhesion) contracts. Waivers are valid as long as they are reasonable but are not designed to encourage negligent conduct. Contract law treats minors differently than adults. Minors may disaffirm most agreements, but they must still place the other party in no worse position than before. Intoxication is not usually a valid defense to a contract since it is a voluntary act.

Discussion and Review Questions

1. Why do some states still have special laws that apply only on Sundays?
2. Why do states regulate the maximum rates of interest on certain loans known as usury laws?
3. Why are minors treated differently than adults in terms of contract formation?
4. What does the term ratification mean in terms of minors and contracts?
5. What are antitrust laws and why are they relevant in the study of contract law?

Critical Thinking Exercises

1. Joe and Pat enter into a same-sex marriage contract in Massachusetts even though they are residents of New York state. As "domestic partners," Joe and Pat have shared personal belongings for many years. After their Massachusetts marriage was considered void (i.e., it was considered illegal in the first place), Joe sought to enforce the premarital contract in New York under New York state law. Do you feel that the New York courts should uphold the premarital agreement?
2. Alison works at a high-powered law firm in Chicago and has developed many relationships during her four years of practice. The law firm has over 300 attorneys and establishes a policy that if lawyers decide to leave the firm they cannot take their clients with them as part of their no-compete policy. Is this legal or ethical for lawyers? Would it make a difference if Alison were a doctor instead of a lawyer?
3. Jim gets his haircut by an unlicensed cosmetologist. He is pleased with the work, and pays the appropriate fee with a 15 percent tip. Thirty days later, Jim reads in the local newspaper that the entire hair salon neglected to renew their cosmetology licenses, and, technically, their services were illegal since they did not renew their license (by an honest mistake). Do you

think that Jim would be successful in claiming that the service was illegal and therefore void and that he should be entitled to a return of his money?

Online Research Exercises

1. Just because one receives a bad deal does not mean it is a contract of adhesion. Explore various credit card agreements online, and take note of the differences in annual rates of interest.
2. McDonald's has many promotions, including the Monopoly game. Why do you feel that it conspicuously states, "NO PURCHASE NECESSARY" as part of the promotion?
3. At the federal level, the Federal Trade Commission (FTC) and the Federal Communications Commission (FCC) often become involved in investigation of false or misleading (and possibly illegal) advertisements. *See* http://www.fda.gov/bbs/topics/NEWS/2005/MUCHfactsheet.html.
4. Explore usury laws in your state (and others) found online.
5. Consider how the state of Texas in 2004 dealt with the validity of a non-compete clause in an employment contract in http://www.supreme.courts.state.tx.us/Historical/2006/oct/031050.pdf.
6. Many cities and towns require a camera crew to obtain a permit to film outdoors. Consider why this type of license is important. Is it primarily to raise revenue or is there another reason for requiring compliance with such governmental regulation? *See* http://www.redondo.org/civica/filebank/blobdload.asp?BlobID=1780.

CASE APPLICATIONS

Case 1

Consider the following Pennsylvania case involving a no compete clause. Was the clause reasonable or was it oppressive? Notice how the concept of consideration was addressed by the court as well in this employment agreement.

FRES-CO SYSTEM USA, INC. v. BODELL

2005 U.S. Dist. LEXIS 28140 (E.D. Pa. Nov. 15, 2005)

DALZELL, J.

In this diversity action to enforce a non-competition clause, plaintiff Fres-co System USA, Inc. filed last summer a motion for a temporary restraining order against its former salesman, Robert Bodell, which we denied after a hearing on July 12, 2005. Fres-co then filed a motion for a preliminary injunction, and we convened a hearing on November 10, 2005. At the close of that hearing, the parties agreed that the matter should be submitted as a trial of the action on the merits, pursuant to *Fed. R. Civ. P. 65(a)(2)*. This memorandum will constitute our findings of fact and conclusions of law under *Fed. R. Civ. P. 52(a)*.

Most of the facts are undisputed. Between July 13, 1998 and May 6, 2005, Robert Bodell worked as a sales representative for Fres-co, which manufactures and distributes flexible packaging materials and packaging machinery. Its principal customers are roasters and packagers of coffee. Before coming to Fres-co, Bodell had worked for PrintPak, another flexible packaging company involved in the coffee industry.

Bodell's sales territory for Fres-co was the southeastern United States and the Caribbean. In 2004, Bodell was responsible for about $4 million of packaging sales and $2.5 million in equipment sales.

On June 25, 1998, about three weeks before he began working at Fres-co, Bodell signed a Confidentiality and Non-Competition Agreement ("the 1998 Agreement"). See Compl. Ex. A. On July 15, 1999, Bodell signed a new

Confidentiality and Non-Competition Agreement ("the 1999 Agreement"). See Compl. Ex. B. Bodell was not paid extra money to sign the 1999 Agreement. All 350 Fres-co employees—from the lowest clerical or maintenance worker to the firm's senior officers—had to sign the same non-compete agreement, and no employee was permitted to negotiate the terms of the 1999 Agreement.

The 1998 Agreement provided, inter alia, that:

> During the course of his/her employment, and for a period of two (2) full years after the termination thereof under any circumstances or for any reason, Employee shall not directly or indirectly solicit business from, engage in, be employed by, contract with, or otherwise do business with any clients, customers, or competitors of Fres-co if such business is of a type which was performed by Fres-co or could be performed by Fres-co without the express specific written consent of Fres-co.

In the 1999 Agreement, the form states that for one year after the employee stops working at Fres-co, he or she would not become an employee of a Fres-co competitor "in any 'Line of Business,'" as defined in the agreement, and that he or she would not "solicit business from, contract with, be employed by, or otherwise do business with any customer of Fres-co or assist any other person or entity in doing so in any 'Line of Business'" (the "non-compete"). *Id.* P7. Paragraph seven of the 1999 Agreement provides that:

> During the course of his/her employment, and for a period of one (1) full year after the termination thereof under any circumstances or for any reason, Employee shall not directly or indirectly whether as owner, shareholder, director, partner or employee or in any other capacity:
>
> a) compete with Fres-co in any "Line of Business";
>
> b) accept employment with or be employed (as an employee, consultant or in any other capacity) by a competitor of Fres-co in any "Line of Business"; or
>
> c) solicit business from, contract with, be employed by, or otherwise do business with any customer of Fres-co or assist any other person or entity in doing so in any "Line of Business."
>
> As used in this paragraph "Line of Business" means and includes:
>
> 1) the manufacture, design, development, service, distribution or sale of flexible packaging equipment and/or materials for use in packaging any products for which customers or prospective customers of Fres-co have, at any time during the two (2) year period immediately preceding termination of employment, purchased or contracted to purchase equipment and/or materials from Fres-co (or any affiliate of Fres-co) and shall in any event include, but not be limited to Coffee, Pet Food, Agricultural Chemicals and polymers; and
>
> 2) any other line of business conducted by Fres-co on the date of termination of employment or then in development by Fres-co.
>
> The foregoing prohibition concerning competition shall apply to the geographic areas in which Fres-co has engaged in any business activities (including but not limited to, product sales, marketing or shipments) during the two (2) year period prior to termination of employment.

The form also calls on the employee not to disclose any of Fres-co's confidential information (the "confidentiality clause").

After leaving Fres-co, Bodell began working for Ultra Flex Packaging Corp. ("Ultra Flex"), a Fres-co competitor. Despite the restrictions contained in the 1999 Agreement, Bodell contacted at least nine of Fres-co's customers, eight of whom had relationships with Ultra Flex prior to Bodell starting at that company. To date, Fres-co has not lost any money as a result of Bodell's departure six months ago.

Fres-co sued Bodell, seeking injunctive and declaratory relief on three counts: (1) breach of contract (based on solicitation); (2) misappropriation of trade secrets and confidential and proprietary information; and (3) tortious interference with existing and prospective contractual and business relations (for which Fres-co also seeks damages). At the same time that it filed the complaint, Fres-co filed a motion for a temporary restraining order and a preliminary injunction, and the temporary restraining order was, as noted, denied after a hearing on July 12, 2005.

After expedited discovery, Fres-co renewed its request for a preliminary injunction, one somewhat narrower than the remedy demanded in the complaint. Fres-co requested that we enjoin Bodell from working in the coffee flexible packaging or machinery business in North America or the Caribbean, and revealing any of Fres-co's trade secrets or confidential information. At the close of a hearing on this motion on November 10, 2005, parties agreed that the record on the motion should be submitted as a trial of the action on the merits, pursuant to *Fed. R. Civ. P. 65(a)(2)*.

Because this case is governed by Pennsylvania law, we first assess whether Fres-co's non-compete language is enforceable under the Commonwealth's law.

I. Non-compete agreements under Pennsylvania law

Pennsylvania courts "permit the equitable enforcement of post-employment restraints only where they are [1] incident to an employment relation between the parties to the covenant, [2] the restrictions are reasonably necessary for the protection of the employer, and [3] the restrictions are reasonably limited in duration and geographic extent." *Sidco Paper Co. v. Aaron, 465 Pa. 586, 351 A.2d 250, 252 (Pa. 1976)*. The Pennsylvania Supreme Court has cautioned that "restrictive covenants are not favored in Pennsylvania and have been historically viewed as a trade restraint that prevents a former employee from earning a living." *Hess v. Gebhard & Co. Inc., 570 Pa. 148, 808 A.2d 912, 917 (Pa. 2002)*. Because restrictive covenants restrain an employee's trade, they "are strictly construed against the employer." *All-Pak, Inc. v. Johnston, 694 A.2d 347, 351 (Pa. Super. Ct. 1997)*.

A. Incident to an employment relation

When evaluating whether a non-compete agreement is "incident to an employment relation," Pennsylvania courts consider whether adequate consideration supports the agreement. "If an employment contract containing a restrictive covenant is entered into subsequent to employment, it must be supported by new consideration which could be in the form of a corresponding benefit to the employee or a beneficial change in his employment status." *Modern Laundry & Dry Clean v. Farrer, 370 Pa. Super. 288, 536 A.2d 409, 411 (Pa. Super. Ct. 1988)*. Since Fres-co and Bodell entered into the 1999 Agreement more than a year after Bodell began working for Fres-co, the non-compete clause cannot be enforced unless Bodell received some "new consideration."

According to the language of the 1999 Agreement, Bodell signed it "in consideration of the nullification of a prior confidentiality and non-competition agreement." Compl. Ex. B, Introduction. The 1999 Agreement differed from the 1998 Agreement in that it (1) reduced the restricted period from two years to one year; (2) introduced and defined the phrase "line of business;" and (3) eliminated a liquidated damages provision. Fres-co characterizes these lessened restrictions as consideration. *See John G. Bryant Co., Inc. v. Sling Testing & Repair, Inc., 471 Pa. 1, 369 A.2d 1164, 1169 (Pa. 1977)* (finding consideration where a later agreement lessened restrictions of an earlier covenant).

However, as Fres-co has conceded, the company had employees sign the 1999 Agreement because it was concerned that the 1998 Agreement might be unenforceably overbroad. If the 1998 Agreement is unenforceable, there were no prior restrictions on Bodell's post-Fres-co activity. In that case the 1999 Agreement's non-compete language would not decrease the period of a restriction (as Fres-co contends), but rather it would increase restrictions on Bodell's post-Fres-co activity by creating a new a one-year restriction where none existed before. This hardly constitutes consideration.

Moreover, Fres-co admits that every employee, however lowly, had to sign the same 1999 Agreement and was not permitted to negotiate any terms. Fres-co argues this was done for consistency across the organization. No doubt this method was administratively convenient and achieved consistency, but whether such an agreement was permissible under Pennsylvania law is quite a different matter. Lacking consideration since gratuitously sought, the 1999 Agreement fails to satisfy Pennsylvania's requirements and is thus unenforceable on this basis alone.

Pennsylvania law recognizes that non-competition agreements can protect legitimate business interests and that these include "trade secrets of an employer, customer goodwill and specialized training and skills acquired from the employer." *Thermo-Guard, Inc. v. Cochran, 408 Pa. Super. 54, 596 A.2d 188, 193-94 (Pa. Super. Ct. 1991)* (footnote added). At the same time, such agreements may not be used to "eliminate or repress[] competition or to keep the employee from competing so that the employer can gain an economic advantage."

Fres-co argues that its non-compete form protects legitimate business interests—customer goodwill and trade secrets. While Fres-co identifies protectable business interests, the terms of the non-compete form far exceed what is reasonably necessary to protect them. The form's language covers not only customers in the coffee market, but all "lines of business" for Fres-co and "any affiliate of Fres-co," "including, but not limited to Coffee, Pet Food, Agricultural Chemicals and polymers." . . . the form language by its terms reaches at least four industries on three continents. This international cross-industry protection is unquestionably broader than is necessary to protect any legitimate concerns Fres-co might have as they relate to a salesperson who sold for them in the coffee market in the southeastern United States and the Caribbean.

A final consideration under Pennsylvania law is whether the restrictions imposed are reasonably limited in duration and geographic extent. Bodell concedes that one year may be reasonable, but takes issue with the geographic scope, which, as already discussed, is international both by its terms and as proposed for our modification.

The non-compete at issue here is not even limited to Bodell's former sales territory (the states of the old Confederacy and the Caribbean), nor even to his industry (coffee packaging products). It is thus impermissibly broad in geographic scope.

Having failed to meet Pennsylvania's standard for enforceability of non-competes, Fres-co cannot succeed on the merits and therefore is not entitled to injunctive relief.

II. Reforming the Non-compete Language

Fres-co asks that if this Court finds the 1999 Agreement overly broad, we should narrow it and apply injunctive relief to the non-compete as we have modified it. While the non-compete is unenforceable because of overbreadth and lack of consideration, we will assume for the purposes of this reformation analysis that Bodell received consideration for the 1999 Agreement. Is reformation warranted in this case?

The Pennsylvania Supreme Court has repeatedly held that "where the covenant imposes restrictions broader than necessary to protect the employer . . . a court of equity may grant enforcement limited to those portions of the restrictions which are reasonably necessary for the protection of the employer." *Sidco, 465 Pa. 586, 351 A.2d 250, 254 (Pa. 1976)* (citing many cases in support of this proposition). Bodell concedes that this Court can exercise its broad discretion in fashioning an injunction that enforces a modified version of the restrictive covenant, but he argues that it should not, relying primarily on *Reading Aviation Service, Inc. v. Bertolet, 454 Pa. 488, 311 A.2d 628 (Pa. 1973)*.

Fres-co contends there is no "intent to oppress" here because the restriction is only for one year and because Bodell's agreement covers only coffee, which is only a portion of the entire flexible packaging industry. However, by its express terms, the non-compete is not limited to the coffee industry, nor to the region in which Bodell worked, nor to the Fres-co customers Bodell contacted while an employee there, nor even to the Fres-co customers in existence when Bodell left. All such limitations could have been included in the 1999 Agreement without sacrificing the consistency that Fres-co sought and still protecting legitimate business concerns.

Fres-co cites several other cases to support its argument that this Court should apply Pennsylvania law to reform the 1999 agreement and enforce it as modified. In two cases, including one this Court decided, the facts differed critically in that the covenants at issue suffered from relatively minor defects. *See Vector Sec., Inc. v. Stewart, 88 F. Supp. 2d 395, 400 (E.D. Pa. 2000)* ("While the covenant limits to some degree the customer base from which the defendants may draw, the clause does not prohibit them from working in the alarm security field or from competing with Vector for new subscribers."); *QVC, Inc. v. Tauman, No. 98-1144, 1998 U.S. Dist. LEXIS 4383, at *8-17 (Apr. 3, 1998) (Dalzell, J.)* (reforming a contract by altering its term after concluding that the fairly narrow restrictive covenant was supported by consideration and, except for a flaw in its duration, was valid and enforceable).

Sitting in equity, a court has broad powers to craft appropriate injunctive relief, but it must carefully weigh all the facts of the case in deciding what is equitable. The cases Fres-co cites are not in the same league as this case, largely because the language of those covenants was narrower. Here we are asked to either enforce the non-compete or completely rewrite it and then enforce it. If we were to do the latter, perhaps Bodell would get some limited relief and Fres-co's legitimate interests would be protected, but we would then sanction Fres-co's choice to make all of its 350 employees sign a gratuitously overbroad non-compete lacking in consideration. This is precisely the "heads the employer wins, tails the employee loses" situation against which the Pennsylvania Supreme Court set its face in *Reading Aviation*.

We cannot ignore the Pennsylvania Supreme Court's admonition that restrictive covenants are disfavored and "historically viewed as a trade restraint that prevents a former employee from earning a living." *Hess, 808 A.2d at 917*. When covenants are included in agreements to "eliminate or repress" competition or to keep the employee from competing so that the employer can gain an economic advantage, the covenant will not be enforced." *Id. at 920-921*. Given the over-reaching terms of Fres-co's non-compete adhesion form, we cannot view it as anything other than a restraint unnecessarily preventing Bodell from earning his living in the business he knows. Even if Bodell had received consideration for the 1999 Agreement, it would be inequitable to reform that form under these highly oppressive circumstances.

Having recognized an overbreadth problem with its 1998 Agreement, Fres-co failed properly to address it. Now it asks this Court to take on a wholesale rewriting that properly belongs to corporate decision-makers working with their counsel. We decline this expansive invitation to exercise our equitable powers to help this employer stifle legitimate competition by a salesman merely seeking to ply his trade.

Conclusion

Fres-co's non-competition language contained in its 1999 Agreement is unenforceable for lack of consideration and overbreadth. Moreover, for the reasons discussed, this is a case in which granting relief would be inequitable. We therefore deny Fres-co's motion for a final injunction. An appropriate Order follows.

Case Questions

1. What is a diversity action?
2. What was the contract remedy that Fres-co wanted the federal court to issue?
3. How long did the 1998 agreement compare to the subsequent 1999 no-compete agreement?
4. What are the three concerns that Pennsylvania courts use to analyze whether a noncompete agreement is enforceable in that state?

Case 2

Consider this Tennessee case involving a waiver and a claim of the tort of negligence. Did the court agree that the waiver violated public policy and should not be enforced?

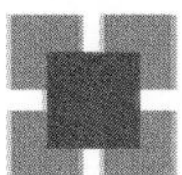

HENDERSON v. QUEST EXPEDITIONS, INC

174 S.W.3D 730 (TENN. 2005)

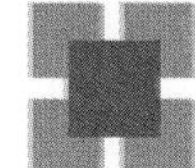

FRANKS, P. J.

In this action for personal injuries allegedly due to defendant's negligence, the Trial Court granted defendant summary judgment on the grounds that plaintiffs had executed a Waiver and Release of Liability which was required by defendant prior to plaintiffs' participation in white water rafting. Plaintiffs have appealed, insisting the Release is void as against the public policy of this State. We affirm.

Plaintiffs' Complaint alleged that Henderson was injured while on a white water rafting expedition operated by defendant. The Complaint alleged that defendant "ferries rafters to and from the Ocoee River by means of a series of dilapidated school buses," and that after Henderson had completed his rafting trip, he and other rafters were put on a bus, and then told to get on another bus, and when disembarking from the first bus he slipped and fell, sustaining severe personal injuries. Plaintiffs further alleged that defendant's negligence was the proximate cause of his injuries.

Defendant in its Answer admitted that Henderson had participated in a rafting trip sponsored by defendant, and among its defenses raised was waiver, because plaintiff had signed a "Waiver and Release of Liability," which defendant attached to its Answer.

In their Answers to Requests for Admissions, plaintiffs admitted that the waiver in question had been signed by Henderson. Defendant then filed a Motion for Summary Judgment, which plaintiffs opposed and Henderson filed his Affidavit which stated that Henderson had no previous white-water rafting experience, and was given a pre-printed document to sign prior to the excursion which was not reviewed with him by an employee of defendant. He further stated that he was not advised whether there were any other rafting companies who would allow him to go rafting without having to sign a waiver, or whether he could pay additional money to not have to sign the waiver.

The Trial Court determined that the waiver in this case did not affect the public interest, and thus the waiver was not void as against public policy. The court noted that *Olson v. Molzen, 558 S.W.2d 429 (Tenn. 1977)* did not apply to this situation and he was guided by the rule adopted in California, which states that "exculpatory agreements in the recreational sports context do not implicate the public interest." Plaintiffs on appeal insist the Waiver is void against public policy, and in the alternative, that the Waiver was void on the grounds it was too excessive in scope.

Plaintiffs concede that if the Waiver is enforceable then this action is barred, but argue the waiver violates the public policy of this State.

As our Supreme Court has explained:

> It is well settled in this State that parties may contract that one shall not be liable for his negligence to another but that such other shall assume the risk incident to

> such negligence. . . . Further, it is not necessary that the word "negligence" appear in the exculpatory clause and the public policy of Tennessee favors freedom to contract against liability for negligence. *Empress Health and Beauty Spa, Inc. v. Turner, 503 S.W.2d 188 (Tenn. 1973).*

An exception to this rule was recognized by the Supreme Court in *Olson v. Molzen*, wherein the Court held that certain relationships required greater responsibility which would render such a release "obnoxious." The Court adopted the opinion of the California Supreme Court in *Tunkl v. Regents of University of California, 60 Cal. 2d 92, 383 P.2d 441, 32 Cal. Rptr. 33 (Ca. 1963)*, which held that where the public interest would be affected by an exculpatory provision, such provision could be held invalid. *Olson, at p. 431.*

Our Supreme Court adopted the six criteria set forth in *Tunkl* as useful in determining when an exculpatory provision should be held invalid as contrary to public policy. *See Olson*. These criteria are:

> (a.) It concerns a business of a type generally thought suitable for public regulation.
>
> (b.) The party seeking exculpation is engaged in performing a service of great importance to the public, which is often a matter of practical necessity for some members of the public.
>
> (c.) The party holds himself out as willing to perform this service for any member of the public who seeks it, or at least for any member coming within certain established standards.
>
> (d.) As a result of the essential nature of the service, in the economic setting of the transaction, the party invoking exculpation possesses a decisive advantage of bargaining strength against any member of the public who seeks his services.
>
> (e.) In exercising a superior bargaining power the party confronts the public with a standardized adhesion contract of exculpation, and makes no provision whereby a purchaser may pay additional reasonable fees and obtain protection against negligence.
>
> (f.) Finally, as a result of the transaction, the person or property of the purchaser is placed under the control of the seller, subject to the risk of carelessness by the seller or his agents. *Olson, at p. 431.*

In *Olson*, the Supreme Court invalidated a contract between a doctor and patient which attempted to release the doctor from liability for his negligence in the performance of medical services. In *Russell*, this Court refused to enforce an exculpatory contract between home buyers and the home inspectors who were hired by the buyers, because the Court found that the home inspectors were professionals whose services affected the public interest, and thus the contracts were offensive to public policy, based on the factors enumerated in *Olson*. In *Carey*, this Court made clear that not all of the factors had to be present in order to invalidate an exculpatory agreement, but generally, the factors were limited to circumstances involving "a contract with a profession, as opposed to 'tradesmen in the marketplace.'" *Carey, at p. 916; cf. Parton v. Mark Pirtle Oldsmobile-Cadillac-Isuzu, Inc., 730 S.W.2d 634 (Tenn. Ct. App. 1987)* (auto repair shop is not "professional" as would qualify it as service affecting public interest in order to invalidate exculpatory contract).

This case is factually different from *Olson*, *Carey*, and *Parton* because the white-water rafting service offered by defendant is not a "professional" trade, which affects the public interest. As discussed in factor number two quoted above, this is not a service of "great importance to the public, which is often a matter of practical necessity for some members of the public." *See Olson*. There is no necessity that one go white-water rafting. In fact, many jurisdictions have recognized that such recreational sporting activities are not activities of an essential nature which would render exculpatory clauses contrary to the public interest. *See Seigneur v. National Fitness Institute, Inc., 132 Md. App. 271, 752 A.2d 631 (Md. Ct. Spec. App. 2000)* (health club services not essential for purposes of holding exculpatory clause unenforceable as offensive to public interest); *Allan v. Snow Summit, Inc., 51 Cal. App. 4th 1358, 59 Cal.Rptr.2d 813 (Cal. Ct. App. 1996)* ("voluntary participation in recreational and sports activities [skiing] does not implicate the public interest"); *Schutkowski v. Carey, 725 P.2d 1057 (Wyo. 1986)* (sky diving and other private recreational businesses generally do not involve services which are necessary to the public such that exculpatory contract would be invalidated).

Plaintiffs argue that the Release in this case does affect the public interest because the business involved, i.e. commercial white-water rafting, is subject to regulation. While this is true, the presence of this factor does not render this Release offensive to the public interest. In fact, recent legislation passed by the Tennessee Legislature "recognizes that the State has a legitimate interest in maintaining the economic viability of commercial white water rafting operations" because the State and its citizens benefit thereby. 2005 Tenn. Pub. Acts 169. This act states the legislative intent is to "encourage white water rafting by discouraging claims based on injury, death or damages resulting from risks inherent in white water rafting." *Id.* Thus, the Tennessee legislature has evidenced that the public policy of this State is that commercial white water rafting companies be protected from claims for injuries to patrons.

Accordingly we affirm the Trial Court's determination that the exculpatory contract in this case does not affect the public interest such that it should be invalidated pursuant to the *Olson* criteria.

Finally, appellants argue that the Release in this case should not operate as a bar to their claims because the injury suffered by Henderson was not within the "inherent risks" of the sport of white water rafting, and thus was not within the contemplation of the parties when the release was signed.

In the cases relied on by the plaintiffs regarding the scope of exculpatory provisions in the context of a sport, there are no provisions in those agreements which purport to release the defendant from its own negligence. For example, in *Johnson v. Thruway Speedways, Inc., 63 A.D.2d 204, 407 N.Y.S.2d 81 (N.Y. App. Div. 1978)*, the Court refused to uphold a grant of summary judgment based on a release signed by the plaintiff prior to the sporting event. The Court stated that language of the release (which was not quoted in the opinion) "could lead to the conclusion that it only applied to injuries sustained by a spectator which were associated with the risks inherent in the activity of automobile racing." The plaintiff in that case was injured when he was hit by a maintenance vehicle not involved in the race. *Id. at 205*. Thus, the Court held that this created a triable issue of fact as to whether the incident was of the type contemplated by the parties when the release was signed. *Id.*

In another case where "negligence" is included in the release, *Sweat v. Big Time Auto Racing, Inc., 117 Cal. App. 4th 1301, 12 Cal.Rptr. 3d 678 (Cal. Ct. App. 2004)*, the plaintiff was injured when the pit-area bleachers collapsed. Plaintiff had signed a release before entering the pit area, which stated that he released the defendant from all liability "whether caused by the negligence of the releasees or otherwise while the undersigned is in or upon the restricted area and/or . . . observing . . . the event." The Court found that the release was ambiguous due to the "and/or" language used, and thus relied on extrinsic evidence in interpreting the release, such as the fact that anyone could enter the pit area without signing the release once the race was over. The Court concluded that the release was only intended to apply to the risks inherent in being in close proximity to a race, and was not intended to cover the type of incident which occurred when the bleachers collapsed due to defective construction/maintenance.

The majority view from sister states is that an exculpatory provision which specifically and expressly releases a defendant from its own negligence will be upheld, without regard to whether the injury sustained is one typically thought to be "inherent in the sport." In fact, there seems to be a split of authority among the states regarding whether the word "negligence" is even required to be present in the exculpation clause for the provision to be construed as releasing the defendant from its own negligence. Cases from Connecticut, for example, have held that in order for an exculpatory provision to be construed as releasing a defendant from its own negligence, the provision must expressly mention negligence. The cases are equally clear, however, that if the provision does expressly release the defendant from its own negligence, then it will be upheld as written.

Most jurisdictions, including Tennessee, have held that if the exculpation contract sufficiently demonstrates the parties' intent to eliminate liability for negligence, the absence of the word "negligence" is not fatal. In these cases, the fact that the injury occurred during an activity that was not foreseeable or not associated with a risk "inherent in the sport" did not matter. *See, e.g., Benedek* (health club member injured when adjusting a television set above exercise machines which fell); *Murphy* (white water rafter injured when her raft tried to engage in rescue of another raft), and Petry (patron of health club injured when exercise machine she was sitting on collapsed).

The Contract under consideration is clear and unambiguous, and states that plaintiffs agreed to release defendant from any and all liability, including defendant's own negligence. Moreover, the Contract specifically mentions that plaintiffs are being furnished and participating in white water rafting and "bus or van transportation" provided by the defendant. The Contract states that plaintiffs realize that they could be injured due to dangers from the rafting as well as the use of white water equipment, forces of nature, or even due to the negligence of defendant's employees and other rafters. The Contract states that defendant is being relieved of any liability caused by its own negligence in no less than four places, the last of which is in bold print above the signature line. This Contract is plain, and enforceable as written. We conclude the Trial Court properly granted summary judgment to defendant on plaintiffs' negligence claims.

The Trial Court's Judgment is affirmed, and the cost of the appeal is assessed to plaintiffs Nathan and Brandy Henderson.

Case Questions

1. According to the appellate court, was the word "negligence" required to be mentioned in the waiver?
2. What state did the court look to for guidance—primarily for the determination as to whether this type of waiver was valid as a matter of public policy?
3. How many criteria did the Tennessee court say that it should look to in analyzing waivers and their relationship to public policy concerns?
4. In the end, did this waiver exceed its legal authority by attempting to waive negligence in the white-water rafting context?

Exercise

Read the following complex employment contract. What provisions did you find interesting and why? What provisions might be added that are not found in this agreement? Is this agreement fair? Why would employers have employees sign such agreements? From this rather complex form, create a basic no-compete agreement with you (as employer) for a potential employee (a recent college graduate) to sign as part of their condition of employment since your company's success thrives based upon confidential information, customer lists, and training methods.

EMPLOYEE AGREEMENT FOR ASSIGNMENT OF RIGHTS, CONFIDENTIALITY, AND NON-COMPETITION

THIS AGREEMENT is made and entered into by and ________________, having an address of ________________, ("Employer") and ________________________, an individual residing at ("Employee"), to be effective as of the ___ day of __________, ___________.

1. Employment by Employer as Sole Occupation. Subject only to the exceptions provided in this Agreement, Employee agrees to devote his/her full business time, attention, skill and effort exclusively to the performance of the duties that Employer may assign to him/her from time to time. Employee may not engage in any business activities or render any services of a business, commercial, or professional nature (whether or not for compensation) for the benefit of anyone other than Employer, unless Employer has given its consent in writing in advance.

2. Noninterference with Third-Party Rights. Employee warrants that (1) he/she is free to enter into employment with Employer and (2) only Employer is entitled to the benefit of his/her work. Employer has no interest in using any other person's patents, copyrights, trade secrets, or trademarks in an unlawful manner. Employee warrants that he/she will not misapply proprietary rights that Employer has no right to use.

3. Continuance of Employment. The faithful observance of this Agreement by Employee is, and shall remain, a condition to Employee's employment. Employee's employment is terminable at will by either Employee or Employer at any time. Employer reserves the absolute right to make any changes in assignment, personnel, or employee benefits at any time.

4. Proprietary Rights Claimed by Employer. For purposes of this Agreement, "Employee Developments" consist of all technological, financial, operating, and training ideas, processes, and materials, specifically including all inventions, discoveries, improvements, enhancements, computer programs, written materials, and developments in any way pertaining to the existing or contemplated business, products or services of Employer, that Employer may develop or conceive of while employed by Employer, alone or with others, during or after working hours, and with or without the use of the resources of Employer. The determination of whether an Employee Development exists should be made according to whether the development has any possible significance to Employer in Employer's existing or contemplated business, regardless of whether it is technically eligible for protection under patent, copyright, or trade secret law; Employee agrees that Employer shall receive the full benefit of Employee's talent, imagination, and ability in its existing or contemplated business.

5. Exclusive Ownership by Employer of Certain Employee Developments; Power of Attorney. Employee is required to devote his/her creative faculties exclusively to Employer during his/her employment. All Employee Developments relating to the existing or contemplated business or interests of Employer shall be considered made for hire by Employee for Employer and prepared within the scope of his/her employment. Employee will promptly disclose all such Employee Developments to Employer and make available to Employer any work papers, models, diskettes, computer tapes, or other tangible incidents of such Employee Developments. Employee specifically agrees that all copyrightable materials generated or developed under this Agreement shall be considered works made for hire under U.S. copyright law and that all such materials shall, upon creation, be owned exclusively by Employer. To the extent that any such material, under applicable law, may not be considered works made for hire, Employee hereby assigns to Employer the ownership of copyright in such materials, without the necessity of any further consideration, and Employer shall be entitled to register and hold in its own name all copyrights in respect of such materials. Employee agrees to assign to Employer in full any right he/she may acquire now or in the future with respect to any such Employee Developments. Employee irrevocably waives and relinquishes any moral rights recognized by any applicable law in any Employee Developments. Employee agrees to perform upon the request of Employer any acts that may be necessary or desirable to transfer ownership of all such Employee Developments to Employer or to establish original ownership of all such Employee Developments on the part of Employer, to the fullest extent possible. When requested, Employee will:

1. Execute, acknowledge and deliver any requisite affidavits and documents of assignment and conveyance;
2. Obtain and aid in the enforcement of patents or copyrights with respect to any patentable or copyrightable Employee Developments in any countries;
3. Provide testimony in connection with any proceeding affecting the right, title, or interest of Employer in any trade secret, patent, patent application, or copyright covering any such Employee Development; and
4. Perform any other acts deemed necessary or desirable to carry out the purposes of this Agreement. Employer will reimburse Employee for any reasonable out-of-pocket expenses incurred at the request of Employer in the process of perfecting ownership by Employer of any Employee Developments or transferring ownership thereof to Employer.

To effectuate the terms of this section, Employee hereby names and irrevocably constitutes and appoints Employer, with full power of substitution therein, as Employee's true and lawful attorney-in-fact to exercise the rights assigned hereby.

6. Consequences of Entrustment with Sensitive Information. Employee acknowledges that his/her position with Employer requires considerable responsibility and trust. Relying on Employee's ethical responsibility and undivided loyalty, Employer expects to entrust Employee with highly sensitive confidential, restricted, and proprietary information involving Trade Secrets and Confidential Information (as defined herein). Employee should recognize that it could prove very difficult to isolate these Trade Secrets and Confidential Information from business activities that Employee might consider pursuing after termination of his/her employment, and in some instances, Employee may not be able to compete with Employer in certain ways because of the risk that Employer's Trade Secrets and Confidential Information might be compromised. Employee is legally and ethically responsible for protecting and preserving Employer's proprietary rights for use only for Employer's benefit, and these responsibilities may impose unavoidable limitations on Employee's ability to pursue some kinds of business opportunities that might interest Employee during or after his/her employment.

7. Definitions of "Trade Secrets" and "Confidential Information." For purposes of this Agreement, the following definitions shall apply:

A. "Trade Secret" means the whole or any portion or phase of any scientific or technical information, design, process, procedure, formula, or improvement that is valuable and secret (in the sense that it is not generally known to competitors of Employer). To the extent consistent with the foregoing definition, Trade Secrets include (without limitation) the specialized information and technology that Employer may develop or acquire with respect to system designs, program materials (including source and object code and system and user documentation), operating processes, equipment designs, and product specifications.

B. "Confidential Information" means any data or information, other than Trade Secrets, that is material to Employer and not generally known by the public. To the extent consistent with the foregoing definition, Confidential Information includes (without limitation):

1. The sales records, profits and performance reports, pricing manuals, sales manuals, training manuals, selling and pricing procedures and financing methods of Employer;
2. Customer lists, the special demands of particular customers, and the current and anticipated requirements of customers generally for the products of Employer;
3. The specifications of any new products under development;
4. The business plans and internal financial statements and projections of Employer; and
5. Any information identified as secret or confidential, or which, from the circumstances in good faith and good conscience ought to be treated as confidential, relating to the business or affairs of Employer.

8. Restrictions on Use and Disclosure of Trade Secrets. During his/her employment with Employer and for so long afterwards as the information or data remain Trade Secrets, Employee agrees not to use, disclose, or permit any person to obtain any Trade Secrets of Employer (whether or not the Trade Secrets are in written or tangible form), except as specifically authorized by Employer.

9. Restrictions on Use and Disclosure of Confidential Information. During his/her employment with Employer and for so long afterwards as the information or data remain competitively sensitive, Employee agrees not to use, disclose, or permit any person to obtain any Confidential Information of Employer (whether or not the Confidential Information is in written or tangible form), except as specifically authorized by Employer.

10. Screening of Public Releases of Information. In addition, and without any intention of limiting Employee's other obligations under this Agreement in any way, Employee will not reveal any nonpublic information concerning the business, services or the proprietary products and processes of Employer (particularly those under current development or improvement), unless Employee has obtained approval from Employer in advance. In that connection, Employee will submit to Employer for review any proposed scientific and technical articles and the text of any public speeches relating to work done for Employer before they are released or delivered. Employer has the right to disapprove and prohibit, or delete any parts of, such articles or speeches that might disclose Employer's Trade Secrets or Confidential Information or otherwise be contrary to Employer's business interests.

11. Return of Materials. Upon the request of Employer and, in any event, upon the termination of Employee's employment, Employee must return to Employer and leave at its disposal all memoranda, notes, records, drawings, manuals, computer programs, documentation, diskettes, computer tapes, and other documents or media pertaining to the business of Employer or Employee's specific duties for Employer (including all copies of such materials). Employee must also return to Employer and leave at its disposal all materials involving any Trade Secrets or Confidential Information of Employer. This Section applies to all materials made or compiled by Employee, as well as to all materials furnished to Employee by anyone else in connection with his/her employment.

12. Restrictions on Competition. After the termination of Employee's employment for any reason, Employee agrees not to compete with Employer, for twenty-four (24) months following the effective date of such termination, by engaging in any activities which Employer was engaged in, or contemplating engaging in, at the time of such termination. Employee will refrain from actually performing or directly managing or supervising such activities, whether as principal, agent, employee, consultant, contractor, or co-venturer.

13. No Interference With Personnel Relations. During his/her employment with Employer and for a period of twenty-four (24) months afterwards, Employee will not knowingly solicit, entice or persuade any other employees of Employer to leave the services of Employer for any reason.

14. Prior Inventions. If, prior to the date of execution hereof, Employee has made or conceived any unpatented inventions, improvements, developments, or original works of authorship whether or not patentable or copyrightable, which Employee desires to have excluded from this Agreement, Employee has written on a complete list thereof on Exhibit "A" hereto.

15. Compliance Not Contingent Upon Additional Consideration. Employee has not been promised, and shall not claim, any additional or special payment for compliance with the covenants and agreements herein contained. If this Agreement was entered into after Employee has commenced employment, Employee acknowledges and agrees that the increased benefits, salary increase and/or continued employment constitute adequate consideration for Employee's obligations hereunder.

16. Specific Performance and Consent to Injunctive Relief. Irreparable harm should be presumed if Employee breaches any covenant in this Agreement. The faithful observance of all covenants in this Agreement is an essential condition of Employee's employment, and Employer is depending upon absolute compliance. Damages would probably be very difficult to ascertain if Employee breached any covenant in this Agreement. This Agreement is intended to protect the proprietary rights of Employer in many important ways. Even the threat of any misuse of the Trade Secrets or Confidential Information of Employer would be extremely harmful, since the Trade Secrets or Confidential Information are essential to the business of Employer. In light of these facts, Employee agrees that any court of competent jurisdiction should immediately enjoin any breach of this Agreement upon the request of Employer, and Employee specifically releases Employer from the requirement of posting any bond in connection with temporary or interlocutory injunctive relief, to the extent permitted by law, in addition to any other remedies to which Employer may be entitled.

17. Notices. All notices required under this Agreement shall be made in writing and shall be deemed given when (1) delivered in person, (2) deposited in the U.S. mail, first class, with proper postage prepaid and properly addressed, or (3) sent through the interoffice delivery service of Employer (if Employee is still employed by Employer at the time).

18. Related Parties. This Agreement shall inure to the benefit of, and be binding upon, Employer and its subsidiaries and its affiliates, together with their successors and assigns, and Employee, together with his/her executor, administrator, personal representative, heirs, and legatees.

19. Severability. Employee agrees that the unenforceability or inapplicability of any one or more provisions of this Agreement shall not affect the remaining provisions of this Agreement or any part thereof. Furthermore, in lieu of any invalid or unenforceable provision, there shall be added automatically as part of this Agreement a provision as similar to such invalid or enforceable provision as may be possible and be valid and enforceable, and the parties hereto request any court or other entity to whom disputes arising under Agreement may be submitted to reform any otherwise invalid or unenforceable provisions in accordance with this provision.

20. Survival. Employee's obligations under this Agreement shall continue in the event his/her employment or work with Employer is terminated, voluntarily or involuntarily, by Employer, with or without cause.

21. Entire Agreement. This Agreement supersedes and merges all previous agreements and discussions relating to the same or similar subject matters between the parties and constitutes the entire agreement between the parties with respect to the subject matter of this Agreement. This Agreement may not be modified in any respect by any verbal statement, representation or agreement made by any employee, officer, or representative of the parties or by any written agreement unless signed by an officer of Employer.

22. Governing Law. The laws of the State ______________________________ will govern the interpretation, validity and effect of this Agreement without regard to the place of execution or the place for performance thereof, and all parties agree that the state and federal courts having jurisdiction in ______________________________ shall have personal jurisdiction over all parties to hear all disputes arising under this Agreement, and that venue shall lie in _________________________ for all purposes.

EMPLOYEE ACKNOWLEDGES THAT, BEFORE SIGNING THIS AGREEMENT, EMPLOYEE WAS GIVEN AN OPPORTUNITY TO READ IT, CAREFULLY EVALUATE IT, AND DISCUSS IT WITH HIS/HER PERSONAL ADVISORS AND WITH REPRESENTATIVES OF EMPLOYER.

IN WITNESS WHEREOF, Employer and Employee have executed this Agreement, effective as of the ________ day of ________________, ______________.

EMPLOYER

By:

This ________ day of _______________, _________

EMPLOYEE

Printed Name:

This _________ day of __________________, ______________.

References

Berger, S.A. *Adding Insult to Injury: How In Re Venture Mortgage Funds Exposes the Inequitable Results of New York's Usury Remedies,* 29 Fordham Urb. L.J. 2193 (2002).

Davis, B., *A Matter of Trust for Rising Stars: Protecting Minors' Earnings in California and New York,* 27 J. Juv. L. 69 (2006).

Graves, S.M. and C.L. Peterson, *Predatory Lending and the Military: The Law and Geography of "Payday" Loans in Military Towns,* 66 Ohio St. L.J. 653 (2005).

Krieg, J., *There's No Business Like Show Business: Child Entertainers and the Law,* 6 U. Pa. J. Lab. & Emp. L. 429 (2004).

Martin, S.L., *Financing Litigation Online: Usury and Other Obstacles,* 1 DePaul Bus. & Comm. L.J. 85 (2002).

Chapter 5

Defenses

After reading this chapter you will be able to:

1. Explain what a defense to a contract means.
2. Compare and contrast the defenses of fraud, duress, and mutual mistake.
3. Describe the phrases *caveat emptor* and *caveat vendor* and why they are important in the study of contracts.
4. Understand the relationship between consumer protection laws and contracts.

Key Terms

Caveat emptor	Intoxication	Puffery
Caveat vendor	Misrepresentation	Statement of fact
Defense	Mutual mistake	Statement of opinion
Duress	Negligent misrepresentation	Undue influence
Fraud		

K = O + A + C + (**Leg. + Cap.**)

After a contract is formed but not yet completed, one or more of the parties to the agreement might believe that the contract should end prematurely. The reasons may vary, but contract **defenses** refer to the various claims available to a party that the contract should no longer exist, they should be excused from performance, or that the contract never really existed in the first place. For example, if one were induced to enter into a contract by fraud, one would expect that the law would free the misled party from the agreement due to this misrepresentation. This chapter explores the three primary defenses to a contract: fraud, duress, and mutual (bilateral) mistake. It is important to understand that the parties have to acknowledge that some sort of agreement existed for these defenses to apply in the first place. A party can certainly allege that the contract never existed due to illegality, lack of capacity, or lack of mutual assent, all previously addressed.

FRAUD

Sometimes referred to as "fraud in the inducement" or **misrepresentation**, the defense of **fraud** is the strongest of the contract defenses and is almost always successful if proved. Courts do not protect those who misled another in order to enter into an agreement. Fraud, then, is an intentional act by the defendant. Could one be considered to be fraudulent for failing to disclose information? Yes, but as a general rule a party to a contract does not have a legal duty to volunteer information to the other side about the nature or terms of the contract. For example, information must be revealed to consumers involving certain types of transactions which are supported by state consumer protection laws, including real estate sales transactions, various types of loans, and even health club contracts. As in tort law, to prove that one was defrauded a plaintiff has to demonstrate that the defendant made a false representation of a material fact and knew that it was false when the statement was made. The plaintiff also will have to demonstrate that the defendant knew that the plaintiff would rely on the misrepresentation (and did) and that the plaintiff suffered damages as a result. If a defendant claims that he or she did not know whether the statement was true or false, then the legal issue would be whether the defendant should have known. If the answer is "yes," then the defendant might still be liable for the false statement of fact even if there was no intent to deceive. This would be characterized as **negligent misrepresentation** rather than intentional misrepresentation—the importance of which focuses on the potential for punitive damages in the latter instance.

The determination of whether fraud occurred might boil down to statements made by one of the parties prior to entering the agreement. **Statements of opinion** (sometimes calling **puffery** or puffing language) sound less like fraud and are usually not actionable. False **statements of fact**, however, present an entirely different scenario. For example, a salesperson who exclaims, "This is the car for you" or "This is the best car on the lot" would likely succeed in their defense that such statements are simply the art of selling goods or services and not statements of fact at all. Consider fine print found in some contracts. The modern approach disallows fine print or even print found on the back of a contract unless the party draws attention to it by boldface type font on the front of an agreement. Many states are now attempting to legislate consumer protection laws related to the practice of predatory lending which might have excessive fees and other "hidden" charges found in the fine print for payday loans. Again, it is possible that one could be held liable for negligent misrepresentation if a statement should have been made (but was not) about the quality of goods or services, and the buyer relies on the seller's expertise, special knowledge, or skill, as well as their advice for a sale.

CAVEATS

When consumers are involved in a contractual relationship, the modern approach is to move away from ***caveat emptor*** (let the buyer beware) and instead toward ***caveat vendor*** (let the seller beware). Misrepresentations (regardless of intent) which induce someone to enter into a contract will generally create a rebuttable presumption that the party should have known that the assertions were false. It is important to note that if a misrepresentation of the *law* is made, that is usually not a valid defense to undo a contract: courts generally stand firm by the Latin expression, *Ignorantia legis non excusat* ("ignorance of the law is no excuse"). One could have sought legal advice from a licensed attorney or even looked up the law itself at the public library or even on the Internet.

DURESS

Another defense to a contract is **duress**. Duress does not mean stress alone. Rather, it means that a party to the agreement really had no choice at all and was essentially forced into the contract. The force must be an immediate force, such as the threat of physical harm (physical duress), severe economic duress, or a form of severe emotional distress such as extortion. Duress, sometimes referred to as **undue influence,** might be valid if an individual is being taken advantage of due to a special and/or fiduciary relationship that involves exceptional trust or confidence. Often cited examples include lawyer-client, doctor-patient, and employer-employee relationships.

MUTUAL MISTAKE

Mistakes in contracts might occur related to price, value, quantity, and quality. However, the least effective defense to a contract is the defense of **mutual mistake** (sometimes referred to as a bilateral mistake or even sometimes a common mistake). This defense demonstrates that there was no real meeting of the minds in the first place because both of the parties were mistaken as to the nature, terms, and/or conditions found in the contract. This is very unlikely to occur. While one party may allege that it was mistaken, it is very unlikely that both parties will admit to this (otherwise, the case would not be involved in litigation). This, of course, differs from a unilateral (one-sided mistake) which is not usually considered a valid defense to a contract. In that case, a party would be asking a court for a remedy for their own error. This is not likely to be successful.

INTOXICATION

As a rule, **intoxication** is no defense to a contract. Generally speaking drunkenness, public and private intoxication, and even drug abuse are considered *voluntary* acts. If these were valid contract defenses, litigants might claim this as a defense on a regular basis (whether true or not). Still, it is possible that the defense of *involuntary* intoxication might be a valid one. For example, if someone's drink were spiked and it affected their judgment (and they could prove it was spiked by someone else), then the possibility does exist that intoxication might be a valid defense though this is not a strong argument. This includes the effects of prescription medication on the mind as well.[1]

CHAPTER SUMMARY

Once a contract has been entered into, one of the parties may wish to try to get out of the agreement by utilizing a contract defense. The primary defenses are fraud, duress, and mutual (bilateral) mistake. Fraud is a very strong defense since courts do not favor those who made misrepresentations or those who make false statements of fact in order to induce someone to enter into an agreement. In addition to contract law remedies, consumers may also be protected by various state laws known as consumer protection laws. The proliferation of consumer protection laws has caused the legal principle *caveat emptor* (let the buyer beware) to evolve today to be better served as *caveat vendor* (let the seller beware).

[1]Even if one claimed that prescription medication was the reason that their judgment was affected, consider the likelihood that one would subsequently enter into a contract thereafter.

Discussion and Review Questions

1. What are the three big defenses to a contract?
2. What is the difference between *caveat emptor* and *caveat vendor*?
3. Why is fraud the strongest of the defenses to a contract?
4. If someone sells something "practically brand new," is that stretching the art of the sale too far if, in fact, it is not really new?

Critical Thinking Exercises

1. Assume that your agreement with your cell phone company requires that you maintain your agreement for a period of two years. However, you are not satisfied with your service. For example, you have frequent dropped calls, and your bills have been wrong on at least three different occasions. What contract defense might be most successful, and could you terminate the agreement?
2. A successful salesperson assists a customer in a large local retail store. The customer is buying a new phone, and asks the salesperson for advice on which phone to get. The salesperson states, "Most people buy this phone." The customer relies on that statement and buys that model. Later the customer finds out that the type of phone she bought is common, but not the leading brand in terms of sales. Could the customer sue? If so, under what legal theories?
3. Explore the case *Jennings v. Radio Station KSCS*, 708 S.W.2d 60 (Tex. Ct. App. 1986). Do you feel that the listener (even though a prisoner) should be entitled to a $25,000 award due to a unilateral mistake when the stationed failed to live up to its promise of "We play at least three-in-a-row or we pay you $25,000"?
4. Music star Vanilla Ice (Rob Van Winkle) was supposedly held over a hotel balcony and threatened to be dropped unless he signed over certain royalty rights to Marion "Suge" Knight. However, Vanilla Ice disputes much of that story. *See* http://www.washingtonpost.com/wpdyn/content/discussion/2006/02/16/DI2006021601769.html?nav=nsc. If someone held you over a balcony in order to get you to sign a contract, do you feel that would constitute duress as a defense to a contract?
5. Have you ever heard an extremely fast disclaimer at the end of a radio commercial? Have you ever seen a scrolling disclaimer after a television advertisement that is so fast that you cannot even read what the language says? Do you feel that such disclaimers are valid? Why or why not?
6. Waivers found on the back of sporting event tickets waive all kinds of liability including being hit by bats, balls, pucks, participants and so on. Do you think that the waivers found on the back of sporting event tickets (and usually in fine print) are valid disclaimers? Are they mere deterrents to filing a lawsuit by an injured party?

Online Research Exercises

1. Explore waivers found on personal or business websites or website providers such as match.com or myspace.com. They can be any type of waiver which disclaims liability of any sort. Do you think that they are well written and valid? Why or why not?
2. What if you went to get a tattoo on your body, and the tattoo artist made a spelling error on your arm? How would you feel and could you sue? Consider http://www.findarticles.com/p/articles/mi_m1571/is_12_15/ai_54246282 and the opinions found in http://archives.thedaily.washington.edu/1999/030299/04.amitojtatt.html.
3. A recent phenomenon involving fraud and the Internet is something known as click fraud in which a website intentionally misrepresents the number of times that a link has been clicked in order to generate more revenue from the advertising company. Visit http://blog.ericgoldman.org/archives/2007/04/google_adwords_1.htm.

CASE APPLICATIONS

Case 1

Consider the following Michigan case involving mass mailings, consumer protection, sweepstakes rewards, and allegations of fraud.

GIBSON v. PUBLISHERS CLEARING HOUSE

2000 U.S. DIST. LEXIS 15227 (W.D. MICH. SEPT. 29, 2000)

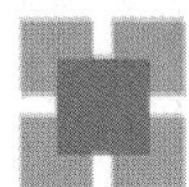

BELL, J.

Plaintiffs Leo Gibson and Ethel Gibson have brought claims that Defendant Publishers Clearing House (PCH) committed fraud, misrepresentation, and breach of contract in denying Plaintiffs' claim to a sweepstakes prize of $5,376,600. Plaintiffs filed in Michigan Circuit Court in Berrien County, Michigan. Defendant removed to this Court.

PCH's primary business involves mass mailings to consumers to market magazine subscriptions. As part of its marketing scheme, PCH employs the use of the well-known Publishers Clearing House Sweepstakes, through which it entices consumers to subscribe to its magazines.

In May 1998 Plaintiff Leo Gibson received one of PCH's solicitations which Gibson asserts led him to believe that he had won a prize of $5,376,600. Subsequently, Plaintiff Ethel Gibson quit her job at the Orchard Grove Extended Care Facility in reliance upon Plaintiffs' belief that Defendant would be forthcoming with the prize money. Despite contacting Defendant several times, Plaintiff was never awarded the $5,376,600 in prize money.

Plaintiff brings three claims, alleging that: (I) Defendant PCH violated the Michigan Consumer Protection Act (*MCL 445.901* et seq.) and the Michigan Pricing and Advertising Act (*MCL 445.351* et seq.); (II) Defendant PCH engaged in fraud and misrepresentation in connection with its solicitation of Plaintiffs; and (III) Defendant PCH breached its contract with Mr. Gibson by failing to award Mr. Gibson a $5,376,600 sweepstakes prize.

Breach of Contract. Plaintiff Leo Gibson alleges that he received correspondence from Defendant PCH in May of 1998 in which Defendant offered to transfer $5,376,600 to Plaintiff if Plaintiff accepted by returning certain documents to Defendant. Plaintiffs maintain that Defendant breached this contract when it did not transfer to Plaintiffs $5,376,600. Defendant argues that Plaintiffs have failed to state a claim upon which relief can be granted because no reasonable person would interpret the mailings received by Plaintiffs to be a valid contract to award Plaintiffs $5,376,600.

The front of the Exhibit 1 letter states (1) recipient is a guaranteed cash winner; (2) Farmers State Bank is transferring $5,376,600; (3) to claim the cash award recipient "must complete and return the Contest Documents that will arrive under separate cover." It is from this information that Plaintiff Leo Gibson apparently drew the inference that he had received a bona fide unilateral offer to accept $5,376,600.

On the back of the letter, however, there is additional information. Included are statements that (1) "This is an official notification that you are guaranteed to win a cash prize of up to $100,000"; (2), in bold type, "ALTHOUGH MOST FOLKS WILL RECEIVE A CHECK FOR $1.00, YOUR PRIZE COULD BE AS MUCH AS $100,000!"; and (3) "No Purchase Necessary."

Plaintiff maintains that the letter received from PCH is an enforceable contract. To establish an enforceable contract in a lottery or drawing an entrant must show (1) the offer of a prize by the sponsor or performance of a specified act; (2) participation in the contest; and (3) performance of the act requested by the sponsor.

Here, a reasonable reading of the materials provided to Plaintiffs indicate that there was an offer to be awarded at least a $1.00 prize if Plaintiffs accepted by sending in the appropriate materials. A reasonable person could not infer that PCH's mailing created an offer for acceptance of a $5,376,600 cash prize. After reading all the information provided in the letter, a reasonable person would realize that the $5,376,600 "Being Transferred" is the total amount of monies being awarded in the contest, and not the amount being awarded to any one person. Plaintiffs either ignored or did not read the disclaimers contained in the letter.

Michigan law requires that all materials in the mailing must be considered as a whole. *See Workmon v. Publishers*

Clearing House, 118 F.3d 457 (6th Cir. 1997). Taking all the statements in this mailing into account, the disclaimer clearly advises the recipient that he has won a cash prize, that it is likely to be $1.00, and that in no event will it be over $100,000.

No reasonable person would assume he had won a prize of $5,376,000. Therefore, as to the breach of contract claim, Plaintiffs have failed to state a claim upon which relief may be granted. The breach of contract claim should be dismissed under *Rule 12(b)(6) of the Federal Rules of Civil Procedure.*

Plaintiff Ethel Gilbert has brought a detrimental reliance claim based on the supposed contract. It is not enough, however, to show reliance alone. Any such reliance must be reasonable. As discussed *supra*, no reasonable person would assume from the materials received by Plaintiffs that there was a valid offer to award $5,376,600. It follows that there could be no reasonable reliance where there can be no reasonable inference of a contract. Because Plaintiff Ethel Gilbert's only claim is based upon the breach of contract allegation, she should be dismissed as a Plaintiff in this case.

Fraud and Misrepresentation. Defendants have also moved to dismiss the fraud and misrepresentation claim under Fed. R. Civ. P. 9(b), which requires that Plaintiff "must allege with particularity a false statement of fact made by defendant" upon which Plaintiff relied. "The purpose undergirding the particularity requirement of Rule 9(b) is to provide a defendant fair notice of the substance of a plaintiff's claim in order that the defendant may prepare a responsive pleading." Plaintiff must "state facts with particularity, and that these facts, in turn, must give rise to a 'strong inference' of the defendant's fraudulent intent." Plaintiffs cite *In re Credit Acceptance Corp., supra,* for the proposition that in considering a motion to dismiss pursuant to Rule 9(b) the Court must "construe the complaint in the light most favorable to the plaintiff" and "accept all factual allegations as true." The proposition is true, but the problem here is that Plaintiffs allege conclusions rather than substantive facts upon which a case may be built. For example, Plaintiffs' primary allegation is that Leo Gibson "received a guaranteed winner notification from defendant and a notice of monetary transfer by Farmers State Bank . . . in the amount of $5,376,600." *See* Plaintiffs' Complaint, at 2 (June 15, 2000); Plaintiffs' *Answer to Defendant's Motion to Dismiss*, at 2 (Sept. 7, 2000). While Plaintiffs make general accusations of fraud and misrepresentation, the crux of Plaintiffs' case is whether the allegation of a guaranteed winner notification and contract for $5,376,600 is supported by the facts. Plaintiffs fail to provide such facts. Exhibit 1, as discussed *supra*, fails to support Plaintiffs' conclusions.

Even after the filing of a complaint and an answer to Defendant's Motion to Dismiss Plaintiffs' Complaint, Plaintiffs have been unable to identify with particularity any representation of Defendant, taken in context, to support their claim that Defendant misrepresented its invitation to make an offer or did so fraudulently. Plaintiffs have had sufficient opportunity to plead the factual basis for believing a fraud occurred as required by Rule 9(b), but have failed to do so. Thus, Counts I and II are dismissed for failure to state a claim upon which relief can be granted, pursuant to Rules 9(b) and 12(b)(6).

It is evident that Publishers Clearing House has taken great pains to craft an invitation that looks remarkably like an offer to accept a multi-million dollar prize. In so doing, it is engaging in highly questionable ethical practices designed to dupe the unsophisticated. These practices do not, however, reach to the Counts articulated in Plaintiffs' complaint.

This Court has also considered Plaintiffs' point that Michigan's Attorney General has filed a similar complaint against Publishers Clearing House (*Granholm v. Publishers Clearing House*, Docket No. 99-90793-CP (Oct. 8, 1999)), and other suits have been filed around the country against Publishers Clearing House. *See, e.g.,* Time *Settles Mailings Complaints, THE DETROIT NEWS, (2000 WL 3489159)* Aug. 25, 2000 (stating that Publishers Clearing House had agreed to pay $18 million in 24 states to settle complaints of deceptive sweepstakes mailings). These cases, however, have either not been decided or have settled out of court. Neither settlements nor mere filings of complaints can have precedential authority for this Court.

Plaintiff has failed to state a claim upon which relief can be granted regarding Count III, and has failed to plead its case with sufficient particularity with regard to Counts I and II. Accordingly, an order consistent with this opinion will be entered.

Case Questions

1. Is this a federal or state case?
2. What two major categories of law did the plaintiffs bring the lawsuit under?
3. Did the court believe that a reasonable person would have expected that they would have won the sweepstakes? Why or why not?

Case 2

In this California decision, consider whether the typographical mistake involving an automobile advertisement gave rise to a legitimate claim for breach of contract. Notice, too, the discussion of the statute of frauds (that certain types of agreements must be in writing to be enforced) which is discussed in greater detail in the next chapter. Do you believe your state court would have analyzed the case in the same way?

DONOVAN v. RRL CORP.

27 P.3D 702 (CAL. 2001)

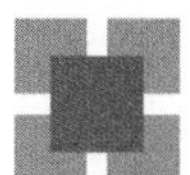

GEORGE, C. J.

Defendant RRL Corporation is an automobile dealer doing business under the name Lexus of Westminster. Because of typographical and proofreading errors made by a local newspaper, defendant's advertisement listed a price for a used automobile that was significantly less than the intended sales price. Plaintiff Brian J. Donovan read the advertisement and, after examining the vehicle, attempted to purchase it by tendering the advertised price. Defendant refused to sell the automobile to plaintiff at that price, and plaintiff brought this action against defendant for breach of contract. The municipal court entered judgment for defendant on the ground that the mistake in the advertisement precluded the existence of a contract. The appellate department of the superior court and the Court of Appeal reversed, relying in part upon *Vehicle Code Section 11713.1*, subdivision (e), which makes it unlawful for an automobile dealer not to sell a motor vehicle at the advertised price while the vehicle remains unsold and before the advertisement expires.

We conclude that a contract satisfying the statute of frauds arose from defendant's advertisement and plaintiff's tender of the advertised price, but that defendant's unilateral mistake of fact provides a basis for rescinding the contract. Although *Vehicle Code Section 11713.1*, subdivision (e), justifies a reasonable expectation on the part of consumers that an automobile dealer intends that such an advertisement constitute an offer, and that the offer can be accepted by paying the advertised price, this statute does not supplant governing common law principles authorizing rescission of a contract on the ground of mistake. As we shall explain, rescission is warranted here because the evidence establishes that defendant's unilateral mistake of fact was made in good faith, defendant did not bear the risk of the mistake, and enforcement of the contract with the erroneous price would be unconscionable. Accordingly, we shall reverse the judgment of the Court of Appeal.

While reading the April 26, 1997, edition of the *Costa Mesa Daily Pilot,* a local newspaper, plaintiff noticed a full-page advertisement placed by defendant. The advertisement promoted a "Pre-Owned Coup-A-Rama Sale!/2-Day Pre-Owned Sales Event" and listed, along with 15 other used automobiles, a 1995 Jaguar XJ6 Vanden Plas. The advertisement described the color of this automobile as sapphire blue, included a vehicle identification number, and stated a price of $25,995. The name Lexus of Westminster was displayed prominently in three separate locations in the advertisement, which included defendant's address along with a small map showing the location of the dealership. The following statements appeared in small print at the bottom of the advertisement: "All cars plus tax, lic., doc., smog & bank fees. On approved credit. Ad expires 4/27/97[.]"

Also on April 26, 1997, plaintiff visited a Jaguar dealership that offered other 1995 Jaguars for sale at $8,000 to $10,000 more than the price specified in defendant's advertisement. The following day, plaintiff and his spouse drove to Lexus of Westminster and observed a blue Jaguar displayed on an elevated ramp. After verifying that the identification number on the sticker was the same as that listed in defendant's April 26 Daily Pilot advertisement, they asked a salesperson whether they could test drive the Jaguar. Plaintiff mentioned that he had seen the advertisement and that the price "looked really good." The salesperson responded that, as a Lexus dealer, defendant might offer better prices for a Jaguar automobile than would a Jaguar dealer. At that point, however, neither plaintiff nor the salesperson mentioned the specific advertised price.

After the test drive, plaintiff and his spouse discussed several negative characteristics of the automobile, including high mileage, an apparent rust problem, and worn tires. In addition, it was not as clean as the other Jaguars they had inspected. Despite these problems, they believed that the advertised price was a very good price and decided to purchase the vehicle. Plaintiff told the salesperson, "Okay. We will take it at your price, $26,000." When the salesperson did not respond, plaintiff showed him the advertisement. The salesperson immediately stated, "That's a mistake."

After plaintiff asked to speak with an individual in charge, defendant's sales manager also told plaintiff that the price listed in the advertisement was a mistake. The sales manager apologized and offered to pay for plaintiff's fuel, time, and effort expended in traveling to the dealership to examine the automobile. Plaintiff declined this offer and expressed his belief that there had been no mistake. Plaintiff stated that he could write a check for the full purchase price as advertised. The sales manager responded that he would not sell the vehicle at the advertised price. Plaintiff then requested the sales price. After performing some calculations, and based upon defendant's $35,000 investment in the automobile, the sales manager stated that he would sell it to plaintiff for $37,016. Plaintiff responded, "No, I want to buy it at your advertised price, and I will write you a check right now." The sales manager again stated that he would not sell the vehicle at the advertised price, and plaintiff and his spouse left the dealership.

Plaintiff subsequently filed this action against defendant for breach of contract, fraud, and negligence. In addition to testimony consistent with the facts set forth above, the following evidence was presented to the municipal court, which acted as the trier of fact.

Defendant's advertising manager compiles information for placement in advertisements in several local newspapers, including the *Costa Mesa Daily Pilot*. Defendant's advertisement published in the Saturday, April 19, 1997, edition of the *Daily Pilot* listed a 1995 Jaguar XJ6 Vanden Plas but did not specify a price for that automobile; instead, the word "Save" appeared in the space where a price ordinarily would have appeared. The following Thursday afternoon, defendant's sales manager instructed the advertising manager to delete the 1995 Jaguar from all advertisements and to substitute a 1994 Jaguar XJ6 with a price of $25,995. The advertising manager conveyed the new information to a representative of the *Daily Pilot* that same afternoon.

Because of typographical and proofreading errors made by employees of the *Daily Pilot*, however, the newspaper did not replace the description of the 1995 Jaguar with the description of the 1994 Jaguar, but did replace the word "Save" with the price of $25,995. Thus, the Saturday, April 26, edition of the *Daily Pilot* erroneously advertised the 1995 Jaguar XJ6 Vanden Plas at a price of $25,995. The *Daily Pilot* acknowledged its error in a letter of retraction sent to defendant on April 28. No employee of defendant reviewed a proof sheet of the revised *Daily Pilot* advertisement before it was published, and defendant was unaware of the mistake until plaintiff attempted to purchase the automobile.

Except for the 1995 Jaguar XJ6 Vanden Plas, defendant intended to sell each vehicle appearing in the April 26, 1997, *Daily Pilot* advertisement at the advertised price. Defendant's advertisements in the April 26 editions of several other newspapers correctly listed the *1994* Jaguar XJ6 with a price of $25,995. In May 1997, defendant's advertisements in several newspapers listed the 1995 Jaguar XJ6 Vanden Plas for sale at $37,995. Defendant subsequently sold the automobile for $38,399.

The municipal court entered judgment for defendant. During the trial, the court ruled that plaintiff had not stated a cause of action for negligence, and it precluded plaintiff from presenting evidence in support of such a claim. After the close of evidence and presentation of argument, the municipal court concluded as a matter of law that a newspaper advertisement for an automobile generally constitutes a valid contractual offer that a customer may accept by tendering payment of the advertised price. The court also determined that such an advertisement satisfies the requirements of the statute of frauds when the dealer's name appears in the advertisement. Nevertheless, the municipal court held that in the present case there was no valid offer because defendant's unilateral mistake of fact vitiated or negated contractual intent. The court made factual findings that defendant's mistake regarding the advertisement was made in good faith and was not intended to deceive the public. The municipal court also found that plaintiff was unaware of the mistake before it was disclosed to him by defendant's representatives.

An essential element of any contract is the consent of the parties, or mutual assent. Mutual assent usually is manifested by an offer communicated to the offeree and an acceptance communicated to the offeror. The determination of whether a particular communication constitutes an operative offer, rather than an inoperative step in the preliminary negotiation of a contract, depends upon all the surrounding circumstances. The objective manifestation of the party's assent ordinarily controls, and the pertinent inquiry is whether the individual to whom the communication was made had reason to believe that it was intended as an offer.

In the present case, the municipal court ruled that newspaper advertisements for automobiles generally constitute offers that can be accepted by a customer's tender of the purchase price. Its conclusion that defendant's advertisement for the 1995 Jaguar did not constitute an offer was based solely upon the court's factual determination that the erroneous price in the advertisement was the result of a good faith mistake.

Because the existence of an offer depends upon an objective interpretation of defendant's assent as reflected in the advertisement, however, the mistaken price (not reasonably known to plaintiff to be a mistake) is irrelevant in determining the threshold question whether the advertisement constituted an offer. In this situation, mistake instead properly would be considered in deciding whether a contract resulted from the acceptance of an offer containing mistaken terms, or whether any such contract could be voided or rescinded.

Some courts have stated that an advertisement or other notice disseminated to the public at large generally does not constitute an offer, but rather is presumed to be an invitation to consider, examine, and negotiate. Nevertheless, certain advertisements have been held to constitute offers where they invite the performance of a specific act without further communication and leave nothing for negotiation. Advertisements for rewards typically fall within this category, because performing the requested act (e.g., returning a lost article or supplying particular information) generally is all that is necessary to accept the offer and conclude the bargain.

Various advertisements involving transactions in goods also have been held to constitute offers where they invite particular action. For example, a merchant's advertisement that listed particular goods at a specific price and included the phrase "First Come First Served" was deemed to be an offer, because it constituted a promise to sell to a customer at that price in exchange for the customer's act of arriving at the store at a particular time. (*Lefkowitz v. Great Minneapolis Surplus Store (1957) 251 Minn. 188 [86 N.W. 2d 689, 691]; Rest.2d Contracts,* §26, com. b, illus. 1, p. 76.) Similarly, external wording on the envelope of an item of bulk rate mail promising to give the recipient a watch "just for opening the envelope" before a certain date was held to constitute an operative offer accepted by performance of the act of opening the envelope. (*Harris v. Time, Inc., supra, 191 Cal. App. 3d 449, 455–456.)* In addition, an advertisement stating that anyone who purchased a 1954 automobile from a dealer could exchange it for a 1955 model at no additional cost constituted an offer that was accepted when the plaintiff purchased the 1954 vehicle. In such cases, courts have considered whether the advertiser, in clear and positive terms, promised to render performance in exchange for something requested by the advertiser, and whether the recipient of the advertisement reasonably might have concluded that by acting in accordance with the request a contract would be formed.

Like the Court of Appeal, we conclude that a licensed automobile dealer's advertisement for the sale of a particular vehicle at a specific price—when construed in light of *Vehicle Code Section 11713.1,* subdivision (e)—reasonably justifies a consumer's understanding that the dealer intends the advertisement to constitute an offer and that the consumer's assent to the bargain is invited and will conclude it.

Vehicle Code Section 11713.1 sets forth comprehensive requirements governing a licensed automobile dealer's advertisements for motor vehicles. This statute requires, among other things, that an advertisement for a specific automobile identify the vehicle by its identification number or license number (*id.,* subd. (a)), disclose the type of charges that will be added to the advertised price at the time of sale (*id.,* subd. (b)), and refrain from containing various types of misleading information (*id.,* subds. (i), (*l*), (o), (p), (r)).

> In addition, *Vehicle Code Section 11713.1,* subdivision (e) (hereafter Section 11713.1(e)), states that it is a violation of the Vehicle Code for the holder of any dealer's license to "[f]ail to sell a vehicle to any person at the advertised total price, exclusive of [specified charges such as taxes and registration fees], while the vehicle remains unsold, unless the advertisement states the advertised total price is good only for a specified time and the time has elapsed."

Although dealers are required by statute to prepare a written contract when selling an automobile, and such a contract contains terms other than the price of the vehicle, we agree with plaintiff that a dealer's advertisement specifying a price for a particular vehicle constitutes a sufficient manifestation of the dealer's assent to give rise to a contract. As we have explained, in light of Section 11713.1(e) such an advertisement objectively reflects the dealer's intention to sell the vehicle to a member of the public who tenders the full advertised price while the vehicle remains unsold and before the advertisement expires. The price almost always is the most important term of the bargain, and the dealer's intention to include other terms in a written contract does not preclude the existence of mutual assent sufficient to conclude a contract.

In sum, because Section 11713.1(e) makes it unlawful for a dealer not to sell a particular vehicle at the advertised price while the vehicle remains unsold and before the advertisement expires, plaintiff reasonably could believe that defendant intended the advertisement to be an offer. Therefore, we conclude that defendant's advertisement constituted an offer that was accepted by plaintiff's tender of the advertised price.

Defendant contends that even if its advertisement constituted an offer that was accepted by plaintiff's tender of the purchase price, plaintiff is not authorized by law to enforce the resulting contract, because there was no signed writing that satisfied the requirements of the statute of frauds for the sale of goods. Plaintiff, on the other hand, maintains that defendant's name, as it appeared in the newspaper advertisement for the sale of the vehicle, constituted a signature within the meaning of the statute.

The applicable statute of frauds states in relevant part: "Except as otherwise provided in this section a contract for the sale of goods for the price of five hundred dollars ($500) or more is not enforceable by way of action or defense unless there is some writing sufficient to indicate that a contract for sale has been made between the parties and *signed by the party against whom enforcement is sought or by his or her authorized agent or broker*. A writing is not insufficient because it omits or incorrectly states a term agreed upon[,] but the contract is not enforceable under this paragraph beyond the quantity of goods shown in the writing." (Cal. U. *Com. Code*, *§2201*, subd. (1), italics added.)

The California Uniform Commercial Code defines the term "signed" as including "any symbol executed or adopted by a party with present intention to authenticate a writing." (Cal. U. *Com. Code*, *§1201*, subd. (38).) The comment regarding the corresponding provision of the Uniform Commercial Code states: "The inclusion of authentication in the definition of 'signed' is to make clear that as the term is used in [the code] a complete signature is not necessary. Authentication may be printed, stamped, or written; it may be by initials or by thumbprint. It may be on any part of the document and in appropriate cases may be found in a billhead or letterhead. No catalog of possible authentications can be complete and the court must use common sense and commercial experience in passing upon these matters. The question always is whether the symbol was executed or adopted by the party with present intention to authenticate the writing." (U. Com. Code com., reprinted at 23A West's Ann. Cal. U. Com. Code (1964 ed.) foll. §1201, p. 65; see 1 Witkin, *supra*, Contracts, §281, p. 273 [citing California decisions generally consistent with this comment]; *Rest.2d Contracts*, *§134*.)

Some decisions have relaxed the signature requirement considerably to accommodate various forms of electronic communication. For example, a party's printed or typewritten name in a telegram has been held to satisfy the statute of frauds. Even a tape recording identifying the parties has been determined to meet the signature requirement of the Uniform Commercial Code. *(Ellis Canning Company v. Bernstein (D.Colo. 1972) 348 F. Supp. 1212, 1228.)*

As established above, defendant's advertisement reflected an objective manifestation of its intention to make an offer for the sale of the vehicle at the stated price. Defendant's printed name in the advertisement similarly evidenced an intention to authenticate the advertisement as an offer and therefore constituted a signature satisfying the statute of frauds.

Having concluded that defendant's advertisement for the sale of the Jaguar automobile constituted an offer that was accepted by plaintiff's tender of the advertised price, and that the resulting contract satisfied the statute of frauds, we next consider whether defendant can avoid enforcement of the contract on the ground of mistake. A party may rescind a contract if his or her consent was given by mistake. (Civ. Code, §1689, subd. (b)(1).) A factual mistake by one party to a contract, or unilateral mistake, affords a ground for rescission in some circumstances.

(See fn. 5.) *Civil Code section 1577* states in relevant part: "Mistake of fact is a mistake, not caused by the neglect of a legal duty on the part of the person making the mistake, and consisting in: [P] 1. An unconscious ignorance or forgetfulness of a fact past or present, material to the contract. . . ."

The Court of Appeal determined that defendant's error did not constitute a mistake of fact within the meaning of *Civil Code section 1577*. In support of this determination, the court relied upon the following principle: "[A] unilateral misinterpretation of contractual terms, without knowledge by the other party at the time of contract, does not constitute a mistake under either *Civil Code section 1577* [mistake of fact] or 1578 [mistake of law]."

. . . California law does not adhere to the original Restatement's requirements for rescission based upon unilateral mistake of fact—i.e., only in circumstances where the other party knew of the mistake or caused the mistake. Consistent with the decisions in *Kemper* and *Elsinore*, the Restatement Second of Contracts authorizes rescission for a unilateral mistake of fact where "the effect of the mistake is such that enforcement of the contract would be unconscionable." (*Rest.2d Contracts*, *§153*, subd. (a).) concluded that a contract properly may be rescinded on the ground of unilateral mistake of fact as set forth in section 153, subdivision (a), of the Restatement Second of Contracts, we next consider whether the requirements of that provision, construed in light of our previous decisions, are satisfied in the present case.

Where the plaintiff has no reason to know of and does not cause the defendant's unilateral mistake of fact, the defendant must establish the following facts to obtain rescission of the contract: (1) the defendant made a mistake regarding a basic assumption upon which the defendant made the contract; (2) the mistake has a material effect upon the agreed exchange of performances that is adverse to the defendant; (3) the defendant does not bear the risk of the mistake; and (4) the effect of the mistake is such that enforcement of the contract would be unconscionable. We shall consider each of these requirements below.

A significant error in the price term of a contract constitutes a mistake regarding a basic assumption upon which the contract is made, and such a mistake ordinarily has a material effect adverse to the mistaken party. (In establishing a material mistake regarding a basic assumption of the contract, the defendant must show that the resulting imbalance in the agreed exchange is so severe that it would be unfair to require the defendant to perform. (*Rest.2d Contracts*, *§152*, com. c, p. 388.) Ordinarily, a defendant can satisfy this requirement by showing that the exchange not only is less desirable for the defendant, but also is more advantageous to the other party. *(Ibid.)*

Measured against this standard, defendant's mistake in the contract for the sale of the Jaguar automobile constitutes a material mistake regarding a basic assumption upon which it made the contract. Enforcing the contract with the mistaken price of $25,995 would require defendant to sell the vehicle to plaintiff for $12,000 less than the intended advertised price of $37,995—an error amounting to 32 percent of the price defendant intended. The exchange of performances would be substantially less desirable for defendant and more desirable for plaintiff. Plaintiff implicitly concedes that defendant's mistake was material.

. . . The final factor defendant must establish before obtaining rescission based upon mistake is that enforcement of the contract for the sale of the 1995 Jaguar XJ6 Vanden Plas at $25,995 would be unconscionable.

Although the standards of unconscionability warranting rescission for mistake are similar to those for unconscionability justifying a court's refusal to enforce a contract or term, the general rule governing the latter situation (Civ. Code, §1670.5) is inapplicable here, because unconscionability resulting from mistake does not appear at the time the contract is made. (*Rest.2d Contracts*, *§153*, com. c, p. 395; 1 Witkin, *supra*, Contracts, §370, pp. 337–338.)

An unconscionable contract ordinarily involves both a procedural and a substantive element: (1) oppression or surprise due to unequal bargaining power, and (2) overly harsh or one-sided results. For example, the Restatement Second of Contracts states that "[i]nadequacy of consideration does not of itself invalidate a bargain, but gross disparity in the values exchanged may be an important factor in a determination that a contract is unconscionable and may be sufficient ground, without more, for denying specific performance." (*Rest.2d Contracts*, *§208*, com. c, p. 108.) In ascertaining whether rescission is warranted for a unilateral mistake of fact, substantive unconscionability often will constitute the determinative factor, because the oppression and surprise ordinarily results from the mistake—not from inequality in bargaining power. Accordingly, even though defendant is not the weaker party to the contract and its mistake did not result from unequal bargaining power, defendant was surprised by the mistake, and in these circumstances overly harsh or one-sided results are sufficient to establish unconscionability entitling defendant to rescission.

In the present case, enforcing the contract with the mistaken price of $25,995 would require defendant to sell the vehicle to plaintiff for $12,000 less than the intended advertised price of $37,995—an error amounting to 32 percent of the price defendant intended. Defendant subsequently sold the automobile for slightly more than the intended advertised price, suggesting that that price reflected its actual market value. Defendant had paid $35,000 for the 1995 Jaguar and incurred costs in advertising, preparing, displaying, and attempting to sell the vehicle. Therefore, defendant would lose more than $9,000 of its original investment in the automobile. Plaintiff, on the other hand, would obtain a $12,000 windfall if the contract were enforced, simply because he traveled to the dealership and stated that he was prepared to pay the advertised price.

These circumstances are comparable to those in our prior decisions authorizing rescission on the ground that enforcing a contract with a mistaken price term would be unconscionable. Defendant's 32 percent error in the price exceeds the amount of the errors in cases such as *Kemper* and *Elsinore*. For example, in *Elsinore, supra, 54 Cal. 2d at page 389*, we authorized rescission for a $6,500 error in a bid that was intended to be $96,494—a mistake of approximately 7 percent in the intended contract price. As in the foregoing cases, plaintiff was informed of the mistake as soon as defendant discovered it. Defendant's sales manager, when he first learned of the mistake in the advertisement, explained the error to plaintiff, apologized, and offered to pay for plaintiff's fuel, time, and effort expended in traveling to the dealership to examine the automobile. Plaintiff refused this offer to be restored to the status quo. Like the public agencies in *Kemper* and *Elsinore*, plaintiff should not be permitted to take advantage of defendant's honest mistake that resulted in an unfair, one-sided contract.

The circumstance that Section 11713.1(e) makes it unlawful for a dealer not to sell a vehicle at the advertised price does not preclude a finding that enforcing an automobile sales contract containing a mistaken price would be unconscionable. Just as the statute does not eliminate the defense of mistake, as established above, the statute also does not dictate that enforcing a contract with an erroneous advertised price necessarily must be considered equitable and fair for purposes of deciding whether the dealer is entitled to rescission on the ground of mistake. In *Kemper, supra, 37 Cal. 2d 696*, we concluded that it would be unconscionable to bar rescission of a bid pursuant to a city charter provision prohibiting the withdrawal of bids, where "it appear[ed] that it would be unjust and unfair to permit the city to take advantage of the company's mistake." *(Id. at p. 703.)* Thus, notwithstanding the public interest underlying the charter provision, our decision in *Kemper* precluded the city from relying upon that provision to impose absolute contractual liability upon the contractor. *(Id. at p. 704.)*

Accordingly, Section 11713.1(e) does not undermine our determination that, under the circumstances, enforcement of the contract for the sale of the 1995 Jaguar XJ6 Vanden Plas at the $25,995 mistaken price would be unconscionable. The other requirements for rescission on the ground of unilateral mistake have been established. Defendant entered into the contract because of its mistake regarding a basic assumption, the price. The $12,000 loss that would result from enforcement of the contract has a material effect upon the agreed exchange of performances that is adverse to defendant. Furthermore, defendant did not neglect any legal duty within the meaning of *Civil Code section 1577* or breach any duty of good faith and fair dealing in the steps leading to the formation of the contract. Plaintiff refused defendant's offer to compensate him for his actual losses in responding to the advertisement. "The law does not penalize for negligence beyond requiring compensation for the loss it has caused." (3 *Corbin, Contracts, supra, §609,* p. 684.) In this situation, it would not be reasonable for this court to allocate the risk of the mistake to defendant.

Having determined that defendant satisfied the requirements for rescission of the contract on the ground of unilateral mistake of fact, we conclude that the municipal court correctly entered judgment in defendant's favor. The judgment of the Court of Appeal is reversed.

Case Questions

1. What brand of car was at issue in the above case?
2. The placement of what word in the advertisement caused all of the confusion?
3. Did the appellate court affirm, reverse, or remand the decision from the lower court?
4. Did you feel that the decision reflected *caveat emptor* or *caveat vendor* or both?
5. In the end, who prevailed in this decision?

Exercise

You are going to organize a local walk/run for a charitable cause of your choice. Review the following participant waiver and modify it accordingly to suit your own needs. Note that while waivers may be effective for ordinary negligence, they will likely fail for conduct considered grossly negligent or reckless.

PARTICIPANT AGREEMENT FORM

Participant's Name ______________________ Date of Birth_______/_______/_______

Address ______________________________ City ________________ Zip__________

Gender M F (circle one) Age _______ Grade_______ School ______________

Home Phone ___________Work Phone ___________ Cell Phone ___________________

Activity Name ___________________ Activity Date(s)_____________

EMERGENCY PHONE # ________________________ Name of EMERGENCY contact _____________

Doctor's Name ______________________ Insurance carrier/number ______________

Special Medical conditions (allergies, etc.) ______________________________

Agreement, Waiver, & Release

In consideration for being permitted by the above district to participate in the above activity, I hereby waive, release, and discharge any and all claims for damage for personal injury, death or property damage which I may have, or which may hereafter accrue to me, as a result of participation in said activity. This release is intended to discharge in advance the above district (its officers, employees, and agents) from any and all liability arising out of or connected in any way with my participation in said activity, even though that liability may arise out of negligence or carelessness on the part of the persons or entities mentioned above. It is understood that this activity involves an element of risk and danger of accidents and knowing those risks I hereby assume those risks. It is further agreed that this waiver, release and assumption of risk is to be binding on my heirs and assigns. I agree to indemnify and to hold the above person or entities free and harmless from any loss, liability, damage, cost, or expense which they may incur as the result of my death or any injury or property damage that I may sustain while participating in said activity.

PARENTAL CONSENT: (to be completed and signed by parent/guardian if applicant is under 18 years of age.)

I hereby consent that my son/daughter, ________________, participate in the above activity, and I hereby execute the Agreement, Waiver, and Release on his/her behalf. I state that said minor is physically able to participate in-said activity. I hereby agree to indemnify and hold the persons and entities mentioned above free and harmless from any loss, liability, damage, cost, or expense that they may incur as a result of the death or any injury or property damage that said minor may sustain while participating in said activity.

I HAVE CAREFULLY READ THIS AGREEMENT, WAIVER, AND RELEASE AND FULLY UNDERSTAND ITS CONTENTS. I AM AWARE THAT THIS IS A RELEASE OF LIABILITY AND A CONTRACT BETWEEN MYSELF AND THE ABOVE DISTRICT AND I SIGN IT OF MY FREE WILL.

Print Name ______________________ Relationship ______________
(Parent/Guardian)

Signature ______________________________ Date ______________

References

Canerday, M., *Alternative Dispute Resolution: The Federal Arbitration Act and Resolving Disputes in Arbitration versus a Court Proceeding,* 81 Denv. U.L. Rev. 597 (2004).

Cherry, M., *A Tyrannosaurus-Rex Aptly Named "Sue": Using a Disputed Dinosaur to Teach Contract Defenses,* 81 N. Dak. L. Rev. 295 (2005).

Goretzke, C., *The Resurgence of Caveat Emptor: Puffery Undermines the Pro-Consumer Trend in Wisconsin's Misrepresentation Doctrine,* 2003 Wis. L. Rev. 171 (2003).

Perna, R.P., *Deceitful Employers: Common Law Fraud as a Mechanism to Remedy Intentional Employer Misrepresentation in Hiring,* 41 Willamette L. Rev. 233 (2005).

Preston, I.L., *Puffery and Other "Loophole" Claims: How the Law's "Don't Ask, Don't Tell" Policy Condones Fraudulent Falsity in Advertising,* 18 J.L. & Com. 49 (1998).

Chapter 6

The Statute of Frauds

After reading this chapter you will be able to:

1. Describe what the statute of frauds is and why it was enacted.
2. Explain why the statute of frauds is or is not important today.
3. Explain the parol evidence rule and exceptions to the rule.
4. Describe the various rules of construction when interpreting contracts.

Key Terms

Contra proferentem	Merger clause	Rules of construction
Guarantor	Parol evidence rule	Statute of frauds
Incorporate by reference	Plain meaning rule	Surety
	Prenuptial agreement	

Certain types of contracts must be in writing if a party later asks a court to enforce that agreement. This written requirement could be evidenced by an invoice, check, fax, e-mail, and so on. Just because an agreement is not in writing or evidenced by some sort of record does not mean that a court will not enforce the agreement, but the lack of a written agreement (when required) allows a court to dismiss a breach of contract case at the outset. The principle that certain contracts must be evidenced by writing is referred to as the **statute of frauds**, and that is the focus of this chapter.[1] Many contracts are oral, but putting them in writing and having the essential terms of an agreement often helps to avoid potential misunderstandings later on. It also assists in the court in the process of resolving contractual disputes if they occur.

STATUTE OF FRAUDS

Historically speaking, the statute of frauds developed from seventeenth-century English law (1677), which was known as *An Act for the Prevention of Frauds and Perjuries*.[2] This principle required that certain kinds of transactions be evidenced by something in writing. The writing also required a signature by the parties (or their agents) in order to deter fraudulent transactions and to provide courts with physical evidence that a transaction occurred. Interestingly, England abolished the statute of frauds in 1954 though it remains visible in the United States.[3] The statute of frauds in the United States is a creature of state rather than federal law.

---

[1]Law students often remember the circumstances requiring a written agreement under the statute of frauds by the mnemonic MYLEGS (marriage, year, land, executor, goods, surety).

[2]*See* G.N. Stepeniak, *The Statute of Frauds as a Bar to an Action in Tort for Fraud*, 53 Fordham L. Rev. 1231 (1985).

[3]E.A. Farnsworth, Farnsworth on Contracts §6.1, at 95 (2d ed. 1998).

Under state law, contracts that require a written agreement in order to be enforceable by a court include:

1. Contracts for the sale of real estate and other interests in land.
2. Contracts that *cannot* by the terms of the agreement be performed within one year.
3. Contracts in which one party acts as **guarantor** or **surety** for another party's debts (aka a "collateral promise").
4. Under the Uniform Commercial Code (UCC), contracts for the sale of goods which cost more than $500.[4]
5. Contracts to be paid by the executor of a will (or estate).
6. Contracts in consideration marriage (e.g., **prenuptial agreements**, various wedding preparation contracts and the like).[5]

EXCEPTIONS

As in many areas of contract law, there are some exceptions to the writing requirement of the statute of frauds. The following list represents exceptions in which there might not be a written agreement, but there could still be evidence that a contract actually existed:

1. Full performance by the seller.
2. Part performance by the buyer.
3. Admission of the existence of a contract by the parties.
4. Promissory estoppel (detrimental reliance).
5. Existence of specialized (customized) or specially manufactured goods.
6. For sureties and guaranties (collateral promises), if it is for their personal benefit.

The above list might allow a court to apply equitable principles such as *quasi-contract* and *quantum meruit* to resolve a contractual dispute in which neither party can actually provide proof of a written agreement.

PAROL EVIDENCE RULE (4-CORNERS RULE)

The **parol evidence rule** is a rule of evidence which holds that when a written agreement represents the final agreement between the parties, courts do not want to hear oral explanations of "he said, she said" which actually *contradict* the terms of the written agreement. To address the courts' reluctance to view statements that

---

[4]The UCC provision is for $500 though the Amended Uniform Commercial Code (AUCC) is for $5,000. As of the time of this writing, no state has yet adopted the AUCC. *See* Bazak Int'l Corp. v. Mast. Indust., 535 N.E.2d 633 (N.Y. 1989) (holding an e-mail sent by one merchant to another purporting to confirm an agreement to purchase goods is sufficient to satisfy the requirements for a writing contained in the statute of frauds).

[5]A prenuptial agreement (aka "prenup") is also known as an antenuptial agreement or even premarital contract. *See* http://www.foxnews.com/story/0,2933,252778,00.html.

contradict the final written agreement, good lawyers and other contract drafters put a **merger clause** in a contract (usually found at the end) to preemptively address this scenario. Though there is a presumption by courts that when a written contract exists it represents the complete and final understanding between the parties a merger clause reinforces this principle. The parole evidence rule does not apply as to whether a right in the contract applies or if the contract exists at all.[6] Still, the following exceptions to the parol evidence rule allow a litigant to bring in evidence that might otherwise be excluded by a court:

1. Evidence of a subsequent modification of the agreement between the parties.
2. Evidence to show fraud, duress, mistake, or illegality.
3. Ambiguous terms may be explained (but not contradicted) by a party.
4. Open terms may be explained to assist the court in filling in the gaps.
5. Evidence of prior course of dealing between the parties.
6. Evidence to explain obvious clerical errors.
7. Evidence to explain orally agreed-upon conditions.

RULES OF CONSTRUCTION

Generally speaking, a role of a court is to uphold contracts, not to undo them. Courts look to the **plain meaning** of the words to an agreement unless there is an ambiguity or if the contract actually contradicts itself. Courts do not want to rewrite contracts, but in some cases the courts have no choice but to try to interpret what was really meant by a word. Though addressed in greater detail at the end of this text in Chapter 16, it may be worth exploring at this point how the following **rules of construction** (i.e., how a court interprets inconsistencies or issues related to words or phrases on the contract itself) apply when having to interpret the words found in a written contract:

1. Words are to be interpreted in their ordinary meaning.
2. Missing terms or words may be incorporated into the contract "by reference." This means that the contract might refer to another document which interprets the proper meaning of the word or even **incorporate by reference** a rather large document itself for efficiency.
3. Courts are to view the intent of the parties as a whole, especially when subportions of the agreement might be contradictory.
4. Where there are contradictory terms, courts must apply the parol evidence rule.
5. Handwritten portions trump typewritten portions which trump preprinted forms.
6. Words always prevail over numbers.
7. Good faith is always implied in any contract.
8. Prior dealings between the parties can be considered.
9. Trade customs (the way others deal in the same or similar industry) may always be considered.

---

[6] *See* Restatement (Second) of Contracts §213.

10. Ambiguities that cannot be resolved by the court may always be construed against the offeror. This is often referred to as construction ***contra proferentem***.[7]

Whether due to good (or poor) contract drafting, courts sometimes have to interpret what the parties intended. Certainly having a written agreement is crucial in this respect, and good contract drafters recognize the importance of the parol evidence rule and the use of a merger clause in contracts as well.

CHAPTER SUMMARY

The principle behind the statute of frauds is that it is a way to ensure stability and certainty in contractual relationships. It requires that certain types of agreements be in writing in order to prevent disagreement or in some cases outright lies in the courtroom over what was actually agreed upon. The statute of frauds has numerous exceptions to it, but at the end of the day the goal of this legal principle is consistent with contract law generally: to provide consistency, stability, and predictability in contractual relationships. In the end, it appears that the statute of frauds is losing ground in the area of contract law. Advances in technology and numerous exceptions to the rule may have something to do with this, and England has largely abolished it altogether.[8]

Discussion and Review Questions

1. What is the statute of frauds and why is it important in contract law?
2. What types of contracts must be in writing (or evidenced by a writing) in order to be enforced?
3. What is the parol evidence rule?
4. Why have courts adopted rules of construction for interpreting a contract?

Critical Thinking Exercises

1. Why do you think that the statute of frauds was abolished for the most part in England, and why do you think that some lawyers, judges, and legal scholars believe that it should be abolished (or tweaked) in the United States as well?
2. Tiffany is a paralegal in a local law firm. She has spent much of the last several weeks preparing a huge real estate document (50 pages) for the lawyers. This document is to be filed at the county register of deeds office and contains all the surveys, rules, and restrictions of a local condominium community that is just being built. Her firm was hired to prepare the real estate documentation filings. Once this document is filed at the register of deeds office (some counties just call it the register's office), what clause might be useful to include in the sales agreement that Tiffany also assists in preparing for the builder to present to buyers of the condominiums so as to avoid a 50-page document having to

[7]The concept of *contra proferentem* encourages those who draft contracts to avoid ambiguities and to be as explicit as possible. It also reflects the general proposition that those in the best position to avoid contractual harm are those who draft the agreements or make offers. *See* Cal. Civ. Code §1654 which codifies this principle as well.

[8]*See* Schara v. Commercial Envelope Mfg. Co., 321 F.3d 240 (1st Cir. 2003).

be delivered at the real estate closing each time a deal is done?

3. Joy, a senior in college and 22 years old, goes with her father to buy a used car at the local dealership. Having grown up in a small town, Joy, her father, and the salesman all know each other and attend the same church. Joy will have to finance about $1,500 of the deal herself. She signs all the documents, but James (the salesman) asks Joy's father to act as a cosigner in the event that Joy cannot pay her loan off. Insulted, the father refuses to sign but insists that he will pay whatever is owed immediately to James if Joy misses even one payment. Local lenders refuse to finance the deal since the father will not sign, so the dealership finances the car itself (without the father's signature) with Joy to close the deal. Do you think that the local dealership could pursue litigation against Joy's father for payment if Joy defaults on her loan to the car dealership? Under what legal theory?

Online Research Exercises

1. Explore your state law and the statutory codification of its statute of frauds.
2. You have a dispute with your professor over your exam grade. You consult your syllabus and it does not state that the professor has the right to deduct points for improper grammar. However, the professor claims that she announced that in class. You were deducted points for an error, but your classmate was not. This was an oversight by the professor who had 100 exams to grade during finals. Could you allege fraud or breach of contract? Is a syllabus actually a contract representing the complete and final agreement between students are professors? *See* http://www.cte.uiuc.edu/Did/Resources/Illini%20Instructor/syllabus.htm and http://www.csun.edu/~newfac/Syllabus.html
3. See if you can find an example of a "merger clause" on the Internet.

CASE APPLICATIONS

Case 1

The following case provides a contemporary example which brings together many of the contract law concepts discussed so far in the text, including issues related to the Statute of Frauds. Notice the various tort (personal injury) claims as well.

LEONARD v. PEPSICO, INC.

88 F.SUPP.2D 116 (S.D.N.Y. 1999)

WOOD, U.S.D.J.

Plaintiff brought this action seeking, among other things, specific performance of an alleged offer of a Harrier Jet, featured in a television advertisement for defendant's "Pepsi Stuff" promotion.

I. BACKGROUND

This case arises out of a promotional campaign conducted by defendant, the producer and distributor of the soft drinks Pepsi and Diet Pepsi. The promotion, entitled "Pepsi Stuff," encouraged consumers to collect "Pepsi Points" from specially marked packages of Pepsi or Diet Pepsi and redeem these points for merchandise featuring the Pepsi logo. Before introducing the promotion nationally, defendant conducted a test of the promotion in the Pacific Northwest from October 1995 to March 1996. A Pepsi Stuff catalog was distributed to consumers in the test market, including Washington State. Plaintiff is a resident of Seattle, Washington. While living in Seattle, plaintiff saw the Pepsi Stuff commercial that he contends constituted an offer of a Harrier Jet.

A. The Alleged Offer

Because whether the television commercial constituted an offer is the central question in this case, the Court will describe the commercial in detail. The commercial opens upon an idyllic, suburban morning, where the chirping of birds in sun-dappled trees welcomes a paperboy on his morning route. As the newspaper hits the stoop of a conventional two-story house, the tattoo of a military drum introduces the subtitle, "MONDAY 7:58 AM." The stirring strains of a martial air mark the appearance of a well-coiffed teenager preparing to leave for school, dressed in a shirt emblazoned with the Pepsi logo, a red-white-and-blue ball. While the teenager confidently preens, the military drumroll again sounds as the subtitle "T-SHIRT 75 PEPSI POINTS" scrolls across the screen. Bursting from his room, the teenager strides down the hallway wearing a leather jacket. The drumroll sounds again, as the subtitle "LEATHER JACKET 1450 PEPSI POINTS" appears. The teenager opens the door of his house and, unfazed by the glare of the early morning sunshine, puts on a pair of sunglasses. The drumroll then accompanies the subtitle "SHADES 175 PEPSI POINTS." A voiceover then intones, "Introducing the new Pepsi Stuff catalog," as the camera focuses on the cover of the catalog.

The scene then shifts to three young boys sitting in front of a high school building. The boy in the middle is intent on his Pepsi Stuff Catalog, while the boys on either side are each drinking Pepsi. The three boys gaze in awe at an object rushing overhead, as the military march builds to a crescendo. The Harrier Jet is not yet visible, but the observer senses the presence of a mighty plane as the extreme winds generated by its flight create a paper maelstrom in a classroom devoted to an otherwise dull physics lesson. Finally, the Harrier Jet swings into view and lands by the side of the school building, next to a bicycle rack. Several students run for cover, and the velocity of the wind strips one hapless faculty member down to his underwear. While the faculty member is being deprived of his dignity, the voiceover announces: "Now the more Pepsi you drink, the more great stuff you're gonna get."

The teenager opens the cockpit of the fighter and can be seen, helmetless, holding a Pepsi. "Looking very pleased with himself" (Pl. Mem. at 3), the teenager exclaims, "Sure beats the bus," and chortles. The military drumroll sounds a final time, as the following words appear: "HARRIER FIGHTER 7,000,000 PEPSI POINTS." A few seconds later, the following appears in more stylized script: "Drink Pepsi—Get Stuff." With that message, the music and the commercial end with a triumphant flourish.

Inspired by this commercial, plaintiff set out to obtain a Harrier Jet. Plaintiff explains that he is "typical of the 'Pepsi Generation' . . . he is young, has an adventurous spirit, and the notion of obtaining a Harrier Jet appealed to him enormously." (Pl. Mem. at 3.) Plaintiff consulted the Pepsi Stuff Catalog. The Catalog features youths dressed in Pepsi Stuff regalia or enjoying Pepsi Stuff accessories, such as "Blue Shades" ("As if you need another reason to look forward to sunny days."), "Pepsi Tees" ("Live in 'em. Laugh in 'em. Get in 'em."), "Bag of Balls" ("Three balls. One bag. No rules."), and "Pepsi Phone Card" ("Call your mom!"). The Catalog specifies the number of Pepsi Points required to obtain promotional merchandise. (See Catalog, at rear foldout pages.) The Catalog includes an Order Form which lists, on one side, fifty-three items of Pepsi Stuff merchandise redeemable for Pepsi Points (see id. [the "Order Form"]). Conspicuously absent from the Order Form is any entry or description of a Harrier Jet. (See id.) The amount of Pepsi Points required to obtain the listed merchandise ranges from 15 (for a "Jacket Tattoo" ["Sew 'em on your jacket, not your arm."]) to 3300 (for a "Fila Mountain Bike" ["Rugged. All-terrain. Exclusively for Pepsi."]). It should be noted that plaintiff objects to the implication that because an item was not shown in the Catalog, it was unavailable. The rear foldout pages of the Catalog contain directions for redeeming Pepsi Points for merchandise. (See Catalog, at rear foldout pages.) These directions note that merchandise may be ordered "only" with the original Order Form. The Catalog notes that in the event that a consumer lacks enough Pepsi Points to obtain a desired item, additional Pepsi Points may be purchased for ten cents each; however, at least fifteen original Pepsi Points must accompany each order.

Although plaintiff initially set out to collect 7,000,000 Pepsi Points by consuming Pepsi products, it soon became clear to him that he "would not be able to buy (let alone drink) enough Pepsi to collect the necessary Pepsi Points fast enough." Reevaluating his strategy, plaintiff "focused for the first time on the packaging materials in the Pepsi Stuff promotion," and realized that buying Pepsi Points would be a more promising option. Through acquaintances, plaintiff ultimately raised about $700,000.

B. Plaintiff's Efforts to Redeem the Alleged Offer

On or about March 27, 1996, plaintiff submitted an Order Form, fifteen original Pepsi Points, and a check for $700,008.50. Plaintiff appears to have been represented by counsel at the time he mailed his check; the check is drawn on an account of plaintiff's first set of attorneys. At the bottom of the Order Form, plaintiff wrote in "1 Harrier Jet" in the "Item" column and "7,000,000" in the "Total Points" column. In a letter accompanying his submission, plaintiff stated that the check was to purchase additional Pepsi Points "expressly for obtaining a new Harrier jet as advertised in your Pepsi Stuff commercial." On or about May 7, 1996, defendant's fulfillment house rejected plaintiff's submission and returned the check, explaining that:

> The item that you have requested is not part of the Pepsi Stuff collection. It is not included in the catalogue or on the order form, and only catalogue merchandise can be redeemed under this program.
>
> The Harrier jet in the Pepsi commercial is fanciful and is simply included to create a humorous and entertaining ad. We apologize for any misunderstanding or confusion that you may have experienced and are enclosing some free product coupons for your use.

Plaintiff's previous counsel responded on or about May 14, 1996, as follows:

> Your letter of May 7, 1996 is totally unacceptable. We have reviewed the video tape of the Pepsi Stuff commercial . . . and it clearly offers the new Harrier jet for 7,000,000 Pepsi Points. Our client followed your rules explicitly. . . .
>
> This is a formal demand that you honor your commitment and make immediate arrangements to transfer the new Harrier jet to our client. If we do not receive transfer instructions within ten (10) business days of the date of this letter you will leave us no choice but to file an appropriate action against Pepsi. . . .

(This letter was apparently sent onward to the advertising company responsible for the actual commercial, BBDO New York ("BBDO"). In a letter dated May 30, 1996, BBDO Vice President Raymond E. McGovern, Jr., explained to plaintiff that:

> I find it hard to believe that you are of the opinion that the Pepsi Stuff commercial ("Commercial") really offers a new Harrier Jet. The use of the Jet was clearly a joke that was meant to make the Commercial more humorous and entertaining. In my opinion, no reasonable person would agree with your analysis of the Commercial.

On or about June 17, 1996, plaintiff mailed a similar demand letter to defendant.

Defendant's Advertisement Was Not an Offer

1. Advertisements as Offers

The general rule is that an advertisement does not constitute an offer. The Restatement (Second) of Contracts explains that:

> Advertisements of goods by display, sign, handbill, newspaper, radio or television are not ordinarily intended or understood as offers to sell. The same is true of catalogues, price lists and circulars, even though the terms of suggested bargains may be stated in some detail. It is of course possible to make an offer by an advertisement directed to the general public (see §29), but there must ordinarily be some language of commitment or some invitation to take action without further communication.

Restatement (Second) of Contracts §26 cmt. b (1979). Similarly, a leading treatise notes that:

The exception to the rule that advertisements do not create any power of acceptance in potential offerees is where the advertisement is "clear, definite, and explicit, and leaves nothing open for negotiation," in that circumstance, "it constitutes an offer, acceptance of which will complete the contract." *Lefkowitz v. Great Minneapolis Surplus Store, 251 Minn. 188, 86 N.W.2d 689, 691 (Minn. 1957).* In Lefkowitz, defendant had published a newspaper announcement stating: "Saturday 9 AM Sharp, 3 Brand New Fur Coats, Worth to $100.00, First Come First Served $1 Each." *86 N.W.2d at 690.* Mr. Morris Lefkowitz arrived at the store, dollar in hand, but was informed that under defendant's "house rules," the offer was open to ladies, but not gentlemen. See id. The court ruled that because plaintiff had fulfilled all of the terms of the advertisement and the advertisement was specific and left nothing open for negotiation, a contract had been formed. See id.; see also *Johnson v. Capital City Ford Co., 85 So. 2d 75, 79 (La. Ct. App. 1955)* (finding that newspaper advertisement was sufficiently certain and definite to constitute an offer).

The present case is distinguishable from Lefkowitz. First, the commercial cannot be regarded in itself as sufficiently definite, because it specifically reserved the details of the offer to a separate writing, the Catalog. The commercial itself made no mention of the steps a potential offeree would be required to take to accept the alleged offer of a Harrier Jet. The advertisement in Lefkowitz, in contrast, "identified the person who could accept." Corbin, supra, §2.4, at 119. See generally *United States v. Braunstein, 75 F. Supp. 137, 139 (S.D.N.Y. 1947)* ("Greater precision of expression may be required, and less help from the court given, when the parties are merely at the threshold of a contract."); Farnsworth, supra, at 239 ("The fact that a proposal is very detailed suggests that it is an offer, while omission of many terms suggests that it is not."). Second, even if the Catalog had included a Harrier Jet among the items that could be obtained by redemption of Pepsi Points, the advertisement of a Harrier Jet by both television commercial and catalog would still not constitute an offer. As the Mesaros court explained, the absence of any words of limitation such as "first come, first served," renders the alleged offer sufficiently indefinite that no contract could be formed. See *Mesaros, 845 F.2d at 1581.* "A customer would not usually have reason to believe that the shopkeeper intended exposure to the risk of a multitude of acceptances resulting in a number of contracts exceeding the shopkeeper's inventory." Farnsworth, supra, at 242. There was no such danger in Lefkowitz, owing to the limitation "first come, first served."

The Court finds, in sum, that the Harrier Jet commercial was merely an advertisement. The Court now turns to the line of cases upon which plaintiff rests much of his argument.

2. Rewards as Offers

In opposing the present motion, plaintiff largely relies on a different species of unilateral offer, involving public offers of a reward for performance of a specified act. Because these cases generally involve public declarations regarding the efficacy or trustworthiness of specific products, one court has aptly characterized these authorities as "prove me wrong" caseshe most venerable of these precedents is the case of *Carlill v. Carbolic Smoke Ball Co., 1 Q.B. 256* (Court of Appeal, 1892), a quote from which heads plaintiff's memorandum of law: "If a person chooses to make extravagant promises . . . he probably does so because it pays him to make them, and, if he has made them, the extravagance of the promises is no reason in law why he should not be bound by them." *Carbolic Smoke Ball, 1 Q.B. at 268* (Bowen, L.J.).

Other "reward" cases underscore the distinction between typical advertisements, in which the alleged offer is merely an invitation to negotiate for purchase of commercial goods, and promises of reward, in which the alleged offer is intended to induce a potential offeree to perform a specific action, often for noncommercial reasons. In *Newman v. Schiff, 778 F.2d 460 (5th Cir. 1985),* for example, the Fifth Circuit held that a tax protestor's assertion that, "If anybody calls this show . . . and cites any section of the code that says an individual is required to file a tax return, I'll pay them $100,000," would have been an enforceable offer had the plaintiff called the television show to claim the reward while the tax protestor was appearing. See *id. at 466–67.* The court noted that, like Carbolic Smoke Ball, the case "concerns a special type of offer: an offer for a reward." *Id. at 465. James v. Turilli, 473 S.W.2d 757 (Mo. Ct. App. 1971),* arose from a boast by defendant that the "notorious Missouri desperado" Jesse James had not been killed in 1882, as portrayed in song and legend, but had lived under the alias "J. Frank Dalton" at the "Jesse James Museum" operated by none other than defendant. Defendant offered $10,000 "to anyone who could prove me wrong." See *id. at 758–59.* The widow of the outlaw's son demonstrated, at trial, that the outlaw had in fact been killed in 1882. On appeal, the court held that defendant should be liable to pay the amount offered. See *id. at 762;* see also *Mears v. Nationwide Mutual Ins. Co., 91 F.3d 1118, 1122-23 (8th Cir. 1996)* (plaintiff entitled to cost of two Mercedes as reward for coining slogan for insurance company).

In the present case, the Harrier Jet commercial did not direct that anyone who appeared at Pepsi headquarters with 7,000,000 Pepsi Points on the Fourth of July would receive a Harrier Jet. Instead, the commercial urged consumers to accumulate Pepsi Points and to refer to the Catalog to determine how they could redeem their Pepsi Points. The commercial sought a reciprocal promise, expressed through acceptance of, and compliance with, the terms of the Order Form. As noted previously, the Catalog contains no mention of the Harrier Jet.

C. An Objective, Reasonable Person Would Not Have Considered the Commercial an Offer

Plaintiff's understanding of the commercial as an offer must also be rejected because the Court finds that no objective person could reasonably have concluded that the commercial actually offered consumers a Harrier Jet.

1. Objective Reasonable Person Standard

In evaluating the commercial, the Court must not consider defendant's subjective intent in making the commercial, or plaintiff's subjective view of what the commercial offered, but what an objective, reasonable person would have understood the commercial to convey. See *Kay-R Elec. Corp. v. Stone & Weber Constr. Co., 23 F.3d 55, 57 (2d Cir. 1994)* ("We are not concerned with what was going through the heads of the parties at the time [of the alleged contract]. Rather, we are talking about the objective principles of contract law."); *Mesaros, 845 F.2d at 1581* ("A basic rule of contracts holds that whether an offer has been made depends on the objective reasonableness of the alleged offeree's belief that the advertisement or solicitation was intended as an offer."). On the other hand, if there is no indication that the offer is "evidently in jest," and that an objective, reasonable person would find that the offer was serious, then there may be a valid offer. See *Barnes, 549 P.2d at 1155* ("If the jest is not apparent and a reasonable hearer would believe that an offer was being made, then the speaker risks the formation of a contract which was not intended."); see also *Lucy v. Zehmer, 196 Va. 493, 84 S.E.2d 516, 518, 520 (Va. 1954)* (ordering specific performance of a contract to purchase a farm despite defendant's protestation that the transaction was done in jest as "'just a bunch of two doggoned drunks bluffing'"). . . .

3. Whether the Commercial Was "Evidently Done In Jest"

Plaintiff's insistence that the commercial appears to be a serious offer requires the Court to explain why the commercial is funny. Explaining why a joke is funny is a daunting task; as the essayist E.B. White has remarked,

"Humor can be dissected, as a frog can, but the thing dies in the process. . . ." The commercial is the embodiment of what defendant appropriately characterizes as "zany humor."

First, the commercial suggests, as commercials often do, that use of the advertised product will transform what, for most youth, can be a fairly routine and ordinary experience. The military tattoo and stirring martial music, as well as the use of subtitles in a Courier font that scroll terse messages across the screen, such as "MONDAY 7:58 AM," evoke military and espionage thrillers. The implication of the commercial is that Pepsi Stuff merchandise will inject drama and moment into hitherto unexceptional lives. The commercial in this case thus makes the exaggerated claims similar to those of many television advertisements: that by consuming the featured clothing, car, beer, or potato chips, one will become attractive, stylish, desirable, and admired by all. A reasonable viewer would understand such advertisements as mere puffery, not as statements of fact, see, e.g., *Hubbard v. General Motors Corp., 1996 U.S. Dist. LEXIS 6974, 95 Civ. 4362 (AGS), 1996 WL 274018,* at *6 (S.D.N.Y. May 22, 1996) (advertisement describing automobile as "Like a Rock," was mere puffery, not a warranty of quality); *Lovett, 207 N.Y.S. at 756;* and refrain from interpreting the promises of the commercial as being literally true.

Second, the callow youth featured in the commercial is a highly improbable pilot, one who could barely be trusted with the keys to his parents' car, much less the prize aircraft of the United States Marine Corps. Rather than checking the fuel gauges on his aircraft, the teenager spends his precious preflight minutes preening. The youth's concern for his coiffure appears to extend to his flying without a helmet. Finally, the teenager's comment that flying a Harrier Jet to school "sure beats the bus" evinces an improbably insouciant attitude toward the relative difficulty and danger of piloting a fighter plane in a residential area, as opposed to taking public transportation.

Third, the notion of traveling to school in a Harrier Jet is an exaggerated adolescent fantasy. In this commercial, the fantasy is underscored by how the teenager's schoolmates gape in admiration, ignoring their physics lesson. The force of the wind generated by the Harrier Jet blows off one teacher's clothes, literally defrocking an authority figure. As if to emphasize the fantastic quality of having a Harrier Jet arrive at school, the Jet lands next to a plebeian bike rack. This fantasy is, of course, extremely unrealistic. No school would provide landing space for a student's fighter jet, or condone the disruption the jet's use would cause.

Fourth, the primary mission of a Harrier Jet, according to the United States Marine Corps, is to "attack and destroy surface targets under day and night visual conditions." United States Marine Corps, Factfile: AV-8B Harrier II (last modified Dec. 5, 1995) <http://www.hqmc.usmc.mil/factfile.nsf>. Manufactured by McDonnell Douglas, the Harrier Jet played a significant role in the air offensive of Operation Desert Storm in 1991. See id. The jet is designed to carry a considerable armament load, including Sidewinder and Maverick missiles. See id. As one news report has noted, "Fully loaded, the Harrier can float like a butterfly and sting like a bee—albeit a roaring 14-ton butterfly and a bee with 9,200 pounds of bombs and missiles." Jerry Allegood, Marines Rely on Harrier Jet, Despite Critics, News & Observer (Raleigh), Nov. 4, 1990, at C1. In light of the Harrier Jet's well-documented function in attacking and destroying surface and air targets, armed reconnaissance and air interdiction, and offensive and defensive antiaircraft warfare, depiction of such a jet as a way to get to school in the morning is clearly not serious even if, as plaintiff contends, the jet is capable of being acquired "in a form that eliminates [its] potential for military use." (See Leonard Aff. P 20.)

Fifth, the number of Pepsi Points the commercial mentions as required to "purchase" the jet is 7,000,000. To amass that number of points, one would have to drink 7,000,000 Pepsis (or roughly 190 Pepsis a day for the next hundred years—an unlikely possibility), or one would have to purchase approximately $700,000 worth of Pepsi Points. The cost of a Harrier Jet is roughly $23 million dollars, a fact of which plaintiff was aware when he set out to gather the amount he believed necessary to accept the alleged offer. Even if an objective, reasonable person were not aware of this fact, he would conclude that purchasing a fighter plane for $700,000 is a deal too good to be true.

D. The Alleged Contract Does Not Satisfy the Statute of Frauds

The absence of any writing setting forth the alleged contract in this case provides an entirely separate reason for granting summary judgment. Under the New York Statute of Frauds,

> a contract for the sale of goods for the price of $500 or more is not enforceable by way of action or defense unless there is some writing sufficient to indicate that a contract for sale has been made between the parties and signed by the party against whom enforcement is sought or by his authorized agent or broker. N.Y.U.C.C. §2-201(1).

Without such a writing, plaintiff's claim must fail as a matter of law. See *Hilord Chem. Corp. v. Ricoh Elecs., Inc., 875 F.2d 32, 36-37 (2d Cir. 1989)* ("The adequacy of a writing for Statute of Frauds purposes `must be determined from the documents themselves, as a matter of law."')

There is simply no writing between the parties that evidences any transaction. The commercial is not a writing; plaintiff's completed order form does not bear the signature of defendant, or an agent thereof; and to the extent that plaintiff seeks discovery of any contracts between defendant and its advertisers, such discovery would be unavailing: plaintiff is not a party to, or a beneficiary of, any such contracts. Because the alleged contract does not meet the requirements of the Statute of Frauds, plaintiff has no claim for breach of contract or specific performance.

E. Plaintiff's Fraud Claim

To properly state a claim for fraud, "plaintiff must allege a misrepresentation or material omission by defendant, on which it relied, that induced plaintiff" to perform an act. "General allegations that defendant entered into a contract while lacking the intent to perform it are insufficient to support the claim." Instead, the plaintiff must show the misrepresentation was collateral, or served as an inducement, to a separate agreement between the parties. Plaintiff in this case does not allege that he was induced to enter into a contract by some collateral misrepresentation, but rather that defendant never had any intention of making good on its "offer" of a Harrier Jet. (See Pl. Mem. at 23.) Because this claim "alleges only that the defendant entered into a contract with no intention of performing it," *Grappo, 56 F.3d at 434,* judgment on this claim should enter for defendant.

III. CONCLUSION

In sum, there are three reasons why plaintiff's demand cannot prevail as a matter of law. First, the commercial was merely an advertisement, not a unilateral offer. Second, the tongue-in-cheek attitude of the commercial would not cause a reasonable person to conclude that a soft drink company would be giving away fighter planes as part of a promotion. Third, there is no writing between the parties sufficient to satisfy the Statute of Frauds.

Case Questions

1. Where did Pepsi test market the commercial in question before taking the campaign at a national level?
2. How many Pepsi Points were required to be collected to be able to (allegedly) claim a Harrier Jet?
3. In New York state, what elements must a plaintiff claim to successfully succeed in a claim for fraud?
4. In the end, did the court believe that the commercial constituted an offer to the viewer-plaintiff?

Case 2

The following Indiana case involves a dispute over the legitimacy of a faxed memo and whether (or not) it constituted the final agreement between the parties or was simply part of the negotiation process to ultimately reach an agreement.

COCA-COLA CO. v. BABYBACK'S INT'L, INC.

841 N.E.2D 557 (IND. 2006)

DICKSON, J.

This opinion centers on the enforceability of an alleged business agreement reflected in a memo prepared and faxed by one party to another. The trial court's certification order described the "fundamental issue" as: whether a legally sufficient written contract was signed for the alleged national co-marketing agreement to satisfy the requirements of Indiana's Statute of Frauds. . . . If an adequate writing is determined to not exist, a question of law remains whether the equitable doctrines of part performance or promissory estoppel can support plaintiff's claims for lost future profits. If an adequate writing is determined to exist, these alternative positions of plaintiff need not be litigated.

This business controversy arises from a complaint by Babyback's International, Inc., presenting various claims for relief. The underlying facts are not in dispute. Early in 1997, Babyback's, a processor and seller of barbeque meat products, entered into an agreement with Hondo, Incorporated, d/b/a Coca-Cola Bottling Company Indianapolis, a/k/a Coca-Cola Bottling Company of Indianapolis, Inc. ("Coke Indy"), a bottler of Coca-Cola products with its main office in Chicago, and its market area including Indianapolis [CCE]. Under this agreement, Coke Indy was to pay Babyback's to arrange for and prominently place coolers in grocery stores in and around Indianapolis, displaying Babyback's products side-by-side in the coolers with Coca-Cola products. After Babyback's and Coke Indy experienced success with this "meals to go" concept in Indianapolis, CCE and Babyback's began discussions about similarly co-marketing their products in the Louisville market, which was outside the Coke Indy territory but within that of CCE. Babyback's thereafter arranged to have coolers delivered to several Louisville area grocery stores. At this time, Babyback's and CCE did not have a written contract regarding this arrangement. Babyback's and CCE representatives met on October 24, 1997, to discuss further expanding the arrangement into other CCE market areas. Following this meeting, Babyback's faxed to CCE a proposed contract. This contract, however, was never signed. On November 18, 1997, Babyback's and CCE representatives met again, this time at CCE's Atlanta headquarters, to discuss expanding their co-marketing arrangement to stores on a nationwide basis. Following the November 1997 Atlanta meeting, a representative of CCE drafted and faxed to Babyback's a memo, which Babyback's contends summarizes the parties' oral agreement to co-market their food and drink products in mutual coolers in stores in Atlanta and across the nation. Babyback's claim asserts that CCE breached the agreement when it refused to perform under the purported terms, refused to pay allegedly agreed-upon up-front fees, and denied the existence of a contractual relationship between the parties.

CCE contends on appeal that its motion for partial summary judgment should have been granted because the multiple-year agreement alleged by Babyback's is unenforceable under the Statute of Frauds because it could not be performed within a year and no written contract was ever signed by the parties. CCE argues that the faxed memo following the November 1997 meeting is insufficient to satisfy the statute because it fails to contain the essential terms of a contract, and further, because it shows that no agreement was reached. Finally, CCE asserts that there is no evidence supporting an adequate substitute for a writing in the form of part performance or based upon a theory of estoppel.

Babyback's responds that the trial court properly denied CCE's motion for partial summary judgment because of the existence of genuine issues of determinative fact regarding whether the faxed memo was sufficiently comprehensive and evinced the parties' intention to contract. Alternatively, Babyback's asserts that the Statute of Frauds should not apply to bar enforcement of the parties' agreement because of (a) Babyback's part performance, (b) promissory estoppel, (c) constructive fraud, and (d) an oral agreement to memorialize in writing within one year. Because the trial court's certification of this interlocutory appeal did not include the latter two alternative arguments, its denial of summary judgment thereon is not considered in this appeal.

STATUTE OF FRAUDS WRITING REQUIREMENT

This case centers on the application and requirements of the Indiana Statute of Frauds, which provides in relevant part:

> A person may not bring any of the following actions unless the promise, contract, or agreement on which the action is based, or a memorandum or note describing the promise, contract, or agreement on which the action is based, is in writing and signed by the party against whom the action is brought or by the party's authorized agent:
>
> * * *
>
> (5) An action involving any agreement that is not to be performed within one (1) year from the making of the agreement.

Ind. Code §32-21-1-1(b). It is undisputed that the alleged agreement is one that could not be performed within one year. And CCE's invocation of the Statute of Frauds does not claim a lack of signature. Rather, CCE claims that the faxed memo fails to contain the essential terms of the contract sufficient to satisfy the statute's requirement of a writing and that the memo demonstrates that "no agreement had in fact been reached." Brief of Appellant CCE at 12. To satisfy the Statute of Frauds, either the agreement sought to be enforced must be in writing, or there must be "a memorandum or note describing the promise, contract, or agreement." *Ind. Code §32-21-1-1(b)*. Whether the undisputed language of a document constitutes a contract is a question of law.

CCE asserts that the faxed memo of the alleged agreement with Babyback's was insufficient to satisfy the Statute of Frauds because as a matter of law it did not contain the essential terms of the agreement, specifically claiming no indication of a meeting of the minds regarding the commencement date and duration of the program; whether and how much "up-front money" Babyback's was to receive; the identity and location of stores to be involved; and the allocation of responsibilities for advertising, promotion, and delivery and installation of the coolers. CCE also emphasizes several passages in the memo indicating that CCE did not intend to agree upon a contract with Babyback's and that the memo only reflected preliminary discussions. Thus, the statute, according to CCE, precludes enforcement of any alleged agreement between the parties in Louisville, where there was clearly no written agreement, as well as in Atlanta, where the only purported writing is the faxed message.

Claiming that the memo was sufficient under the statute, Babyback's refers to content in the memo and its attachments that discuss when the program was to begin, that CCE agreed to pay Babyback's "up front and on an annual basis," that the duration was to be "multi-year," that CCE was to purchase coolers and provide advertising and promotion, and that the parties understood that store identification would occur later.. And Babyback's disputes CCE's claim that the memo demonstrates no contract was formed by pointing to various words and phrases in the memo such as "we do agree," "alliance," and "agreed in principle."

We note that, notwithstanding the memorialization of numerous details, the memo also specifies various other preliminary details remaining to be resolved. More importantly, the specific language and overall tenor of the memo unequivocally establish that no final agreement had been reached between CCE and Babyback's.

The fax CCE sent to the plaintiff following the November 18, 1997, meeting was prepared by Dan Marr of CCE and addressed to Phillipe Rouas, the President of Babyback's International. The first page of the fax contained a memo, which stated:

> We enjoyed our meeting yesterday with you and believe *we have made further strides toward coming to agreement* on a 'quiet' partnership with your company. *Your objectives however to have absolute agreement by Friday may be difficult to achieve.* Nonetheless, *we will move as quickly as possible given the complexities which must be worked through.* As we have stated several times, we do agree that the complimentary merchandising of Babyback's with the # 1 brand in the world, Coca-Cola, does make sense.
>
> Attached is a recap on the discussion yesterday and also a copy of the directive sent out by Kroger—Atlanta to its stores. You will note, as did we, that *the communication is a nice recommendation to the store managers, but certainly falls well short of being a mandate.* We are concerned that the memo does not indicate to the stores that they must maintain placement of the cooler for any length of time.

As the memo indicated, attached to it was a recap of the topics covered in the meeting earlier that day. The recap described that those in attendance at the meeting included Rouas, Marr, and two other CCE representatives.

The cover memo, the recap, and the Kroger memo made up the entire fax message and the only writing evidencing the purported agreement between the plaintiff and CCE. Both CCE and Babyback's refer to other correspondence between the parties subsequent to the faxed memo to form arguments related to CCE's intent whether to enter into a contract and with regard to the terms of such an agreement. However, before any of this other evidence may be considered, the threshold issue—whether an agreement was satisfactorily reduced to a writing—must be resolved because an agreement required to be in writing must completely contain the essential terms without resort to parol evidence in order to be enforceable.

Considering the totality of the faxed memo and its attachments, we conclude that it establishes that the parties were still in the process of negotiating and had not yet reached a final agreement. For example, the fax cover memo states: "we have made further strides toward coming to agreement"; "your objectives however to have absolute agreement by Friday may be difficult to achieve"; "we will move as quickly as possible given the complexities which must be worked through"; and "[the Kroger manager memo] is a nice recommendation to the store managers, but certainly falls well short." The recap of the parties' meeting attached to the cover memo further includes: "our legal department will need to advise and recommend;" and "we will need an audited financial statement from Babyback's in order to proceed with the transaction."

To satisfy the Statute of Frauds, either "the promise, contract, or agreement on which the action is based," or "a memorandum or note describing the promise, contract, or agreement," must be "in writing and signed by the party against whom the action is brought or by the party's authorized agent." *Ind. Code* §*32-21-1-1(b)*. The writing proffered by Babyback's, the faxed memo from CCE along with its attachments, does not constitute a promise, contract, or agreement. It merely reflects preliminary negotiations. Nor does it constitute a memorandum or note describing a promise, contract or agreement. To the contrary, the fax establishes that no final agreement had yet been reached. We need not evaluate the parties' claims regarding the presence or absence of specific terms of the alleged agreement because it is clear that the writing constitutes only preliminary negotiations and does not establish that the parties had reached a final contract.

This writing does not satisfy the Statute of Frauds, and thus, unless there remains a genuine issue of determinative fact regarding an exception to the statute, Babyback's may not bring an action involving the alleged multi-year national co-marketing agreement. *Ind. Code 32-21-1-1(b)(5)*.

PART PERFORMANCE

Supplementing its contention that enforcement of the alleged agreement fails for lack of an adequate writing under the Statute of Frauds, CCE maintains that it is entitled to partial summary judgment despite Babyback's assertion that the doctrine of part performance removes the agreement from the Statute of Frauds. Babyback's asserts that, even if the faxed memo is insufficient to satisfy the Statute of Frauds, part performance "prevents CCE from escaping its obligations under the National Contract." The "modern rule" of part performance, according to Babyback's is: Where one party to an oral agreement has partially performed in reliance on the contract and it would be perpetrating a fraud upon him to allow the other party to repudiate the contract, equity removes the agreement from the Statute of Frauds and enforces the contract.

Babyback's maintains that its conduct in reliance on CCE's promises could only be explained by the existence of a contract, thereby providing evidence normally supplied by a writing of an enforceable agreement. Babyback's argues that application of the part performance doctrine "avoids the harm" that is the concern of the Statute of Frauds, which it describes as the "pitting of one person's word against another's as to the existence of the contract." CCE argues that any evidence of reliance by Babyback's on CCE's alleged promises is immaterial because Indiana law does not recognize part performance as an exception to the Statute of Frauds when the contract is one that cannot be performed within a year.

A considerable body of Indiana case law recognizes that some oral contracts may be excepted from the Statute of Frauds by the doctrine of part performance. But the doctrine has been found to apply only to some of the six types of transactions specifically governed by the subsections of the Statute of Frauds. *Ind. Code* §*32-21-1-1(b)(1)-(b)(6)*. For example, Tolliver, cited by Babyback's as expressing the rule on part performance, involved an effort to charge a person upon a promise to answer for the debt of another, invoking *subsection (b)(2)*. And the part performance exception to the Statute of Frauds is frequently noted as applicable in actions involving a contract for the sale of land, otherwise governed by *subsection (b)(4)*. In contrast, however, in actions "involving any agreement that is not to be performed within one (1) year from the making of the agreement," *subsection (b)(5)* of the Statute of Frauds, the doctrine of part performance has generally been held not to apply.

CCE also cites cases from many jurisdictions demonstrating this majority approach. Included among those jurisdictions is Florida, where the court rejected a plaintiff's argument that part performance removed an oral multi-year contract from the Statute of Frauds. The court considered the purpose of the Statute of Frauds "to intercept the frequency and success of actions based on nothing more than loose verbal statements or mere innuendos," and it concluded that the statute's requirements of a writing signed by the party to be charged "should be strictly construed to prevent the fraud it was designed to correct." *Id. at 154* (quoting *Yates v. Ball, 132 Fla. 132, 138, 181 So. 341, 344 (1938)*). The court also suggested that as long as the statute can be used to effectuate its purpose, "courts should be reluctant to take cases from its protection." *Id.* (quoting *Yates, 181 So. at 344*). Therefore, part performance, according to the Florida court, would take only oral contracts for transfers of land out of the Statute of Frauds because the proof required for part performance in such cases shows regard for the statute's purpose. *Id. at 155*. Such proof would include the payment of consideration, taking of possession, and making of improvements by the transferee with the consent of the transferor. *Id.* (citing *Miller v. Murray, 68 So.2d 594, 596 (Fla. 1953)*). Thus, the court refused to support the plaintiff's claim for damages on an oral multi-year agreement that did not involve a transfer of land. *Id. at 158*.

Babyback's argues that "if the party alleging the existence of an oral contract that would ordinarily fall within the Statute of Frauds has engaged in conduct that can only be explained by the existence of the contract, the contract is taken out of the statute." Br. of Appellee at 33. This approach is similar to that taken in *Nelson v. Elway, 908 P.2d 102 (Colo. 1995)*, in which the Colorado Supreme Court held, "The part performance doctrine will apply if there is part performance of an oral contract which is: (1) substantial; and (2) required by, and fairly referable to no other theory besides that allegedly contained within the oral agreement." *Id. at 108*. The court cites as the rationale for its conclusion that the conduct constituting the part performance must evidence the existence of some oral agreement. *Id. at 109*.

The part performance doctrine represents an impingement upon the express provisions of the Statute of Frauds. We decline to enlarge that constriction by adopting the minority approach as reflected by the Colorado opinion. The underlying purpose of the Statute of Frauds is "to preclude fraudulent claims that would likely arise when the word of one person is pitted against the word of another." *Brown v. Branch, 758 N.E.2d 48, 51 (Ind. 2001)*. This purpose would be undermined if a party's conduct could form the basis for establishing and enforcing a claimed oral agreement not to be performed within one year simply because the same party's conduct arguably provided the only explanation for the agreement. Such an approach would invite persons to concoct and seek enforcement of fictitious contracts on grounds that the existence of an agreement would provide the only possible explanation for such persons' conduct. In contrast to real estate contracts, where evidence of part performance is relatively clear, definite, and substantial, the nature of evidentiary facts potentially asserted to show part performance of an agreement not performable within one year would be vague, subjective, imprecise, and susceptible to fraudulent application. We choose to retain Indiana's existing rule that the doctrine of part performance may not be used to satisfy *subsection (b)(5)* of the Statute of Frauds governing contracts not to be performed within one year.

Because the doctrine of part performance is not applicable to exempt oral contracts that cannot be performed within one year, this doctrine does not provide a basis for the trial court's denial of CCE's motion for partial summary judgment.

PROMISSORY ESTOPPEL

CCE further supports its claim that the trial court erred in denying its motion for partial summary judgment by asserting that the doctrine of promissory estoppel is not available to Babyback's in this case. CCE contends that promissory estoppel does not remove a case from the Statute of Frauds where the promise allegedly relied upon is the very promise that the statute requires be in writing, and where the damages allegedly suffered are not so substantial and independent as to constitute unconscionable injury and loss.

Oral promises that are not enforceable under the Statute of Frauds may nonetheless be enforced under the equitable doctrine of promissory estoppel. *Brown, 758 N.E.2d at 51*. Prior cases have addressed the "problem" when "it is the very promise which the statute declares unenforceable that the [plaintiffs] assert should remove their claim from the statute's operation." *Whiteco Indus., Inc. v. Kopani, 514 N.E.2d 840, 844 (Ind. Ct. App. 1987)*. In *Ohio Valley Plastics v. Nat'l City Bank, 687 N.E.2d 260, 264 (Ind. Ct. App. 1997)*, the court emphasized as "well-settled authority, that a claim of estoppel or fraud will not operate to remove a case from the Statute of Frauds where the promise relied upon is the very promise that the Statute declares unenforceable if not in writing."

The promise explicitly identified by Babyback's as the basis for its claim of promissory estoppel is the alleged promise of CCE to perform the national contract. Babyback's is seeking to obtain the benefit of the precise bargain that is rendered unenforceable by the Statute of Frauds. Under the above quoted rule of Brown and Whiteco, the doctrine of promissory estoppel will thus not apply except as to a "reliance injury so substantial and *independent* as to constitute an unjust and unconscionable injury and loss." *Id.* (emphasis added).

This requirement for "independent" injury and loss is not further explained in Brown or Whiteco. But it appears to mean independent from the benefit of the bargain that would have resulted from the oral agreement unenforceable under the Statute of Frauds. If this is so, the language of Whiteco, as quoted with approval in Brown, may be understood to express that for the promissory estoppel doctrine to limit application of the Statute of Frauds, the reliance injury must be not only (1) independent from the benefit of the bargain and resulting incidental expenses and inconvenience, but also (2) so substantial as to constitute an unjust and unconscionable injury. To separately require such independence from the benefit of the bargain, however, has not to our knowledge been specifically implemented in Indiana case law. And some decisions of the Court of Appeals appear to have granted relief from the Statute of Frauds under the promissory estoppel doctrine without consideration of such a separate requirement that the reliance injury be independent.

Resolution of the present case, however, does not require us to further address the requirement of independent reliance injury. While the damages sought by Babyback's may not be independent from the benefit of the bargain, the doctrine of promissory estoppel clearly does not apply here for a separate reason, the clear absence of any genuine issue of determinative fact regarding one of its essential elements—that the alleged promise must induce "reasonable reliance by the promisee." *Brown, 758 N.E.2d at 52.*

The following facts are undisputed. On the day following CCE's November 17, 1997, faxed memo, the president of Babyback's faxed a letter to CCE declaring that Babyback's was "taking pride in having reached an agreement with Coca-Cola Enterprises," and to which was attached a "new revised agreement which has been modified with all the changes that we all have agreed." Appellants' Joint App'x at 330-336. But CCE immediately replied the same day with a fax to Babyback's that explicitly stated, "We . . . feel compelled to remind you that contrary to your cover letter, we have not reached an agreement with your company." *Id.* at 337 (emphasis in original). The CCE reply fax proceeded to identify various issues still in dispute, and then stated that CCE would treat Babyback's "proposal with high priority, but unfortunately we will be unable to finalize an agreement with you in the timeframe you have outlined." *Id.*

In light of CCE's immediate and unequivocal denial of the national agreement sought by Babyback's, it clearly was not reasonable for Babyback's to take any actions in reliance upon its belief that CCE had promised to perform the alleged national agreement. On this issue there is no genuine issue of fact. Because the alleged promise of CCE did not induce reasonable reliance by Babyback's, one of the essential elements of the doctrine of promissory estoppel is absent as a matter of law, and the doctrine thus cannot support the denial of CCE's motion for partial summary judgment.

CONCLUSION

After denying CCE's motion for partial summary judgment, the trial court certified this interlocutory appeal, specifically identifying three issues for appellate consideration: (1) the sufficiency under the Statute of Frauds of the written memorandum of the alleged national co-marking agreement; (2) the availability of the doctrine of part performance; and (3) the availability of the doctrine of promissory estoppel. As to each of these issues, we hold that there is no genuine issue of determinative fact and that CCE is entitled to summary judgment as a matter of law. The denial of CCE's motion for partial summary judgment is reversed, and this cause is remanded to the trial court for further proceedings consistent with this opinion.

Case Questions

1. What was the name of the new city that Babyback's and Coca-Cola Bottling Company discussed about comarketing their products which had previously proved successful in the Indianapolis area?
2. What were Babyback's claims that it tried to support in its assertion that the fax was a legally binding agreement?
3. Did the Indiana court ultimately hold that the fax was a preliminary negotiation or a legally binding agreement?

Exercise

Using the Internet as a reference, draft a simple prenuptial agreement for your jurisdiction. Here is an extremely basic example for starters with a few considerations as well.

PRENUPTIAL AGREEMENT

This Agreement made this ____________ day of ____________, 2_____, by and between ______________________________________ AND ____________________, __________

WHEREAS, the parties contemplate legal marriage under the laws of the State of _____; and

WHEREAS, it is their mutual desire to enter into this Agreement whereby they will regulate their relationships toward each other with respect to the property each of them own and in which each of them has an interest.

Now, therefore, the parties agree:

1. That all properties of any kind or nature, real, personal or mixed, wherever the same may be found, which belong to each party, shall be and forever remain the personal estate of said party, including all interest, rents and profits which may accrue therefrom.
2. That each party shall have at all times the full right and authority, in all respects the same as each would have if not married, to use, enjoy, manage, convey and encumber such property as may belong to him or her.
3. That each party may make such disposition of his or her property as the case may be, by gift or will during his or her lifetime, as each sees fit; and in the event of the decease of one of the parties, the survivor shall have no interest in the property of the estate of the other, either by way of inheritance, succession, family allowance or homestead.
4. That each party, in the event of a separation, shall have no right as against the other by way of claims for support, alimony, attorney fees, costs, or division of property.

______________________________ ____________

Signature Date

______________________________ ____________

Signature Date

Note: The parties also consider the following issues (if relevant):

1. Children
2. Real property
3. Financial assets (stocks, bonds, savings, pensions, 401(k), IRA)
4. Financial liabilities (credit card, student loans)
5. Furniture
6. Life insurance
7. Written, oral and moral obligations (college education, wedding costs)
8. Previous relationship costs (prior spouse)

9. Automobile issues
10. Employment concerns (no competes, trade secrets)
11. Parental obligations
12. Religious commitments and considerations
13. Inheritance
14. Periodic modifications and revisions

References

East, W.D., *The Statute of Frauds and the Parol Evidence Rule under the NCCUSL 2000 Annual Meeting Proposed Revision of U.C.C. Article 2*, 54 SMU L. Rev. 867 (2001).

Feinman, J.M. and S.R. Brill, *Is an Advertisement an Offer? Why It Is, and Why It Matters*, 58 Hastings L.J. 61 (2006).

Haroutunian, L., *Employee, You Have a Job for Life: But Is This Oral Promise Enforceable under the Statute of Frauds*? 50 Baylor L. Rev. 493 (1998).

Kim, N.S., *Evolving Business and Social Norms and Interpretation Rules: The Need for a Dynamic Approach to Contract Disputes*, 84 Neb. L. Rev. 506 (2005).

O'Connell, Jr., J.J., *Boats against the Current: The Courts and the Statute of Frauds*, 47 Emory L.J. 253 (1998).

Pompian, S., *Is the Statute of Frauds Ready for Electronic Contracting*? 85 Va. L. Rev. 1447 (1999).

Rowley, K.A., *Contract Construction and Interpretation: From the "Four Corners" to Parol Evidence (and Everything in Between)*, 69 Miss. L.J. 73 (1999).

Chapter 7

Third Parties

After reading this chapter you will be able to:

1. Describe who a third party is in the study of contracts.
2. Explain the phrase "privity of contract" and why it is (or is not) important in the study of contracts in today's business environment.
3. Understand the difference between an intended beneficiary and an incidental beneficiary.
4. Differentiate between an assignment and a delegation.
5. Define what a personal services contract is and how it might be relevant to third parties and contracts.

Key Terms

Assignment
Assignee
Assignor
Delegation
Delegator
Delegee
Incidental beneficiary
Intended beneficiary
Personal services contract
Privity of contract
Third party

Third parties to an existing contractual relationship are those who are not the offeror or offeree but who might still have rights in or be entitled to receive benefits from the agreement. While a third party might not be privy to the private bargaining relationship (also known as **privity of contract**), it is certainly possible that the contract could have an impact or effect on the third party. Whether the third party may have legal rights to that contract depends on whether the third party is classified as an **intended beneficiary** or an **incidental beneficiary**. Third party issues in contract law are quite prevalent when contract rights are assigned to a third party, or, as in many cases, duties are delegated. Understanding the difference between an **assignment** of rights and a **delegation** of duties is vital to understanding the relationship between third parties and existing contracts.

PRIVITY OF CONTRACT

The privity of contract concept can only occur between parties to the contract itself. This can involve either the sale of goods or services or both. However, American law now allows consumers to sue manufacturers or any third party in the stream of commerce involving the sale of the good.[1] This contract law concept developed along with tort law, and the two legal theories came to a head in 1916 when a New York state court held that no privity of contract is necessary between a manufacturer and

[1]The classic distribution of goods model might be characterized as where a manufacturer sells to wholesaler to distributor to retailer to consumer (M-W-D-R-C). In this regard, the consumer would technically not have privity of contract with the manufacturer but rather the retailer.

a consumer, especially when a product is dangerous or defective.[2] While there historically has been very little privity of contract between a manufacturer and a consumer, certainly the advent of the Internet has provided for virtual relationships between these parties. The traditional stream of commerce distribution model has been somewhat turned on its head and privity of contract is virtually irrelevant in this context. In fact, many consumers today deal directly with the manufacturer as a result of the Internet.

ASSIGNMENT

After a deal is made, a party to a contract might wish to assign his or her rights in an agreement to a third party. An assignment is the transfer of a legal right and is quite common in loans, mortgages, and other contractual relationships in which money is owed or money needs to be raised quickly. One may assign rights to a contract in almost any scenario.[3] The one who assigns a contract is known as the **assignor**. The one who receives the assignment is known as the **assignee,** and they acquire the same rights (i.e., stand in the same shoes) as the assignor. Barring a state statute that mandates that an assignment must be in writing, assignments may be oral or written as long as there is the intent to assign. Notice of an assignment must be given in cases where the contract itself requires prior notification. However, there are instances in which the law says that an assignment is *not* valid. For example, one may not assign rights to a contract:

1. If a statute expressly prohibits it.
2. If it is against public policy.
3. If it involves the right to receive workers' compensation benefits.
4. If it is a **personal services contract** for those who have unique talents, abilities, skills.
5. If it involves insurance policies (due to the unique nature of each "risk").
6. If the contract prohibits it or limits assignment.[4]

DELEGATION

While an assignment of a contract eliminates the assignor from the contractual relationship and replaces it with the assignee instead, a delegation of duties does not relieve the **delegator** from ultimate liability on the contract. A delegation occurs when duties are transferred to another person (a **delegee**) who must perform them. In the event that the delegee does not perform, the delegator would still be liable under the contract, unlike an assignment. Just as one may not assign

[2]*See* MacPherson v. Buick Motor Co., 111 N.E. 1050 (N.Y. 1916).

[3]Assignment of a patent, however, is governed by federal law and is found at 35 U.S.C. §261.

[4]As a general rule, one cannot restrict the right to receive money, negotiable instruments, or interests in real estate.

all types of contracts, one cannot delegate certain contractual responsibilities either, including:

1. Personal services contracts (including expertise for someone's unique talents, abilities, and skills).
2. When a contract prohibits it.
3. When it is against public policy.
4. When the delegate has a substantial interest in the personal performance by the delegator.

Assignments and delegation relationships often occur in construction contracts and home modeling projects which require subcontractors.

THIRD-PARTY BENEFICIARIES

A classic example of third parties and their relationship to contracts is found in the insurance industry. When one purchases life insurance, the contract is between the insurer (the insurance company) and the insured (the one who pays the premiums) so that when the insured dies that another (a third party) will benefit from the contract. This is an intended beneficiary relationship. This is a much different scenario than an incidental beneficiary who claims that they were intended to benefit from the private contract, but the facts and circumstances do not substantiate their claim. An incidental beneficiary might be one who purchases a parcel of land adjacent to where a city plans on building a new shopping mall. If the mall is constructed, presumably the price of land will increase. However, if the project does not go through, the incidental beneficiary would not then have the right to sue for breach of contract. Thus, the types of third party beneficiaries include:

1. *Intended:* Have rights in a contract because the benefits of the agreement were intended to benefit the third party.[5]
2. *Incidental:* Do not have rights in a contractual relationship because a reasonable person would not believe that this third party was intended to receive a benefit under the contract.

CHAPTER SUMMARY

One may assign rights while one delegates duties. The assignment of a right eliminates the assignor from the contractual relationship. A delegation of duties allows a third party to participate in the contract. However, if the delegee does not perform as promised, the delegator is still held responsible. Further, when a contract is formed it is possible that third parties have legal rights to that contract as well. An intended beneficiary is one who was intended to benefit from the contractual relationship. This occurs frequently in insurance contracts. An incidental beneficiary is one who benefits from a contract but does not have rights that could be enforced in the agreement.

[5] *See* Restatement (Second) of Contracts §302.

Discussion and Review Questions

1. How does an assignment differ than a delegation?
2. What is the difference between an intended and incidental beneficiary?
3. What does the phrase "privity of contract" mean?
4. Do you feel that incidental beneficiaries should not have the right to sue for breach of contract?

Critical Thinking Exercises

1. Katie and Josh are about to be married. Much planning went into their big day, including the hiring of a local wedding singer for the postcelebration party. The wedding singer has had numerous personal issues in the last month which have interfered with his ability to perform on the weekends. The wedding singer notifies Katie and Josh three days prior to their big day that he cannot attend their reception, but he knows another wedding singer in the area who covers the same songs that he sings. He does not sing his own material. The contract between Katie, Josh, and the wedding singer did not address assignment or delegation. What do you think would be the likely outcome of this situation, especially if the singer recommends the replacement singer instead?
2. Omar is a talented minor league baseball player. Though he is a professional athlete, he has not yet made it to a Major League roster. One day he and the head coach have a falling out. Omar sends an e-mail to the coach that he is delegating his responsibilities to his first cousin Ivan who is talented (but not under contract with any team). Do you think that Omar can do this? Why or why not?
3. Ken builds homes for a living. He is the general contractor and has hundreds of subcontractors assist him in building the homes and condominiums throughout the state. As the general contractor, is Ken responsible for the actions of his subcontractors? Why or why not? On a similar note, do you feel that Ken has to provide workers' compensation insurance for the subcontractors who are not his employees? Consider how North Carolina deals with this issue, http://www.comp.state.nc.us/ncic/pages/bus&ind.htm.

Online Research Exercises

1. Explore the Internet and see if you can find an example of a nonassignment clause.
2. See if you can find an example of a personal services contract on the Internet as well—one for *unique* talents, abilities, or skills.

CASE APPLICATIONS

Case

The following case from Georgia demonstrates the difference between an incidental beneficiary and an intended beneficiary in the context of both tort and contract law.

DONNALLEY v. STERLING

689 S.E.2D 639 (GA. APP. 2005)

ADAMS, J.

Joseph and Carole Sterling, individually and as administrators of the estate of their deceased son, Daniel Sterling, filed this wrongful death suit against Mike Donnalley and the Cobb County School District. The trial court subsequently granted summary judgment on the Sterlings' tort claims, finding that Donnalley and the District were shielded from liability on the grounds of sovereign and official immunity. But the trial court denied the motion as to the Sterlings' breach of contract claim, and Donnalley and the District appeal that holding. Because we find as a matter of law that Daniel Sterling was not intended as a third-party beneficiary under the contract at issue, we reverse.

Here, the evidence shows that in 1999, Donnalley was the head football coach at Wheeler High School in Cobb County. In August 1999, the Wheeler High School football team traveled to the Athens YMCA Camp in Tallulah Falls, Georgia, for a three-day training camp. On the first day of camp, Daniel Sterling, along with several teammates, was riding a "zip line" into the camp's lake. The boys would drop off into the lake from the zip line and swim either to the dock or to the shore. The campers were supervised by Steve Brown, an assistant football coach, who was standing on a dock approximately 30 feet away. Brown had been entrusted with responsibility for patrolling the lake for the three years Wheeler High had held the football camp at the Athens "Y" Camp. In the past, Brown had undergone CPR, lifesaving and water rescue instruction and had been certified to teach first aid, but he had never received a certificate in lifesaving or water rescue.

After his second trip down the zip line, Daniel Sterling surfaced, swam clear, and began treading water. A few minutes later, however, Daniel began to struggle in the water. One of his teammates, Breon Segree, tried to help him but was unable to hold him above the water. Segree yelled for help and another teammate, Chase Paris, tried to help Segree pull Daniel from underneath the water. Brown also dove into the water and helped Paris bring Daniel to shore. He was quickly joined in the water by Donnalley and a third coach.

Daniel was unconscious and was not breathing when he was brought to shore. The coaches administered CPR until an ambulance arrived, and Daniel was eventually evacuated by helicopter from a local hospital to Scottish Rite Children's Hospital in Atlanta, where, tragically, he died two days later.

1. The Sterlings' breach of contract claim arises from a one-page rental contract that Donnalley signed with the YMCA for the use of the Athens "Y" Camp. Donnalley signed the agreement as a "group official" and is listed as the "person responsible." Under this contract, Donnalley agreed that the football team, and not the YMCA, was responsible for providing "qualified personnel" to supervise the lake during water activities, although that term was not defined in the agreement. The Sterlings' contract claim asserts that Daniel was a third-party beneficiary of the rental contract, and they argue that a jury question exists as to whether Donnalley and the District breached the requirement of providing "qualified personnel" by failing to have a certified lifeguard patrol at the lake.

In denying summary judgment on this claim the trial court stated that it could not "find as a matter of law that Daniel Sterling was not a third-party beneficiary of the contract." The trial judge stated that the language of the contract—in particular, the use of the pronoun "we" when referring to the party renting the camp—made it appear as if Donnalley entered into the contract on behalf of the entire Wheeler Football Team. From this language, the judge inferred an intent to confer a direct benefit upon the members of the football team, including Daniel Sterling. We disagree.

"In order for a third party to have standing to enforce a contract . . . it must clearly appear from the contract that it was *intended* for his or her benefit. The mere fact that the third party would benefit from performance of the agreement is not alone sufficient." *Culberson v. Fulton-DeKalb Hosp. Auth., 201 Ga. App. 347, 349 (1) (d) (411 SE2d 75) (1991)*. Accordingly, "[a]lthough the third-party beneficiary [does not need to] be specifically named in the contract, the contracting parties' intention to benefit the third party must be shown on the face of the contract." Thus, "in personal injury cases, an injured party may not recover as a third-party beneficiary for failure to perform a duty imposed by a contract unless it is apparent from the language of the agreement that the contracting parties intended to confer a direct benefit upon the plaintiff to protect him from physical injury."

Applying these principles, we recently held that an inmate injured on a work detail was not a third-party beneficiary to a contract between Stone Mountain Memorial Association and the Department of Corrections. Although that contract required the Association to provide a safe workplace for inmate work details and to furnish safety gear, we held that these provisions did not evidence an intent to benefit the inmates directly as the Association did not agree to render any specifically identified performance to the inmates. Instead, we found that any benefit to the inmates was merely incidental to the contract. See also *Anderson v. Atlanta Committee for the Olympic Games, 273 Ga. 113, 118 (4) (537 SE2d 345) (2000)* (park visitors not third-party beneficiaries of security contract between security company and Olympic committee); *Brown v. All-Tech Investment Group, 265 Ga. App. at 897 (2) (a) (i), 900 (2) (b)* (tenant's visitors not third-party beneficiaries to contracts between tenant and property manager and property manager and security service provider).

Similarly, we find that any benefit to Daniel Sterling from the rental contract was merely incidental and did not render him a third-party beneficiary to the contract. It is clear that the contract, when read as a whole, was intended to delineate the relative duties and responsibilities of the parties. The form agreement designates the time and length of the rental, the rental fee and divides responsibilities between the Athens "Y" Camp and the Wheeler Football Team. After assigning responsibilities for meals and cleaning of the facilities, the contract provides, in pertinent part:

> 4) We will be responsible for administering *First Aid along with supplying the needed medical supplies. Also we will have qualified personnel to patrol the water front areas.*
>
> 5) The Athens "Y" Camp *has no responsibility or liability concerning any lake activities.*

The pronoun "we" refers to the Wheeler Football Team as the group renting the camp.

We find that the intent of these sections is merely to clarify that it was the football team, and not the camp, that had the responsibility over the lake area and its associated activities and specifically to relieve Athens "Y" Camp of this responsibility. While the members of the football team may have incidentally benefitted from this agreement, we find nothing in the language indicating an intent to confer a direct benefit upon the individual players to protect them from physical harm. For example, there is no agreement to render any specific performance for the benefit of the individual football players. And the use of the pronoun "we" does not alter this analysis.

Accordingly, Donnalley and the District were entitled to summary judgment on the Sterlings' breach of contract claim. Judgment reversed.

Case Questions

1. What legal theories in tort law are also part of this breach of contract case?
2. What sport was Donnalley the head coach of?
3. Did the Court of Appeals agree with the trial court decision?
4. Under contract law principles, was Daniel Sterling an intended beneficiary of the YMCA contract?

Exercise

Review the following complex web hosting agreement. Your firm asked you to draft a paragraph to be included in the agreement which will prevent the hosting company from assigning its rights or delegating its duties to another company unless the hosting company obtains prior and written approval (i.e., a nonassignment clause). This is important to your firm because the Web site changes frequently during the week, and the corporation (your firm) really wants the ability to notify the provider of the web services with frequent and informal e-mails requesting the same. Use the Internet as a starting point and framework.

Hosting Agreement

THIS HOSTING AGREEMENT (the "Agreement") is entered into and effective of this ____________ day of ________________, 200____, by and between ________________, a ____________________ corporation (the "Customer"), and Hosting Company, a __________________ corporation ("Provider").

The parties desire to have the Provider host Customer's Web site. In consideration of the mutual covenants and agreements set forth herein, Provider and Customer (each a "Party" and collectively, the "Parties") hereby agree as follows:

Definitions

"Confidential Information" shall have the meaning set forth in Section 0 of this Agreement.

"Content" means all text, pictures, sound, graphics, video and other data supplied by Customer to Provider in connection with the hosting services to be provided by Provider, as such materials may be modified from time to time.

"Domain Name" means the domain name specified for the Web Site (defined herein) by Customer from time to time.

"Intellectual Property Rights" means any and all now known or hereafter known tangible and intangible (a) rights associated with works of authorship throughout the universe, including but not limited to copyrights, moral rights, and mask-works, (b) trademark and trade name rights and similar rights, (c) trade secret rights, (d) patents, designs, algorithms and other industrial property rights, (e) all other intellectual and industrial property rights (of every kind and nature throughout the universe and however designated) including logos, "rental" rights and rights to remuneration), whether arising by operation of law, contract, license, or otherwise, and (f) all registrations, initial applications, renewals, extensions, continuations, divisions or reissues hereof now or hereafter in force (including any rights in any of the foregoing).

"User Content" means all text, pictures sound, graphics, video and other data provided by Web Site users.

"User Information" means any information collected about a Web Site user, including, without limitation: (i) navigational information, including but not limited to usage of hyperlinks within or available through the Web Site; (ii) transactional information, including but not limited to billing information, method of payment and the subject matter of the transaction; and (iii) users' Internet address and/or other identifying information such as actual name and address.

"Web Site" means the user interface, functionality and Content made available on pages under the Domain Name.

Web Hosting

Services. Provider shall provide the following web hosting services:

Contact Control. Customer shall have sole, control over the Content. Provider shall not supplement, modify or alter any Content (other than modifications strictly necessary to upload the Content to, or maintain the full and error-free functionality of, the Web Site) except with Customer's prior written consent. Provider shall upload all Content, including updates, to the Web Site within 24 hours of delivery to Provider. Provider shall also permit Customer to electronically transmit or upload Content directly to the Web Site.

Standards. Provider's hosting standards shall confirm to the following:

Response Time. The mean response time for server response to all accesses to the Web Site shall not exceed more than _____ seconds during any 1 hour period.

Uptime. The Web Site shall be available 99.99% of the time, measured on a monthly basis, except for scheduled maintenance periods.

Bandwidth. The bandwidth representing the Web Site's connection to the Internet shall be operating at a capacity no more than _____ minutes in any 24 hour period.

Security. Provider shall prevent unauthorized access to restricted areas of the Web Site and any databases or other sensitive material generated from or used in conjunction with the Web Site; and Provider shall notify Customer of any known security breaches or holes.

Inapplicability of Force Majeure. The foregoing standards shall apply regardless of the cause of the interruption in service, even if the interruption in service was beyond the control of Provider.

Remedies. In addition to other applicable remedies, Customer may immediately terminate the Agreement without a further cure period if: (x) any breach of this Section 0 is not cured within the later of the next measurable period (only if applicable) or 10 days, (y) the same subsection is breached a second time, or (z) there are 2 breaches of separate subsections (even if cured) within any 6 month period.

Customer License. During the period that Provider provides web hosting services pursuant to this Section 0, Customer hereby grants to Provider a non-exclusive, non-sublicensable, royalty-free, worldwide license to reproduce, distribute, publicly perform, publicly display and digitally perform the Content only on or in conjunction with the Web Site. Customer grants no rights other than explicitly granted herein, and Provider shall not exceed the scope of its license.

Trademarks. Subject to the terms and conditions of the Agreement and this Agreement, each Party hereby grants to the other Party a limited, non-exclusive, non-sublicensable, royalty-free, worldwide license to use such Party's trademarks, service marks, trade names, logos or other commercial or product designations (collectively, "Marks") for the purposes of creating content directories or indexes and for marketing and promoting the Web Site. The trademark owner may terminate the foregoing license if, in its sole discretion, the licensee's use of the Marks does not confirm to the owner's standards. Title to and ownership of the owner's Marks shall remain with the owner. The licensee shall use the Marks exactly in the form provided and in conformance with any trademark usage policies. The licensee shall not form any combination marks with the other Party's Marks. The licensee shall not take any action inconsistent with the owner's ownership of the Marks and any benefits accruing from use of such marks shall automatically vest in the owner.

Electronic Mail. Nothing in the Agreement will prohibit Customer from sending commercial e-mail, bulk e-mail and/or messages containing advertising, provided the recipients of such messages have consented to receipt of such messages.

Term and Termination

Term and Termination for Cause. The term of the Agreement shall be for one year. In addition to Section 4 of the original Agreement, the Agreement will terminate, without notice, (i) upon the institution by or against either Party of insolvency, receivership or bankruptcy proceedings or any other proceedings for the settlement of the party's debts; (ii) upon either party's making an assignment of substantially all of its assets for the benefit of creditors; (iii) upon either party's dissolution or cessation of business; or (iv) in the event a party materially breaches any material term, condition or representation of this Agreement or materially fails to perform any of its material obligations or undertakings hereunder, and fails to remedy such default within thirty (30) days after being notified in writing by the non-breaching party of such breach or failure.

Termination During Web Site Hosting. In the event of expiration or termination of the Agreement while Provider is providing Web hosting services pursuant to Section 0, Provider shall download all material on the Web Site to a medium of Customer's choosing and deliver such materials to Customer by 5:00 p.m. EST the same business day. In addition, at no cost to Customer, provider shall: (a) keep the Web Site publicly accessible for a period of 90 days following the date of termination of the Agreement; (b) if the transfer requires a change in the Domain Name, immediately upon the date that the Web Site is no longer publicly accessible, and for a period of 12 months thereafter, maintain the Web Site's URL and, at such URL, provide 1 page (including a hypertext link) that Customer may use to direct its users to its new Web Site or some other URL of Customer's choosing; and (c) if the transfer does not require a change in the Domain Name, cooperate with Customer in assigning a new IP address to the Domain Name as Customer may request and transferring all operations of the Web Site to a new Provider.

Effect of Termination. Sections __, 0, 5 and 0 through 0 shall survive termination of the Agreement. Except as provided in Section 0, upon the termination of the Agreement for any reason and upon request by Customer at any time, Provider shall promptly return, in their original form, all Content and copies thereof. Subject to Provider's obligations pursuant to Section 0, Provider shall remove all copies of the Content from servers within its control and use reasonable efforts to remove any references to Customer or the Content from any site which caches, indexes or links to the Web Site.

Provider Warranties and Covenants

Provider Warranties. Provider warrants that: (a) there is no outstanding contract, commitment or agreement to which Provider is a Party or legal impediment of any kind known to Provider which conflicts with the Agreement or this Agreement, or might limit, restrict or impair the rights granted to Customer hereunder; and (b) it has full authority to enter into this Agreement and this Agreement.

Performance. Provider covenants that, at all times: (a) each of its employees assigned to perform the Services shall have the proper skill, training and background so as to be able to perform in a competent and professional manner; and (b) it shall allocate and provide to Customer a sufficient number of employees and other resources to perform the Services within the time periods set forth in the Agreement and to otherwise fulfill all of Provider's obligations under the Agreement and this Agreement.

Promotional Materials/Press Releases. Provider shall not publish or release any press releases, public announcements or other promotional materials related to or referencing the Agreement without the prior written consent of Customer. Notwithstanding, Provider may, within the sole discretion of Customer, give itself credit by providing a hypertext link at the foot of Customer's Web Site home page.

Disclaimer of Warranties. Except as set forth in the Agreement or this Agreement, each party expressly disclaims all warranties or conditions of any kind, express or implied, including without limitation the implied warranties of title, non-infringement, merchantability and fitness for a particular purpose.

Ownership

Ownership of Web Site. All services and work provided by Provider hereunder are "works made for hire" by Provider. Provider hereby irrevocably assigns to Customer all right, title and interest in and to the Web site including, without limitation, all applicable Intellectual Property Rights thereto. If Provider has any such rights that cannot be assigned to Customer, provider waives the enforcement of such rights, and if Provider has any rights that cannot be assigned or waived, Provider hereby grants to Customer an exclusive, irrevocable, perpetual, worldwide, fully paid license, with right to sublicense through multiple tiers, to such rights. Provider acknowledges and agrees that Customer shall own all right, title and interest in and to the elements of graphics, design, organization, presentation, layout, user interface, navigation and stylistic convention (including the digital implementations thereof) and the total appearance and impression substantially formed by the combination, coordination and interaction of such elements, which are generally associated with online areas specifically within the Web Site.

Ownership of Content and User Information. As between Provider and Customer, any Content given to Provider by Customer under the Agreement or otherwise, and all user Content, shall at all times remain the property of Customer or its licensor. Further, Customer shall retain all rights, title and interest in any and all User Information. Provider shall have no rights in such Content, User Content or User Information other than the Limited right to use such content only as required for Provider to perform in accordance with the Agreement and this Agreement.

Indemnity

Provider Indemnity. Provider shall defend Customer against any third party claim, action, suit or proceeding resulting from Provider's acts, omissions or misrepresentations under the Agreement or this Agreement (including without limitation Provider's breach of the warranties contained in Section 0). Subject to Section 0, Provider shall indemnify Customer of all losses, damages, liabilities and all reasonable expenses and costs incurred by Customer as a result of a final judgment entered against Customer in any such claim, action, suit, or proceeding.

Mechanics of Indemnity. The indemnifying Party's obligations are conditioned upon the indemnified Party: (a) giving the indemnifying Party prompt written notice of any claim action, suit or proceeding for which the indemnified Party is seeking indemnity; (b) granting control of the defense and settlement to the indemnifying Party; and (c) reasonably cooperating with the indemnifying Party at the indemnifying Party's expense.

Confidential Information. Customer's "Confidential Information" are any passwords used in connection with the Web Site, User Information, any Content which Customer designates as confidential, and any other materials of Customer which Customer designates as confidential or which Provider should reasonably believe to be confidential. Customer's "Confidential Information" also includes the Web Site itself until such time as Customer decides to make the Web Site publicly available to users. Provider's Confidential Information means any materials or information of Provider designated as confidential or which Customer should reasonably believe is Confidential. Provider understands and agrees that Customer does not want any other Confidential Information of Provider, and should the parties agree that additional confidential information of Provider needs to be disclosed to Customer, the parties shall execute a separate non-disclosure agreement regarding such information. Each Party shall hold the other Party's Confidential Information in confidence and shall not disclose such Confidential Information to third parties nor use the other Party's Confidential Information for any purposes other than as necessary to perform under the Agreement or this Agreement. The foregoing restrictions on disclosure shall not apply to Confidential Information which is (a) already known by the recipient, (b) becomes, through no act or fault of the recipient, publicly known, (c) received by recipient from a third party without a restriction on disclosure or use, or (d) independently developed by recipient without reference to the other Party's Confidential Information.

Limitations on Liability. In no event shall either Party be liable for any lost profits or special incidental or consequential damages (however arising, including negligence) arising out of or in connection with the Agreement or this Agreement. This provision supercedes any limitation of liability provisions in the Agreement.

General Provisions

Governing Law. The Agreement and this Agreement will be governed and construed in accordance with the laws of the State of ____________ without giving effect to principles of conflict of laws. Both parties submit to the personal jurisdiction in ____________ and further agree that any cause of action arising under the Agreement or this Agreement may be brought in a court in _________, _________.

Further Assurances. Provider shall cooperate with Customer, both during and after the term of the Agreement, in the procurement and maintenance of customer's rights to intellectual property created hereunder and to execute, when requested, any other documents deemed necessary or appropriate by Customer to carry out the purpose of the Agreement.

Compliance with Laws. Provider shall ensure that its Web Site design and its web hosting services will comply with all applicable international, national and local laws and regulations.

Severability; Waiver. If any provision of the Agreement or this Agreement is held to be invalid or unenforceable for any reason, the remaining provisions will continue in full force without being impaired or invalidated in any way. The parties agree to replace any invalid provision with a valid provision which most closely approximates the intent and economic effect of the invalid provision. The waiver by either Party of a breach of any provision of the Agreement or this Agreement will not operate or be interpreted as a waiver of any other or subsequent breach.

Headings. Headings used in the Agreement or this Agreement are for reference purposes only and in no way define, limit, construe or describe the scope or extent of such section or in any way effect the Agreement or this Agreement.

Independent Contractors. The parties to the Agreement are independent contractors, and no agency, partnership, joint venture or employee-employer relationship is intended or created by the Agreement or this Agreement. Neither Party shall have the power to obligate or bind the other Party. Personnel supplied by Provider shall work exclusively for Provider and shall not, for any purpose, be considered employees or agents of Customer. Provider assumes full responsibility for the acts of such personnel while performing services hereunder and shall be solely responsible for their supervision, direction and control, compensation, benefits and taxes.

Notice. Any notices required or permitted hereunder shall be given to the appropriate Party at the address specified below or at such other address as the Party shall specify in writing. Such notice shall be deemed given: upon personal delivery if sent by telephone facsimile, upon confirmation of receipt; or if sent by certified or registered mail, postage prepaid, 5 days after the date of mailing.

Counterparts. The Agreement and this Agreement may be executed in one or more counterparts, each of which shall be deemed an original and all of which shall be taken together and deemed to be one instrument.

Injunctive Relief. Provider hereby waives any right to injunctive relief or rescission and agrees that its sole and exclusive remedy for any breach or alleged breach, termination or cancellation of the Agreement by Customer shall be an action for damages and termination of its services hereunder. Customer shall be entitled, in additional to such monetary relief as may be recoverable by law, to such injunctive or other relief as may be necessary to restrain any threatened, continuing or further breach by Provider, without showing or proving actual damage sustained by customer and without posting a bond.

Entire Agreement. The Agreement and this Agreement, including any exhibits attached hereto, sets forth the entire understanding and agreement of the parties and supersedes any and all oral or written agreements or understandings between the parties as to the subject matter of the Agreement and this Agreement. It may be changed only by a writing signed by both parties. Neither Party is relying upon any warranties, representations, assurances or inducements not expressly set forth herein.

IN WITNESS WHEREOF, the Parties hereto have executed this Agreement as of the date first written above.

______________________________ (Provider)

By: ______________________

Title: ______________________

Address: ______________________

Fax: ______________________

______________________________ (Customer)

By: ______________________

Title: ______________________

Address: ______________________

Fax: ______________________

References

Burnham, S.J., *How to Read a Contract,* 45 Ariz. L. Rev. 133 (2003).

Eisenberg, M.A., *Third Party Beneficiaries,* 92 Colum. L. Rev. 1358 (1992).

Garvin, L.T., *Uncertainty and Error in the Law of Sales: The Article Two Statute of Limitations,* 83 B.U.L. Rev. 345 (2003).

Holdych, T.J., A *Seller's Responsibilities to Remote Purchasers for Breach of Warranty in the Sales of Goods under Washington Law,* 28 Seattle Univ. L. R. 239 (2005).

Powers, J.F., *Expanded Liability and the Intent Requirement in Third Party Beneficiary Contracts,* 1993 Utah L. Rev. 67 (1993).

Chapter 8

Performance, Completion, and Discharge

After reading this chapter you will be able to:

1. Define the term condition and describe its role in contract law.
2. Explain the role of substantial performance in contracts.
3. Understand what anticipatory repudiation is and why it is important.
4. Identify and consider a few special contract clauses that might be included in a contract.
5. Understand the role of bankruptcy and its relationship to contract law.

Key Terms

Accord and satisfaction
Adequate assurance of performance
Anticipatory repudiation
Automatic stay
Bankruptcy
BAPCPA
Breach
Commercial impracticability
Condition
Condition concurrent
Condition precedent
Condition subsequent
Creditors
Debtor
Discharge
Frustration of purpose
Good faith
Hazardous activity clause
Impossibility of performance
Impracticability of performance
Liquidation
Material breach
Mitigation of damages
Novation
Petition
Preferential transfer
Reorganization
Rescission
Statute of limitations
Temporary impossibility
Trustee
Unclean hands doctrine
Unilateral alteration

Most of the time, the parties to a contract live up to their responsibilities and perform under the terms of their agreement. Once the terms have been fulfilled, the contract has been completed, and the legal obligations come to an end. The **discharge** of a contractual obligation by the parties performing the terms of their agreement is the most common way that a party's obligations end. When a party does not fulfill their end of the agreement, however, the party is considered to have breached the contract. A **breach**, then, is the nonperformance of a contractual duty. Still, there might have been legitimate reasons not to perform as one had originally agreed. For example, contractual relationships are often riddled with conditions that might excuse performance though one may not normally decide unilaterally that they do not wish to further perform their obligations. This chapter explores various aspects of conditions and the manner in which a party might be excused from performing their obligations altogether.

CONDITIONS

A **condition** is a possible future event whose occurrence will trigger the performance of a legal obligation or terminate an existing obligation. In other words, an event, stipulation, or prerequisite must occur before an obligation is triggered. There are several different types of conditions.

Condition Precedent

A **condition precedent** is a condition that must occur before one party has an obligation to perform under a contract. For example, party A contracts with party B to purchase real estate. However, Party A must first obtain financing from a lender, such as a bank, precedent to the sale. This is quite common. Consider, also, where a contract might say that payment is not due until one's "personal satisfaction." Performance of the obligation to pay is conditioned upon the subjective satisfaction of the party (or of someone else). Is that a valid condition precedent? The answer is usually "yes" as long as that is what the parties actually bargained for. Most courts require the work to be satisfactory to a "reasonable" person who is a third party, but not all courts agree.

Condition Subsequent

A **condition subsequent** is an act or event that could occur after the parties have agreed to a contract which then triggers some obligation or relieves a party from a duty. For example, A contracts with B to sell real estate "as long as the property remains zoned residential."[1] If the property zoning changes (e.g., within the first year), it might be possible to void the contract.

Condition Concurrent

A **condition concurrent** is the most common form of condition and is found in most bilateral contracts. For example, when you purchase groceries at the store, the duty to pay arises when at essentially the same time (i.e., contemporaneously) that the duty of the store relinquishes the goods to you.

PERFORMANCE

Most of the time, parties are excused from their contractual responsibilities when the parties have performed as promised. In some cases, courts will discharge responsibilities in a contract even if the performance is not totally finished. If an event occurs that is unforeseen by either party, which makes the performance of the contract either impossible, illegal, or would require a modification by the parties, it is possible that the nonperformance can be discharged as well. This is often characterized as the **frustration of purpose** doctrine.[2] The following examples represent the ways in which a contract may be completed or when the parties are excused from their duties:

1. *Complete Performance:* Performance finished just as agreed. Sometimes referred to as strict performance.
2. *Substantial Performance:* One has acted in good faith and has performed substantially all the terms of the contract. If performance is not at least

---

[1]Other catch phrases that identify conditions subsequent might include "so long as" and "but if."

[2]Frustration of purpose as a defense is often used by buyers who have no desire to complete the contract while the concepts of impossibility or temporary impossibility are more associated with sellers.

substantial, then it is called a **material breach.**[3] A material breach is where the nonbreaching party is substantially harmed and it would be difficult to compensate them without discharging the contract entirely. In a contract for services, when a party substantially performs it will receive full payment minus the cost of the uncompleted task (and any defects). When there is not a substantial performance, the breaching party only gets the market value of the work completed, not the promised contract price. **Good faith** is a theme that runs throughout contract law and the UCC.[4]

3. *Anticipatory Repudiation:* Sometimes referred to as anticipatory breach, **anticipatory repudiation** is a form of a preemptive strike. If one of the parties has reason to believe that the other party will not perform, then the nonbreaching party can suspend their own performance as well without it being considered a breach. For example, this could involve unexpected or drastic changes in stock or gas prices, transportation costs, and so on, which upset the purpose of the agreement. One has to ask for an **adequate assurance of performance** if reasonable grounds for insecurity arise.[5]
4. *Discharge:* The end of contractual responsibilities. Examples include:
   - A. **Accord and Satisfaction** (similar to a waiver, a form of settlement that essentially releases someone from a debt obligation for less than what was originally owed).
   - B. **Bankruptcy**(federal law that had big changes in 2005 for individual debtors).
   - C. **Impossibility of Performance** (outrageously costly to perform or it would take a much longer time because of some external force such as bad weather or other acts of God.), but this is not **impracticability of performance.** (It would be outrageously costly to do so, or it would take a much longer time because of some external force such as the weather or other acts of God.[6] This is also sometimes called **commercial impracticability**, the frustration of purpose doctrine, or **temporary impossibility.**)
   - D. **Novation** (a substituted agreement, or even replacing a party to the contract).
   - E. **Rescission** (the parties agree set aside the contract).
   - F. **Unilateral alteration** (unilateral price or quantity increases for example) could excuse the nonbreaching party if this clearly represented bad faith.

UNCLEAN HANDS DOCTRINE

When a defendant attempts to show that the plaintiff should not be entitled to equitable relief for a breach of contract, the defendant might prove that the plaintiff acted in bad faith or unethically. This attempt to show that the plaintiff is

[3]If a breach is considered "material," then the other party may stop performing as well. If the breach is considered "minor," then the party must still perform and sue for the difference later. (Consider *quantum meruit*, etc., and **mitigation of damages**, a concept which requires that the non-breaching party not make matters any worse.)

[4]Found in the Restatement (Second) of Contracts §205.

[5]*See also* UCC §2-609, 610.

[6]Also known as *force majeure* clauses.

partially at fault is referred to as the **unclean hands doctrine**. If a court believes that the plaintiff is in part at fault for a breach or nonperformance of a contract, the court might then not award an injunction, specific performance, or other remedies or damages for breach of contract. Thus, one who asks a court for relief must come to court with clean hands, so to speak.

CONTRACT CLAUSES

Parties to a contract might stipulate by means of various clauses in a contract other legitimate means of ending the contractual relationship. These could include simple satisfaction clauses,[7] morals clauses, best efforts clauses, **hazardous activity clauses** (or "dangerous activity") in sports contracts, and so on.[8] Consider the "conduct detrimental to the team" clause found in National Football League player contracts, for example.[9] These clauses might create conditions subsequent in which a team or league could terminate a contractual relationship with a player.

STATUTE OF LIMITATIONS

The phrase **statute of limitations** is the amount of time one has to bring a lawsuit following an injury in tort law or breach of contract in contract law, for example. The amount of time varies greatly among the states. Some states say that the statute of limitations for contracts is three years from the date of the breach while others hold that it is four or five years. For the sale of goods, the UCC offers that it is is four years. Under California law, a party has four years in which to file suit for breach of a written contract.[10] In contrast, the statute of limitations is only two years in California if the contract is an oral agreement while it is six years under both Tennessee[11] and New York[12] law, and five years in Florida.[13] Oral contracts, of course, will require substantially more evidence to overcome the burden of proving that a contract actually existed.[14]

OPTIONAL MATERIAL

BANKRUPTCY

Bankruptcy laws are codified in the federal Bankruptcy Code. Bankruptcy law is federal law and is certainly an important consideration in the law of contracts because when a person or organization files for bankruptcy, virtually no contract

---

[7]Such as money-back guarantees.

[8]This is a hot topic in sports law. With so much money being spent on professional athletes, teams and leagues are requiring that certain types of activities must be avoided altogether out of fear that participation in such conduct (playing recreational basketball, riding a motorcycle without a helmet, bungee-jumping) will likely lead to some injury that affects the professional athlete's career.

[9]NFL Collective Bargaining Agreement, *NFL Player Contract,* Paragraph 15. *See* http://www.nflpa.org/CBA/CBA_Complete.aspx and http://www.nflpa.org/pdfs/Agents/CBA_Amended_2006.pdf.

[10]Cal. Civ. Proc. Code §312 et seq.

[11]Tenn. Code Ann. §28-3-101 et seq.

[12]N.Y. Civ. Prac. Laws & Rules §201 et seq.

[13]Fla. Stat. Ann. §95.011 et seq.

[14]Also note that unlike tort law, one *cannot* pursue punitive (exemplary) damages for breach of contract.

is protected from dismissal or **discharge**.[15] If an individual or business files for bankruptcy, it is quite possible that the contractual obligations will be terminated under the authority of the bankruptcy court.[16]

THE PETITION

Voluntarily **petitioning** the bankruptcy court for financial relief is an option for debtors who cannot live up to contractual obligations. This could be due to any number of reasons. Three major causes of bankruptcy include losing a job, having a spousal divorce or death, and large medical bills. Bankruptcy courts are quite lenient for petitioners who seek relief, and the **trustee** in bankruptcy has great power. Whether Chapter 7 (**liquidation**) or 11 and 13 (the **reorganization** chapters), the trustee has the ultimate say as to whether to discharge contractual obligations owed to creditors.

Once a petition for bankruptcy has been filed, all creditors must immediately stop pursuing collection of their debts under the **automatic stay** provision (11 U.S.C. §362). The trustee in bankruptcy then is in charge of handling the petition and the bankruptcy estate. Ultimately, the goal of bankruptcy law is to give debtors a fresh start while at the same time being as fair as possible to the various creditors. Bankruptcy law, then, focuses on which contractual obligations might be legally affirmed (upheld) by the trustee, legally discharged (excused) from performance, or, alternatively, modified in some other way, including extending payment over time with a lower monthly payment plan. Bankruptcies actually broke the 2 million filing mark in calendar year 2005, though this is likely due to the major bankruptcy overhaul taking effect in October of that year.[17]

THE BANKRUPTCY PROCESS

When studying bankruptcy, consideration must also be given to Article 9 of the UCC, *Secured Transactions*. Generally speaking, secured **creditors** are paid first when the bankruptcy estate is administered by the trustee. Unsecured creditors are paid last, if at all. The petitioner (**debtor**) must list all of their property and give the information to the trustee who is in charge of the administration of the bankruptcy estate. The trustee makes certain that no one creditor gets favored (preferential) treatment over another creditor, sometimes known as an "insider." Trustees carefully examine payments made from petitioners to creditors within the 90-day (3-month) period prior to filing bankruptcy so as to avoid these preferred or **preferential transfers**.

BAPCPA

The most recent modification to the Bankruptcy Code was in 2005 under the **Bankruptcy Abuse Prevention and Consumer Protection Act of 2005 (BAPCPA)**.[18] This change was signed into law by President Bush on April 20,

---

[15]Article I, Section 8 of the U.S. Constitution confers the power to establish uniform bankruptcy laws to the federal government.

[16]http://articles.moneycentral.msn.com/Banking/BankruptcyGuide/WhenBankruptcyIsBest.aspx?GT1=9115&wa=wsignin1.0.

[17]http://www.uscourts.gov/bnkrpctystats/bankrupt_f2table_dec2005.xls.

[18]http://www.uscourts.gov/bankruptcycourts/abuseprotection.pdf.

2005. Prior to that, the bankruptcy law was not modified since the Bankruptcy Reform Act of 1978 almost thirty years prior, and before that the Bankruptcy Act. BAPCPA went into effect on October 17, 2005. The new law was promoted (lobbied) for eight years by the banking, credit card, and retailing industries. BAPCPA focused on the consumer end of bankruptcy law, but changes were made throughout. While American bankruptcy law used to look at debtors as victims of sorts of financial difficulty, now bankruptcy looks at petitioners with a curious eye. Anyone seeking bankruptcy protection now, for example, must have credit counseling as part of the process. Additionally, attorneys who prepare bankruptcy forms must certify that they have performed a "reasonable investigation" into the petitioner's finances. There was a mad rush to file before the deadline, and the numbers were staggering.[19] The following information summarizes the major chapters of the Bankruptcy Code as it was modified in 2005. The three major chapters of the code are 7, 11, and 13. In addition to businesses and individuals, the bankruptcy code also addresses bankruptcy concerns involving farmers and even cities and counties (municipalities).

Bankruptcy Code Chapters

Chapter 7: Liquidation—often used by debtors with high credit card debt and few assets

Chapter 9: Municipalities

Chapter 11: Reorganization for Business—allows business to continue to operate—reorganizes debts

Chapter 12: Family Farmers/Family Fishermen

Chapter 13: Reorganization for Individual Debtors—like Chapter 11, it focuses on repayment plan rather than complete discharge

CHAPTER SUMMARY

Most contracts are performed as agreed, and therefore the parties' duties are discharged by performance. While a contract is finalized, there may be conditions attached to it. For example, conditions precedent, subsequent, and concurrent all represent situations in which a duty to perform might begin or may terminate. In other situations, a party might be discharged from performing if they have substantially performed. In other instances and out of fear of nonperformance by the other party, one might ask for an adequate assurance for performance from the other party in anticipation that the party might not perform. The statute of limitations to bring a lawsuit for breach of contract varies from state to state. Consideration must be given to the role of bankruptcy in contract law since contracts might be set aside as part of the bankruptcy process by the trustee.

[19]http://www.uscourts.gov/bnkrpctystats/bankrupt_f2table_dec2005.xls. *See also,* http://www.ocregister.com/ocr/2005/08/21/sections/nation_world/nation_world/article_643051.php.

Discussion and Review Questions

1. What are the differences between conditions concurrent, precedent, and subsequent?
2. What is the concept of anticipatory repudiation?
3. What are other examples of how a contract might be discharged under the law?
4. What is the statute of limitations for breach of contract in your state?

Critical Thinking Exercises

1. Heather is having trouble falling asleep one night. She watches television and sees an advertisement for a piece of fitness equipment that is supposed to strengthen her abdominal muscles, and the advertisement says, "30-day money back guarantee if you are not satisfied." Heather buys the equipment and is not satisfied. All things being equal, if Heather complies with the offer and returns the goods within the 30-day time period, should she be entitled to her money back even if she does not give a reason? Similarly, why do sellers of goods offer such money-back guarantees in the first place? Have retailers changed their return policies out of abuse of such policies?
2. Matt and Adam are roommates, but they have a disagreement which causes Matt to vacate the apartment. Adam is not only a tenant, but he is also the owner of the high-rise apartment. Matt realizes that he still has three months of rent that is due to Adam, but rather than pay Adam, Matt just leaves. Does Adam have any responsibility whatsoever to mitigate his damages?
3. Frank is a Major League Baseball pitcher. As part of his multiyear contract, he is to refrain from snow and waterskiing, rock climbing, skydiving, bungee-jumping, and any other activity that involves a high potential of risk for injury. One day, Frank goes to a local video game store and buys a video game that comes with a special guitar that similutes the playing of many pop songs. Frank is really excited and hammers away to the music only to play the guitar so hard that he injures his pitching elbow. Could the team legitimately argue that this video game injury is covered under its "hazardous activity" clause even though it was not specifically mentioned? *See* http://www.msnbc.msn.com/id/16212095/. *See* also http://sports-law.blogspot.com/2006_12_01_archive.html.
4. Gene owes Raymond $1,500. One day, Gene writes Raymond a check for $1,200 and tells Raymond that he will pay him the difference later. Raymond says "that is fine," and deposits the check in his local bank. Unbeknown to Raymond, Gene had written "paid-in-full" in the memo section of the check. By depositing the check, did that constitute a waiver of the $300 difference on Raymond's part? In other words, was it an accord and satisfaction? *See* http://www.winstonandwinston.com/art%2016%20paid%20in%20full%20checks.htm.

Online Research Exercises

1. Consider the legitimacy of the claim involving wrongful termination of an employment contract involving a popular sports television personality: http://www.thesmokinggun.com/archive/1031061espn1.html.
2. Consider the termination of another entertainment industry personality as well and potential contract issues that could arise as a result. *See* http://www.eonline.com/news/article/index.jsp?uuid=a0cb7f17-d2f9-43f2-9861-795f8fa2d498.
3. Explore corporate franchise agreements: http://contracts.onecle.com/type/79.shtml. Consider also http://www.freep.com/apps/pbcs.dll/article?AID=2006612100595.
4. Explore employee contracts and employee rights on the Internet including http://

employment. findlaw. com/employment/ employment-employee-job-loss/.

5. Consider the odd weather patterns in the United States which forced delays or cancellations of some Major League Baseball games at the beginning of the 2007 season. Consider how good contract drafters might address future issues such as weather clauses involving sporting events. *See* http:// www. usatoday. com/sports/baseball/ 2007-04-16-weather_N. htm.

6. Explore the Internet for instances involving professional athletes, coaches, and sport broadcasters and off-the-field misconduct which caused them to lose their role or even their job as it violated their employment contract. For starters: http://www .newsday. com/sports/baseball/yankees/ny-ndbase1349306650ct13,0,3347025. story.

7. Sports Contracts are really interesting for discussion. Consider the recent issues involving Major League baseball player Roger Clemens. He signed a contract with the New York Yankees which actually allows him to be away from the team on days that he is not pitching. This "freedom clause" as some may call it really created waves in 2007. *See* http:// sports.espn.go.com/espn/page2/ story?page=jackson/070516&sportCat=mlb. *See also* http://www. associatedcontent .com/article/244292/ roger_clemens_ contract_is_ridiculous. html

CASE APPLICATIONS

Case

Consider how the New Jersey Supreme Court dealt with a contract issue related to a "satisfaction clause" found in an employment contract.

SILVESTRI v. OPTUS SOFTWARE

814 A.2D 602 (N.J. 2001)

This is a breach of contract action. Defendant Optus Software, Inc. ("Optus"or "the company"), a small computer software company, hired plaintiff Michael Silvestri as its Director of Support Services, responsible for supervising the provision of technical support services to the company's customers. Silvestri's two-year employment contract contained a clause that reserved to the company the right to terminate his employment for failure to perform to the company's satisfaction (the "satisfaction clause").

Nine months into the contract, Silvestri was terminated under the satisfaction clause by the chief executive officer of Optus, Joseph Avellino. Silvestri filed this action, contending that the company's dissatisfaction was objectively unreasonable and that therefore his termination was a breach of the employment contract. The trial court granted summary judgment to the company. The Appellate Division reversed, however, holding that an employer must meet an objective standard for satisfaction in order to invoke a right to terminate pursuant to a satisfaction clause in an employment contract.

The question presented then is whether the employer's satisfaction is subject to an objective or subjective evaluation. We conclude that, absent language to the contrary, a subjective assessment of personal satisfaction applies and that the trial court's grant of summary judgment to the company was appropriate. We therefore reverse the contrary holding of the Appellate Division.

Optus hired Silvestri for a two-year period commencing January 4, 1999, at an annual salary of $70,000. According to the company's president and chief executive officer, defendant Avellino, Silvestri's duties as a manager in this small business encompassed all tasks assigned to him by the board of directors. Specifically, Silvestri was charged with supervision of the support services staff, responsibility for communication with resellers of the Optus computer software to end-users, and coordination of ongoing training for support staff and resellers of the company's products in order to maintain their proficiency in assisting end-users. The employment contract contained a clause allowing termination of Silvestri for "failure or refusal to perform faithfully, diligently or completely his duties . . . to the satisfaction"of the company. Termination under that clause relieved the company of any further payment obligation to Silvestri.

The record indicates that Silvestri enjoyed the full support of Avellino during the first six months of his employment. Avellino's communications within and without the organization praised Silvestri's abilities and underscored his role as leader of the support services group. As late as July 16, 1999, Avellino sent an e-mail message to all members of the group, exhorting them to support their new supervisor. The e-mail referred to the problems Optus had been having in providing technical support to resellers and end-users, stressed that Optus had hired Silvestri to help alleviate those problems, and again asked the staff to support Silvestri.

Although Avellino repeatedly expressed his belief in Silvestri's ability and efforts during those early months, his attitude started to change during the summer months of 1999. In June, July, and August, several clients and resellers communicated to Avellino their disappointment with the performance and attitude of the support services staff generally, and several complaints targeted Silvestri specifically. Avellino informed Silvestri of those criticisms. As the criticisms mounted, Avellino's concerns and frustrations grew, as evidenced by his e-mail exchanges with Silvestri and others. Finally, on September 3, 1999, Avellino told Silvestri that they needed to have a "heart-to-heart" talk about his performance. On September 17, 1999, Silvestri was terminated.

Silvestri filed an action for breach of contract and tortious interference, naming Optus and Avellino as defendants. The complaint named another terminated support services employee as a co-plaintiff, but that employee's claim was dismissed and is not part of this appeal.

Both parties moved for summary judgment relying on copies of the numerous e-mail communications between them. Defendants submitted copies of e-mail messages received from customers expressing difficulties with the delivery of support services, and with Silvestri's attitude toward them. One from Peter Mittler, a large reseller of Optus products, complained to Avellino, as well as to another manager of Optus, about Silvestri's lack of cooperation and his "dour, condescending attitude on the phone [that] made [Mittler] feel like [he] shouldn't be bothering him."Complaints were received from others both outside and within the company who were having difficulty interacting with the support services unit.

In a certification in support of his motion, Avellino explained that he terminated Silvestri because Silvestri had failed to "exhibit the leadership and management skills necessary to perform his duties to the Company's satisfaction."He cited the objective evidence of the complaints received from the various customers and resellers as well as the concerns and frustrations he communicated to Silvestri at the time those complaints increased. The implication of the certification was that Avellino's dissatisfaction was not an after-the-fact justification for termination. The relationship had been deteriorating over time and finally reached a breaking point after Silvestri failed, in the company's judgment, to respond adequately to the numerous customer complaints. Optus is a small company in the business of customer services, and difficulty with support to resellers and end-users of Optus's products carries the potential for significant consequences in such a business.

Silvestri did not assert that there was any reason for his termination other than Avellino's genuine dissatisfaction with his performance. Rather, Silvestri challenged the reasonableness of that dissatisfaction. He portrayed Avellino as a meddling micromanager who overreacted to any customer criticism and thus could not reasonably be satisfied. By way of example, Silvestri focused on the legitimacy of Avellino's concern about the criticism leveled at Silvestri and his support services group by Mittler, characterizing Mittler as someone who simply would not wait his turn for assistance when requesting technical support. It is undisputed that one of Silvestri's innovations was a "queue"system for prioritizing and addressing customer requests for support service assistance. According to Silvestri, Avellino's overreaction to Mittler's criticism demonstrated that the dissatisfaction with his performance was not objectively reasonable, or that at the very least it presented a question for a jury to determine.

On summary judgment, the trial court refused to substitute its judgment for that of the president and CEO of Optus in respect of whether Silvestri's performance was satisfactory to the company. The Appellate Division, on the other hand, relying on this Court's per curiam decision in *Fitzmaurice v. Van Vlaanderen Machine Co., 57 N.J. 447, 273 A.2d 561 (1971)*, concluded that an employer must meet an objective, reasonable-person test when invoking a satisfaction clause permitting termination of employment. Finding a triable issue of fact concerning the reasonableness of Avellino's dissatisfaction with Silvestri's performance, the court held that summary judgment was inappropriate, and reversed. We granted certification, *171 N.J. 445, 794 A.2d 183 (2002)*, and now reverse the Appellate Division.

Agreements containing a promise to perform in a manner satisfactory to another, or to be bound to pay for satisfactory performance, are a common form of enforceable contract. Such "satisfaction"contracts are generally divided into two categories for purposes of review: (1) contracts that involve matters of personal taste, sensibility, judgment, or convenience; and (2) contracts that contain a requirement of satisfaction as to mechanical fitness, utility, or marketability. The standard for evaluating satisfaction depends on the type of contract. Satisfaction contracts of the first type are interpreted on a subjective basis, with satisfaction dependent on the personal, honest evaluation of the party to be satisfied. Absent language to the contrary, however, contracts of the second type—involving operative fitness or mechanical utility—are subject to an objective test of reasonableness, because in those cases the extent and quality of performance can be measured by objective tests. A subjective standard typically is applied to satisfaction clauses in employment contracts because "there is greater reason and a greater tendency to interpret [the contract] as involving personal satisfaction,"rather than the satisfaction of a hypothetical "reasonable"person.

In the case of a high-level business manager, a subjective test is particularly appropriate to the flexibility needed by the owners and higher-level officers operating a competitive enterprise. When a manager has been hired to share responsibility for the success of a business entity, an employer is entitled to be highly personal and idiosyncratic in judging the employee's satisfactory performance in advancing the enterprise.

Although broadly discretionary, a satisfaction-clause employment relationship is not to be confused with an employment-at-will relationship in which an employer is entitled to terminate an employee for any reason, or no reason, unless prohibited by law or public policy. In a satisfaction clause employment setting, there must be honest dissatisfaction with the employee's performance. The employer may not claim "dissatisfaction"as the reason for termination when another reason is the actual motivation, even if that other reason is neither discriminatory nor contrary to public policy and would therefore pass muster as the basis for discharge of an at-will employee. Moreover, the dissatisfaction with the discharged employee must be honest and genuine. If, however, the employer's dissatisfaction is honest and genuine, even if idiosyncratic, its reasonableness is not subject to second guessing under a reasonable-person standard. In other words, standing alone, mere dissatisfaction is sufficient so long as it does not mask any other reason for the adverse employment action.

Thus, as in an at-will employment setting, the burden of persuasion is on the employee challenging termination under a satisfaction clause in an employment contract. The employee prevails in such a cause of action "if he proves that he was discharged before the expiration of . . . the contract, and either (1) that the employer was not dissatisfied with him, or (2) that the employer, whether dissatisfied or not, did not discharge him on account of the dissatisfaction."

We hold that a subjective test of performance governs the employer's resort to a satisfaction clause in an employment contract unless there is some language in the contract to suggest that the parties intended an objective standard. There is no such language here. Nothing in the text of the satisfaction clause suggests that dissatisfaction was to be measured by any standard other than the employer's good faith, unilateral judgment. We are, moreover, persuaded that in the circumstances before us, application of another's notion of satisfactory performance would undermine recognized and accepted notions of business judgment and individualized competitive strategy, as well as principles of freedom of contract. Idiosyncratic judgments as to what constitutes satisfactory performance are expected and should be permitted. The employer, not some hypothetical reasonable person, is best suited to determine if the employee's performance is satisfactory. Accordingly, notwithstanding the thoughtful dissent by our colleagues who favor application of an objective test, a subjective test shall apply generally to satisfaction employment contracts, unless the language of the contract signals otherwise.

Turning then to application of the subjective test in this setting, and granting Silvestri the benefit of all inferences in this motion record as we must, *Gaines v. Bellino, 173 N.J. 301, 303-04, 801 A.2d 322 (2002)*, we conclude that the entry of summary judgment in favor of defendants was appropriate. The only issue available to Silvestri is whether the dissatisfaction with his performance was genuine, and he has failed to make a *prima facie* showing that it was not. Indeed, he does not even assert that it was not genuine, and he neither pleaded nor raised any issue of illegal or improper motivation for his dismissal. His moving papers attacked only the reasonableness of Avellino's dissatisfaction by contending that another more reasonable person would have otherwise viewed the merits of his performance. Consistent with that position, Silvestri sought to show that even when he did encounter difficulties with resellers and customers of Optus, the problems were not entirely his fault. Thus, applying the test of genuineness, and not reasonableness, we conclude based on the overwhelming evidence in this record that Silvestri has not demonstrated that a dispute exists requiring submission of the matter to jury trial. The judgment of the Appellate Division is reversed and the matter remanded for entry of summary judgment in favor of defendants.

Case Questions

1. How long was the original employment agreement?
2. How many months into the agreement was Silvestri actually terminated?
3. Did the court hold that the correct view of satisfaction clauses is a subjective or an objective standard?

Exercise

Consider the validity of this arbitration clause below, which one might find in an employment agreement. After reading, review *E.E.O.C. v. Waffle House,* 534 U.S. 279 (2002), and discuss whether you agree with the final decision. How might you draft the arbitration clause differently, if at all?

> "The parties agree that any dispute or claim concerning Applicant's employment with Waffle House, Inc., or any subsidiary or Franchisee of Waffle House, Inc., or the terms, conditions or benefits of such employment, including whether such dispute or claim is arbitrable, will be settled by binding arbitration. The arbitration proceedings shall be conducted under the Commercial Arbitration Rules of the American Arbitration Association in effect at the time a demand for arbitration is made. A decision and award of the arbitrator made under the said rules shall be exclusive, final and binding on both parties, their heirs, executors, administrators, successors and assigns. The costs and expenses of the arbitration shall be borne evenly by the parties."

References

Belcher, J.R., *Archer v. Warner: Circuit Split Resolution or Contractual Quagmire?,* 61 Wash. & Lee L. Rev. 1801 (2004).

Di Gennaro, M.J. and H.J. Goldstein, *Can Ipso Facto Clauses Resolve the Discharge Debate?: An Economic Approach to Novated Fraud Debt in Bankruptcy,* 1 DePaul Bus. & Comm. L.J. 417 (2003).

Foreman, R.J., *Employee Stock Options in Personal Bankruptcy,* 72 U. Chi. L. Rev. 1367 (2005).

Garvin, L.T., *Adequate Assurance of Performance: Of Risk, Duress, and Cognitision,* 69 U. Colo. L. Rev. 71 (1998).

Krieger, M.S., *"The Bankruptcy Court Is a Court of Equity": What Does That Mean?* 50 S.C. L. Rev. 275 (1999).

Loeb, B.M., *Deterring Player Holdouts: Who Should Do It, and Why It Has to Be Done,*11 Marq. Sports L.Rev. 275 (2001).

Rowley, K.A., *A Brief History of Anticipatory Repudiation in American Contract Law,* 69 U. Cin. L. Rev. 565 (2001).

Snyder, D.V., *The Law of Contract and the Concept of Change: Public and Private Attempts to Regulate Modification, Waiver, and Estoppel,* 1999 Wis. L. Rev. 607 (1999).

Weiskop, N.R., *Frustration of Contractual Purpose-Doctrine or Myth?* 70 St. John's L. Rev. 239 (1996).

Chapter 9

Breach of Contract and Remedies

After reading this chapter you will be able to:

1. Explain what a breach of contract is.
2. Describe the various remedies associated with a breach of contract.
3. Discuss the various damages associated with a breach of contract.
4. Understand why punitive damages are not awarded for breach of contract.
5. Discuss the remedy of specific performance and when it is used.

Key Terms

Compensatory damages
Consequential damages
Damages
General damages
Liquidated damages
Mitigate damages
Punitive damages
Rescission
Reformation
Remedies
Restitution
Special damages
Specific performance
Waiver of a breach

When there is a breach of an agreement, contract law allows for a variety of methods to remedy or "repair" the damage caused by the breach. Courts often attempt to place the injured party (i.e., the nonbreaching party) ultimately in the position that he or she would have been in had the contract been performed. A breach of contract, then, is the failure to act or perform under the terms of the agreement. This chapter explores the various remedies and damages available to parties seeking relief from the judicial system as a result of a breach of contract. It is important to recall that courts utilize the objective theory of contracts to determine what was meant by the parties to a contract based upon the written agreement or by their conduct—and by objective evidence only. It also is important to remember that the parties may have determined prior to the execution of the agreement that any disputes might be resolved by means other than litigation. This is referred to as alternative dispute resolution or ADR for short.

REMEDIES

When one party has breached the contract, the nonbreaching party may seek numerous types of **remedies** from a court. Remedies represent the breadth of possibilities that a court might impose on the parties since they were unable to resolve their dispute themselves. The following judicial remedies are often pursued by those who have been done wrong by a breach of contract:

1. **Damages** of various types. This usually means monetary damages to compensate for the loss of the bargain.
2. **Reformation**: This allows a court to keep a contract intact but with modified terms or conditions especially if parts of the contract are deemed unconscionable.[1] Consider, for example, contracts that are legal except for the fact that one party is charging an excessive rate of interest on a loan in

[1] *See* UCC §2-701 through §2-715 for a discussion of buyer and seller remedies as they relate to the sale of goods. Visit AUCC §2-703 for recent changes regarding cover and resale.

violation of a state usury law.[2] A court might reduce the rate of interest to a legal rate rather than undo the entire agreement.

3. **Rescission**: This means the setting aside of a contract either because there was no meeting of the minds or due to the existence of a state statute (such as a consumer protection law) which makes the contract illegal. Rescission often returns the parties to their position *status quo ante* (i.e., before they entered into the contract).
4. **Restitution**: The returning of the goods or value of the goods/services. This can occur if a minor, for example, wants to avoid contractual responsibilities while still a minor. The minor can escape from the agreement, but has to return goods, services, or their equivalent value back to the other party.
5. **Specific Performance**: An equitable remedy, it forces someone to perform. This is not available for personal services contracts.

DAMAGES

When a party seeks monetary damages for a breach of contract, courts attempt to compensate a party for harm suffered as a result of the others' wrongful act. Damages compensate the nonbreaching party for the "loss of the bargain" and to put the innocent party either *back* to where they were prior to the contract being entered into or *forward* to where they could be had the contract been performed. This might even include lost profits for a business if they can be proven with reasonable certainty. There are several kinds of contract damage remedies available to the victim of a breach of contract, including compensatory damages, consequential damages, and liquidated damages. Punitive damages are not available, however, for a breach of contract.

Compensatory Damages

Compensatory damages can be defined as the amount of money necessary to make up for the economic loss caused as a result of the breach of contract. These monetary damages are intended to compensate the plaintiff for losses suffered as a result of a breach. **General damages** (or noneconomic damages) include compensation for pain, suffering, mental anguish, disability, and disfigurement. **Special damages** (or economic damages) consist of medical expenses, loss of income, and other direct economic losses. Both general and special damages are specific attempts to deal with the unique situation between the parties.

Consequential Damages

Consequential damages are economic losses caused *indirectly* by a breach of contract.[3] Consequential damages are those which arise from the intervention of special circumstances. As a general rule, they are compensable only if it is

---

[2]http://www.lectlaw.com/files/ban02.htm. For example in Michigan, http://www.michigan.gov/documents/cis_ofis_ceilings_24956_7.pdf.

[3]Law school professors often cite the old English case Hadley v. Baxendale, 9 Exch. 341, 156 Eng. Rep. 145 (1854), which established the basic rule for determining the scope of consequential damages arising from a breach of contract (related to a broken crankshaft and a mill).

determined that the circumstances were within the contemplation of both parties at the time the contract was executed, and therefore foreseeable by both. When an alleged breach is due to an unexcused delay in completion of a project or performances, damages as a result of the delay (or breach) could be recoverable such as lost profits.

LIQUIDATED DAMAGES

Good contract drafters predict that these unforeseeable causes for nonperformance or delay of performance might occur. As such, drafters provide for this in their agreements and such clauses are often referred to as liquidated damages. **Liquidated damages** are damages specified in the contract itself and may also be referred to as "agreed-upon" damages. These damages represent a sum of money agreed upon by both a buyer and a seller prior to signing a contract as a substitute for actual damages for a breach. While not considered a penalty, the parties to the contract do agree prior to performance of the contract what the damages would be for a breach. Liquidated damages clauses are wise considerations for contract drafters as they provide certainty, but courts do not like to characterize them as a penalty.[4] They are often found in construction contracts and prenuptial agreements.

PUNITIVE DAMAGES

Punitive damages (sometimes called exemplary damages) are damages that compensate the wrongdoer in a personal injury (tort) action for intentional or willful misconduct. As a general rule, punitive damages are *not* recoverable in a contract action since the goal of contract law is to make "whole" rather than to punish (the goal of the criminal law). Unlike compensatory damages, punitive damages are designed to make an example out of a party for wrongful misconduct. Such damages are often used to send a message to the community (or society) at large that such conduct is unacceptable. This is not the goal of contract remedies, however. Still, punitive damages are possibly recoverable in antitrust cases or if a state statute allows for it as in the case of a violation of consumer protection statutes.

MITIGATION OF DAMAGES

The duty to **mitigate damages** means that the nonbreaching party in a breach of contract action cannot simply let economic losses pile up and later sue the other party to pay for all of those losses as well. The "victim" of a breach of contract must attempt to minimize the amount of economic loss.[5]

---

[4]This is consistent with the lack of recovery for punitive damages in breach of contract cases.

[5]This principle was established in the classic contract case Rockingham County v. Luten Bridge Co., 35 F.2d 301 (4th Cir. 1929) (discussion of the duty to mitigate damages after a breach of contract). *See also,* In re WorldCom, Inc., 2007 Bankr. LEXIS 383 (Bankr. S.D.N.Y. Feb. 13, 2007) (case involving former NBA star Michael Jordan and his agent and their duty to mitigate damages after WorldCom filed for bankruptcy).

WAIVER OF BREACH

A contract **waiver of a breach** is the voluntary relinquishment of a legal right due to the defective performance by a party to a contract as opposed to a waiver such as a disclaimer, exculpatory clause, or covenant not to sue or compete (discussed in Chapter 1). Sometimes individuals or businesses might waive breaches of contract to maintain lasting business relationships or simply to avoid conflict. For example, a landlord and a tenant may have had a great working relationship for many years. One month the tenant is late in paying rent due to the fact that she was out of town visiting her mother. She returned to town two days after the rent was due and owed the landlord $10 in late fees. After talking about the reason for being late, the landlord tells the tenant, "Don't worry about it. I'll let this one slide." This would be an example of a waiver of a breach of the late fees (i.e., liquidated damages). Waiving a breach is often a wise choice for individuals or businesses who wish to preserve personal or business relationships.

SPECIFIC PERFORMANCE

Specific performance is an order by a court requiring the party that breached the contract to perform its obligation.[6] Assuming a court orders specific performance as a remedy for a breach of contract, the breaching party must then do what it agreed to do in the contract. This remedy is *not* afforded to personal services contracts as a remedy since forcing someone to perform would constitute a modern-day form of enslavement or involuntary servitude.[7] Specific performance, as a remedy, may occur in the buying and selling of real estate. Ultimately, courts do not favor this remedy unless it involves "unique" things such as sale of land, paintings by artists, rare coins, cards, and so on.

CHAPTER SUMMARY

When a breach of contract occurs, the nonbreaching party has a host of legal remedies that they can pursue with the help of the judicial system if necessary. From monetary damages to rescission to specific performance, ultimately the role of the courts is to place the party who did not breach the contract in the position they would have been in had the contract been performed. In addition to contract remedies, courts may award monetary damages, but not punitive damages. Good contract drafters will often insert a liquidated damages clause in a contract in the anticipation of a future breach. Also it may be a good business practice to waive a breach of contract in some cases, especially if the nonbreaching party desires to maintain a business relationship with the other party.

---

[6]Similar to an injunction, specific performance orders performance whereas an injunction often orders nonperformance. *See* UCC §2-716.

[7]Abolished by U.S. Const. amend. XIII, 1.

Discussion and Review Questions

1. What are the various types of damages awardable for a breach of contract?
2. Describe the differences in the various types of remedies associated with a breach of contract?
3. What is the purpose of mitigating contract damages?
4. Why might a business waive a breach of contract?
5. How might a liquidated damages clause be advantageous for a business owner?
6. Why do you feel that some courts disfavor liquidated damages as a remedy?

Critical Thinking Exercises

1. Jenna wants cosmetic surgery on her nose. New to the town, a local cosmetic surgeon offers a deal that for no money down, a patient can have certain types of cosmetic surgery to improve their appearance. After surgery, Jenna is unhappy and refuses to pay the doctor. She also sues for breach of contract, alleging that he breached the contract in his promise to "improve" her look. The words "improve" and "improvement" were used throughout the Web site advertisement. How do you think the court would rule in this breach of contract case and why? Should she be entitled to damages? Is not all cosmetic surgery subject to serious risk? Consider the classic Massachusetts case of *Sullivan v. O'Connor*, 296 N.E.2d 183 (Mass. 1973) which involved a tort and breach of contract action brought by a plaintiff against her surgeon for failure to improve her appearance.
2. Monica wishes to have her lower back tattooed with her boyfriend's name, Jacques. She chooses the style at a local parlor and the tattoo artist provides an excellent design. Unfortunately, the artist spelled the name Jacqes and left out the "u." What type of legal claims, remedies, damages, or other resolution might Monica pursue in this unilateral error? Consider http://www.cnn.com/US/9908/26/fringe/tattoo.update/.
3. April owns a web hosting and design company. She is an entrepreneur and broke away from her nine-to-five job as a human resources coordinator to start her own business. She now has 30 clients and is quite profitable. As part of her web hosting agreement, she has a clause that allows her to charge $250 per week for each week that a customer is late in paying their monthly hosting and design fee. One of her smaller clients is going through tough times and is even considering filing bankruptcy. They notify April by e-mail that they are extremely sorry, but if she can give them more time they will pay her. Technically, they are in breach of contract. What would you do if you were April at this point since there is a breach of contract, and they are now three weeks late? Would it be worth litigating?

Online Research Exercises

1. Consider Domino's Pizza's promise to deliver pizza within a certain time frame after ordering: http://www.gtla.org/public/news/dominos.html.
2. Consider punitive damage awards that are not directly related to a breach of contract such as fraud or failure to warn. See, for example, the case involving a smoker and alleged fraud by a tobacco company: http://www.law.com/jsp/article.jsp?id=1161853524385. Also, explore the discussion and various points of view of the now infamous McDonald's coffee cup case found at http://www.atla.org/pressroom/FACTS/frivolous/McdonaldsCoffeecase.aspx.

3. Consider the Federal Arbitration Act as a means to resolve contract disputes found at http://www.law.cornell.edu/uscode/html/uscode09/usc_sup_01_9_10_1.html.

4. Tattoo misspellings seem to be frequent these days. What is the deal? *See* http://www.thesmokinggun.com/archive/years/2007/0501072cards1.html.

CASE APPLICATIONS

Case

Consider how the Ninth Circuit Court of Appeals dealt with a claim of employment discrimination by an employer in Washington State and the role that arbitration played in resolving employment disputes.

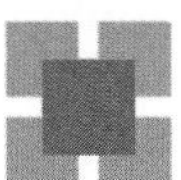

MOHAMMED AL-SAFIN v. CIRCUIT CITY

394 F.3D 1254 (9TH CIR. 2004)

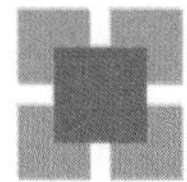

TASHIMA, Circuit Judge

Circuit City Stores, Inc. ("Circuit City"), appeals the district court's denial of its motion to dismiss and compel arbitration of Mohammed Al-Safin's employment discrimination claims. The district court held that the arbitration agreement between Circuit City and Al-Safin is unconscionable under Washington state law, and thus unenforceable.

BACKGROUND

In June 1997, Al-Safin applied for a job at a Circuit City store in the state of Washington. Before Circuit City would consider his application, Al-Safin was required to sign an arbitration agreement entitled "Circuit City Dispute Resolution Agreement" ("DRA"). By signing the DRA, Al-Safin agreed to resolve all disputes arising out of his employment relationship with Circuit City through arbitration in accordance with the "Circuit City Dispute Resolution Rules and Procedures" ("DRRP").

While Al-Safin was still employed by Circuit City, the DRRP was amended, effective December 31, 1997 (the "1998 DRRP"). The 1998 DRRP was essentially the same as the 1997 DRRP, except that Rule 19 was amended to state that "all claims arising before alteration or termination shall be subject to the [DRA] and corresponding [DRRP] *in effect at the time the Arbitration Request Form and accompanying filing fee is received by the Company*." (Emphasis added.) The result of this modification would be that any arbitration filed in 2003 would be governed by the DRRP in effect in 2003, as opposed to the DRRP in effect when the claim arose.

Al-Safin continued to work for Circuit City after the 1998 modification until his employment was terminated in November 1998.

On December 2, 1999, Al-Safin filed a complaint against Circuit City in the United States District Court for the Western District of Washington alleging violations of both federal and state anti-discrimination laws. Circuit City filed a motion to compel arbitration, which was denied, and Circuit City appealed.

In an unpublished disposition, we reversed the district court's decision and held that: (1) the district court improperly relied on *Duffield v. Robertson Stephens & Co., 144 F.3d 1182 (9th Cir. 1998)*, "to hold that the compulsory arbitration contract was unenforceable"; (2) "to the extent that the district court relied on the 'knowing waiver' requirement of *Prudential Ins. Co. v. Lai, 42 F.3d 1299 (9th Cir. 1994)*, our examination of the relevant contract reveals that the requirement was met as a matter of law"; and (3) "although we express no opinion as to the enforceability of particular provisions, we are unable to agree with the suggestion that illegal provisions so infected the contract as to render it invalid as a matter of *federal law*." *Al-Safin v. Circuit City Stores, Inc., 46 Fed. Appx. 446 (9th Cir. 2002)* (emphasis added) ("*Al-Safin I*"). We explicitly remanded the case for the district court to consider "the validity of these contracts under state law."

Effective December 31, 2002, long after Al-Safin was terminated by Circuit City, and over three years into this litigation, the DRRP was again amended (the "2003 DRRP"). The 2003 DRRP modified many of the provisions that have been deemed unconscionable or unenforceable in other proceedings. One week after adopting the 2003 DRRP, Circuit City renewed its motion to compel arbitration and argued that under the new DRRP the arbitration agreement is enforceable. The district court held that the 1997 DRRP, and not the 1998 or 2003 DRRP, applies, and that the arbitration agreement is unenforceable because it is unconscionable under Washington law. After its motion for reconsideration was denied, Circuit City appealed.

DISCUSSION

The *Federal Arbitration Act* ("FAA") was enacted "to reverse the longstanding judicial hostility to arbitration agreements . . . and to place arbitration agreements upon the same footing as other contracts." *Gilmer v. Interstate/Johnson Lane Corp., 500 U.S. 20, 24, 114 L. Ed. 2d 26, 111 S. Ct. 1647 (1991)*. The FAA applies to arbitration agreements, like the one here, that cover employment-related claims. The FAA provides that arbitration agreements generally "shall be valid, irrevocable, and enforceable," but courts may decline to enforce them when grounds "exist at law or in equity for the revocation of any contract." *9 U.S.C. § 2*. "Thus, generally applicable contract defenses, such as fraud, duress, or unconscionability, may be applied to invalidate arbitration agreements without contravening" federal law. *Doctor's Assocs., Inc. v. Casarotto, 517 U.S. 681, 687, 134 L. Ed. 2d 902, 116 S. Ct. 1652 (1996)*.

Accordingly, we review Al-Safin's arbitration agreement with Circuit City in light of the "liberal federal policy favoring arbitration agreements," and consider its enforceability according to the laws of the state of contract formation.

The parties dispute whether: (1) we previously decided that the arbitration agreement is enforceable; (2) the agreement is unconscionable under Washington law; and (3) any unenforceable contract provisions are severable.

I. Law of the Case

Circuit City contends that our prior decision instructed the district court to determine if any particular contract terms are unenforceable under Washington law, while enforcing the core contractual obligation to arbitrate. We disagree.

"The law of the case doctrine requires a district court to follow the appellate court's resolution of an issue of law in all subsequent proceedings in the same case." The doctrine applies to both the appellate court's "explicit decisions as well as those issues decided by necessary implication." However, "the doctrine does not apply to issues not addressed by the appellate court."

Our prior disposition consists of two paragraphs. The first addresses the validity of the arbitration agreement under federal law. By citing *Duffield, 144 F.3d 1182*, and *Prudential Ins. Co. v. Lai, 42 F.3d 1299*, we determined that Circuit City could compel arbitration of Al-Safin's federal employment discrimination claims, and that Al-Safin knowingly agreed to arbitrate his federal claims. *Al-Safin I, 46 Fed. Appx. at 446*. Although we expressed "no opinion as to the enforceability of particular provisions," we concluded that we were "unable to agree with the suggestion that illegal provisions so infected the contract as to render it invalid *as a matter of federal law*." *Id.* (emphasis added).

The second paragraph discusses what we did not decide. We began with the general proposition that to be enforceable, an arbitration contract "must meet the requirements of generally applicable state [contract] law." *Id.* We then remanded the case for the district court to determine the "validity of [the agreement] under [Washington] state law." *Id. at 446–47*.

The plain meaning of our decision is that: (1) the arbitration agreement is valid under federal law; but (2) the district court was to determine in the first instance whether it is valid under state contract law. We did not address whether the arbitration agreement is enforceable under state law and the district court followed our mandate by determining unconscionability under Washington law.

II. Washington Law of Unconscionability

"Unconscionability is a doctrine under which courts may deny enforcement of all or part of an unfair or oppressive contract based on abuses during the process of forming a contract or within the actual terms of the contract itself." David K. DeWolf, et al., 25 Wash. Practice Series, *Contract Law & Practice* § 9.5 (2003). Washington recognizes two classifications of unconscionability, substantive and procedural.

> "Substantive unconscionablity involves those cases where a clause or term in the contract is alleged to be one-sided or overly harsh. . . ." "'Shocking to the conscience', 'monstrously harsh', and 'exceedingly calloused' are terms sometimes used to define substantive unconscionability." Procedural unconscionability is the "lack of a meaningful choice, considering all the circumstances surrounding the transaction including "the manner in which the contract was entered," whether the party had "a reasonable opportunity to understand the terms of the contract," and whether "the important terms [were] hidden in a maze of fine print."

In Washington, a contract generally may be invalid based on either substantive or procedural unconscionability. In the employment context, the Washington Supreme Court, while "holding that substantive unconscionability alone can support a finding of unconscionability," has recently "declined to consider whether [procedural unconscionability] alone will support a claim of unconscionability." *Adler, 2004 Wash. LEXIS 930, 2004 WL 3016302, at *5.*

III. Substantive Unconscionability

Whether a contract is substantively unconscionable is a question of law determined as of the time the contract was made, as opposed to the time when the contract is enforced.

A. Which DRRP Controls

As a threshold issue, Circuit City contends that Rule 19 of the DRRPs permitted it to amend the arbitration agreement each year, and that under the 1998 DRRP, Al-Safin's dispute is governed by the rules in effect when he files for arbitration. Because Al-Safin has not yet filed for arbitration, Circuit City contends that his dispute is governed by the most recent rules and procedures and that we should analyze the 2003 DRRP to determine whether the agreement is enforceable.

We are not persuaded. Even if we assume that Circuit City validly amended the 1997 DRRP and is seeking to enforce Rule 19 of the 1998 DRRP, we could not conclude that the 2003 DRRP applies to Al-Safin. First, we have held that the modification provision of Rule 19 of the 1998 DRRP is unenforceable under California law. *See Mantor, 335 F.3d at 1107; Ingle, 328 F.3d at 1179.* The modification provision allows Circuit City to alter the rules and procedures governing arbitration almost at will. For example, here, Circuit City has attempted to implement new rules and procedures over three years after the onset of this litigation, and over four years after terminating Al-Safin's employment. We conclude that Rule 19, which permits this conduct, is substantively unconscionable under Washington law and that the modification provision is therefore unenforceable.

Second, even if we were to accept that the 1998 DRRP requires us to look at the DRRP in effect when Al-Safin files for arbitration, we would conclude that the 2003 DRRP is not effective as to Al-Safin.

Under Washington law, contract modifications are subject to the general "requisites of contract formation, offer, acceptance and consideration." Employers in Washington have been permitted to "unilaterally amend or revoke policies and procedures established in an employee hand-book."

> The handbook language constitutes the offer; the offer is communicated by the dissemination of the handbook to the employee; the employee's retention of employment constitutes acceptance; and by continuing to stay on the job, although free to leave, the employee supplies the necessary consideration.

Id. (citing *Pine River State Bank v. Mettille, 333 N.W.2d 622 (Minn. 1983))*. "However, an employer's unilateral change in policy will not be effective until employees receive reasonable notice of the change" and accept the change.

Applying the principles set forth in*Gaglidari*, we conclude that Circuit City did not properly amend the 1998 DRRP, at least as to Al-Safin. Circuit City's offer to amend the 1998 DRRP consisted of posting a written notice at Circuit City locations and by including a copy of the modification in its Applicant Packet. Even if this provided "reasonable notice" to current and prospective employees, it was not "reasonable notice" to former employees like Al-Safin. That is, it is not reasonable to expect former employees of Circuit City to check the postings at a Circuit City store every December, nor is it reasonable to expect that a terminated employee would review an Applicant Packet, to determine if Circuit City decided to amend its arbitration rules and procedures. Thus, as to former employees like Al-Safin, there was no valid offer to amend the 1998 DRRP. Moreover, Al-Safin did not continue his employment with Circuit City, sign an acceptance, or accept the modification of the 1998 DRRP in any other way.

Therefore, because no contract was formed between Circuit City and Al-Safin regarding the 2003 DRRP, the 2003 DRRP never went into effect as to Al-Safin and the 1998 DRRP controls the parties' dispute.

B. Substantive Unconscionability of the 1998 DRRP

In *Mantor, Ingle,* and *Adams*, we held that Circuit City's arbitration agreement is substantively unconscionable under California law and rejected contract provisions: (1) forcing employees to arbitrate claims against Circuit City, but not requiring Circuit City to arbitrate claims against employees.

California applies virtually the same definition of substantive unconscionability as Washington. *Compare Ingle, 328 F.3d at 1172* (stating that under California law, substantive unconscionability refers to whether terms of the agreement "are so one-sided as to shock the conscience" (quoting *Kinney v. United Healthcare Servs., Inc., 70 Cal. App. 4th 1322, 83 Cal.Rptr.2d 348, 353 (Ct. App. 1999)) with Nelson, 896 P.2d at 1262* (stating that under Washington law, substantive unconscionability refers to contract terms that are "one-sided or overly harsh" and "shocking to the conscience" (quoting *Schroeder, 544 P.2d at 23*)). Each of the provisions we held unconscionable under California law is present in the 1998 DRRP at issue here. Thus, we conclude that *Mantor, Ingle,* and *Adams* are persuasive authority that the arbitration agreement is substantively unconscionable under Washington law. And, in fact, the Washington Supreme Court recently cited *Ingle, 328 F.3d at 1175*, and *Adams, 279 F.3d 889 at 894–95*, with approval, in holding that a 180-day limitations provision in an employment arbitration agreement was substantively unconscionable.

Moreover, the United States Supreme Court has explained that "by agreeing to arbitrate a statutory claim, a party does not forgo the substantive rights afforded by the statute; it only submits to their resolution in an arbitral, rather than a judicial, forum." *Gilmer,*

500 U.S. at 26 (quoting *Mitsubishi Motors Corp. v. Soler Chrysler-Plymouth, Inc., 473 U.S. 614, 628, 87 L. Ed. 2d 444, 105 S. Ct. 3346 (1985)). Gilmer* requires arbitration agreements to embody "basic procedural and remedial protections so that claimants can effectively pursue their statutory rights." *Adams, 279 F.3d at 895.* In *Adams,* we explained that Circuit City's arbitration agreement does not meet these minimum requirements because it limits the remedies that would otherwise be available in a judicial forum, and fails to ensure that employees do not have to pay unreasonable fees, costs, or expenses "as a condition of access to the arbitration forum." *Id.* Here, we again conclude that Circuit City's arbitration agreement requires employees to forgo essential substantive and procedural rights and that the clauses regarding coverage of claims, remedies, arbitration fees, cost-splitting, the statute of limitations, class actions, and modifications, render the arbitration agreement excessively one-sided and unconscionable.

IV. Severability

Like California law, Washington law grants courts discretion to sever unconscionable contract provisions or refuse to enforce the entire contract. *Compare Ingle, 328 F.3d at 1180* (explaining that under California law the court may "refuse to enforce the contract in its entirety") *with Schroeder, 544 P.2d at 24, 86 Wn. 2d at 262* (stating that under Washington law "the court may refuse to enforce the contract" (quoting *Wash. Rev. Code § 62A.2-302*)).

In each of the California cases—*Mantor, Ingle,* and *Adams*—we held that the unconscionable terms rendered the arbitration agreement unenforceable. In *Ingle,* we specifically determined that the 1998 arbitration agreement was "permeated with unconscionable provisions" and was unenforceable in its entirety because "any earnest attempt to ameliorate the unconscionable aspects of Circuit City's arbitration agreement would require this court to assume the role of contract author rather than interpreter." *Ingle, 328 F.3d at 1180; see also Adams, 279 F.3d at 895–96* (reaching the same result regarding an earlier version of the arbitration agreement). Applying Washington law, we also conclude that the unconscionable provisions of the 1998 DRRP pervade the entire arbitration agreement and any attempt to sever those provisions would render the procedure unworkable.

CONCLUSION

For the foregoing reasons, we conclude that the arbitration agreement between Circuit City and Al-Safin is substantively unconscionable. Although we have serious doubts about whether the agreement is procedurally unconscionable as well, we do not decide this issue because the agreement's substantive unconscionability alone renders it invalid under Washington law. Therefore, the judgement of the district court is **AFFIRMED.**

Case Questions

1. What federal circuit decided this case?
2. What form of ADR was at issue?
3. What was the acronym (i.e., abbreviation) for the Circuit City dispute resolution program?
4. How did the state of Washington courts define unconscionability?
5. How did this court ultimately rule?

References

Anderson, E.G., *The Restoration Interest and Damages for Breach of Contract,* 53 Md. L. Rev. 3 (1994).

Kreshek, B.H., Students or Serfs? *Is Mandatory Community Service a Violation of the Thirteenth Amendment?* 30 Loy. L.A. L. Rev. 809 (1997).

Kull, A., *Restitution as a Remedy for Breach of Contract,* 67 S. Cal. L. Rev. 1465 (1994).

Schmitz, A.J., *Confronting ADR Agreements' Contract/No-Contract Conundrum with Good Faith,* 56 DePaul L. Rev. 55 (2006).

Chapter 10

Electronic Contracts

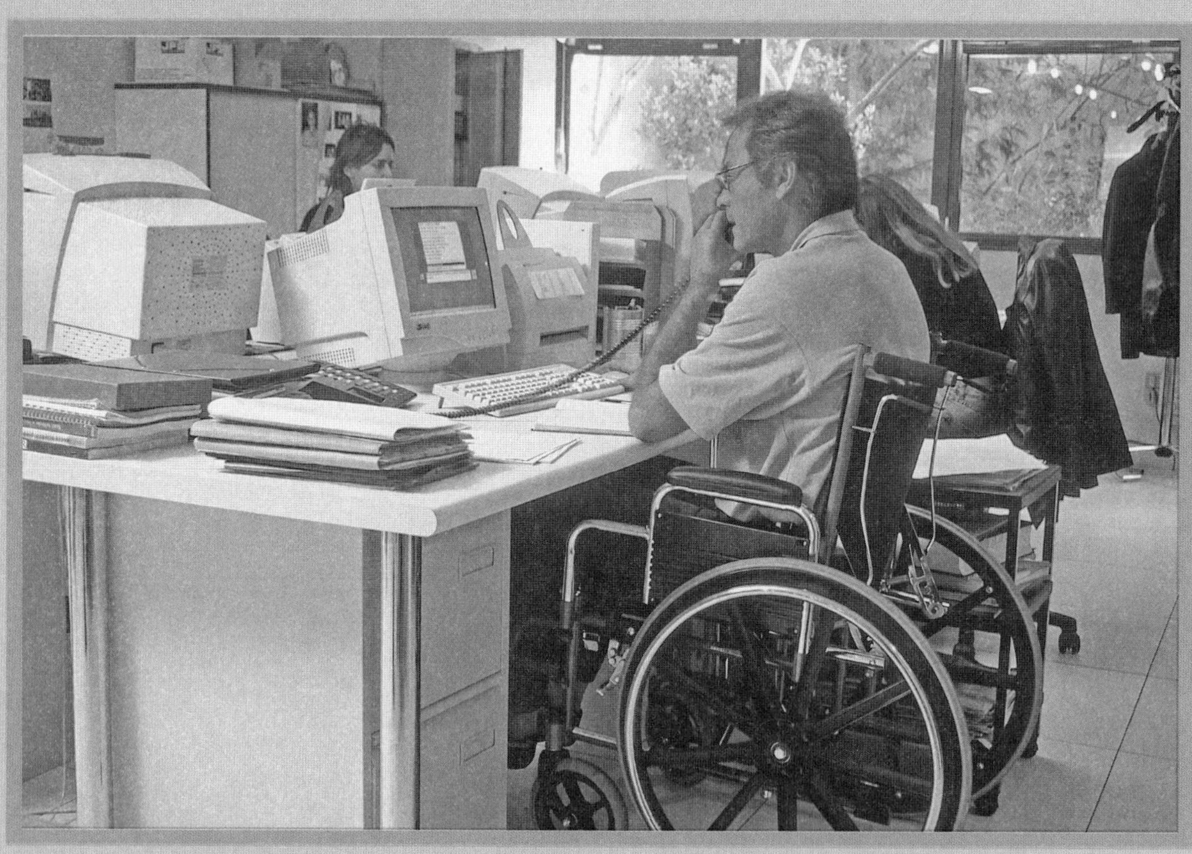

After reading this chapter you will be able to:

1. Explain what an electronic contract is and why it is important in today's world.
2. Discuss the importance of the forum selection and ADR clauses in today's virtual environment.
3. Define what a click-on agreement is.
4. Discuss the role of computer software and licensing issues in e-contracts.
5. Understand the difference between UETA and UCITA.

Key Terms

Access contract	End-user	NCCUSL
ADR clause	E-SIGN	Partnering agreement
Attribution	Forum selection clause	Shrink-wrap agreement
Browse-wrap	License	Signature dynamics
Click-on agreement	Licensor	UCITA
Cybernotary	Licensee	UETA
Electronic signature	Mass-market license	

Advances in technology in the last few decades have forced lawyers, judges, court clerks, and numerous others to adapt and address issues related to contract law in the context of cyberspace. Contracts transacted (or transmitted) electronically are referred to as electronic contracts (e-contracts). Electronic contracts, then, represent and reflect the modern era of contract law principles in a virtual world of transmission and communication. It is very common to transact business and secure contracts via e-mail today in addition to utilizing a fax machine. While electronic contract law is fundamentally the same as traditional paper-based common law of contracts, much of the terminology is different. This area of contract law is still evolving. This brief chapter focuses on the language of e-commerce and its role in contract law.

ONLINE OFFERS

Offers in the online world involving software are often done by what is termed a **click-on agreement**. You are probably familiar with the I AGREE or I DECLINE buttons on a Web site. These click-on agreements are akin to **shrink-wrap** agreements between a manufacturer and the buyer of a product which is literally surrounded by shrink wrap. When a buyer opens the box, the buyer agrees to the terms by keeping the merchandise. These agreements state the contract terms, warranties, and remedies, and had to be conspicuous. A buyer's failure to object to terms contained in a shrink-wrapped software package (or an online offer) may constitute acceptance of the terms by conduct (i.e., opening it). It is also important to consider the **browse-wrap** terms/license found in online agreements as well.[1] These are the subdued "mini-click-on agreements" as one moves through a software package during installation of software. Nothing needs to be done to proceed, however. While the general rules of offer and acceptance apply equally in the online world as in the traditional hard-copy contract-environment, two contract clauses are particularly important when contracts are entered into online.

1. **Forum selection clause.** A forum selection clause demonstrates where (geographically) a dispute would be settled if there is a need for litigation. This clause is normally enforced, but not if a court feels it was inconspicuous. Some forum selection clauses favor the offeror while others are quite fair to the offeree. For example, this clause might be particularly important when a party from the state of Maine forms an agreement with a party from Arizona, and the deal was all done online. If there is a subsequent dispute, this clause would address where the dispute would be resolved.
2. **ADR (alternative dispute resolution) clause.** ADR is an important topic in contract law. With the advent of the Internet and the high costs of litigation, many companies such as cell phone service providers and cable companies require that their users agree to binding arbitration rather than litigation in order to resolve disputes. The two primary methods of ADR are mediation and arbitration. Arbitration is a binding process whereas the goal of a mediation is to attempt to get the parties to settle their dispute on their own and then form a contract representing their settlement.

Good contract drafters should consider the inclusion and clarity of such provisions in a contract today. The role of ADR in e-contracts is vital. The following outlined items use terms frequently mentioned in the online world of contracts. It is important that students of today become familiar with these terms if they have not already done so.

SOFTWARE

Software contracts can be performed online (and usually are) or can be installed on a computer by a CD or DVD.[2] Customers are called **end-users**, and their relationship to the software provider is based upon a special contract known as a license. A **license** grants one the right to use the software. The seller is the **licensor**, and the buyer is the **licensee**. The licensing of software is a very important and sometimes very time consuming process. Licenses might even contain automatic update provisions and, of course, billing issues as well.

[1] *See* Specht v. Netscape Commc'ns Corp., 150 F. Supp. 2d 585 (S.D.N.Y., 2001). *See also*, http://blog.ericgoldman.org/archives/2005/09/specht_v_netsca.htm.

[2] Originally rules related to electronic contracts were going to be instituted in Article 2 B of the UCC, but that effort by the National Conference of Commissioners on Uniform State Laws (NCCUSL) failed.

MASS-MARKET LICENSE

A **mass-market license** (MML) is an e-contract that is presented with a package of computer information in the form of a click-on license or shrink-wrap license.[3] It is essentially a standard form contract (i.e., a boilerplate agreement) used for transactions with the general public where the information is generic and the software is the same for every customer.[4]

E-SIGNATURES

An **electronic signature** is defined as "an electronic sound, symbol or process attached to or logically associated with a record and executed or adopted by a person with the intent to sign the record."[5] Many people recognize an electronic signature as a PIN number. Electronic signatures include a digital signature (called asymmetric cryptosystem) which uses two different keys, one private and one public. A **cybernotary** is a legally recognized certification authority which confirms digital signatures. **Signature dynamics** is the process of signing with a stylus on a computer pad. Electronic signatures attempt to ensure that a party to an e-contract is verified.

ATTRIBUTION

Attribution is the term used in electronic business transactions referring to the procedures that may be used to ensure that the person sending an electronic record is the same person whose e-signature accompanies the record. This is often the user name/password that is used to access a Web site.

UETA

The **Uniform Electronic Transactions Act** (of 1999) is a model act put forth by the **NCCUSL**. Almost all of the states have adopted UETA. It states that a signature may not be denied legal effect (meaning it is legal) solely because of its electronic form.[6] Similarly, **E-SIGN** (Electronic Signatures in Global and National Commerce Act) was enacted in 2000 to promote commerce over the Internet and provide that a contract which is electronically signed may not be denied its legal effect.[7] In the event that a state enacts UETA, then E-SIGN is superceded. E-SIGN is a federal law only and admittedly modeled after UETA.

---

[3]UCITA 102(a)(43).

[4]http://www.nccusl.org/nccusl/uniformact_qanda/uniformacts-q-ucita.asp.

[5]UETA 2(8).

[6]15 U.S.C. §7001 et seq. *See also* UCC §2-211–213.

[7]*See* http://www.ftc.gov/os/2001/06/esign7.htm. Exceptions include eviction and divorce papers.

UCITA

Only Maryland and Virginia have adopted the **Uniform Computer Information Transactions Act** (UCITA) since 1999. It is generally not considered consumer friendly by many, and it allegedly promoted the desire of the software companies instead of consumers.[8] It was also originally proposed by the NCCUSL.

PARTNERING AGREEMENT

A **partnering agreement** is a simple agreement in which the buyer and seller (both online) agree in advance on their terms and conditions subsequently conducted online and electronically. For example, consider Internet banking agreements wherein customers must usually complete various steps online as part of the contractual agreement between the bank and the customer before the online agreement takes effect.

ACCESS CONTRACT

An **access contract** is one formed for the purpose of obtaining, by electronic means, access to another's database or information processing system. Consider that both LexisNexis™ and Blackboard™ among thousands of other companies require an access contract of some sort.

CHAPTER SUMMARY

Changes in technology have brought the law of contracts to a new and evolving era. While the vocabulary is different, the fundamental basis of offer, acceptance, consideration, and so on remains the same. Those involved in contracts must recognize how technology has modified how business is done and how effective electronic contracts are in today's world. Forum selection and ADR clauses are two of the most important clauses in the e-contract environment. The NCCUSL has been successful in promoting its Uniform Electronic Transactions Act (UETA) as well to adapt to these technological changes and peculiar forms of terminology.

Discussion and Review Questions

1. Why are electronic contracts important today?
2. Why do you think that forum selection and ADR clauses are important in e-contracts?
3. What is a click-on agreement?
4. What is the difference between UETA and UCITA?

Critical Thinking Exercises

1. Company A and Company B are engaged in e-mail correspondence related to the sale of a fleet of trucks. Negotiations over e-mail are going well, but there are many issues unresolved such as how many trucks the buyer wants, the cost per truck, and so on. Other than that, however, the parties seem very eager to close the deal next month. Company B is pleased with the negotiations to this point, and sends an e-mail to

[8] http://www.ucita.com/. *See also* http://www.nccusl.org/nccusl/ucita/UCITA_Standby_Comm.htm.

Company A stating, "Let's Roll!" in the context that things are going well. Do you believe that that statement alone is enough to establish that there was a legally binding agreement, or would it be better stated that such a phrase merely constituted a preliminary negotiation? Consider the alleged breach of contract issues involving e-mail transmissions found in *PFT Roberson, Inc. v. Volvo Trucks N. Am., Inc.*, 2005 U.S. App. LEXIS 20316 (7th Cir. Ill. Sept. 19, 2005).

2. A company that designs computer software has a forum selection clause as part of the click-wrap agreement that a user must consent to if he or she wishes to use the software. In fact, there is a warning in bold face and capitalized font stating, among other things, that "**USER HEREBY AGREES TO SETTLE ANY AND ALL CLAIMS IN THE COURTS OF VIRGINIA USING VIRGINIA LAW**." The user clicks through and agrees to all the terms. Unfortunately, a dispute arises later, and the user files suit in his or her home state of Idaho, alleging misrepresentation and breach of warranty. How effective do you think that the forum selection clause warning will be? Explore *Salco Distribs. LLC v. Icode, Inc.*, 2006 U.S. Dist. LEXIS 9483, 1056 (M.D. Fla. Feb. 21, 2006).

Online Research Exercises

1. For e-commerce issues that generally are kept up-to-date, visit: http://lawprofessors.typepad.com/contractsprof_blog/ecommerce/index.html.
2. Explore the eBay User Agreement: http://pages.ebay.com/help/policies/user-agreement.html.
3. Review the LexisNexis end user licensing agreement online. *See* http://www.lexisnexis.com/toolbar/eula.asp.
4. Read the importance of the CyberNotary Project to the American Bar Association, http://www.abanet.org/scitech/ec/cn/cybernote.html.

CASE APPLICATIONS

Case

Consider how the Ohio Court of Appeals dealt with a dispute involving an alleged ambiguities and breach of contract involving eBay, Inc. and its user agreement.

DURICK v. EBAY, INC.

2006 Ohio App. LEXIS 4773 (Ohio Ct. App. Sept. 11, 2006)

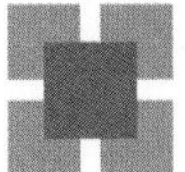

DONOFRIO, J.

Plaintiff-appellant, Dr. Robert J. Durick, appeals from a Mahoning County Common Pleas Court decision granting summary judgment in favor of defendant-appellee, eBay, Inc. Appellee operates as an online market place where members can place for sale and/or bid on a wide variety of goods and services. Appellant, a licensed dentist, registered as a member of appellee in January of 1999. Appellant agreed to the terms and conditions of appellee's user agreement.

Appellant offered for sale a number of items on appellee's website. For each listing, appellant chose the exact title and description of the item. Twelve of appellant's listings described prescription drugs, controlled substances, or hazardous materials. Many of the descriptions contained the amount of the drug that remained in the bottle. Appellee removed these 12 listings and issued a warning for each listing, claiming that the listings violated either its Prescription Drugs and Devices Policy or its Hazardous, Restricted, and Perishable Items Policy.

In November 2002, after issuing 12 warnings over a period of two years, appellee suspended appellant's account for 30 days. In two emails, appellee informed appellant that he had the opportunity to write to appellee at the end of the 30-day period to request an account review to reinstate his account. Appellant did not request reinstatement of his account.

Instead, appellant filed a complaint for breach of contract against appellee. Appellant stated that he acted within appellee's policies and procedures and, therefore, appellee improperly terminated his account. Appellant sought reinstatement of his account and damages.

Appellee moved for summary judgment on appellant's breach of contract claim. Appellee argued that because its user agreement is clear and unambiguous, and appellant violated the terms of the user agreement, appellee was justified in suspending appellant's account. Therefore, appellee argued that there was no genuine issue of material fact to be determined and it was entitled to judgment as a matter of law. Appellant responded by arguing that there existed genuine issues of material fact concerning whether the items removed by appellee were prohibited under the user agreement and whether appellee acted in good faith in suspending his account.

On September 29, 2005, the trial court awarded summary judgment in appellee's favor. The court reasoned that appellant "clearly breached the agreement between himself and Defendant by repeatedly posting item descriptions clearly prohibited by the agreement" and found there was no just cause for delay. Appellant filed this timely appeal on October 28, 2005.

In a breach of contract claim, the plaintiff must prove the existence of a contract, the plaintiff's performance under the contract, the defendant's breach, and damages.

There is no dispute that a contract existed between appellant and appellee. In support of its summary judgment motion, appellee submitted the affidavit of Suza Capps, a customer care specialist for the office of the president of eBay. Capps explained the registration process. In order to become a member of appellee, an individual must register by completing an online registration form. To finalize the online registration process, individuals must accept the user agreement, and all of the policies and procedures incorporated therein, by clicking on a button that says "I Accept." (Capps Aff. P3). The user agreement states that a member must "read, agree with and accept all of the terms and conditions contained in this user agreement * * *, which include those terms and conditions expressly set out below and those incorporated by reference, before you may become a member of eBay." (Capps Aff. Ex. A). Appellant agreed to be bound by the terms and conditions of appellee's user agreement, therefore creating a binding contract between appellant and appellee.

However, appellant argues that there is a dispute as to whether either party breached the terms of the agreement. Specifically, appellant argues that a genuine issue of material fact exists concerning the meaning of appellee's user agreement, and the policies and procedures contained therein.

When terms of a contract are clear and unambiguous, the contract's "interpretation is a matter of law and there is no issue of fact to be determined." However, "when contract terms are ambiguous and one interpretation supports some recovery for plaintiff, the trial court may not enter summary judgment for defendant." Whether a contract is ambiguous is a question of law.

Appellant contends that the terms of the user agreement are ambiguous, and create a genuine issue of material fact for a jury to decide. Appellee, on the other hand, argues that the terms of its user agreement are clear and unambiguous, thus interpretation of the contract is a matter of law as opposed to a matter of fact.

Appellee's user agreement explains the terms and conditions governing the relationship between appellee and its members. Section 5.1 of the agreement expressly provides that a member "must be legally able to sell the item(s)" listed for sale on appellee's website. Likewise, Section 6.2(d) of the agreement states that any items listed on the website shall not "violate any law, statute, ordinance or regulation."

In accordance with the terms of sections 5.1 and 6.2(d), section 18 of the agreement incorporates a Restricted and Prohibited Items Policy, which sets forth items that are prohibited from being listed for sale on the website. The policy includes a Prescription Drugs and Devices Policy as well as a Hazardous, Restricted, and Perishable Items Policy. These policies provide that prescription medications and hazardous materials are prohibited from being sold on appellee's website.

The Prescription Drugs and Devices Policy specifically states that appellee "does not permit the listing of any controlled drug or item that requires a prescription from a licensed practitioner (such as a doctor, dentist, or optometrist) to dispense." (Capps Aff. Ex. C). The policy further states that appellee "does not permit the listing of any components of prescription or over-the-counter drugs unless the sale of such components without a prescription has been approved by the Food and Drug Administration." (Capps Aff. Ex. C). The policy also references a link to the FDA's website, where members can determine whether a particular drug requires a prescription by searching the database by drug name.

The Hazardous, Restricted, and Perishable Items Policy defines hazardous or dangerous goods as "items that may pose a danger to health, safety, or property while being transported, such as * * * toxic substances." The policy specifically states that "such items are not allowed on eBay." The policy provides a link to the U.S. Postal Service website for members to obtain details on hazardous substances and transportation requirements.

Appellee's user agreement provides notice to its members of the consequences for breaching the agreement. Section 9 of the agreement states:

"Without limiting other remedies, we may immediately remove your item listings, warn our community of your actions, issue a warning, temporarily suspend, indefinitely suspend or terminate your membership and refuse to provide our services to you if:

"a. you breach this Agreement or the documents it incorporates by reference;

"b. * * *

"c. we believe that your actions may cause financial loss or legal liability for you, our users or us." (Capps Aff. Ex. A).

The language contained in appellee's user agreement is clear and easily understandable. The agreement also lists and explains prohibited items with specificity and detail. Therefore, the terms of appellee's user agreement are clear and unambiguous. Thus, interpretation of the user agreement is a matter of law to be decided by the court, and no genuine issue of material fact remains to be tried concerning the meaning of the user agreement.

In this case, the appellant offered only a self-serving affidavit to refute the evidence presented by appellee. Despite appellant's claims that the bottles were merely collectibles and only had nostalgic value, appellee offered evidence that appellant described the items listed for sale as hazardous materials and bottles filled with substantial amounts of prescription drugs, such as full or half-full bottles. The user agreement does not state that appellee will inquire into the value of an item to determine whether the item is being sold as a prescription drug or hazardous material. Therefore, even if the value of the items that appellant was offering for sale was purely nostalgic, appellant was still in violation of the user agreement because he listed prescription drugs and hazardous materials on appellee's website. Therefore, appellant's self-serving affidavit is not sufficient to preclude summary judgment in this case.

Appellant further argues that he did not materially breach the agreement because the prescription bottles contained only traces of drugs, and appellee therefore improperly suspended appellant. However, by attempting to sell any amount of prescription drugs, controlled substances, and hazardous and restricted materials on appellee's website, appellant was in direct violation of Sections 5.1, 6.2(d), and 18 of the user agreement. Further, appellee offered evidence that the bottles offered for sale contained more than mere traces of drugs.

Appellant finally argues that the issue of whether appellee acted in good faith in suspending his account is a genuine issue of material fact for the jury to decide. However, appellee has shown that appellant directly violated the terms of its user agreement by listing prescription drugs and hazardous materials on its website, and that it properly suspended appellant in accordance with the agreement. Therefore, there is no genuine issue of material fact concerning whether appellee acted in good faith.

Based on the above analysis, no genuine issue of material fact exists. Therefore, the trial court properly granted summary judgment in favor of appellee. Accordingly, appellant's sole assignment of error is without merit. For the reasons stated above, the trial court's judgment is hereby affirmed.

Case Questions

1. Who is the appellee in this case?
2. How many warnings did eBay give the appellant before suspending his account?
3. Did the court find that there was, in fact, a contract between the parties?
4. Were the bottles ultimately considered nostalgic and collectibles or did the court feel that the bottles contained substances which violated the terms of the user agreement?

References

Anderson, T., *An Analysis of Personal Jurisdiction and Conflict of Laws in the Context of Electronically Formed Contracts,* 37 Idaho L. Rev. 477 (2001).

Brown, L., *Out with the Old, In with the New?: Articles 2 and 2A of the Uniform Commercial Code: Panel 2: Article 2 and Revised Article 2, UETA & E-Sign-Contract Formation & Enforcement—What Law Governs a "Goods" Transaction?* 3 DePaul Bus. & Comm. L.J. 539 (2005).

Daniel, J.L., *Electronic Contracting under the 2003 Revisions to Article 2 of the Uniform Commercial Code: Clarification or Chaos,* 20 Santa Clara Computer & High Tech. L.J. 319 (2004).

Jentz, G.A., R.L. Miller & F.B. Cross, WEST'S BUSINESS LAW ALTERNATE EDITION (Thomson/West, 10th ed. 2007).

Towle, H.K., *E-Signatures-Basics of the U.S. Structure,* 38 Hous. L. Rev. 921 (2001).

Twomey D.P. & Jennings, M.M., BUSINESS LAW: PRINCIPLES FOR TODAY'S COMMERCIAL ENVIRONMENT (Thomson/West, 2e, 2008).

Part II

The Uniform Commercial Code

Chapter 11

The Uniform Commercial Code

After reading this chapter you will be able to:

1. Explain what the Uniform Commercial Code (UCC) is.
2. Understand the differences among the various UCC articles.
3. Describe why a sale of goods is important and relevant to the study of contract law.
4. Discuss what a hybrid sale is and why it is relevant to commercial transactions.
5. Explain the difference between Article 2 and Article 2A of the UCC.
6. Understand why a merchant's firm offer is an important concept under the UCC.

Key Terms

American Law Institute	Goods	Sale
Article 2	Hybrid sale	Shipping terms
AUCC	INCOTERMS	Statute of limitations
Boilerplate	Merchant	Uniform Commercial Code
Cure	NCCUSL	
Firm offer	Nonconforming	
Good faith	Record	

After the industrial revolution arrived and transportation of goods via railroad, truck, and airplane became quite commonplace, the American legal system modified to adapt to modern trade and shipping issues and concerns. As such, the **Uniform Commercial Code** (UCC) was developed to address contract deals involving parties that might be several states apart or even across the entire country. Developing uniform systems of contracts and contract interpretation for the sale and distribution of goods addressed the potential legal minefields involving interstate commerce, jurisdiction, and contract remedy disputes. Though the UCC has been modified several times since its original enactment in 1951, it has provided a statutory framework for trade that reflects the modern contracts environment in the United States today.[1] Because so many changes were made to the most recent amended version of the UCC in 2003, this text will try to clarify which section of the UCC it refers to.

THE UCC DEFINED

The Uniform Commercial Code is a model act only. It is not federal or state law, but all the states have adopted this model act just as they have numerous other model acts.[2] The UCC is the byproduct of the efforts of two organizations of lawyers and

[1]The UCC (and the AUCC) are American model acts. Consider the international version of the UCC known as the CISG (the United Nations Convention on Contracts for the International Sale of Goods). It was enacted in 1980 and has been adopted by at least sixty-two countries. *See* http://www.cisg.law.pace.edu/cisg/biblio/cook.html.

[2]*See* http://nccusl.org/Update/DesktopDefault.aspx?tabindex=2&tabid=60.

legal scholars: the **American Law Institute** (ALI) and the National Conference of Commissioners on Uniform State Laws (**NCCUSL**). The original version of the UCC first appeared in Pennsylvania in 1953 and eventually was adopted throughout the country. The UCC deals with the sale of goods, but not real estate or services. While all states have adopted the UCC, Louisiana has enacted only parts of the Code and has not adopted Article 2.[3] This makes sense since the legal history of the state of Louisiana is much different than other states. Louisiana traces its legal history back to France's Napoleonic Code rather than the English common law system of most states.

ARTICLES

Nine major articles (11 total) make up the UCC. The most studied and discussed of the nine articles of the UCC is Article 2 which governs the sale of goods. Other UCC articles address negotiable instruments (sometimes referred to as commercial paper), bank deposits and collections, letters of credit, documents of title such as bills of lading and warehouse receipts, investment securities, and secured transactions. In fact, the UCC deals with every stage of the contractual relationship from buying the goods to delivering the goods to paying for the goods. Thus, the UCC attempts to provide a consistent framework of rules to deal with all the phases of a sales transaction from start to finish. If there is a conflict between the UCC and state common law interpretation, the UCC generally controls. However one of the most important principles of the UCC is that it comes into play *only* when the parties to a contract fail to provide otherwise in their contract which later results in a dispute.[4]

The Articles of the UCC Include:

Article 1: General Provisions (groundwork and definitions such as "good faith," "sale," "good," and "merchant")
Article 2: Sales
Article 2A: Leases
Article 3: Commercial Paper (negotiable instruments)
Article 4: Bank Deposits and Collections
Article 4A: Funds Transfers
Article 5: Letters of Credit
Article 6: Bulk Transfers[5]
Article 7: Warehouse Receipts, Bills of Lading and Other Documents of Title
Article 8: Investment Securities[6]
Article 9: Secured Transactions, Sales of Accounts and Chattel Paper

[3]Louisiana has not yet adopted Articles 2 or 2A as it uses legal foundations developed from its statutory Civil Code instead.

[4]In fact, throughout both the UCC (and the AUCC) the code notes that the UCC applies only as a default reference "unless otherwise" expressly agreed upon. *See* UCC §1-302.

[5]Most states have repeated this section entirely.

[6]Stocks and bonds are included here because they can be negotiated (transferred by signing on the back of the instrument).

SALE OF GOODS

As already mentioned, one of the most important parts of the UCC is **Article 2**, the sale of goods.[7] This represents a codification of common law contract principles. The UCC, unlike common law contracts, is more flexible when it comes to contract formation, interpretation, and modification. All of this is designed to promote commerce in commercial transactions. For example, according to UCC §2-204, the parties to a contract may agree in *any* manner that is sufficient to show an agreement. This reflects the black-letter law concept of mutual assent but demonstrates that even the conduct of the parties (rather than a written agreement) could show evidence of a contract.

PRE-UCC

Before the enactment of Article 2 of the UCC, the seller and the buyer of goods had to comply with the "mirror image" rule established in the black-letter law of contracts. This meant that an acceptance of an offer had to exactly match the terms of the offer. If the acceptance differed in any way, this would be recognized as a counteroffer, and no contract would have yet been established. In practice, a seller's (or buyer's) **boilerplate** (i.e. standard) contract terms might be modified in the agreement in some way from the original offer (by disclaiming warranties, limiting remedies, pursuing arbitration instead of litigation, and so on).[8] The UCC, however, recognizes that parties often intend to be bound to a contract even if there were these standard or even different or additional boilerplate contract terms (standardized forms).[9] Therefore, only if the additional terms are considered to be *material* alterations of the contract as a whole would they not then become part of the resulting agreement under the UCC. The following terms are important concepts to understanding Article 2 of the UCC and should be given special attention:

Sale: The passing of title from the seller to a buyer for a price (UCC §2-106).

Goods: Tangible and moveable items at the time of sale (real estate is excluded) (UCC §2-102). Food is not usually considered a "good" under the UCC, but can be considered under the UCC for the purpose of an implied warranty of merchantability.[10]

Merchant: A person who regularly deals in goods of the kind involved in the sales contract (retailer, wholesaler, and manufacturer).[11] A merchant also is a person who holds him/herself out as having knowledge and skill unique to the practices of goods involved in the transaction. A merchant is one who possesses or uses an expertise related to the goods being sold. This is not always a clear-cut definition. (UCC §2-104).

---

[7]Things attached to realty such as window air conditioners and tables and stools (unless bolted down) are considered goods and therefore not real estate.

[8]Boilerplate contracts are sometimes referred to as standard form contracts. There is usually no room to bargain by the offeree, and the contract is essentially given as a take-it-or-leave it proposition. Boilerplate contracts are often the result of collective bargaining agreements (CBAs) or standard form contracts involving large corporations. To avoid the take-it-or-leave-it aspect of boilerplate contracts, many states have enacted statutes to address boilerplate contracts requiring minimum font size and a particular font so as to make the terms conspicuous.

[9]Referred to as the "battle of the forms" in the event litigation resulted as a matter related to the difference in contract terms.

[10]UCC §2-314 (implied warranty of merchantability). *See also* §2-108.

[11]Someone who is not a merchant is often referred to as a non-merchant.

Good faith: For merchants, this means "honesty in fact," plus using reasonable commercial standards of fair dealing (UCC §2-103).

OFFERS AND THE UCC

When it comes to contract offers, the UCC is much more flexible than common law contract principles. For example, one can have "open" terms and still have a legally binding contract (open terms include the price, payment options, delivery, duration of the agreement, and so on that might be ambiguous). While common law contract principles might say that vague contracts with open terms could be void due to vagueness or the lack of definiteness, the UCC says that as long as the parties intended to make a contract and there is a reasonably certain basis for a court to grant an appropriate remedy, then there is still a legally binding agreement. This occurs frequently in requirements and output contracts in which the quantity element is missing. The UCC imposes a "good faith limitation" on these special contracts.[12] A **firm offer** is when a merchant gives assurances in a signed writing that the offer will remain open.[13] It is irrevocable for the stated period or a reasonable period (not to exceed three months according to UCC §2-205).[14]

ACCEPTANCE AND THE UCC

When the offeror does not specify how to accept, the acceptance can be made by any reasonable means under the circumstances. Even an acceptance that adds or alters terms will often create a contract between merchants.[15] Essentially, then, the UCC dispenses with the "mirror-image" rule found in common law contracts. Therefore, buyers and sellers of goods should take great care to make sure that during the negotiation phase of a contract their correspondence conspicuously states the words "offer" or "counteroffer" to provide evidence later (in court if necessary) whether their precontract discussions actually intended to enter into an agreement at that point.[16] When both parties are merchants, additional terms

---

[12]Requirements contracts and output contracts can be found at UCC §2-306. *See also* Chainworks, Inc., v. Webco Indus., Inc., 2006 U.S. Dist. LEXIS 9194 (W.D. Mich., Feb. 24, 2006).

[13]*See* http://www.law.cornell.edu/ucc/2/2-205.html.

[14]The actual language is "an offer by a merchant to buy or sell goods in a signed writing which by its terms gives assurance that it will be held open is not revocable, for lack of consideration, during the time stated or if no time is stated for a reasonable time, but in no event may such period of irrevocability exceed three months; but any such term of assurance on a form supplied by the offeree must be separately signed by the offeror." UCC §2-205.

[15]UCC §2-207. Also note that many states use what is known as the "knock-out" rule: conflicting terms cancel each other out. Then UCC §2-509 would fill in the gaps.

[16]This is often referred to as the "battle of the forms" in which the seller accepts the buyer's offer, but there are additional or different terms as part of the acceptance (UCC §2-207). This may happen frequently, in fact, if the seller and buyer use their own standard forms and then later there is a conflict which results in an interpretation question as to whose form is most valid. If the buyer and seller agree to terms but then there is a battle of the forms dispute later, many states utilize the "knockout rule" in which the conflicting terms are canceled (i.e., "knocked out"). Most of the time, the parties are unaware at the time of contracting that there is a conflict. This often occurs with jurisdictional disputes which have arisen as a result of an alleged breach of contract. *See* Roto-Lith, Ltd., v. F.P. Bartlett & Co., 297 F.2d 497 (1st Cir. 1962), for starters. *See also*, McJunkin Corp. v. Mechanicals, Inc., 888 F.2d 481 (6th Cir. 1989).

become part of the deal unless there is clear language insisting on no additional terms. This occurs frequently when there are preprinted (boilerplate) forms.[17] Consider the issue of conforming or **nonconforming** goods: shipping nonconforming goods is a breach of contract, but still allows the buyer the chance to accept them even though the order is wrong (i.e., nonconforming). This is designed to promote commerce, one of the major themes found throughout the UCC.

CONSIDERATION AND THE UCC

An agreement modifying a contract for the sale (or lease) of goods needs no consideration to be binding.[18] This is different than the common law contract principles, and modifications by the parties must be made in good faith. According to UCC §2-209, contract modifications need no additional consideration to be valid and this can be done orally, too. This situation might occur in extreme market shifts that cause the parties' agreement to be come so out-of-balance that the original purpose of the contract becomes frustrated. This can be limited of course ahead of time by including a modification clause in a contract.

STATUTE OF FRAUDS AND THE UCC

The statute of frauds (discussed earlier in this text) requires that certain sales agreements be evidenced by a written agreement or some written document. This concept has not changed under the UCC except that the AUCC increases the minimum dollar amount from $500 to $5,000 to be evidenced by a **record** of some sort.[19] Also, if a contract is between merchants, then a signed written confirmation by only one of the parties is sufficient. The merchant who receives the written confirmation must object within 10 days. Exceptions to the statute of frauds requirement under the UCC include situations involving specially manufactured goods, admissions by one of the litigants, and part performance that can be proved. Courts will often look at prior course of dealing and usage of trade for interpretations in addition to course of performance. That is, the actual conduct between the parties to a commercial contract.

STATUTE OF LIMITATIONS

For breach of contract under the UCC, the **statute of limitations** is four years. For the AUCC, it is no longer than five years and begins to run once the seller tenders delivery to the buyer. This statute of limitation does not exclude the fact that a plaintiff could pursue a tort action (i.e., personal injury) as well, which might have a different statute of limitations.

---

[17]Some have characterized UCC §2-207 as the worst section in the entire UCC. *See* http://www.drbilllong.com/Sales/Forms.html.

[18]UCC §2-209(1).

[19]AUCC §2-201. For a lease, it is $1,000. The AUCC also replaces the term "writing" to "record" to reflect changes in technology and commercial transactions over the Internet and via email. It should also be noted that in AUCC §2-201(4), the provision of the statute of frauds which had required evidence of a writing if it could not be performed within a year has been essentially repealed.

HYBRID SALES

A **hybrid sale** describes when both goods and services are combined in a sale. A hybrid sale is sometimes referred to as a "mixed contract." Most courts use the "most predominant" test or "predominant purpose" test to determine the nature of the contract. This means if the sale was more goods related, then the UCC applies. If it was more services related, then the UCC does not apply. Instead, common law contract principles would apply. This determination would most likely be made by a court.

2003 AMENDMENTS

While an amended UCC (that is, the **AUCC**) does not become effective until it is approved in state legislatures, it is likely to occur in the future.[20] The original version of Article 2 required that any contract for the sale of goods priced at $500 or more had to be evidenced by a writing of some form. This most recent version of the UCC increases that minimum amount to $5,000 as part of its moderinizing amendments. Other changes include the fact that the term "writing" has been replaced by the term "record," which includes not only traditional paper writings but also electronic forms.[21] For example, the AUCC allows a contract to be evidenced by electronic records, including e-mails.

SHIPPING TERMS

Article 2 also contains sections dealing with transportation and shipping acronyms (discussed in Chapter 12) such as CIF (cost, insurance, and freight), FOB (free on board), and so on that would determine at what point the risk of loss of the goods passed from the seller to the buyer.[22] These sections have been deleted from the 2003 version, and the revision does not replace them with new terms. Rather, the UCC suggests that **shipping terms** generally accepted in commerce should be recognized (e.g., **INCOTERMS** created by the International Chamber of Commerce) and widely used in international transactions.[23]

OTHER CHANGES

When a buyer rejects a shipment goods because they are nonconforming, Article 2 allowed the seller to **cure** the defect by repairing or replacing the goods, assuming time remained under the contract. The "cure" section of the UCC only applied if the buyer rejected the goods. If the buyer accepted the goods but later discovered defects, the buyer was entitled to revoke its acceptance of the goods. The AUCC allows the seller

[20]Also known as the revised UCC, amended UCC, or simply AUCC.

[21]AUCC §1-201(b)(31).

[22]AUCC §2-509, 510. These terms were found at UCC §§2-319-324 but are repealed entirely in the latest version of the UCC.

[23]http://www.export911.com/e911/export/comTerm.htm (INCOTERMS).

to cure defects even after the buyer has revoked acceptance of the goods if time for performance still remains under the contract.[24] This 2003 revision also clarifies warranty obligations where the buyer purchases the goods from a distributor but finds warranties from the manufacturer with whom the buyer has not directly dealt inside the box. Other changes include the fact that the original statute of limitations of four years is extended to up to five years under the AUCC in certain situations, and terms such as telegram and honor are deleted.[25] Terms that are added to the AUCC include definitions of consumer, authenticate, record, state, good faith, and bank.[26]

ARTICLE 2A

When leases of goods (such as furniture, cars, and so on) became quite common in the 1980s, the UCC was modified in 1990 to address commercial lease transactions rather than sales of the goods. Article 2A was established and governs commercial leases.[27] This Article governs any transaction that creates a lease or sublease of goods.

CHAPTER SUMMARY

Originally promulgated in 1951, the Uniform Commercial Code represents a model act designed to incorporate fundamental contract law principles into a uniform code for the states to adopt. The purpose of the UCC is to promote commerce and trade and to avoid the pitfalls of having 50 individual state laws which might conflict with each other. Understanding that the UCC is more flexible than common law contracts is important because sellers and buyers may have opportunities to repair or remedy conflicts that would otherwise be considered breaches of contract leading to litigation. The most often discussed and studied article of the UCC is Article 2, which involves the sale of goods. This is to be distinguished from the sale of services or real estate for which the UCC does not directly apply. Article 2A, which was originally enacted in 1990, represented the adaptation of the UCC to incorporate commercial leases as opposed to the sale of goods. Then, in 2003, the UCC was amended in several significant ways although adoption of the Amended UCC has been quite slow and as of the time of this writing no state has adopted it.

Discussion and Review Questions

1. Why (and when) was the UCC enacted?
2. How many articles are there in the UCC?
3. How does the UCC differ from common law contracts?
4. What is a hybrid sale?
5. What are some of the changes brought by the 2003 amendments?
6. What is a merchant's firm offer and why is it important?

---

[24]In both the original and revised versions, more time for cure is permitted if the seller has reasonable grounds to believe that it would still be entitled to cure after the original contract time expires. This would typically be based on the prior dealings between the parties.

[25]Western Union sent its last telegram in 2006. *See* http://www.msnbc.msn.com/id/11147506/. The term "honor" refers to honoring a negotiable instrument (commercial paper) such as a check.

[26]AUCC §1-201 for a complete list.

[27]Also revised in 2003.

Critical Thinking Exercises

1. Jaime has a garage sale as part of her process of beginning to move from Michigan to Wisconsin where she has a new job. Do you believe that Jaime would be characterized as a "merchant" under the UCC? Why or why not? If Jaime regularly had garage sales (such as once per month) would this change your opinion?
2. Todd has his Jeep repaired by a local auto mechanic. The mechanic tells him that he needs a new transmission and that he has it in stock. Would the installation of the transmission constitute the sale of goods, the sale of services, or both (i.e., a hybrid sale). Justify your reasoning. Would an oil change constitute a hybrid sale?
3. When someone sells an item on eBay, would such a sale be governed by the UCC? Why or why not? Might other uniform acts apply? Might a separate agreement such as a user agreement supersede the UCC anyway?

Online Research Exercises

1. For an overview of the Uniform Commercial Code, visit http://www.law.cornell.edu/ucc/2/overview.html.
2. For a state-by-state listing of relevant UCC statutes, visit http://www.law.cornell.edu/uniform/ucc.html.

CASE APPLICATIONS

Case

Consider this New Jersey case involving the alleged breach of contract and personal injury involving a beauty parlor, hair products, and their services in a hybrid sale.

NEWMARK v. GIMBELS, INC.

258 A.2D 697 (N.J. 1969)

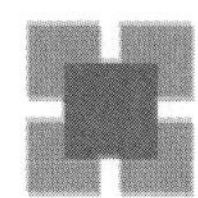

This appeal involves the liability of a beauty parlor operator for injury to a patron's hair and scalp allegedly resulting from a product used in the giving of a permanent wave. The action was predicated upon charges of negligence and breach of express and implied warranty. Trial was had before the county district court and a jury. At the close of the proof, the court ruled as matter of law that the warranty theory of liability was not maintainable because in giving a permanent wave a beauty parlor is engaged in rendering a service and not a sale; hence responsibility for injurious results could arise only from negligence. Consequently the court dismissed the warranty counts and submitted the issue of negligence for the jury's determination. Upon the return of a verdict for defendants, plaintiffs appealed. The Appellate Division reversed holding that a fact issue existed requiring jury decision as to whether there was an implied warranty of fitness of the lotion applied to Mrs. Newmark's hair and scalp for the purpose of producing the permanent wave. *Newmark v. Gimbel's Inc., 102 N.J. Super. 279 (App. Div. 1968).* Thereafter we granted defendants' petition for certification.

The defendants, who by stipulation were to be considered as one, operated a number of beauty parlors where permanent waves were offered to the public for a consideration. For about a year and a half prior to the incident in question, Mrs. Newmark had been a patron of one of defendants' shops where she had a standing appointment every week to have her hair washed and set. She was usually attended by the same operator, one William Valante. During that period plaintiffs' brief asserts and defendants do not deny that she had purchased permanent waves there, at least one having been given by Valante, and she had not experienced any untoward results.

On November 16, 1963, pursuant to an appointment, Mrs. Newmark went to the beauty parlor where she inquired of Valante about a permanent wave that was on special sale. He told her that her fine hair was not right for the special permanent and that she needed a "good" permanent wave. She agreed to accept the wave suggested by him. Valante conceded that the wave she received was given at his suggestion and that in accepting it she relied on his judgment as to what was good for her hair. Both Valante and Mrs. Newmark testified there was nothing wrong with her hair or scalp before the wave was given.

Valante proceeded to cut and wash her hair after which he put her head under a dryer for about 10 minutes. The hair was then sectioned off, a permanent wave solution marketed under the name "Helene Curtis Candle Wave" was applied with cotton and the hair was rolled section by section. Following this, more of the waving solution was put on by an applicator-bottle. Then a cream was placed along the hairline and covered with cotton. About three to five minutes after the last of the waving solution had been applied Mrs. Newmark experienced a burning sensation on the front part of her head. She complained to Valante who added more cream along the hairline. This gave some relief but after a few minutes she told him that it was burning again. The burning sensation continued but was alleviated when Valante brought her to a basin and rinsed her hair in lukewarm water. The curlers were then removed, a neutralizing solution was applied and allowed to remain for about seven minutes, and her hair was again rinsed. After this Valante set her hair and again put her under the dryer where she remained for about 25 minutes. The burning sensation returned and she promptly informed Valante who reduced the heat of the dryer thereby giving her partial relief. When the dryer operation was completed her hair was combed, and she left the parlor.

That evening her head reddened, and during the following day her entire forehead was red and blistered. A large amount of hair fell out when it was combed. On November 19 she returned to defendants' place of business where Valante gave her, without charge, a conditioning treatment which he told her is given when the hair is dry. Mrs. Newmark testified that it made her hair feel singed at the hairline.

Six days after the permanent wave Mrs. Newmark consulted a dermatologist who diagnosed her condition as contact dermatitis of the scalp and loss of hair resulting therefrom. On the basis of his experience, he concluded that the sole cause of her condition was the permanent wave solution. The redness and tenderness of the scalp diminished under his treatment. When he last saw her on December 13, 1963 the loss of hair on the top of her head was still present and he could not estimate the time it would take for replacement.

Defendants' dermatologist examined plaintiff over four months after the incident. He noticed several areas of diminution of hair which he attributed to Mrs. Newmark's use of wire brush curlers. The agreed statement of facts does not say expressly that the doctor denied plaintiffs' physician's assertion that the permanent wave solution caused the dermatitis. Since defendants argue that there was insufficient proof of the solution's defectiveness, presumably their contention is that their doctor's attribution of the diminution of hair to Mrs. Newmark's use of wire brush curlers warrants an inference that such curlers were the original producing cause of her dermatitis. Such an inference is rather insubstantial in view of Mrs. Newmark's assertion that she never had any such condition before the solution was applied on the occasion in question, and in the absence of any testimony by Valante or any of defendants' beauticians who gave her waves for a long time before the injurious event, that her use of wire brush hair curlers had caused or would cause damage to her scalp or loss of hair. Moreover, plaintiffs' dermatologist acknowledged that wire brush curlers could cause breakage of hair but expressly denied that they could cause dermatitis.

Valante identified the permanent wave solution as "Candle Glow," a product of Helene Curtis. He said the liquid was mild but could damage a scalp which had scratches on it or could cause a sting if the solution were rubbed into the scalp. He applied the solution as it came from the original package or container, and his experience had shown that a tingling or burning sensation, the degree varying with different persons, was fairly common. The label on the package contained a caveat for the beauty operator. It said:

> "Always wear rubber gloves when giving a wave. Make sure patron's hair and scalp are in condition to receive a cold wave. Never brush or rub the scalp vigorously either before or after shampooing. If the scalp is excessively tender or shows evidence of sores or abrasions, the wave should not be given. Ask the patron her previous experience with cold waves to be sure she does not have a sensitivity to waving lotion."

Mrs. Newmark did not see this label, and there is nothing in the record to indicate Valante asked her about any previous experience with cold waves. It does appear, however, that she had four permanent waves without ill effects after the incident involved here and before trial of this case.

In dismissing the cause of action based on warranty, the trial court expressed the view that the transaction with Mrs. Newmark was not a sale within the contemplation of the Uniform Commercial Code, *N.J.S.A. 12A:2-106(1)*, but rather an agreement for the rendition of services. Therefore, it was not accompanied by any warranty of fitness of products used in rendering the services, and the liability of the beauty parlor was limited to the claim of negligence. Having in mind the nature of a permanent wave operation, we find that the distinction between a sale and the rendition of services is a highly artificial one. If the permanent wave lotion were sold to Mrs. Newmark by defendants for home consumption or application or to enable her to give herself the permanent wave, unquestionably an implied warranty of fitness for that purpose would have been an integral incident of the sale. Basically defendants argue that if, in addition to recommending the use of a lotion or other product and supplying it for use, they applied it, such fact (the application) would have the effect of lessening their liability to the patron by eliminating warranty and by limiting their responsibility to the issue of negligence. There is no just reason why it should. On the contrary by taking on the administration of the product in addition to recommending and supplying it, they might increase the scope of their liability, if the method of administration were improper (a result not suggested on this appeal because the jury found no negligence).

The transaction, in our judgment, is a hybrid partaking of incidents of a sale and a service. It is really partly the rendering of service, and partly the supplying of goods for a consideration. Accordingly, we agree with the Appellate Division that an implied warranty of fitness of the products used in giving the permanent wave exists with no less force than it would have in the case of a simple sale. Obviously in permanent wave operations the product is taken into consideration in fixing the price of the service. The no-separate-charge argument puts excessive emphasis on form and downgrades the overall substance of the transaction. If the beauty parlor operator bought and applied the permanent wave solution to her own hair and suffered injury thereby, her action in warranty or strict liability in tort (*Santor v. A. & M. Karagheusian, Inc., 44 N.J. 52, 64-65 (1965))* against the manufacturer-seller of the product clearly would be maintainable because the basic transaction would have arisen from a conventional type of sale It does not accord with logic to deny a similar right to a patron against the beauty parlor operator or the manufacturer when the purchase and sale were made in anticipation of and for the purpose of use of the product on the patron who would be charged for its use. Common sense demands that such patron be deemed a consumer as to both manufacturer and beauty parlor operator.

A beauty parlor operator in soliciting patronage assures the public that he or she possesses adequate knowledge and skill to do the things and to apply the solution necessary to produce the permanent wave in the hair of the customer. When a patron responds to the solicitation she does so confident that any product used in the shop has come from a reliable origin and can be trusted not to injure her. She places herself in the hands of the operator relying upon his or her expertise both in the selection of the products to be used on her and in the method of using them. The ministrations and the products employed on her are under the control and selection of the operator; the patron is a mere passive recipient.

Defendants suggest that there is no doctrinal basis for distinguishing the services rendered by a beauty parlor operator from those rendered by a dentist or a doctor, and that consequently the liability of all three should be tested by the same principles. On the contrary there is a vast difference in the relationships. The beautician is engaged in a commercial enterprise; the dentist and doctor in a profession. The former caters publicly not to a need but to a form of aesthetic convenience or luxury, involving the rendition of non-professional services and the application of products for which a charge is made. The dentist or doctor does not and cannot advertise for patients; the demand for his services stems from a felt necessity of the patient. In response to such a call the doctor, and to a somewhat lesser degree the dentist, exercises his best judgment in diagnosing the patient's ailment or disability, prescribing and sometimes furnishing medicines or other methods of treatment which he believes, and in some measure hopes, will relieve or cure the condition. His performance is not mechanical or routine because each patient requires individual study and formulation of an informed judgment as to the physical or mental disability or condition presented, and the course of treatment needed. Neither medicine nor dentistry is an exact science; there is no implied warranty of cure or relief. There is no representation of infallibility and such professional men should not be held to such a degree of perfection. There is no guaranty that the diagnosis is correct. Such men are not producers or sellers of property in any reasonably acceptable sense of the term. In a primary sense they furnish services in the form of an opinion of the patient's condition based upon their experienced analysis of the objective and subjective complaints, and in the form of recommended and, at times, personally administered medicines and treatment. Compare, *Gagne v. Bertran, 43 Cal. 2d 481, 275 P.2d 15 (1954).* Practitioners of such callings, licensed by the State to practice after years of study and preparation, must be deemed to have a special and essential role in our society, that of studying our physical and mental ills and ways to alleviate or cure them, and that of applying their knowledge, empirical judgment and skill in an effort to diagnose and then to relieve or to cure the ailment of a particular patient. Thus their paramount function—the essence of their function—ought to be regarded as the furnishing of opinions and services. Their unique status and the rendition of these *sui generis* services bear such a necessary and intimate relationship to public health and welfare that their obligation ought to be grounded and expressed in a duty to exercise reasonable competence and care toward their patients. In our judgment, the nature of the services, the utility of and the need for them, involving as they do, the health and even survival of many people, are so important to the general welfare as to outweigh in the poliiy scale any need for the imposition on dentists and doctors of the rules of strict liability in tort.

In arguing against strict liability in tort or liability under the Uniform Commercial Code for breach of implied warranty, defendants point out further that the permanent wave solution is bought from the manufacturer and applied to their patrons from the original package. Thus they say they have no greater opportunity to discover any injurious or defective quality than does the patron. But they occupy the status of retailers, and lack of opportunity to inspect the goods they supply to the publicly solicited customer does not relieve them of liability. 2 *Restatement, Torts 2d, supra,* §402*A, comment f, p.* 350. It has long been settled that retailers and those whose relationship with their patrons or consumers place them in that classification, are subject to a heavy burden of liability. The liability has been predicated upon breach of implied warranty of fitness or more recently in terms of strict liability in tort. As Chief Justice Traynor noted in *Vandermark, supra,* retailers are engaged in the distribution of goods to the public. They select the manufacturer whose products they wish to sell, and thus they become part of the overall producing and marketing enterprise that should bear the cost of injuries resulting from defective products. Moreover, from a practical standpoint the strict liability of the dealer may move him to put pressure on the manufacturer to make the products safe.

Accordingly, in light of all of the above, and particularly the testimony of the plaintiffs' dermatologist attributing the hair and scalp injury to the permanent wave solution, in our judgment a factual issue was presented at trial for jury determination as to (1) whether the permanent wave solution was defective, and (2) whether it was the proximate cause of the dermatitis. An affirmative answer by the jury would warrant a verdict for the plaintiffs. The judgment of the Appellate Division is affirmed for the reasons stated, and the cause is remanded for a new trial.

Case Questions

1. What color did the plaintiff's hair turn after use of the treatment product?
2. Did the court feel that licensed beauticians should be treated the same as doctors or dentists for purposes of standards of care under the UCC?
3. What warranty theory under the UCC was at issue in this case?
4. When a case such as this one is remanded, what does that mean?

References

Brown, L., *Out with the Old, In with the New?: Articles 2 and 2A of the Uniform Commercial Code: Panel 2: Article 2 and Revised Article 2, UETA & E-Sign-Contract Formation & Enforcement—What Law Governs a "Goods" Transaction?* 3 DePaul Bus. & Comm. L.J. 539 (2005).

Dubroff, H., *The Implied Covenant of Good Faith in Contract Interpretation and Gap-Filling: Reviling a Revered Relic,* 80 St. John's L. Rev. 559 (2006).

Effross, W.A., *The Legal Architecture of Virtual Stores: World Wide Web Sites and the Uniform Commercial Code,* 34 San Diego L. Rev. 1263 (1997).

Hymson, E.B. and J.A. Zavaletta, *Widgets to Windows: The "Webolution" of Commercial Sales,* 6 Comp. L. Rev. & Tech. J. 243 (2002).

Jentz, G.A., R.L. Miller & F.B. Cross, WEST'S BUSINESS LAW ALTERNATE EDITION (Thomson/West, 10th ed. 2007).

Kissman, L., *Revised Article 2 and Mixed Goods/Information Transactions: Implications for Courts,* 44 Santa Clara L. Rev. 561 (2004).

Owings, R., *UCC: Output Contracts and the Unreasonably Disproportionate Clause of Section 2-306,* 59 Mo. L. Rev. 1051 (1994).

Rusch, L.J., *Is the Saga of the Uniform Commercial Code Article 2 Revisions Over? A Brief Look at What the NCCUSL Finally Approved,* 6 Del. L. Rev. 41 (2003).

Twomey D.P. & Jennings, M.M., BUSINESS LAW: PRINCIPLES FOR TODAY'S COMMERCIAL ENVIRONMENT (Thomson/West, 2e, 2008).

Chapter 12

Shipping and Delivery Issues

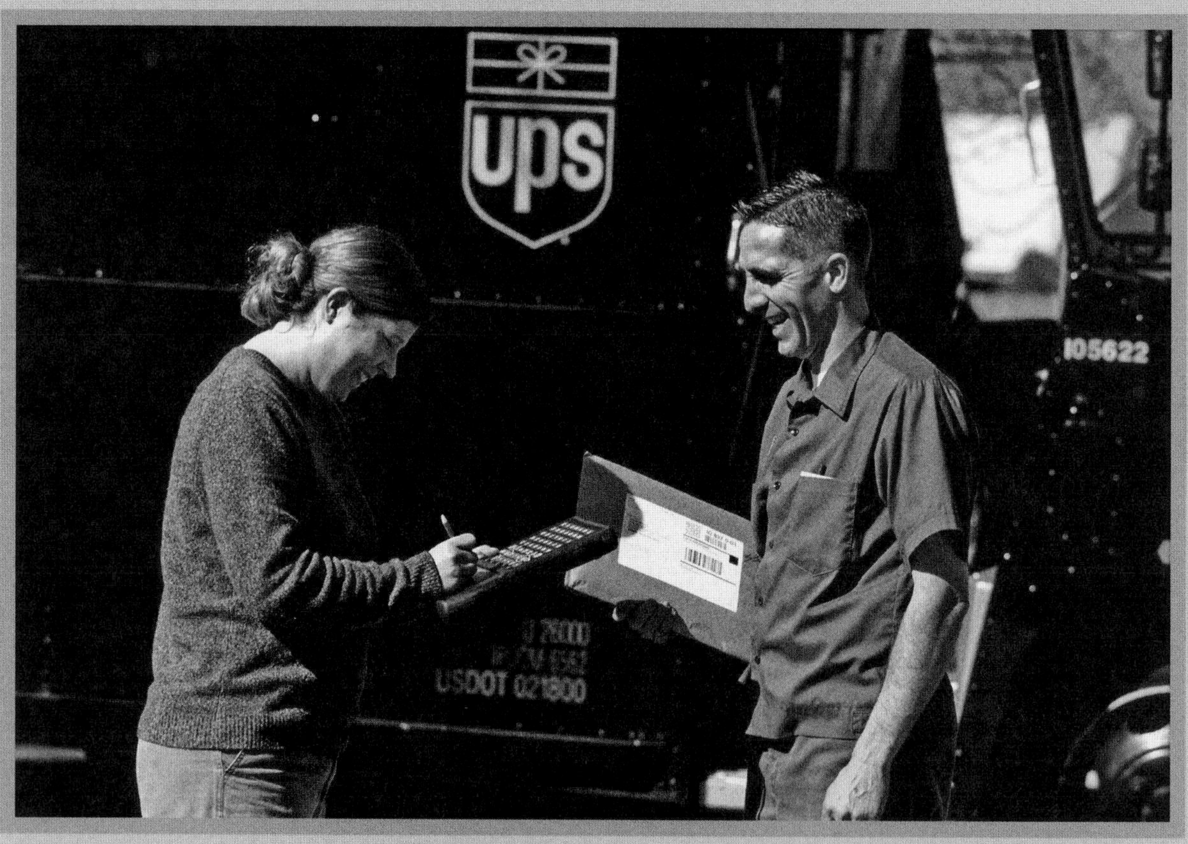

After reading this chapter you will be able to:

1. Discuss the concept of risk of loss and its relationship to shipping, delivery, and title.
2. Differentiate between a shipment contract and a destination contract.
3. Define the term bill of lading and discuss its importance in shipping contracts.
4. Discuss the term insurable interest.
5. Define the term bailment, and describe the bailment relationship.
6. Understand the difference between a sale or return and a sale on approval.
7. Explain what a consignment is and why it is important in commercial transactions.

Key Terms

Airbill
Bailee
Bailment
Bailor
Bill of lading
Carrier
CIF or C&F (cost, insurance, freight)
Consignee
Consignment sales
Consignor
Delivery
Delivery ex-ship
Existing goods
FAS (free alongside)
FOB (destination point; free on board; shipping point)
Future goods
Identification of goods
Insurable interest
Part of a larger mass
Recipient
Risk of loss
Sale on approval
Sale or return
Shipment contract
Shipper
Title
Warehouse receipt

This chapter addresses issues that may arise when delivering goods from one location to another. It also deals with who is responsible for the delivery along the way. The seller (sometimes referred to as the **shipper**) delivers goods by a **carrier** to the buyer (sometimes referred to as the **recipient**). When goods are shipped, usually the parties agree who is responsible for the entire delivery in advance. When it comes to who "owns" the goods, however, the UCC takes a somewhat different approach and instead focuses more on who is responsible for the goods along the way. Understanding the similarities between the concepts of bailment and consignment sales is important when considering the sale and delivery of goods as well.

DELIVERY

While the deterimination as to who owns the goods during a shipment is important under the UCC, it is less important than determining who is responsible for the goods along the way. This determination involves sellers, buyers, and possibly even third parties involved in a sales transaction. Since the delivery of goods by a carrier can cause all sorts of problems, including damage to the goods or delays in delivery due to natural disasters, the UCC focuses on snapshots in time which allocate responsibility for the goods during delivery and the respective rights between the parties themselves. The UCC considers three things as part of the **delivery** process involving goods:

1. Identification of the goods.
2. Risk of loss (damage).
3. Insurable interest.

GOODS

Under the UCC, **identification of goods** must be specified in the sales contract. One reason for this is so that the seller or buyer can obtain insurance on the goods to protect against a possible loss. When it comes to identifying the goods, they then fall into one of three categories.[1] Goods either "exist," or are "future goods" or are "part of a larger mass." **Existing goods** are tangible and moveable at the time of a sale.[2] This is not normally a problem since goods can be identified in various ways including, for example, product serial numbers, vehicle identification numbers (VIN), and so on. **Future goods** are interesting because these are goods that do not yet exist, but will. They are goods which are not yet existing or identified.[3] This includes unborn animals and crops to be harvested within 12 months, for example. The identification of these animals begins as soon as they are conceived. Identification of crops begin when they are planted or start to grow.

In relation to goods, the phrase **part of a larger mass** simply means, as an example, a case within a whole lot such as wheat, oil, or wine. Thus, if there are 1,000 boxes of the same wine, a lot of 100 boxes may be identified when they are separated or differentiated from the rest of the lot as a whole.[4]

RISK OF LOSS

Who assumes the responsibility for damage when goods are delivered is crucial in the UCC framework. This is known as the **risk of loss**. Under traditional property law concepts, one demonstrates ownership of goods by either possessing it or by evidencing **title** to the goods. UCC §2-401 says that title passes in any manner that the parties agree upon when the goods are physically delivered by the seller "unless otherwise explicitly agreed."[5] In the following types of contracts which are specifically mentioned in the UCC, goods are being moved (i.e., shipped) by a carrier.

SHIPMENT CONTRACT

According to the UCC, all contracts are presumed to be **shipment contracts** unless otherwise stated in a sales contract.[6] This means that title to the goods

[1] *See* UCC §2-105.

[2] *See* UCC §2-105.

[3] *See* UCC §2-105.

[4] There is an exception for goods characterized as "fungible goods" under UCC §2-105(4) in which title and risk of loss may still pass event though the goods have not yet been separated from the lot. Examples frequently cited fungible goods include specific grades of wine, oil, or wheat.

[5] *See* UCC §2-401(2).

[6] *See* UCC §2-504.

and the risk of loss passes to the buyer when the goods are given to a carrier such as a trucking company. This is often referred to as **FOB shipping point**.

DESTINATION CONTRACT

Under a **destination contract**, the title passes when the goods are actually delivered (i.e., "tendered") to the buyer wherever that may be at a designated point such as a physical location. This is often referred to as an **FOB destination point**. The buyer can then pick up and take delivery of the goods.[7]

TERMS FOR SHIPMENT CONTRACTS

Though the AUCC abolishes the following traditional shipping terms, the UCC uses them and they are very important to understand in modern commercial transactions and other logistics involving the delivery of goods:

1. **FOB (free on board):** FOB will always have a geographic location associated with it. FOB Flint, for example, would mean that when the goods get to the city of Flint, title to the goods *and* risk of loss switches to the buyer. Interestingly, the geographic point does not have to be where the goods are ultimately delivered.[8]
2. **FAS (free alongside):** FAS is more involved in shipping (water) contracts involving a vessel. Title passes when Carrier Ship A pulls literally next to Carrier Ship B.
3. **Delivery ex-ship:** This terminology is similar to FAS, but title does not pass until goods are literally leaving one ship for either the dock (quay) or the other ship.
4. **CIF or C&F (cost, insurance, freight):** The seller delivers goods to the carrier. The price of the goods normally includes a lump sum of cost of goods, plus insurance and/or freight (CIF). C&F obviously does not include insurance. These are essentially pricing terms.

BILL OF LADING

A **bill of lading** is a document of title that identifies the goods that are being carried by the carrier, displays who owns the goods, and describes when title transfers. A bill of lading is referred to as an **airbill** when goods are being transported by air. Similarly, a **warehouse receipt** is a bill of lading involving goods that are stored as opposed to goods that are being delivered. Bills of lading might utilize an abbreviation such as BOL or B/L.[9]

---

[7]*See* UCC §2-503(1). Also, note that when goods are held by the seller for the buyer to pick up, a document of title is not usually used.

[8]In some circles, the acronym FOB might sometimes be referred to as "freight on board."

[9]*See* UCC §2-509(2) for the situation involving risk of loss when the buyer is picking up the goods held by a bailee rather than a seller using the goods to be delivered to the buyer.

IMPERFECT TITLE

If the seller of goods is a thief (and therefore the goods are stolen goods), the title remains with the true owner since the seller's alleged title would be considered void from the very beginning. Similarly, if the goods are obtained fraudulently (e.g., by a bad check), the buyer would have title as long as they are a good faith purchaser and did not know that the goods were obtained fraudulently.

INSURABLE INTEREST

The only way insurance can be purchased on the goods is if there is an **insurable interest** over identifiable goods by a party who might have something to lose financially. The buyer obtains an insurable interest in goods when they are identified to the contract.[10] A seller retains an insurable interest in goods as long as title to the goods or a security interest is retained in them (UCC §2-501(2)).[11]

BAILMENT

The concept of **bailment** involves entrusting personal property or goods (sometimes referred to as chattels) to someone else. A bailment is not a sale or a gift, but it is a special relationship between parties. While it involves delivering goods, it does not involve the transfer of title. It only involves transferring possession of the goods, and therefore it is not normally a concern for the Uniform Commercial Code except when a seller (the **bailor**) delivers goods to a **bailee** for the buyer to pick up on their own. In this case, a document of title is used and is most likely to be the warehouse receipt. Who is responsible for the goods if they are damaged while bailed? It depends, but most often the bailee will be held responsible.

Bailor → Goods → Bailee (evidenced by a receipt of some sort)

Bailment often occurs with valet parking, dry cleaning clothes, and coat checks at restaurants.[12] A common example of a bailment ticket disclaimer for a sports event parking lot might look like this:

THIS CONTRACT LIMITS OUR LIABILITY SO PLEASE READ

Owner/Operator shall not be responsible and expressly does not assume any responsibility for loss or damage by fire, storm, theft, or accident to any person or vehicle, or for any loss or damage to articles left in vehicles. Only a license is granted hereby and no bailment is created in respect to any vehicle or its contents, on these premises. Articles left in vehicle are at owner's risk.

[10] *See* UCC §2-501.

[11] Security interests (secured transactions) are addressed in Article 9 of the UCC.

[12] For a thorough discussion of bailment issues in New York state, explore Garlock v. Multiple Parking Servs. Inc., 1980 N.Y. Misc. LEXIS 2228 (N.Y. City Ct. Jan. 15, 1980).

CONSIGNMENT

Consignment sales certainly are part of the Uniform Commercial Code and are quite similar to bailments. One major difference, however, is that the consignee (unlike the bailee) has the authority to sell the goods. The owner of the goods (**consignor**) delivers the goods to another (**consignee**) to sell or keep. While the goods are in possession of the consignee, the consignee actually holds title to them.[13] Consider sale of artwork, for example, in which a retail store often displays pictures and paintings from local artists for the customers to buy even though there is often no direct relationship between the sale of artwork and the retail store's business at hand.[14] In essence, a sale on consignment is considered a conditional sale. The two examples of conditional sales include the sale or return and the sale on approval.

SALE OR RETURN

A **sale or return** is a special type of conditional sale for the buyer (such as a local mini-mart) who intends to resell the goods to a customer. The buyer has the right to return the goods to the seller within a specified time to undo the "sale" and receive a full refund or credit of some sort, however. If the buyer does not return the goods within that time frame, then a sale is complete. Who risks damage to the goods in this situation? Well, when B receives the goods, risk passes to B until (if) B returns the goods to S. B retains an *option* to return some or all of the goods. This is essentially the same as a consignment sale and therefore the UCC treats them in the same manner.[15]

SALE ON APPROVAL

A **sale on approval** is not really a sale at first. It is a sale on a 'trial basis' only. It is more akin to a conditional offer. You see this on late night and weekend television advertisements. This is similar to a money-back guarantee.[16] Title and risk of loss remain with the seller until the buyer accepts (approves) the deal.

Sometimes it still might be unclear as to whether the deal is a sale or return or sale on approval. The UCC states that "if the goods are primarily for resale" then that is considered a sale or return.[17]

CHAPTER SUMMARY

The delivery of goods from point A to point B is crucial in today's commercial world. So, too, is determining who is responsible for the delivery at the points

[13] *See* UCC §2-326. Note that the AUCC moves consignments to Article 9, secured transactions.

[14] For example, a prominent local health club might display in its hallways artwork from local artists to be eligible to be purchased by the members. In this way, the health club does not have to buy paintings at all.

[15] *See* UCC §§2-326, 327.

[16] *See* UCC §2-326. Note that "sale or return" consignments have been moved to revised Article 9 under the AUCC.

[17] *See* UCC §§2-326, 327.

along the way. The UCC specifically addresses responsibility for delivery of the goods in terms of who is responsible for the risk of loss rather than ownership. Parties to a contract may always agree otherwise in their own contract, but the UCC provides for default provisions for shipping (and destination) contracts. Understanding the differences between FOB shipping point, destination point, FAS, and so on is important in the study of the UCC. The common law contract principle of bailment still exists today especially in special consignment relationships such as a sale or return or sale on approval involving goods.

Discussion and Review Questions

1. Why do you think the UCC concerns itself with who is responsible for the risk of loss of goods rather than the concept of ownership (i.e., title) of the goods?
2. What are the differences in the shipping terms FOB, FAS, ex-ship, and CIF?
3. What is the difference between a shipping contract and a destination contract?
4. Why are bills of lading important when goods are being delivered?
5. What is the difference between a bailment and a consignment sale under the UCC?
6. How is a sale or return and a sale on approval similar or different?

Critical Thinking Exercises

1. Henry owns a local gas station which also sells all sorts of food products and even magazines. Much of the goods on display inside the store are considered to be a sale or return. What products do you feel might fit into that category, assuming Henry's store is typical of local gas station/food stores? Why do you think that a distributor might require Henry to return unsold monthly magazines back for a store credit, but Henry must first rip the cover off of the magazine in order to do so?
2. Julie watches much late night television. Having received her paycheck for the week, she decides that she can afford the exercise equipment being sold on a cable channel at 2 A.M. She is very encouraged to purchase the product especially since she has a 30-day free trial and money back guarantee within the 30 days. What type of special conditional sale is this?
3. Why do you feel that in order for a seller or buyer to have an insurable interest that the goods must be identified or exist?
4. Why do you think that the AUCC has abolished the acronyms FOB and the like when such terms have become engrained in commercial transactions and will not go away quietly?

Online Research Exercises

1. Consider whether you believe that CD Baby, a Web site for independent music, is an example of a bailment or consignment, especially under the part in which the Web site will help you sell the CD. Visit http://www.cdbaby.com/.
2. See if you can find an example of a sale or return or sale on approval on the Internet.
3. Do you feel that parking your car in a parking lot constitutes a bailment, a consignment, or neither? Why? What circumstances would make it appear to be more akin to a bailment, if at all? *See* Garlock v. Multiple Parking Services, Inc., 1980 N.Y. Misc. LEXIS 2228 (N.Y. City Ct. Jan. 15, 1980).

CASE APPLICATIONS

Case

Consider how the California Court of Appeals addressed the issue of risk of loss and conditional sales involving the sale of clothes through a mail order sales company. Notice the impact of the phrase, "unless otherwise agreed" on the decision.

WILSON v. BRAWN OF CALIFORNIA, INC.

2005 CAL. APP. LEXIS 1393 (CAL. APP. 1ST DIST. DEC. 14, 2005)

STEIN, J.

The San Francisco Superior Court entered judgment against Brawn of California, Inc. (Brawn), a mail order company, ruling that Brawn had engaged in a deceptive business practice by charging its customers an "insurance fee" of $1.48 with every order placed. The ruling presumed that Brawn, rather than its customers, bears the loss of risk in transit, so that its customers received nothing of value in return for paying the fee. The court also awarded plaintiff litigation expenses in the amount of $24,699.21 and attorney fees in the amount of $422,982.50.

We reverse, concluding that Brawn did not bear the risk of loss of goods in transit under the applicable California Uniform Commercial Code sections discussed, *post*.

BACKGROUND

Brawn markets clothing through its catalogs and over the Internet. When a customer places an order, Brawn packages it, and holds it at its warehouse, where it is picked up by a common carrier and delivered to the customer, using an address provided by the customer. At all times relevant, the terms of Brawn's mail order form required the customer to pay the listed price for the goods purchased, plus a delivery fee and a $1.48 "insurance fee." As to the last, the form recited: "INSURANCE: Items Lost or Damaged in Transit Replaced Free." Brawn based the insurance fee on the costs to it of replacing any goods lost in transit, and Brawn did indeed replace, without further cost to the customer, any goods that had been lost in transit. Brawn rarely, if ever, sold its goods to a customer unwilling to pay the insurance fee.

On February 5, 2002, and again on February 7, 2002, plaintiff Jacq Wilson (plaintiff) purchased items from Brawn's catalogue, each time paying the insurance fee. On February 13, 2002, Wilson, acting on behalf of himself and all other similarly situated persons, brought suit against Brawn, contending that in charging the fee, Brawn violated the unfair competition law, *Business and Professions Code section 17200 et seq.*, prohibiting unfair competition, and *Business and Professions Code section 17500 et seq.*, prohibiting false advertising.

Plaintiff's suit was premised on the theory that by charging customers an insurance fee, Brawn suggested to them that they were paying for and receiving a special benefit—insurance against loss in transit—when in fact, customers did not need insurance against loss in transit because Brawn already was required to pay for that loss as a matter of law. The trial court agreed, finding that irrespective of the insurance fee, Brawn bore the risk of loss of goods in transit, reasoning that the fee was an "illusory" benefit. The court found that Brawn's customers were likely to be deceived by the insurance fee, and that Brawn therefore had engaged in a deceptive business practice, entitling its customers to restitution.

DISCUSSION

Neither party has cited any significant source of law concerning mail order sales or the risk of loss in mail order consumer sales, resting their contentions on provisions of the California Uniform Commercial Code. As the California Uniform Commercial Code, and the cases cited there, typically involve arm's-length sales between fairly sophisticated parties, the fit is not perfect. Nonetheless, there appears to be little legislation or case law specifically concerned with mail order sales or risk of loss in consumer sales contracts, and we, too, turn to the California Uniform Commercial Code's provisions.

California Uniform Commercial Code section 2509 sets forth the general rules for determining which party bears the risk of loss of goods in transit when there has been no breach of contract. *Subdivision (1) of section 2509* provides, as relevant: "(1) Where the contract requires or authorizes the seller to ship the goods by carrier [P] (a) If it does not require him to deliver them at a particular destination, the risk of loss passes to the buyer when the goods are duly delivered to the carrier . . . ; but [P] (b) If it does require him to deliver them at a particular destination and the goods are there duly tendered while in the possession of the carrier, the risk of loss passes to the buyer when the goods are there duly so tendered as to enable the buyer to take delivery."

Shipment Contract or Destination Contract

Official Code comment 5 to *Uniform Commercial Code section 2-503*, concerning the seller's manner of tendering delivery, explains: "[U]nder this Article the 'shipment' contract is regarded as the normal one and the 'destination' contract as the variant type. The seller is not obligated to deliver at a named destination and bear the concurrent risk of loss until arrival, unless he has specifically agreed so to deliver or the commercial understanding of the terms used by the parties contemplates such a delivery." Of course, a seller will have to provide the carrier with shipping instructions. It follows that a contract is not a destination contract simply because the seller places an address label on the package, or directs the carrier to "ship to" a particular destination. "Thus a 'ship to' term has no significance in determining whether a contract is a shipment or destination contract for risk of loss purposes." The point is illustrated in *La Casse v. Blaustein (1978) 93 Misc. 2d 572 [403 N.Y.S.2d 440]*, where the plaintiff, a student in Massachusetts, purchased 23 pocket calculators by telephone from a New York manufacturer. The method of shipment was left to the seller, but the plaintiff wrote a check to cover postage, and directed the seller to ship the goods to the plaintiff's residence. The court held: "Under the Uniform Commercial Code, the sales contract which provides for delivery to a carrier is considered the usual one and delivery to a particular destination to a buyer the variant or unusual one. In view of the foregoing, the request of the plaintiff's letter to ship to his residence is insufficient to convert the contract into one requiring delivery to a destination rather than one to a carrier. The request was nothing more than a shipping instruction and not of sufficient weight and solemnity as to convert the agreement into a destination contract."

In addition, although the risk of loss does not necessarily pass at the same time title to the goods passes, *California Uniform Commercial Code section 2401, subdivision (2)(a)*, provides that "[i]f the contract requires or authorizes the seller to send the goods to the buyer but does not require him to deliver them at [a] destination, title passes to the buyer at the time and place of shipment." This section, therefore, also distinguishes between the seller's obligation to deliver goods to a carrier, and the seller's obligation to deliver goods to the buyer.

It is not at all uncommon for a contract to shift the risk of loss to the buyer at the point at which the seller delivers the goods to a common carrier, while calling for the seller to pay for delivery and insurance. The California Uniform Commercial Code recognizes this type of contract in its provisions pertaining to the term "C.I.F." "The term C.I.F. means that the price includes in a lump sum the cost of the goods and the insurance and freight to the named destination." (*Cal. U. Com. Code, §2320, subd. (1)*.) Official comment 1 to the section explains that "[t]he C.I.F. contract is not a destination but a shipment contract with risk of subsequent loss or damage to the goods passing to the buyer upon shipment if the seller has properly performed all his obligations with respect to the goods. Delivery to the carrier is delivery to the buyer for purposes of risk and 'title.'" Official Code comment 5 to *Uniform Code section 2-503*, similarly, explains that a term requiring the seller to pay the freight or the cost of delivery is not to be interpreted as the equivalent of a term requiring the seller to deliver to the buyer or to an agreed destination. In a standard "C.I.F." contract, then, the buyer bears the risk of loss in transit even though the cost of insurance is rolled into the purchase price and is in fact paid by the seller. By breaking out the cost of insurance, and requiring the buyer to pay it, Brawn's mail order contracts even more clearly place the risk of loss in transit on the buyer.

Other evidence, while not determinative, is consistent with the conclusion that Brawn, at least, intended the contracts to be shipment contracts. Brawn's own insurance covers goods lost while in Brawn's possession, but does not cover goods destroyed or lost after the goods left Brawn's physical possession. Brawn pays California use tax, rather than sales tax, on the theory that the goods were "sold" when they left Brawn's place of business, located outside of California. Brawn records the revenue for the goods sold at the point of shipment, and removes the goods from its inventory at the time of shipment.

In sum, nothing in Brawn's conduct, and nothing in the delivery or insurance terms of Brawn's mail order forms, suggests that it was offering anything other than a standard, C.I.F.-type shipment contract, which the customers agreed to when they used Brawn's mail order form to purchase goods.

Sales on Approval

Plaintiff, however, contended, and the trial court agreed, that Brawn's mail order contracts were "sales on approval," where, as a general rule, the seller bears the risk of loss in transit. The contention was and is based on the provision that Brawn's customers are entitled to return any goods with which they are not satisfied for a refund of the purchase price or credit toward another purchase. Plaintiff also contended that the practice of allowing customers to return goods for a full refund is so common in the industry as to establish a trade usage, asserting that even if the written terms of Brawn's contracts establish that they are shipment contracts, the written terms must be modified by trade usage so as to make the contracts "sales on approval."

The legal support for the claim that Brawn's contracts are "sales on approval" is contained in *California Uniform Commercial Code sections 2326* and *2327*. *Section 2326, subdivision (1)* provides: "Unless otherwise agreed, if delivered goods may be returned by the buyer even though they conform to the contract, the transaction is [P] (a) A 'sale on approval' if the goods are delivered primarily for use, and [P] (b) A 'sale or return' if the goods are delivered primarily for resale." *California Uniform Commercial Code section 2327, subdivision (1)(a)* provides that unless otherwise agreed, under a sale on approval, "the risk of loss and the title do not pass to the buyer until acceptance."

The initial flaw in plaintiff's contention is that a "sale on approval" places the risk of loss in transit on the seller "unless otherwise agreed." Brawn's contract specifically and expressly calls for the buyer to pay for shipping and insurance, placing the risk of loss in transit on the buyer.

It also is well established that the express terms of the agreement control usage of trade. (*Cal. U. Com. Code, §2208, subd. (2).*) Therefore, even if plaintiffs established that most contracts in the trade are "sales on approval" (and they did not), the express terms of Brawn's contract control.

In any event, *California Uniform Commercial Code section 2326* is designed to distinguish between two forms of bailment, not to convert ordinary retail sales contracts into "sales on approval." The section addresses transactions where the parties intend the goods in question to continue to be the seller's property after the buyer takes possession of them. A common example is the consignment sale, where the buyer's responsibility is to sell the goods on behalf of the seller, or return them if they cannot be sold. Another example arises when the parties intend to postpone the change in ownership until sometime after delivery to allow the buyer an opportunity to decide whether or not to accept the goods. *Section 2326* provides a means of distinguishing between these kinds of transactions, explaining that a sale is "on approval" when the goods are intended for the buyer's own use, and is a "sale or return" when the goods are to be resold by the buyer. (*Id., subd. (1)(a) & (b).*) A "sale on approval" is a bailment that gives the purchaser the right to use and the option to purchase after a reasonable period of time.

One reason for distinguishing between these types of transactions involves the competing interests of the buyer's creditors and the seller. *California Uniform Commercial Code section 2326, subdivision (2)* provides: "Goods held on approval are not subject to the claims of the buyer's creditors until acceptance; goods held on sale or return are subject to such claims while in the buyer's possession." Under plaintiff's interpretation, then, Brawn retains an interest in any goods shipped to its customers, superior to the rights of the customers' creditors, until some time after shipment, when the customers signal their approval of the goods.

It also has been recognized that a common attribute of "sales on approval" is that the obligation to pay for the goods does not arise until the goods have been tested and approved by the buyer. In *Copy Service, Inc. v. Florida Copy Corp. (1988) 527 So. 2d 247*, a purchaser argued that the sale of a copy machine was a sale on approval because the seller agreed that it would adjust the copier to the customer's satisfaction or replace it with a new unit. The court rejected the argument. It reasoned that the contract's denomination as an "Equipment and Sales Contract,"and its recitation that the buyer entered an order for the equipment and agreed to pay cash for it, was "wholly inconsistent with a 'sale on approval' transaction."

While we are not prepared to say that a sale on approval *never* can occur when the buyer pays for the goods before shipment, we think that for such a purchase to be a sale on approval there must be some provision or objective fact demonstrating an intent that, notwithstanding that the buyer has paid for the goods, they do not "belong" to the buyer until the buyer approves them, so that the seller's rights in the goods are superior to the rights of the buyer's creditors until the approval period has passed. That Brawn, or any other retailer, permits a customer to return goods for a refund is a benefit to the customer, but does not in and of itself suggest that the parties intended the seller to retain an interest in the goods until sometime after they are delivered to the customer, and does not convert a routine sale with a right to return into a sale on approval.

CONCLUSION

The judgment is reversed. The order awarding litigation expenses and attorney fees is reversed. Brawn is awarded its costs on appeal.

Case Questions

1. Did Brawn ultimately bear the risk of loss in delivering goods?
2. How much did a customer have to pay as part of an "insurance fee"?
3. Why did the trial court rule in favor of Brawn originally?
4. Did the court hold that this contract was a sale on approval arrangement?

Exercise

Review the following complex consignment sales agreement. Prepare a basic agreement between a seller of a stationary bicycle and a retail store which specializes in selling used athletic equipment on a consignment basis to third parties.

CONSIGNMENT AGREEMENT

THIS AGREEMENT ("Agreement") is dated __________, 2005 by and between ________, with an address at _________________________ ("Consignor"), and _________________________, with an address at ____ ("Consignee").

Recitals

A. Consignor desires to sell or otherwise place for profit certain products identified on **Exhibit A** attached hereto as may be amended from time to time by the agreement of the parties (collectively, "Products"; and individually, "Product"); and

B. Consignor desires to deliver Products to Consignee as a consignee of the Products, and Consignee desires to accept the Products on a consignment basis for sale or other placement for profit.

THEREFORE, in consideration of the premises and the mutual covenants and agreements set forth herein, the receipt and sufficiency of which are hereby acknowledged, the parties agree as follows:

1. Consignment of Products. Promptly after execution hereof, Consignor shall deliver Products on consignment to Consignee at Consignee's premises located at (the "Premises") in the amounts specified on **Exhibit A** as the "Maximum Amount" for each Product. Consignee may, but shall not be required to, sell or otherwise place for profit the Products delivered to it hereunder (each such sale or other placement, a "Disposition") in any manner determined by Consignee, including, without limitation, separately or in connection with other products sold or otherwise placed for profit by Consignee, for cash or credit, for any price and upon any terms or documentation determined by Consignee. Consignor shall audit the location where the Products are stored at reasonable times mutually agreeable to the parties to determine the type and number of Products subject to Disposition during the immediately preceding calendar **[month][quarter]**. While on the Premises, Consignor shall comply at all times with Consignee's rules, regulations, policies and procedures. Consignor shall, promptly replenish any type of Product to its Maximum Amount after learning (through audit or notification from Consignee) that the quantity of any such Products is equal to or less than the amount specified on **Exhibit A** as the "Minimum Amount" for such Product.

2. Compensation; Payment. Consignee's compensation for each Disposition shall be equal to the balance of the price it obtains for the Disposition of such Products in excess of the amount specified on **Exhibit A** as the "Consignor's Portion of the Proceeds." Consignor will submit a correct and itemized invoice **[monthly][quarterly]** to Consignee specifying the Consignor's Portion of the Proceeds for all Dispositions made in the preceding calendar **[month][quarter]** and Consignee shall pay all undisputed amounts within sixty (60) days of receipt of the applicable invoice. Consignee may withhold payment of particular charges subject to a good faith dispute pending resolution thereof.

3. Term; Termination. The term of this Agreement shall commence upon the date hereof and shall continue thereafter until terminated in accordance with the provisions hereof. This Agreement may be terminated as follows: (a) by either party by delivering thirty (30) days prior written notice to the other party; or (b) by Consignor immediately and without prior notice if, Consignee files a voluntary petition in bankruptcy or petition seeking reorganization or an arrangement with the creditors; or files an answer admitting the material allegations of a petition against Consignee in any bankruptcy, reorganization or insolvency proceeding; or an order, judgment, or decree shall be entered (without Consignee's application or consent) by any court of competent jurisdiction approving a petition seeking reorganization of Consignee or appointing a receiver, trustee or liquidator of Consignee or of all or a substantial part of its assets, and such order, judgment, or decree shall continue unstayed and in effect for a period in excess of one hundred twenty (120) consecutive days (each, a "Bankruptcy Event").

4. Effect of Termination. Upon termination of this Agreement for any reason, Consignee shall, at its option, within thirty (30) days following the effective date of termination, either (a) make available for pick-up by Consignor or its designee, at a reasonable time, all Products previously delivered to Consignee hereunder but not Disposed of by it; or (b) purchase all Products previously delivered to it hereunder but not Disposed of by it for an amount equal to the amount specified on **Exhibit A** as the "Consignor's Portion of the Proceeds."

5. Delivery of, and Title to Products; Risk of Loss. Consignor shall deliver Products itself or select a common carrier to deliver Products to Consignee and shall pay all freight and transportation costs of such Products to the Premises FOB destination. CONSIGNOR SHALL RETAIN TITLE TO EACH PRODUCT AT ALL TIMES PRIOR TO THE DISPOSITION OF SUCH PRODUCT BY CONSIGNEE IN ACCORDANCE WITH THE TERMS HEREOF OR THE PURCHASE OF SUCH PRODUCT BY CONSIGNEE FROM CONSIGNOR.Except as otherwise expressly provided herein, Consignee shall, upon receiving possession of any Product, pay all further expenses incident thereto, including all expenses of handling, storage, selling and delivering the Product pursuant to any Disposition. Consignee shall bear all risk of loss of and damage to Products delivered to it hereunder. If any Product is lost, missing, stolen, destroyed or damaged while in the possession of Consignee, such occurrence shall be considered a Disposition hereunder and Consignee shall compensate Consignor in the amounts and at the time specified in Section 2 hereof.

6. Default. The following shall constitute a default under this Agreement: (a) Consignee's failure to remit payment to Consignor as required pursuant to Section 2 hereof, if such nonpayment continues for ten (10) business days after Consignee's receipt from Consignor of written notice of such nonpayment, (b) any representation or warranty made by either party shall be incorrect in any material respect as of the date made or either party shall fail or refuse to comply with any other covenant, agreement, term, or provision of this Agreement that is of a material nature and is required to be kept or performed by such party or to make reasonable provision for such compliance within thirty (30) days after such party's receipt from the other party of a written demand for the performance thereof; or (c) the occurrence of a Bankruptcy Event or an event occurs with respect to Consignor that would constitute a Bankruptcy Event if it had occurred with respect to Consignee. In the event of default, each party shall have all rights and remedies at law, in equity, or under applicable statute including, in the event of a default by Consignee, those rights and remedies of a secured party provided for pursuant to the Uniform Commercial Code.

7. Security Agreement. As security for all of Consignee's obligations under this Agreement, Consignee hereby grants, bargains, sells and coveys to Consignor a security interest in and lien upon any Product delivered to Consignee hereunder but not in any proceeds therefore. Upon the request of Consignor, Consignee shall execute such instruments and documents as Consignor may reasonably request to protect the rights of Consignor in the Products under applicable law. Consignee grants Consignor the right to file any financing statement or related document in appropriate governmental offices necessary to perfect or maintain perfection of the consignment and security interest granted herein. Consignee acknowledges that Consignor intends to obtain a first-priority security interest in the Products delivered to Consignee hereunder equivalent to a first-priority purchase money security interest in inventory and shall take all actions required by Consignor in connection therewith including, without limitation, notifying existing creditors of Consignee of such intent.

8. Taxes. Consignee shall collect and pay all sales, use and other taxes arising out of the Disposition of Products. Consignor shall pay all personal property or ad valorem taxes asssessed against, and other taxes relating in any way to, the Products.

9. Representations and Warranties. As of the date hereof and at all times during the term hereof, each party represents and warrants to the other party as follows: (a) it is duly organized, validly existing and in good standing under the laws of the state of its formation and any other state necessary to carry on its business as it is presently being conducted; (b) it has full power to enter into this Agreement and to satisfy its obligations hereunder; (c) the execution, delivery and performance of this Agreement and all other agreements, instruments and documents to be executed or delivered in connection herewith have been duly authorized by all necessary action; and (d) this Agreement has been duly executed and delivered by it and constitutes its legal, valid and binding obligation, enforceable against it in accordance with its terms.

10. Independent Contractor. Consignee is an independent contractor of Consignee. Nothing in this Agreement shall constitute or establish an agency, joint venture, partnership or other relationship between the parties.

11. Choice of Law; Jurisdiction; Jury Trial Waiver. This Agreement shall be governed in all respects by, and construed and enforced in accordance with, the laws of the State of ________, excluding conflicts-of-law principles. EACH OF CONSIGNOR AND CONSIGNEE HEREBY WAIVES ALL RIGHTS TO TRIAL BY JURY IN ANY LITIGATION ARISING UNDER THIS AGREEMENT OR REGARDING THE PRODUCTS. For purposes of any action or proceeding involving this Agreement, each party hereby expressly submits to the jurisdiction and venue of all federal and state courts located in the State of ________ and consent to be served with any process on paper by registered mail or by personal service within or without said state in accordance with applicable law, provided a reasonable time for appearance is allowed. All parties hereby waive, to the fullest extent it may effectively do so, the defense of an inconvenient forum to the maintenance of any such action or proceeding. Nothing in this paragraph shall affect the right of any party to serve legal process in any other manner permitted by law or affect the right of any party to bring any action or proceeding in the courts of any other jurisdiction.

12. General Provisions. All representations, warranties and agreements made herein by any of the parties hereto shall survive consummation of the transactions contemplated hereby. Neither this Agreement nor any term or provision hereof may be changed, modified, waived, discharged or terminated orally or in any manner other than by an instrument in writing, signed by the party against whom the enforcement of such change, modification, waiver, discharge or termination is sought. The provisions of this Agreement shall be severable and if any provision shall be invalid, void or unenforceable in whole or in part for any reason, the remaining provisions shall remain in full force and effect. Each party shall perform any further acts and execute and deliver any documents which may be reasonably necessary to carry out the provisions of this Agreement. The exhibits annexed hereto are incorporated herein by this reference and made a part hereof as if contained in the body of this Agreement. This Agreement has been drafted by Consignee's counsel as a convenience to the parties only and shall not, by reason of such action, be construed against Consignee or any other party. Consignor acknowledges and agrees that its has had full opportunity to review this Agreement and have had access to counsel of its choice to the extent it deems necessary in order to interpret the legal effect hereof. Whenever the expression "satisfactory to Consignee", "in Consignee's judgment" or similar words are used, or Consignee is granted the contractual or right to choose between alternatives or to express its opinion, the satisfaction, judgment, choices and opinions are to be made in

Consignee's sole and absolute discretion. This Agreement may be executed in any number of counterparts, which together shall constitute a single fully executed agreement. In no event shall Consignee's total aggregate liability to Consignor under this Agreement exceed the total amount paid and owing by Consignee to Consignor pursuant to Sections 2 and 4(b) hereof. This Agreement may not be assigned by either party without the other prior written consent of the other party, but shall be binding upon and shall inure to the benefit of the parties and their successors and permitted assigns, and no other person shall acquire or have any right under or by virtue of this Agreement. Any failure by either party at any time or from time to time to enforce and require the strict performance of any of the terms and conditions of this Agreement shall not constitute a waiver on that occasion and shall not constitute a waiver of the same or similar term or condition at any future time. All waivers must be in writing and signed by each party hereto. Any notice or other communication required or desired to be given shall be in writing and shall be sent by certified mail, return receipt requested, by a nationally recognized express courier service (such as FedEx) or personally served. Each such notice shall be deemed to be duly given when mailed upon deposit in any depository maintained by the United States Post Office, when deposited with a nationally recognized express courier service or when personally served. Each such notice shall be addressed to the parties at the addresses set forth on page one hereof or to any other address as may be specified by a party by a notice given as provided herein.

IN WITNESS WHEREOF, the parties have executed this Agreement as of the date shown on the first page hereof.

CONSIGNOR

By: ______________________________

Name: ______________________________

Title: ______________________________

CONSIGNEE

By: ______________________________

Name: ______________________________

Title: ______________________________

EXHIBIT A

PRODUCTS AND COMPENSATION

References

Bouley, S.E., *Where's the Beef? Allocating the Burden of Proof in Bailment Agreements Involving Missing Cattle Grazed on Public Rangeland: Cornia v. Wilcox*, 1996 Utah L. Rev. 1031 (1996).

Burns, J.W., *New Article 9 of the UCC: The Good, the Bad, and the Ugly*, 2002 U. Ill. L. Rev. 29 (2002).

Crowley, M.E., *The Uniqueness of Admiralty and Maritime Law: The Limited Scope of the Cargo Liability Regime Covering Carriage of Goods by Sea: The Multimodal Problem*, 79 Tul. L. Rev. 1461 (2005).

Darby Dickerson, A.D., *Bailor Beware: Limitations and Exclusions of Liability in Commercial Bailments*, 41 Vand. L. Rev. 129 (1988).

Donnelly, S.J.M. and M.A. Donnelly, *Survey: Commercial Law*, 49 Syracuse L. Rev. 271 (1999).

King, B.A., *Ships as Property: Maritime Transactions in State and Federal Law*, 79 Tul. L. Rev. 1259 (2005).

Rusch, L.J., *Is the Saga of the Uniform Commercial Code Article 2 Revisions Over? A Brief Look at What the NCCUSL Finally Approved*, 6 Del. L. Rev. 41 (2003).

Scott, K.J.L., *Bailment and Veterinary Malpractice: Doctrinal Exclusivity, or Not?* 55 Hastings L.J. 1009 (2004).

Walker, G.C., *Trade Usages and the CISG: Defending the Appropriateness of Incorporating Custom into International Commercial Contracts*, 24 J.L. & Com. 263 (2005).

Chapter 13

Performance of UCC Contracts

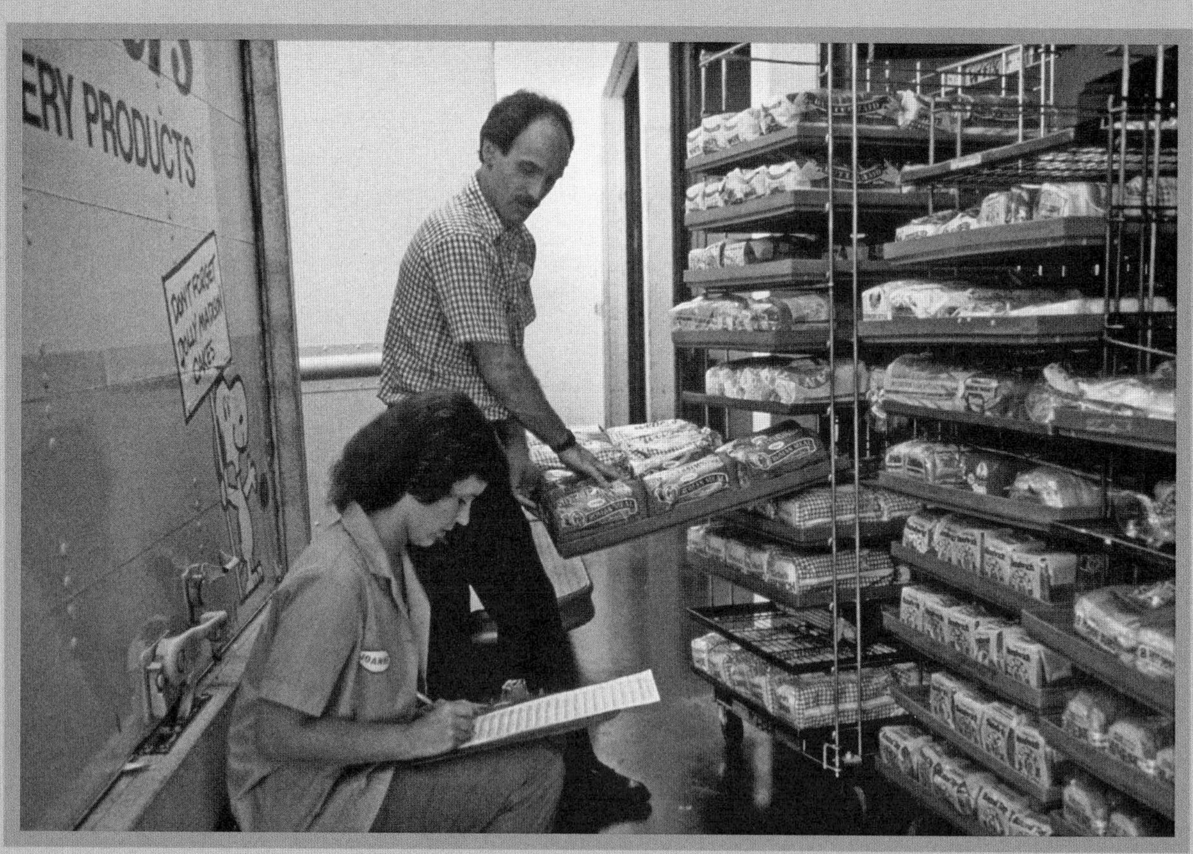

After reading this chapter you will be able to:

1. Discuss why performing a contract under the UCC is more flexible than common law contracts.
2. Describe the perfect tender rule and explain why it is (or is not) important in the study of contract law.
3. Explain the term "cure" in the context of contract law and the UCC.
4. Define the phrase "good faith" when it comes to the UCC.
5. Understand what an adequate assurance of performance is and why it is important in the study of the sale of goods.
6. Define and describe what an installment contract is.
7. Discuss the role of a letter of credit in a commercial transaction.

Key Terms

Account party
Adequate assurance of performance
Beneficiary
Commercially impracticable
Conforming goods
COD
Cooperate
Cure
Defects
Good faith
Issuer
Letter of credit
Nonconforming goods
Perfect tender rule
Substantially impair

As alluded to previously, when performing contracts that involve the UCC, the rigidity of the interpretation process and application of common law of contract principles does not necessarily apply. Under common law contract law principles, for example, a seller would have to deliver the exact goods in the exact manner in the exact order in the exact time. This was called the **perfect tender rule**. Under the UCC, though the seller still must transfer and deliver conforming goods as part of the tender of delivery, the UCC allows for opportunities to correct errors in the delivery process even if there was technically a breach of contract.[1] The payment for the goods can come in various ways. This chapter focuses on the performance and execution of sales contracts in the context of the UCC, including the obligations of the seller and buyer in a transaction. In the end, this chapter demonstrates how pro-commerce the UCC really is.

PERFECT TENDER RULE

The perfect tender rule does not necessarily exist today in the UCC environment because there are so many exceptions to the rule. This rule required that the seller's tender of delivery in a sales contract must conform *exactly* to the terms of the contract. **Conforming goods** meet the exact specification of the buyer's order. The UCC takes a different approach when the delivery is not exact. According to UCC §2-601, if the seller delivers goods that fail in any respect to the order, the buyer

[1]"Seller" may be interchangeably used with "lessor" if considering application of Article 2A (leases).

may accept the goods, reject the whole shipment, or accept part and reject part. These three alternatives are designed to promote commerce rather than promote litigation. It is also one of the hallmarks of how the UCC differs from common law contract principles. After all, if the goods failed to meet the specifications of the order in any respect, then common law black-letter contract law principles would hold that there was a breach of contract and one could immediately sue for the breach. In essence, then, the UCC creates exceptions to the perfect tender rule. These include:

1. *By agreement*: The parties can waive the breach if they so choose.
2. *By curing the defect(s)*: Though the UCC does not define the term **cure**, the UCC says that the seller may repair, adjust, or replace defective or nonconforming goods.[2]

The seller's right to cure any **defects** prevents the buyer from saying, "I just do not want them anymore." Still, many manufacturers or sellers will take the goods back as a matter of company policy and usually within a specified period of time after sale and delivery. A seller might even deliver **nonconforming goods** with a price reduction (allowance), and it is possible the buyer would accept the goods in their nonconforming condition. For example, if a buyer ordered 50 XL shirts and 25 L shirts, but the seller flip-flopped the quantity elements, it is still possible for the buyer to say, "Don't worry, I will take them anyway." Again, this promotes commerce and might even solidify future business relationships between the same two parties. Of course, if the buyer does not accept, then seller has the right to cure within a reasonable amount of time.

BUYER'S OBLIGATIONS

If the contract between the buyer and seller is unclear in terms of performance, the courts will then call upon the UCC to fill in the gaps. According to the UCC, the buyer owes a duty to the seller to accept and pay for conforming goods. However, the buyer generally has the right to inspect the goods before accepting and then paying for them.[3]

GOOD FAITH

All sales contracts require good faith between the seller and buyer. **Good faith** means honesty in fact. For a merchant, it means "honesty in fact *and* the observance of reasonable commercial standards of fair dealing in the trade."[4] Still, who decides what "good faith" means? A judge or jury will have to decide after the fact.

---

[2]*See* UCC §2-508.

[3]*See* UCC §2-513.

[4]*See* UCC §2-103(1)(b).

DUTY OF COOPERATION

Similar to one of the hallmark themes found throughout the UCC (i.e., good faith), the parties to a contract for the sale of goods must **cooperate.**[5] For example, if A and B contract to sell and deliver goods somewhere in Michigan, but the contract states, "at a destination to be agreed upon later," B must eventually tell A where exactly this location is. Again, while this may seem obvious by now, the UCC was designed to promote commerce not to frustrate it.

ADEQUATE ASSURANCE OF PERFORMANCE

If one of the parties believes the other party might breach the sales contract, the nonbreaching party may demand in writing an **adequate assurance of performance.**[6] If it is not given within a reasonable time (usually 30 days), then it can be considered an anticipatory repudiation and the nonbreaching party can suspend performance.[7] This is similar to a preemptive strike, but the idea is to get the parties to communicate with each other to resolve a potential dispute rather than just rush to the courthouse and ask for a remedy.

PLACE OF DELIVERY

When the seller delivers goods to the buyer (with or without a carrier), the goods must be delivered wherever the contract states or the buyer must pick them up at seller's place of business or residence. Commercial law presumes that shipments will be made in one delivery unless otherwise agreed. Recall the concepts of shipment contracts and destination contracts in the previous chapter. In a shipment contract, seller agrees to ship goods by a carrier. In a destination contract, the seller agrees to ship the goods at a particular destination.[8] Sometimes the seller and buyer will agree to deliver goods in installments involving a series of performances (lots). A buyer can only reject the entire contract if either the parties agree or one or more nonconforming installments **substantially impairs** the whole contract.[9] Again this is designed to promote commerce rather than litigation.

COMMERCIAL IMPRACTICABILITY

If an unforeseen occurrence happens that makes delivery **commercially impracticable**, or if a supervening event occurs that is not within the parties contemplation when they made the agreement, then performance of the contract may be

[5] *See* UCC §2-311.

[6] *See* UCC §2-609.

[7] *See* Chapter 8.

[8] Also, recall that the parties can always otherwise agree on delivery terms.

[9] *See* UCC §2-612.

excused. The seller must notify the buyer as soon as possible that there will be a delay or nondelivery (strike, war, terrorism, *force majeure*, etc.).[10] However, excusable reasons for not performing do not normally include recovery for increased costs due to inflation or increased costs due to market forces unless they are so extreme that neither party would have reasonably expected such possibilities.

PAYMENT

Unless otherwise agreed, the buyer must pay when goods are received. Sometimes seller requires cash on delivery (**COD**), and the buyer does not have the right to first inspect the goods.[11] Other times, the seller might accept credit (e.g., 30, 60, 90 days). Payment can be made by cash or any other method acceptable in the commercial world.[12] It is wise to purchase insurance to protect against the destruction of the goods if they are damaged en route or destroyed by fire, for example.

LETTERS OF CREDIT

Letters of credit usually exist when the parties have not done business together before or are just not familiar with each other's line of business.[13] A **letter of credit** is a commercial instrument drawn by a bank on behalf of one of its customers (known as an **account party**) to make payments or accept drafts drawn by a **beneficiary** when such beneficiary has complied with the stipulations contained in the letter. The seller may ask a bank for a letter of credit on behalf of the buyer. The bank is often referred to as the **issuer**.

CHAPTER SUMMARY

The goal of this chapter is to provide insight into the process of completing the performance of the UCC contract for the sale of goods. There are several exceptions to the perfect tender rule and the UCC was designed to promote commerce rather

[10]*See* UCC §2-615.

[11]*See* UCC §2-513(3).

[12]For example, consider payment terms of 2/10, net 30, in which the Buyer buys on credit and must pay it all in 30 days. However, the Buyer will also receive a 2 percent discount if it is paid within 10 days.

[13]*See* UCC Article 5. Letters of credit can be especially important in international transactions.

than litigation. Buyers and sellers have various obligations, and the UCC requires that the parties always act in good faith and cooperate with each other. If either the buyer or seller is concerned that the other party might not perform, it is appropriate to ask for an adequate assurance of performance in writing. There may be times when delivering goods is commercially impracticable. Parties that have not dealt with each other in the past might ask for a letter of credit.

Discussion and Review Questions

1. Why does the UCC allow for more flexibility than the perfect tender rule?
2. What is an adequate assurance of performance?
3. Define commercial impracticablity, and explain why it is important.
4. What is a letter of credit and why is it used?

Critical Thinking Exercises

1. Why do you believe that the UCC allows a buyer to accept nonconforming goods even though they do not meet the buyer's original expectations or specifications?
2. Why do you think that for deliveries made COD that the buyer may not inspect the goods prior to accepting them? Do you feel that COD payments are becoming a thing of the past? Why or why not?
3. Can you provide examples of contractual relationships involving the sale of goods which would require deliveries made in installments rather than in one lot.
4. Why do you feel that the perfect tender rule has so many exceptions to it?
5. Rachel and Alissa form a contract for the sale of Rachel's kitchen sink to Alissa. Rachel, the seller, does not have a place of business since she just started this in-home kitchen business. Assuming that Rachel and Alissa neglect to state anything about the delivery of the kitchen sink in the agreement, where should delivery of the kitchen sink normally take place according to the UCC?

Online Research Exercises

1. Find an example of a letter of credit online.
2. Find an example of a document of title online such as an airbill, bill of lading, or warehouse receipt.
3. In 2007, United Parcel Service (UPS) added a special feature allowing a sender to actually stop a deliver while in transit, for a small fee, known as UPS Delivery Intercept. Explore http://www.ups.com/content/us/en/resources/service/support/delivery_intercept.html.

CASE APPLICATIONS

Case

In this Michigan decision, consider how the Sixth Circuit Court of Appeals dealt with various contract performance issues, including the right to cure defects, installment contracts, breach of contract, the perfect tender rule, and even promissory estoppel.

STAR MACHINE v. FORD MOTOR CO.

1998 U.S. APP. LEXIS 15392 (6TH CIR. MICH. JULY 7, 1998)

PER CURIAM

Plaintiff-appellant Star Machine, Incorporated ("Star") brought a diversity action against defendant-appellee Ford Motor Company ("Ford") alleging breach of contract. The district court granted summary judgment in favor of Ford and Star filed this appeal. For the reasons that follow, we affirm the judgment of the district court.

Star designs and manufactures customized machines for manufacturing and assembly processes. In March 1990, Star, which had previously done work for Ford, was contacted by engineers at Ford's Sandusky, Ohio plastics facility to discuss the possibility of designing and building a fully automatic machine that would affix mass air flow sensors to air cleaner covers to be installed in Ford cars for the 1992 model year. Star was eventually awarded the contract to build the machine.

The contract specifications mandated that the machine have a "production rate of 700 assemblies per hour at 100% efficiency and reliability target of 85% to achieve 595 net yield." The machine also had to have a gross cyclic rate per station pallet of 5.1 seconds, and it had to operate at an air pressure of 60 PSIG (Pounds per Square Inch Gauge). The contract also required Star to purchase the torque guns for the machine from a company called Advanced Fastening Systems ("AFS"). When Ford officially awarded the project to Star on January 30, 1991, the parties agreed that July 8, 1991 was to be the date of delivery for the machine.

In accordance with the contract, Star purchased the torque guns for the machine from AFS. Star also decided to subcontract to AFS the design and manufacture of the individual stations on the machine where the torque guns would be mounted. Star did this because "of the delivery time" and the "complexity of the stations." Star's engineers were concerned from the outset about whether AFS would be able to design stations that met the necessary requirements. To simplify the project, engineers at AFS and Star decided to alter the design of the machine so that it operated at 80 PSIG.

For various reasons, including the need to lower the cycle time of the AFS torque gun stations, Star was unable to have the machine ready by the July deadline. This resulted in Ford having to purchase semi-automatic screw machines to begin assembly-line work that the Star machine was intended to perform. Ford also granted Star additional time to finish the machine and set "a firm delivery date of October 30, 1991." In the letter granting this extension, Ford stated that on October 30, following a run-off to test the adequacy of the system, it would do one of the following: "(1) sign-off and accept the machine; (2) terminate order based on breach of contract by Star; (3) allow Star to continue their efforts and consider means of compensating Ford for Star's inability to perform to their contractual agreements."

A run-off of Star's machine was performed towards the end of October and the machine again failed to satisfy the hourly assembly rates and cycle times specified in the contract. Ford employees visited with Star employees in November to discuss the problems with the machine that had to be fixed for the machine to meet the contract requirements. Once again, Ford granted Star additional time to cure the problems with the machine. During this time, most of Star's efforts focused on altering the AFS stations to make their cycle times meet the rates specified in the contract. On January 7, 1992, Star wrote Ford stating that they had performed a trial in which the machines "were run in automatic," as they had to be for the upcoming run-off, and that the trial showed that the hourly production rates and cycle times of the torque gun stations were now up to the specifications "in the purchase order." Star's letter recommended that the machine be "run off and implemented into the Ford Sandusky production facility." February 3, 1992 was set as the date for the machine's final run-off. Star, however, requested the run-off be delayed until February 10 and Ford agreed. Due to electrical problems at Star's plant, the run-off was not performed until February 11. Star concedes that its machine failed to meet the contract specifications at the February run-off. The record supports this conclusion. In a letter dated February 18, 1992, Ford confirmed to Star that its machine had failed to satisfy the contract specifications during the February run-off.

Ford further stated:

> To protect our production requirements during the delays on this system, we were forced to make other commitments to semi-automatically assemble the air cleaners. Ford Motor Company is unable to wait any longer for completion and accordingly we are terminating our purchase order with you for the machine.

Star eventually sued Ford, alleging that: (1) Ford breached its contract with Star by refusing "to accept the substantially completed Assembly System"; (2) Ford breached oral promises to pay for labor and materials related to development changes in the machine; and (3) Ford misrepresented its desire to obtain the machine after it had already decided it was going to produce the air cleaners with semi-automatic equipment and that Star was entitled to exemplary damages for this misrepresentation.

On appeal, Star raises five assignments of error, which it claims mandate reversing the district court's grant of summary judgment in favor of Ford. We hold that none of these arguments has any merit.

Star first argues that the district court failed to recognize that under the Michigan commercial code, Star had an absolute right to a reasonable amount of time to cure the defects in the machine after the February 1992 runoff. Furthermore, Star argues, after Ford's termination of the project in its February 1992 letter it was unnecessary for Star to actually provide perfect tender because Ford's termination of the project constituted a breach of the contract.

For purposes of Michigan's commercial code, the sales agreement between Star and Ford was not an installment contract. Rather, it was a single delivery contract to which the "perfect tender" rule applies. Section 2-601 of the MCLA provides that a buyer may reject a seller's tender "for any trivial defect, whether it be in the quality of the goods, the timing of performance, or the manner of delivery." However, Star is correct that this harsh rule is tempered by section 2-508 which grants the seller a right to cure an imperfect tender if he "seasonably notifies the buyer of the intent to do so, and either 1) the time for performance has not yet passed, or 2) the seller had reason to believe that the goods were in conformity with the contract."

Thus, it is clear that Ford had already given Star two chances to cure the defects in the machine. It is also clear that, under Michigan law, Star was not entitled to additional time to cure after the February run-off because the time for performance had passed and Star had no legitimate basis for believing at the time of the February run-off that its machine satisfied the required hourly production rates or cycle times. It does not matter whether the machine's performance is measured against the 595 gross units per hour production rate Star now claims it had to meet to satisfy the contract or the 700 gross units per hour rate stipulated in the purchase agreement. This is because even when the parts Ford rejected as unfit for various reasons and refused to count are counted as part of the hourly total the machine produced, Star's machine never operated at a rate greater than 502 units per hour. Star had its opportunity to cure the defects in the machine. It failed to do so. Under Michigan law, there is no basis for granting Star *ad infinitum* an opportunity to cure. Thus, the issue of whether Star was required to tender a conforming machine is moot.

Breach of Alleged Modifications to the Contract

We also find no merit in Star's contention that Ford first modified and then breached its contract with Star. Star claims that Ford altered the initial contract in two respects and then breached one of the altered terms. The first modification Ford allegedly made was requiring Star to subcontract to AFS construction of the stations into which the AFS torque guns would be placed. The second modification Ford allegedly made was authorizing these stations to operate at 80 PSIG. Star asserts that Ford breached this second modified term by refusing to allow the stations to operate at 80 PSIG during the February run-off.

In sum, the record belies Star's claim that Ford agreed to accept a machine that operated at 80 PSIG. Furthermore, the statements of Star's president and a Star engineer noted in the previous discussion of time to cure show that even if Ford did modify the contract to permit the torque gun stations to operate at 80 PSIG, there is no basis for finding that Star could have tendered a conforming machine that operated at 80 PSIG or any other air pressure level.

Promissory Estoppel

Star also argues that the district court improperly dismissed its claim of promissory estoppel. It claims the court erred because it did not recognize that Ford's alleged oral promises to pay for alterations to the machine constituted extra-contractual modifications under which Star could seek to be compensated despite the parties' express contract. For instance, the machine was altered to produce air cleaners for six car lines instead of the three car lines originally contemplated. This added an additional $143,985 to the contract price.

The general rule under Michigan law is that when parties have "an enforceable contract and merely dispute its terms, scope or effect, one party cannot recover for promissory estoppel and unjust enrichment." However, a party to a contract can bring a claim of promissory estoppel where it has "performed services not covered by the contract." The purchase order contract between Star and Ford contained a provision stating "additions and/or engineering changes requested by Buyer prior to completion of the Purchase Order will be negotiated based on rates submitted in Seller's letter." The contract also provided that if any changes were made, the "Buyer shall adjust purchase price. . . ." It is clear that the parties' contract did contemplate design changes to the machine. Therefore, Star cannot claim that it performed work not contemplated by the contract and, therefore, cannot seek quasi-contractual recovery based on promissory estoppel.

Furthermore, even if Star was deemed to have performed extra-contractual work, under Michigan law, promissory estoppel requires reasonable reliance. The parties' contract clearly indicates that any additions would be reflected in the final purchase price. Star does not cite, and independent review does not show, any basis for Star believing that the purchase price or any portion thereof, whether adjusted for design changes or not, would be forthcoming if they did not produce a machine that satisfied the requirements of the contract. Additionally, an unjust enrichment claim is untenable here because Ford has not received anything of value since Star is still in possession of the machine.

Miscellaneous Factual Disputes

Star also claims that several alleged factual disputes preclude summary judgment. These disputes involve: (1) whether the parties had the same understanding of the hourly production requirements for the machine under the terms of the contract; (2) whether Ford had agreed to allow the machine to operate at 80 PSIG; and (3) whether Ford sabotaged the February 1992 runoff.

As previously explained, any factual dispute about whether the parties had the same understanding of the hourly production rate requirements for the machine are immaterial because it is undisputed that the machine never operated near even the level at which Star claims it was required to operate. Likewise, the alleged factual dispute about whether Ford had agreed to allow the stations on the machine to operate at 80 PSIG has already been addressed. Nor does Star's allegation that Ford sabotaged the February 1992 runoff create a triable issue of fact.

Misrepresentation and Exemplary Damages

Star's last argument also fails. Star claims it is entitled to tort damages because Ford misrepresented to Star that Ford would accept the machine if it successfully completed the February run-off. According to Star, Ford had decided long before the February run-off that it would terminate its contract with Star and not accept the machine under any circumstances. Star claims that Ford's bad faith and misrepresentation of its willingness to accept a conforming machine at the February 1992 runoff is evidenced in a letter by Ford's Sandusky engineers to Ford purchasing in Michigan. The problem with this theory is that the letter of the Sandusky Engineers to Ford purchasing cannot rationally be viewed as a decision by Ford purchasing to abandon the project. The letter stated:

> It is our opinion that an estimated three to six months will be required for Star to resolve all the major issues. This situation is unacceptable to the Sandusky plant. . . . we are proceeding with the procurement of semi-automatic screw driving machines. Based on all of the above we are recommending that the company take the necessary actions to terminate the order based on breach of contract by Star.

Clearly, this was just the engineers' recommendation to the purchasing office to abandon the project. When it came to such matters, the engineers were clearly subordinate to the purchasing office and the engineers could not terminate the contract. Only the purchasing office could terminate the contract which it had entered into with Star. There is absolutely no evidence, however, that Ford purchasing decided to do so until its letter after the run-off dated February 18, 1992. Therefore, there is no triable issue of fact on Star's misrepresentation claim.

For the foregoing reasons, the judgment of the district court granting Ford summary judgment is **AFFIRMED**.

Case Questions

1. What does the phrase "diversity action" mean?
2. What was the original date that Star was actually to deliver the machine to Ford?
3. Who did Star subcontract with?
4. According to this court, how many chances did Ford give Star to cure the defects in the machine?
5. Do you believe that Star acted in good faith?

References

Krabacher, G.J., *Revocation of Tripartite Rolling Contracts: Finding a Remedy in the Twenty-first Century Usage of Trade*, 66 Ohio St. L.J. 397 (2005).

Jenkins, S.H., *Evolving Sales Law: Highlights of the Shifting Landscape of Arkansas Purchasing Law*, 57 Ark. L. Rev. 835 (2005).

Moses, M.L., *Letters of Credit and the Insolvent Applicant: A Recipe for Bad Faith Dishonor*, 57 Ala. L. Rev. 31 (2005).

Norwood, J.M., *A Summary of Statutory and Case Law Associated with Contracting in the Electronic Universe*, 4 DePaul Bus. & Comm. L.J. 415 (2006).

Schlechtriem, P., *Subsequent Performance and Delivery Deadlines-Avoidance of CISG Sales Contracts Due to Non-Conformity of the Goods*, 18 Pace Int'l. L. Rev. 83 (2006).

Chapter 14

UCC Remedies

After reading this chapter you will be able to:

1. Describe what a remedy is in commercial law.
2. Differentiate between buyer and seller remedies.
3. Describe the term "cover" and why it is important.
4. Explain what lemon laws are.
5. Discuss how a court might calculate damages for a breach of a sales contract.

Key Terms

AS IS	Lemon laws	Lost profits
Cover	Liquidated damages	Remedies

When a breach of contract occurs between a buyer and seller of goods, the aggrieved party often looks for **remedies** such as when a seller cures a defect in the delivery of a buyer's order as discussed in the previous chapter. The general purpose of remedies is to put the aggrieved party in as close to a position as if the other party had fully performed. Remember that under the UCC the parties could have agreed on remedies prior to a breach in their own contract.[1] When the parties agree to damages for breach of contract ahead of time these are referred to as **liquidated damages**.[2] Sellers and buyers can also agree to the exclusive remedies of the right to repair or replace the defective goods or parts (i.e., warranties provided by the seller). **Lost profits** (sometimes referred as consequential damages) may also be pursued as a result from a breach of contract. Still, claims for these damages will only be successful if they were reasonably foreseeable at the time the breach occurred. When the sale of goods involves a consumer, then various state consumer protection laws might come into play in terms of remedies as well. Ultimately the UCC provides for remedial actions for both sellers and buyers, all designed to be pro-commerce.

SELLER'S REMEDIES

The UCC provides a scheme for remedies for both sellers[3] and buyers.[4] When the goods that will be delivered are still in the possession of the seller, and the buyer breaches the contract, the seller may:

1. Cancel the contract and notify the buyer.
2. Withhold delivery of the goods if:
   a. Buyer wrongfully rejects or revokes acceptance.
   b. Buyer fails to pay.
   c. Buyer repudiates part of the contract.

---

[1]"Unless otherwise agreed. . . . "

[2]*See* UCC §2-718.

[3]*See* UCC §2-701–710.

[4]*See* UCC §2-711–717.

3. Resell or dispose of the goods (holding buyer liable for any loss).[5]
4. For unfinished (partly done) goods, seller can:
   a. Stop making the goods and scrap them.
   b. Complete manufacture and resell or dispose of the goods, holding the buyer responsible for any deficiency (contract price minus resale price) and incidental damages.

SELLER'S RESALE OF GOODS

For the resale of goods, the seller must give the buyer reasonable notice of the resale unless the goods are perishable and rapidly declining in value.[6] If the seller is unable to resell, the seller can pursue the original purchase price plus incidental costs. To determine damages, courts will normally take the contract price MINUS market price (i.e., fair market value) PLUS incidental costs. If this is not enough to put the seller in the position that he or she would have been in had the contract been performed, courts can consider lost profits and reasonable allowances for overhead and other expenses.[7]

When the goods are actually in transit and being delivered by a carrier (or bailee), but the buyer has not yet received the goods, the seller can actually stop the delivery to the buyer if the buyer has breached or confirms that it will breach the agreement. To stop the delivery, the seller must notify the carrier in a timely manner. Still, sellers generally cannot stop the delivery of the goods if the bill of lading has already been transferred to the buyer, the buyer obtains possession of the goods, the carrier stores the goods, or a bailee stores the goods for the buyer. When goods are already in the possession of the buyer and the buyer breaches the contract, the seller can sue for the entire purchase price (if they have paid nothing already) plus incidentals. Sellers can demand a return of the goods within a reasonable time.

BUYER'S REMEDIES

The buyer, of course, has a host of remedies as well when there is a breach of contract on the part of the seller.[8] For example, the buyer can:

1. Cancel the contract if Seller does not deliver the goods.
2. Reject the goods.
3. Obtain specific performance (i.e., an injunction) when a remedy at law is inadequate.
4. Cover with substituting goods. Still, this must be done in good faith and without unreasonable delay.

[5] *See* UCC §2-705, 706.
[6] *See* UCC §2-508.
[7] *See* UCC §2-708.
[8] *See* UCC §2-711–717.

5. Keep the conforming goods and reject the rest of the goods.
6. Recover other damages.

If buyer rejects the goods, seller must be notified "seasonably."[9] Remember, the seller still has the right to cure a defect in the delivery process according to the UCC.

COVER

The word **cover** in the context of the UCC applies to buyers of goods. It means the buying or leasing substitute goods for those that were due under the contract when the seller repudiates the contract, fails to deliver, or the buyer otherwise rightfully rejects the goods. Covering is similar to the mitigation of damages concept under common law contract principles. The buyer can then recover the difference between the contract price and the cover price, plus incidental and consequential damages, minus expenses saved.[10] Acceptance of goods by the buyer can be revoked if nonconformities are later discovered and they "substantially impair" the value of the lot.[11] In such an instance, a revocation is not effective until notice is given to the seller, however.

LEMON LAWS

While not specifically addressed in the UCC itself, looming in the background of all sales of goods are the various state **lemon laws** which are designed to protect consumers against unfair or deceptive practices by sellers of goods or services.[12] In terms of motor vehicles, the lemon laws can vary greatly, but if a car has a defect and it has not been remedied by the seller within a specified number of opportunities (such as three or four), the buyer may be entitled to their money back or a new car. This is the reason that sellers will often sell used cars **AS IS**, conspicuously displayed, as this waives all warranties that may have run with the sale. Lemon laws are one of the various consumer protection statutes that were developed by the state and federal governments beginning in the late 1970s.

CHAPTER SUMMARY

This chapter explored the remedies and damages associated with the breach of a commercial contract. Certainly the seller and buyer can always agree as to what the damages might be in the event of a breach (i.e., liquidated damages), but the UCC offers specific seller and buyer remedies as well. Though not clearly defined by the UCC, the term "cover" allows either the buyer to mitigate its damages during a

---

[9]The term "seasonably" is used throughout the UCC. *See* §2-508, 2-602, 605, 607, 608.

[10]*See* UCC §2-712, 713.

[11]The phrase "substantially impair" is used throughout the UCC as well as found in §2-608, 610, 612, 616.

[12]http://www.lemonhelpers.com/learn_about_lemon_laws.htm.

breach of contract situation. When dealing with consumer transactions, states have enacted lemon laws to deal with defective goods sold to the general public as a matter of consumer protection particularly with regard to motor vehicles.

Discussion and Review Questions

1. Compare and contrast the seller and buyer remedies in the UCC when a breach of contract occurs.
2. What is the concept of cover and why is it important in a commercial transaction?
3. Discuss why you feel lemon laws are important?
4. When it comes to remedies, do you see why the UCC continually references "unless otherwise agreed" by the parties? Why do you think this is so?

Critical Thinking Exercises

1. Tracie forms a written contract with Jim to have him build a new countertop in her home. Tracie, however, changes her mind and breaches the contract *before Jim can begin work* (and Jim has not even started to purchase materials yet). What remedy(ies) can Jim most probably seek in this instance?
2. Jason contracts to buy Todd's entire trading card collection (about 5,000 cards). Todd ships the cards to Jason exactly as stipulated in their agreement. Jason receives the cards and has no objection whatsoever. What are Todd's options if, however, Jason fails to pay for the delivery or even stops payment on the check he wrote to Todd?

Online Research Exercises

1. Compare state lemon laws: http://autopedia.com/html/HotLinks_Lemon.html.
2. Find examples of liquidated damages clauses in contracts found on the Internet.

CASE APPLICATIONS

Case

In the following state case, consider the role that the Michigan Consumer Protection Act played (or did not play) involving the sale of a truck.

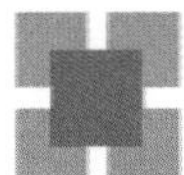

ZINE v. CHRYSLER CORP.

600 N.W.2D 384 (MICH. 1999)

WHITBECK, J.

Zine bought a new Dodge truck in May 1994. The Terrys bought a new Plymouth minivan in July 1995. Purchasers of an automobile in some states are entitled to receive information about their rights under their state's "lemon law." However, other states do not require the manufacturer to provide such information. Chrysler provides one booklet in each vehicle that contains information relevant to the lemon laws of those states that require the manufacturer to provide such information. It does not contain similar information relevant to the lemon laws of other states, such as Michigan, that do not require the manufacturer to provide such information. The booklet also contained a notice to all consumers, regardless of location. It provided in pertinent part:

> To ensure customer satisfaction, Chrysler Corporation and its dealers offer a Customer Arbitration Board which supplements the other Chrysler Corporation customer relations handling procedures. This Board is independent of both Chrysler Corporation and its dealers. The Board resolves complaints through arbitration. (ARBITRATION IS THE PROCESS BY WHICH TWO OR MORE PARTIES AUTHORIZE A THIRD PARTY OR PANEL TO RESOLVE THEIR DISPUTE.)
>
> We encourage you to discuss your problem with your dealer and the Chrysler Corporation Service and Parts Zone Office before filing a complaint with the Customer Arbitration Board. You do, however, have the right to take your problem directly to the Customer Arbitration Board, which will make a determination about your problem in a fair and equitable manner. . . .
>
> Chrysler's dispute settlement procedure does not take the place of any state or Federal legal remedies available to you. Whether or not you decide to submit your dispute to the Board, you are free to pursue other legal remedies.

After detailing the steps that should be followed to resolve a vehicle problem, the notice goes on to state:

> If you're unable to resolve your problem through these two steps, you may choose to contact the Chrysler Customer Arbitration Board (CAB) in your area. . . . This service is strictly voluntary, and you need not submit your problem to the CAB before taking other actions.
>
> NOTE: In some states, laws have been enacted that permit you to obtain a replacement vehicle or a refund of the vehicle purchase price under certain circumstances. The provisions of these laws vary from state to state. If allowed by state law in your state, Chrysler requires that you first provide us with a written notification of any service difficulty you may have experienced so that we may have an opportunity to make any needed repairs before you are eligible for remedies provided by these laws. In all other states, we request that you give us a written notice of any service difficulty. . . .

In February 1996, Zine filed a proposed class action, claiming that the various information documents—and in particular the lemon law booklet—that Chrysler supplied to its dealers for distribution to purchasers of new cars was misleading in that it "caused the probability that Plaintiffs would believe that the state of Michigan does not have a 'lemon law' and that the Chrysler Arbitration Board was or is their only remedy for defective Chrysler vehicles." As a result, according to the complaint, Chrysler "systematically refused to provide a repurchase or replacement . . . for defective vehicles," "Plaintiffs were led to forego seeking remedies pursuant to Michigan's Lemon Law," and "Plaintiffs were led to believe notice of the defect to the manufacturer was not a prerequisite to seeking redress." Zine alleged that such conduct constituted a violation of the MCPA.

In May 1996, the Terrys filed suit against Chrysler, claiming that their new car was defective and sought damages for breach of warranty (count I), breach of good faith (count III), violation of the Magnuson-Moss Warranty Act, *15 USC 2301 et seq.* (count IV), and violation of the MCPA (count VII). They also sought to revoke their acceptance of the vehicle and to compel Chrysler to take it back and refund the purchase price (count II). Count VII included the same allegations pleaded by Zine relative to the lemon law. The *Terry* case was assigned to the same trial court to which the *Zine* case was assigned, and the Terrys subsequently moved to consolidate their case with the *Zine* case. The trial court granted that motion in early October 1996.

In the meantime, in late June 1996, Chrysler filed a motion for summary disposition pursuant to *MCR 2.116(C)(10)* in the *Zine* case, asserting that the MCPA was inapplicable because Zine purchased his truck primarily for use in his business, that it was not required to provide information regarding the lemon law to Michigan car buyers and Zine received and ignored the lemon law information provided by the Secretary of State's office, that the information provided was not misleading, that any misleading information it did provide was not material to the sale of the vehicle because it related solely to the remedies available after sale, and that a claim under the MCPA must be predicated on affirmative representations rather than omissions. Zine responded that he purchased the truck primarily for personal use but sometimes used it for work, that Chrysler voluntarily undertook an obligation to provide information and therefore had to provide accurate information, that the information was misleading because it did not disclose information about Michigan's lemon law, that the documents were material because they were supplied at the time he took possession of the vehicle, and that a claim under the MCPA can be predicated on omissions of fact as well as misrepresentations of fact.

The trial court rejected Chrysler's claim that the MCPA did not apply because the evidence showed that, while Zine used his truck primarily for business, it was his only vehicle and was used for personal reasons as well. The trial court also rejected Chrysler's argument that any representations were not material to the sale because they related to remedies after the sale, they did not induce Zine to buy the truck, and Zine would have bought the truck with or without them. Finally, the trial court rejected Chrysler's argument that Zine could not have reasonably relied on any omissions because he received and ignored the lemon law information provided by the Secretary of State's office.

The MCPA prohibits the use of unfair, unconscionable, or deceptive methods, acts, or practices in the conduct of trade or commerce. *MCL 445.903(1)*; MSA 19.418(3)(1). It defines the term "trade or commerce" as "the conduct of a business providing goods, property, or service primarily for personal, family, or household purposes and includes the advertising, solicitation, offering for sale or rent, sale, lease, or distribution of a service or property, tangible or intangible, real, personal, or mixed, or any other article, or a business opportunity." *MCL 445.902(d)*; MSA 19.418(2)(d). The intent of the act is "to protect consumers in their purchases of goods which are primarily used for personal, family or household purposes."

The MCPA prohibits unfair, unconscionable, or deceptive methods, acts, or practices in the conduct of trade or commerce and defines such prohibited methods, acts, or practices to include the following:

> Causing a probability of confusion or of misunderstanding as to the legal rights, obligations, or remedies of a party to a transaction. [*MCL 445.903(1)(n)*; MSA 19.418(3)(1)(n).]
>
> Failing to reveal facts that are material to the transaction in light of representations of fact made in a positive manner. [*MCL 445.903(1)(cc)*; MSA 19.418(3)(1)(cc).]

The crux of Zine's claim is that Chrysler violated the above subsections of the MCPA by voluntarily undertaking to provide information about some states' lemon laws without disclosing the existence or terms of Michigan's lemon law. Some states require the manufacturer to provide information about their residents' rights under their lemon laws. Thus, Chrysler provided the booklet containing the requisite information pertaining to those states' laws. Michigan does not require the manufacturer to provide this information with the vehicle. Instead, it requires the Secretary of State to provide the information with the vehicle's certificate of title. *MCL 257.1408*; MSA 9.2705(8). The notice must provide substantially the following information:

> IMPORTANT: IF THIS VEHICLE IS DEFECTIVE YOU MAY BE ENTITLED UNDER STATE LAW TO REPLACEMENT OF IT OR A REFUND OF ITS PURCHASE PRICE. TO OBTAIN REPLACEMENT OR A REFUND YOU MUST FIRST REPORT THE DEFECT IN WRITING TO THE MANUFACTURER AND YOU MAY BE REQUIRED TO FIRST ARBITRATE THE DISPUTE.

The notice must also tell the consumer what to do to protect the consumer's rights under this law. *MCL 257.1408*; MSA 9.2705(8).

Motor vehicle manufacturers do not have a duty to provide lemon law information to Michigan consumers, and the MCPA does not impose any duty on them to do so. It provides only that, when such information is provided, it not be done in a misleading or confusing or otherwise deceptive manner. Clearly, had Chrysler not provided any information regarding lemon laws, it could not be charged with violating the MCPA. The trial court nevertheless found that defendant's failure to provide that information could violate the MCPA because it interpreted Chrysler's provision of the lemon law booklet as a voluntary assumption of the duty to provide lemon law information. We see at least two problems with this reasoning.

First, the trial court erroneously assumed that Chrysler had voluntarily assumed a duty it did not otherwise have. Chrysler did not undertake to provide any information about lemon laws to residents of Michigan or any other states in which it was not required to provide such information. It provided all consumers, including Michigan residents, with information about the company's arbitration procedure for settling disputes. It then went on to provide information to certain consumers about their rights under their states' lemon laws. Chrysler did this not because it was assuming a duty to provide information to residents of Michigan (or any other state) but because it was fulfilling a duty imposed by the laws of other states. It fulfilled this duty by printing one booklet for all states that had imposed such a duty and placing that booklet inside each vehicle so that, regardless of which state the vehicle was shipped to, Chrysler would have complied with the obligations imposed on it by that state.

Second, the voluntary assumption of a duty is a concept applicable to negligence law. To prove negligence, the plaintiff must first prove that the plaintiff was owed a particular duty by the defendant. "Duty is an obligation that the defendant has to the plaintiff to avoid negligent conduct." When a person voluntarily assumes a duty not otherwise imposed by law, "that person is required to perform it carefully, not omitting to do what an ordinarily prudent person would do in accomplishing the task."

Here, Zine did not claim that Chrysler was negligent, and therefore principles relating to the imposition of a duty for purposes of negligence liability have little application. The case cited by Zine, *Baker v Arbor Drugs, Inc, 215 Mich. App. 198; 544 N.W.2d 727 (1996)*, is distinguishable on that basis. Here, Zine's claim that Chrysler failed to include information applicable to Michigan residents in the lemon law booklet is predicated on an alleged duty to provide that information. Because Chrysler was not obligated to provide lemon law information to Michigan consumers and was not purporting to do so by providing that information to consumers in other states as required by law, the trial court erred in denying Chrysler's motion for summary disposition on this ground.

As noted, the MCPA prohibits unfair, unconscionable, or deceptive methods, acts, or practices in the conduct of trade or commerce and defines such prohibited methods, acts, or practices to include the following:

> Causing a probability of confusion or of misunderstanding as to the legal rights, obligations, or remedies of a party to a transaction. [*MCL 445.903(1)(n)*; MSA 19.418(3)(1)(n).]
>
> Failing to reveal a material fact, the omission of which tends to mislead or deceive the consumer, and which fact could not reasonably be known by the consumer. [*MCL 445.903(1)(s)*; MSA 19.418(3)(1)(s).]
>
> Failing to reveal facts that are material to the transaction in light of representations of fact made in a positive manner. [*MCL 445.903(1)(cc)*; MSA 19.418(3)(1)(cc).]

The warranty materials checklist provides spaces for the dealer to mark which items have been distributed to the buyer. One of those items is the "Consumer Law or 'Lemon Law' pamphlet for State of ——— (Refer to Owner's Rights Under State Lemon Law book)." That item was not checked on Zine's checklist, although Chrysler's omnibus lemon law booklet was in the truck. That booklet is entitled "Owner's Rights Under State Lemon Laws" and is described as a "supplement to owner's & warranty manuals." The warranty manual described the limited warranties on the vehicle and added the following statement:

NOTE: In some states, laws have been enacted that permit you to obtain a replacement vehicle or a refund of the vehicle purchase price under certain circumstances. The provisions of these laws vary from state to state. *If allowed by state law in your state, Chrysler requires that you first provide us with a written notification of any service difficulty you may have experienced so that we may have an opportunity to make any needed repairs before you are eligible for remedies provided by these laws.* In all other states, we request that you give us a written notice of any service difficulty. . . . [Emphasis in the original.]

This same note appears in the lemon law booklet. Because the note clearly states that written notice of problems is required by Chrysler if state law allows it to require written notice and that written notice is requested even if state law does not allow Chrysler to require written notice, we conclude that reasonable minds could not differ in concluding that the documents clearly made it known that written notice was to be given before seeking a replacement vehicle or refund of the purchase price.

The warranty manual indicates that some states have lemon laws, the provisions of which vary from state to state. The lemon law booklet says the same thing. It then goes on to provide certain information regarding certain states' lemon laws, but does not state that those laws are the only lemon laws in the country. Therefore, we find that the lemon law booklet was not misleading. Even if one could reasonably infer that the states omitted from the booklet did not have lemon laws, the fact that Michigan does have a lemon law should become known by any Michigan resident upon receipt of title to the vehicle. Because that normally occurs within weeks of purchase, it is the rare consumer who would not have knowledge of Michigan's lemon law by the time the consumer experienced so many problems with a vehicle as to have a claim under the law. Therefore, we observe that the allegedly misleading nature of the booklet would not, in most cases, be a proximate cause of any damages. Moreover, as noted above, because the omission was not a material fact, the misleading nature of the omission is irrelevant.

The common question here is whether the new car documents supplied by Chrysler violated the MCPA. Even if that question were to be resolved in plaintiffs' favor, the trial court would have to determine for each class member who had purchased a new vehicle whether the vehicle was bought primarily for personal, family, or household use, *MCL 257.1401(a)(i)*; MSA 9.2705(1)(a)(i), whether the plaintiff had a defective vehicle and reported the defect to the manufacturer or dealer, *MCL 257.1402*; MSA 9.2705(2), had the vehicle in for a reasonable number of repairs, *MCL 257.1403(1)*, (3); MSA 9.2705(3)(1), (3), was unaware of Michigan's lemon law, read the documents supplied by Chrysler, and was led to believe that Michigan did not have a lemon law, and chose not to pursue a remedy under the lemon law because of that belief. These factual inquiries, all of which were subject to only individualized proof, predominate over the one common question and would render the case unmanageable as a class action. Therefore, we hold that the trial court properly denied the motion for class certification on this ground as well.

We reverse the trial court's denial of Chrysler's motion for summary disposition and remand for further proceedings consistent with this opinion. We affirm the trial court's denial of class certification. We do not retain jurisdiction.

Case Questions

1. Did Chrysler try to show that Zine used his truck primarily for business or personal reasons? Why is this important?
2. Did the state of Michigan require that the manufacturer of a vehicle include (as part of the sale) the existence or terms of the state lemon law?
3. Did the court ultimately grant Zine's and the Terrys' class action status?

References

Barnes, D.W., and D. Zalesne, *A Unifying Theory of Contract Damage Rules,* 55 Syracuse L. Rev. 495 (2005).

Griffithe, M.R., *Computer Lemon Laws: An Evaluation of Existing Defective Computer Remedies and the Proposed Computer Lemon Act,* 27 S. Ill. U. L. J. 575 92003).

Lloyd, R.M., *Contract Damages in Tennessee,* 69 Tenn. L. Rev. 837 (2002).

Plass, S.A., *Bargain Avoidance in a Competitive Bargain Market: The Car Sales Conundrum,* 2 Wyo. L. Rev. 1 (2002).

Warren, D.A., *Car Trouble: Some Help for the Uninformed Buyer,* 66 Ohio St. L.J. 441 (2005).

Chapter 15

Warranties

After reading this chapter you will be able to:

1. Define the term warranty.
2. Describe why warranties are important in the sale of goods.
3. Understand the difference between express and implied warranties.
4. Define the phrase implied warranty of merchantability.
5. Explain the role of the Magnuson-Moss Warranty Act in consumer transactions.
6. Describe why disclaimers of warranties are so important in contract law and under the UCC.

Key Terms

Express warranty
Extended warranty
Full warranty
Implied warranty
Implied warranty of fitness for a particular purpose
Implied warranty of merchantability
Lien
Lifetime warranty
Limited warranty
Magnuson-Moss Warranty Act
Third parties
Warranty
Warranty of title

A **warranty** is an assurance by one party of the existence of a fact on which the other party to a transaction can rely. It is part of the seller's promise to the buyer related to the extent it stands behind its product. Warranties can come in various sorts depending on the nature of the transaction. In consumer transactions, for example, a warranty is a promise by the seller to repair or replace a product usually within a specific time frame, if necessary. There are three general warranties: warranty of title, express warranties, and implied warranties. Warranties provide a measure of confidence in a sales transaction that the goods will work for their intended purposes. Warranties impose more obligations on sellers than buyers and are a very important part of the UCC structure.[1]

TYPES OF WARRANTIES

WARRANTY OF TITLE

When a seller sells goods to a buyer, the **warranty of title** automatically passes to the buyer. If there was a **lien** on the goods, the buyer did not know it, and the goods are then repossessed, the buyer can sue the seller for breach of warranty. Of course, one can always disclaim the warranty of title if it is conspicuous. However, who would want to buy goods with that disclaimer attached?[2]

---

[1]Consistent with general contract law principles, warranties can be cumulative. For example, buying a new car may have "warranted to be free from defects for 36,000 or thirty-six months, whichever occurs first."

[2]*See* UCC §2-312. Consider, too, a sheriff's sale in which a buyer knows that the goods have been seized from another.

Express Warranty

An **express warranty** is an affirmative statement by the seller regarding the quality, condition, description, or performance potential of the goods. These warranties are often found in the seller's advertisements and brochures and can be oral or written. The words warranty or guarantee do not have to be used since any affirmation of fact or promise made by the seller will do.[3] However, statements of opinion do not create an express warranty. Rather, these are considered puffery or "puffing" language. Puffery is part of the sales pitch by salespersons though buyers might later allege that certain statements became a basis of the bargain between the seller and buyer. Consumer protection and tort laws might also be relevant if the buyer alleges that there was an intentionally misleading statement by the seller about the goods themselves.

Implied Warranty

Implied warranties naturally flow from the sales transaction between the buyer and seller regardless as to whether statements were actually made by the seller. The law, then, derives an inference from the nature of the transaction and imposes liability on the seller. The following implied warranties should be considered.

Implied Warranty of Merchantability

The **implied warranty of merchantability** automatically arises in every sale of goods made by a merchant.[4] It ultimately holds sellers more responsible than buyers when it comes to these commercial transactions. This warranty can be disclaimed, but the word "merchantability" must be used and it must be conspicuous.[5] Merchantable goods means that the goods must be "reasonably fit for the ordinary purposes for which such goods are used." In other words, the goods should work when the buyer purchases them and uses them for ordinary purposes. For example, when televisions are turned on, they should not explode. This applies to merchantable food, too, in the sense that the food must be fit to eat.[6] Many states prohibit the disclaimer of implied warranties in the sale of consumer goods.[7]

Implied Warranty of Fitness for a Particular Purpose

The **implied warranty of fitness for a particular purpose** is very unique and will depend on the nature of the facts of each case or circumstance.[8] This warranty comes into play if the seller knows the particular purpose for which a buyer will use the goods and knows that the buyer is relying on the seller's skill and judgment.[9] For example, if the buyer needs a particular type or quality of paint, tires, gun, computer,

---

[3] *See* UCC §2-313.

[4] *See* UCC §2-314.

[5] *See* UCC §2-316.

[6] *See* UCC §2-314.

[7] *See* UCC §2-719 for limitation of remedies. For an interesting case involving the UCC and the serving of food, see Webster v. Blue Ship Tea Room, Inc., 198 N.E.2d 309 (Mass. 1964).

[8] Sometimes just referred to as the implied warranty of fitness.

[9] *See* UCC §2-315. *See* http://www.law.cornell.edu/ucc/2/2-315.html.

and so on, and the seller was aware of this need, then an implied warranty of fitness for a particular purpose would certainly apply if the product was inappropriate for the intended purpose. Unlike the implied warranty of merchantability, the implied warranty of fitness for a particular purpose applies to *all* sellers—not just merchants.

Extended Warranty

An **extended warranty** is a warranty that a purchaser buys to extend the warranty of a product beyond the time limitation for the repair or replacing of the goods after the original date of sale. Even third parties such as retail stores offer extended warranties of their own on products that they sell on behalf of the various manufacturers.[10] Essentially the purchaser pays a premium at or near the time of sale as an insurance policy of sorts so that if the product needs repair after the warranty period then the seller or manufacturer must oblige. In exchange, sellers get extra cash up-front from the buyer.

THIRD PARTIES

It is often unclear whether **third parties** (aka "remote purchasers") who were not part of the original purchase but now use the product are covered under a manufacturer or seller's original warranty. There is just no clear-cut answer because there is sharp disagreement among the states. The UCC and the AUCC give three alternatives for which states can select (alternatives A, B, and C).[11] It is a worthwhile exercise to check your own state law.

MAGNUSON-MOSS WARRANTY ACT

Sometimes called the Federal Lemon Law, the **Magnuson-Moss Warranty Act** (1975) relates to consumer transactions and is enforced by the Federal Trade Comission (FTC).[12] It allows consumers to sue in state courts (and seek attorney fees).[13] Under this federal law, if a seller chooses to make an express warranty and the cost of the consumer goods is $10 or more, the warranty must be labeled or designated as "full" or "limited." If the goods cost $15 or more, the FTC says the warranty must be conspicuous, in a single document, and with specific information in "readily understood language."[14] A **full warranty** allows free repair or replacement of any defective part. If it cannot be repaired in a reasonable amount of time, the consumer can ask for a refund, too. A full warranty usually does not have a time

[10]Sometimes referred to as a service agreement (or service contract). Consider http://www.edmunds.com/apps/vdpcontainers/do/vdp/articleId=47681/pageNumber=1. Further, service agreements do not have to have the words "full" or "limited." *See* http://www.ftc.gov/bcp/conline/pubs/buspubs/warranty.htm.

[11]*See* UCC §2-318 (one of three alternatives is provided by the UCC for the individual states to adopt).

[12]15 U.S.C. §2301-2312. Note that virtually all states have their own consumer protection acts as well.

[13]An individual may actually file a claim in a federal district court if the amount in controversy exceeds $50,000 exclusive of interest and costs (§2310[d][3]). Still, no criminal sanctions are offered under this act, only civil remedies.

[14]15 U.S.C. §2302.

limitation. A **limited warranty** is anything other than a full warranty, and it must be conspicuous as well. A limited warranty usually has a time limitation associated with it. **Lifetime warranties** are less clear because it is unclear whether it is for the lifetime of the company, the lifetime of the product, or the lifetime of the purchaser! As a result of the Magnuson-Moss Warranty Act, most manufacturers will disclaim warranties of their goods or provide conspicuous limited warranties.

CHAPTER SUMMARY

Understanding what a warranty is and why it is important involving the sale of goods is vital in the study of the Uniform Commercial Code. Whether express warranties or implied warranties, the UCC imposes certain responsibilities on sellers or manufacturers of goods once they are placed into the stream of commerce. There are several types of warranties involved in the sale of goods including the implied warranty of merchantability, the implied warranty of fitness for a particular purpose, and express warranties. Whether these warranties apply to remote purchasers usually depends on particular state laws. Disclaimers allow sellers to limit or avoid warranties altogether as long as certain conditions are met. The Magnuson-Moss Warranty Act is essentially a federal version of state lemon laws. Manufacturers of goods usually offer full, limited, or lifetime warranties of their products as well.

Discussion and Review Questions

1. What is a warranty and why is it important in the sale of goods?
2. What is "puffing" language and why is it important?
3. What is the difference between the implied warranty of merchantability and the implied warranty of fitness for a particular purpose?
4. Why is the Magnuson-Moss Warranty Act important?
5. Are there any particular goods or industries most infamous for allegedly stretching the truth with regard to claims about their products as part of the art of the sale?

Critical Thinking Exercises

1. Why do you feel that in 2007 powertrain (engine and transmission) warranties were offered by Ford Motor Company (five years, 60,000 miles) and General Motors Corporation (five years or 100,000 miles)? The new warranties are also transferable (goes to new owner/remote purchaser). Formerly they had been three years, 36,000 miles. Note that as of the time of this writing Kia and Hyundai have 10 year, 100,000 miles, with conditions.
2. Some companies that sell products (or even services) are set up in a way that sellers get a commission off of a sale by another seller in their own market who was recruited by them and so on (in a pyramid structure). Often the products that are sold are fine and even have warranties that run with the sale, but the manner in which the organization is set up is often under scrutiny by state regulators. Consider whether your state laws regulate multilevel marketing (MLM) organizations and pyramid schemes as a matter of consumer protection. Common examples of MLM companies include Amway, Avon, Mary Kay Cosmetics, and Tupperware.
3. Consider whether the sale of music online could be a violation of state or federal law in the case of a multi-level (network)

marketing company. See, for example, the case of Burnlounge and allegations by the FTC that it violated consumer protection laws in its network marketing structure by overstating the amount of income one could make as an investor at http://www.thestate.com/426/story/86861.html *See also*, http://corp.burnlounge.com/default/press_articles/ftcFaq.html.

4. Which federal agency has primary responsibility for enforcing the Magnuson-Moss Warranty Act? Why do you feel that this agency (over others) is charged with enforcement at the federal level?

Online Research Exercises

1. Explore the Internet for examples of warranties, including the well-known lifetime warranty offered by Craftsmen™ tools.
2. Analyze the consumer protection statute of your state.
3. Note private organizations that provide consumer protection information such as bbb.org, Nasaa.org, and Nasd.com.
4. For a nice summary of the Magnuson-Moss Warranty Act, visit http://www.ftc.gov/bcp/conline/pubs/buspubs/warranty.htm.
5. The Federal Trade Commission is a federal agency in charge of many things including unfair or deceptive practices when it comes to labeling of products or services to consumers. Explore the Internet and see if you can find examples of where the FTC has had to intervene to order that a company either change its advertising or labeling practices, or discontinue the sale of the product entirely. For starters: http://consumeraffairs.com/news03/bodyflex.html.

CASE APPLICATIONS

Case

In this Sixth Circuit decision, note how the Magnuson-Moss Warranty Act came into play involving the sale of an automobile.

GOLDEN v. GORNO BROS., INC.

410 F.3D 879 (6TH CIR. 2005)

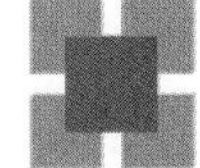

MILLS, District Judge

This case presents a question of first impression in this Circuit. Terrance Golden appeals from the district court's dismissal of his claim pursuant to the Magnuson-Moss Warranty Act, *15 U.S.C. §2301 et seq.*, and several state law claims arising from his purchase of a defective automobile from Gorno Bros., Inc. ("Gorno Ford"). The district court dismissed the Magnuson-Moss Warranty Act claim for lack of subject matter jurisdiction on the basis that it did not satisfy the amount in controversy requirement, and declined to exercise supplemental jurisdiction over the state law causes of action. We AFFIRM.

The sole basis of federal subject matter jurisdiction in this case was Terrance Golden's single claim pursuant to the Magnuson-Moss Warranty Act. In May 2001, Gorno Ford sold a new, customized Ford Mustang to Golden via a retail installment contract totaling $61,708.80, which included more than $14,000 in finance charges. The pre-tax purchase price of the vehicle was $42,903.41. Almost immediately, Golden had to return his Mustang for various repairs. In the five months immediately following the purchase, the vehicle was at Gorno Ford's repair facility for a total of 44 days.

The Ford Mustang began to exhibit obvious mechanical and design problems within one week of its purchase by Golden on May 21, 2001. On May 29, the Mustang was returned to Gorno Ford's repair facility for warranty repairs. The first set of repairs was completed on June 1. Six days later, Golden returned the vehicle to the repair facility for the same problems and other defects. This set of repairs was not completed until July 12, 2001. Gorno Ford had kept the vehicle for 36 days in order to service these defects under warranty.

The persistent problem was that the Mustang's serpentine belt and throttle cable rubbed against the insulation under the hood, causing a burning smell and a risk of fire. Even after the second set of repairs, these problems continued. On the same date that the Mustang was purportedly repaired a second time, July 12, 2001, Golden again returned the vehicle to Gorno Ford's repair facility to be repaired under warranty. On July 13, Gorno Ford replaced the serpentine belt.

According to Golden, the problems with the Mustang did not end. On October 1, 2001, Golden returned the vehicle to Gorno Ford for warranty repairs because it was leaking fuel. The following day, Gorno Ford repaired the Mustang's fuel injector. However, the vehicle continued to experience mechanical problems. On October 22, 2001, Golden's attorney wrote a "Last Chance" letter to former parties Ford Motor Company and Saleen Incorporated and to Gorno Ford.

On March 25, 2002, Golden returned the vehicle to Gorno Ford's repair facility for a fifth time, still hoping that the constant problems would be repaired under warranty. On this occasion, Gorno Ford replaced the entire front hood on the vehicle. This repair was completed on April 10, 2002; Gorno Ford therefore retained possession of the Mustang for more than two weeks. Golden attempted to drive the vehicle, but problems persisted with the cable, the belt, and the interior of the hood. Because of the burning odor and the constant problems with the Mustang, Golden was worried about the possibility of a fire. He determined that he could no longer risk driving a vehicle with such major defects.

Golden filed suit in the Eastern District of Michigan, asserting several claims against Gorno Ford. In addition to his Magnuson-Moss Warranty Act claim, Golden asserted several state law claims (alleging violations of the *Michigan Consumer Protection Act*, the *Michigan Lemon Law* and the *Michigan Motor Vehicle Finance Act*; and claims for breach of contract, breach of warranties, repudiation and revocation of acceptance).

The issue before the district court was whether the entire amount of the contract, including the finance charges, should be included in determining the amount in controversy. The district court entered an order dismissing Golden's action for failure to meet the $50,000 amount in controversy requirement of the Magnuson-Moss Warranty Act. This appeal followed.

The Magnuson-Moss Warranty Act provides that "a consumer who is damaged by the failure of a supplier, warrantor, or service contractor to comply with any obligation under this chapter, or under a written warranty, implied warranty, or service contract, may bring suit for damages and other legal and equitable relief." *15 U.S.C. §2310(d)(1)*. The Act provides for federal district court jurisdiction of certain claims. *See 15 U.S.C. §2310(d)(1)(B)*. However, the jurisdiction of such claims is subject to an amount in controversy requirement. The applicable portion of the Act provides, "No claim shall be cognizable in a suit brought under paragraph (1)(B) of this subsection . . . (B) if the amount in controversy is less than the sum or value of $50,000 (exclusive of interests and costs) computed on the basis of all claims to be determined in this suit." *15 U.S.C. §2310(d)(3)(B)*.

The district court determined that Golden's measure of damages under Michigan warranty law would be considerably less than the purchase price of the Mustang. It concluded, therefore, that he was unable to satisfy the $50,000 amount in controversy requirement of *section 2310(d)(3)(B)*.On appeal, Golden contends that the district court erred in failing to consider revocation of acceptance as an available remedy under the Magnuson-Moss Warranty Act and under Michigan law. He asserts that because revocation of acceptance is an available remedy under Michigan law for breach of warranty, it is therefore an available remedy under the Magnuson-Moss Warranty Act. Pursuant to this remedy, a plaintiff may cancel the entire contract. Accordingly, Golden alleges that the amount in controversy is the entire amount of the contract, including the finance charges. Therefore, he contends that the $50,000 amount in controversy requirement is easily satisfied.

Under certain conditions, Michigan law allows a consumer to revoke the acceptance of a good "whose nonconformity substantially impairs its value to him if he has accepted it." *See M.C.L. §440.2608(1)*. The revocation of acceptance can be based on "the reasonable assumption that its nonconformity would be cured and it has not been seasonably cured." *See M.C.L. §440.2608(1)(a)*. A buyer who revokes his acceptance of goods has the same rights and duties with respect to the goods as if he had rejected them. *See M.C.L. §440.2608(3)*. A buyer who justifiably revokes acceptance may recover as much of the price as has been paid. *See M.C.L. §440.2711(1)*.

How to calculate the amount in controversy in this situation is an issue of first impression in this Court. Recently, the Seventh Circuit addressed how the amount in controversy requirement of the Magnuson-Moss Warranty Act should be determined. *See Schimmer v. Jaguar Cars, Inc., 384 F.3d 402 (7th Cir. 2004).* In addition to his claim under the Magnuson-Moss Warranty Act, the plaintiff in *Schimmer* asserted several claims pursuant to Illinois law, including a claim for revocation of acceptance. The plaintiff had purchased a new 2000 Jaguar XK8, for which he paid $69,513.00 in cash. After encountering several problems which were not repaired to his satisfaction, the plaintiff attempted to revoke acceptance of the Jaguar. Following the defendant's refusal to accept his revocation of acceptance, the plaintiff filed suit in state court. The action was subsequently removed to federal court. *Id. at 403.* On appeal, the Seventh Circuit first considered whether removal to federal court was proper. Although the plaintiff's complaint in *Schimmer* prayed for a full refund of the $69,513.00 purchase price, the Seventh Circuit determined that the amount in controversy could not exceed $50,000. It concluded, therefore, that removal to federal court was improper. *Id. at 404–05.*

The Illinois statutes pertaining to revocation of acceptance contain the same language as do the Michigan statutes in the case *sub judice. See, e.g., 810 Ill. Comp. Stat. 5/2-608, 5/2-711(1); see also* 440 *M.C.L.* §*440.2608* and *440 M.C.L. §2711(1).* In *Schimmer*, the Seventh Circuit concluded that even if Illinois law allowed a full refund of the $69,513.00 purchase price, the amount in controversy would still be less than $50,000. That court explained:

> If the district court were to determine that Schimmer could revoke his acceptance of the car and receive a refund of the purchase price, then Jaguar would also be entitled to re-take possession of the car (now worth only $54,013.00, as explained below). In addition, Jaguar would also be entitled to a credit for the value Schimmer received from his use of the car while it was in his possession. Hence, Schimmer's true money damages—and concomitantly, the true amount in controversy—would equal only the difference between the price of the new car and the worth of the allegedly defective car, reduced by his beneficial use of the defective car. Jaguar could not lose $69,513, any more than Schimmer could gain that amount. We so held in a similar Magnuson-Moss case and calculated damages using the following formula: the price of a replacement vehicle, minus both the present value of the allegedly defective car and the value that the plaintiff received from the use of the allegedly defective car.

A review of the facts of this case and those of *Schimmer* shows that there is actually a stronger argument in favor of federal jurisdiction in *Schimmer*, on the basis that the cost of the vehicle in that case exceeded $50,000. Conversely, the pre-tax purchase price of the Mustang in this case was significantly below the amount required for federal jurisdiction. Golden's argument that the amount in controversy is satisfied depends on adding the interest over the life of the loan to the purchase price. Accordingly, Golden would not dispute that if he had paid cash for the vehicle (like the buyer in *Schimmer*), the amount in controversy would be less than $50,000 and federal subject matter jurisdiction would be lacking. As Gorno Ford notes, it was never entitled to anything more than the $42,903.41 that it received. Certainly, the question of whether federal jurisdiction exists under the Magnuson-Moss Warranty Act should not be determined by whether a finance contract was used in purchasing an automobile. This is particularly true since the Act provides that the amount in controversy does not include interest.

In discussing the amount in controversy requirement of the Magnuson-Moss Warranty Act, the Third Circuit has used the same reasoning as that employed by the Seventh Circuit. *See Samuel-Bassett v. KIA Motors America, Inc., 357 F.3d 392, 402 (3d Cir. 2004).* Quoting *Voelker, 353 F.3d at 521,* that court noted the rule that "the party asserting federal jurisdiction must allege the cost of the replacement vehicle, minus both the present value of the allegedly defective vehicle and the value that the plaintiff received from the allegedly defective vehicle." *Id.* The Third Circuit further stated, "The facts in that Magnuson-Moss case differ from those presented here, but the requirements of allowance for usage and establishing the difference in value, rather than simply the purchase price are the same." *Id.*

According to Golden, the Sixth Circuit case which is most directly on point to this case is *Rosen v. Chrysler Corp., 205 F.3d 918 (6th Cir. 2000).* In *Rosen*, the plaintiff sought rescission of a purchase contract under several theories pursuant to New Jersey law; it did not involve the Magnuson-Moss Warranty Act. The asserted basis for jurisdiction was diversity of citizenship. *See id. at 920.* This Court noted the general rule in diversity cases "that the amount claimed by a plaintiff in his complaint determines that amount in controversy, unless it appears to a legal certainty that the claim is for less than the jurisdictional amount." The Court stated, "Contrary to the reasoning articulated by the District Court, however, in cases where a plaintiff seeks to rescind a contract, the contract's entire value, without offset, is the amount in controversy." It determined, therefore, that the district court erred in offsetting the plaintiff's rescission claim by the resale value of the vehicle. The amount in controversy was the full contract price of almost $30,000. Because revocation of acceptance is similar to rescission, Golden contends that the same analysis should apply to this case and that we should find, therefore, that the amount in controversy is the total contract price of almost $62,000.

We are not persuaded by Golden's argument. Golden contends that there is no reason why a case involving rescission should be analyzed differently than one involving revocation of acceptance. However, this Court in *Rosen* relies in part on *Jadair, Inc. v. Walt Keeler Co., 679 F.2d 131, 133 n.5 (7th Cir. 1982)* for the proposition that the contract's entire value, without offset, is the amount in controversy in a diversity case when a plaintiff seeks rescission. Based on the damages formula in *Schimmer, 384 F.3d at 405-06*, and *Gardynski-Leschuck, 142 F.3d at 957*, and given that *Jadair, Inc.* has not been overruled, it is clear that the Seventh Circuit does not determine the amount in controversy in rescission cases in the same manner as it does in cases involving revocation of acceptance. We agree with the analysis of the Seventh Circuit. Even if Golden is entitled to a refund of the full contract price upon revocation of acceptance, therefore, it does not follow that the amount in controversy requirement has been satisfied.

Golden also relies on *Roberts v. Chandaleur Homes, Inc., 237 F. Supp. 2d 696 (S.D. Miss. 2002)*, in support of his argument that this Court should find that the amount in controversy is the full value of the contract, including the finance charges to be paid over the life of the loan. In *Roberts*, the plaintiffs purchased a defective mobile home and sought rescission of the purchase agreement. Pursuant to the agreement, the amount financed to purchase the mobile home was $30,496.00; the total payments, including interest, required under the agreement were in excess of $120,000. *See id. at 697*. The district court concluded that the amount in controversy was satisfied under the Magnuson-Moss Warranty Act. It also determined that the $75,000 diversity of citizenship amount in controversy requirement had been met. *Id. at 699*. In determining that the amounts in controversy had been satisfied, that court reasoned that the pecuniary consequences on the litigants was in excess of $120,000. *Id. at 698–99*. We decline to follow the reasoning of the district court in *Roberts*.

We conclude that this Court should follow the reasoning of the Third and Seventh Circuits when determining the amount in controversy under the Magnuson-Moss Warranty Act. The finance charges of a contract should not be added when determining if the amount in controversy has been satisfied. Pursuant to that analysis, the amount in controversy here would be calculated by determining the difference between the cost of a replacement vehicle ($42,903.41) and the present value of the Mustang ($25,000). The resulting figure of $17,903.41 would be further reduced by the value that Golden obtained from the Mustang. Even if this amount were $0.00, the most that he could recover and that Gorno Ford could lose would be $17,903.41. Accordingly, the amount in controversy is that amount or a lower figure.

CONCLUSION

Even assuming that Golden continues to make payments on the $61,708.80 contract, the amount in controversy would be further reduced by $25,000 because Gorno Ford would be entitled to the Mustang upon the cancellation of the contract. The district court determined that the vehicle was worth that amount, and that finding has not been contested. Thus, the amount in controversy would not exceed $50,000 even if the finance charges are included in the calculation. Because the amount in controversy between the parties is less than $50,000, this Court lacks jurisdiction under the Magnuson-Moss Warranty Act. We **AFFIRM**.

Case Questions

1. What type of vehicle was at issue in this case?
2. How many times did Golden have to bring his vehicle in for repair before he filed a lawsuit?
3. What was the minimum dollar amount in controversy that Golden had to overcome in order to get his case heard by a federal court?
4. Did this court ultimately grant jurisdiction in this case?

Exercise

Read this excerpt from the Michigan Consumer Protection Act which was originally enacted in the mid 1970s. Notice the variety of concerns related to protecting consumers from unfair or deceptive practices and acts. Should this act be updated due to consumer protection issues related to the Internet? How is your state's law similar or different?

445.903 Unfair, Unconscionable, or Deceptive Methods, Acts, or Practices in Conduct of Trade or Commerce; Rules; Applicability of Subsection (1)(hh).

Sec. 3.

(1) Unfair, unconscionable, or deceptive methods, acts, or practices in the conduct of trade or commerce are unlawful and are defined as follows:

(a) Causing a probability of confusion or misunderstanding as to the source, sponsorship, approval, or certification of goods or services.

(b) Using deceptive representations or deceptive designations of geographic origin in connection with goods or services.

(c) Representing that goods or services have sponsorship, approval, characteristics, ingredients, uses, benefits, or quantities that they do not have or that a person has sponsorship, approval, status, affiliation, or connection that he or she does not have.

(d) Representing that goods are new if they are deteriorated, altered, reconditioned, used, or secondhand.

(e) Representing that goods or services are of a particular standard, quality, or grade, or that goods are of a particular style or model, if they are of another.

(f) Disparaging the goods, services, business, or reputation of another by false or misleading representation of fact.

(g) Advertising or representing goods or services with intent not to dispose of those goods or services as advertised or represented.

(h) Advertising goods or services with intent not to supply reasonably expectable public demand, unless the advertisement discloses a limitation of quantity in immediate conjunction with the advertised goods or services.

(i) Making false or misleading statements of fact concerning the reasons for, existence of, or amounts of price reductions.

(j) Representing that a part, replacement, or repair service is needed when it is not.

(k) Representing to a party to whom goods or services are supplied that the goods or services are being supplied in response to a request made by or on behalf of the party, when they are not.

(l) Misrepresenting that because of some defect in a consumer's home the health, safety, or lives of the consumer or his or her family are in danger if the product or services are not purchased, when in fact the defect does not exist or the product or services would not remove the danger.

(m) Causing a probability of confusion or of misunderstanding with respect to the authority of a salesperson, representative, or agent to negotiate the final terms of a transaction.

(n) Causing a probability of confusion or of misunderstanding as to the legal rights, obligations, or remedies of a party to a transaction.

(o) Causing a probability of confusion or of misunderstanding as to the terms or conditions of credit if credit is extended in a transaction.

(p) Disclaiming or limiting the implied warranty of merchantability and fitness for use, unless a disclaimer is clearly and conspicuously disclosed.

(q) Representing or implying that the subject of a consumer transaction will be provided promptly, or at a specified time, or within a reasonable time, if the merchant knows or has reason to know it will not be so provided.

(r) Representing that a consumer will receive goods or services "free" or "without charge", or using words of similar import in the representation, without clearly and conspicuously disclosing with equal prominence in immediate conjunction with the use of those words the conditions, terms, or prerequisites to the use or retention of the goods or services advertised.

(s) Failing to reveal a material fact, the omission of which tends to mislead or deceive the consumer, and which fact could not reasonably be known by the consumer.

(t) Entering into a consumer transaction in which the consumer waives or purports to waive a right, benefit, or immunity provided by law, unless the waiver is clearly stated and the consumer has specifically consented to it.

(u) Failing, in a consumer transaction that is rescinded, canceled, or otherwise terminated in accordance with the terms of an agreement, advertisement, representation, or provision of law, to promptly restore to the person or persons entitled to it a deposit, down payment, or other payment, or in the case of property traded in but not available, the greater of the agreed value or the fair market value of the property, or to cancel within a specified time or an otherwise reasonable time an acquired security interest.

(v) Taking or arranging for the consumer to sign an acknowledgment, certificate, or other writing affirming acceptance, delivery, compliance with a requirement of law, or other performance, if the merchant knows or has reason to know that the statement is not true.

(w) Representing that a consumer will receive a rebate, discount, or other benefit as an inducement for entering into a transaction, if the benefit is contingent on an event to occur subsequent to the consummation of the transaction.

(x) Taking advantage of the consumer's inability reasonably to protect his or her interests by reason of disability, illiteracy, or inability to understand the language of an agreement presented by the other party to the transaction who knows or reasonably should know of the consumer's inability.

(y) Gross discrepancies between the oral representations of the seller and the written agreement covering the same transaction or failure of the other party to the transaction to provide the promised benefits.

(z) Charging the consumer a price that is grossly in excess of the price at which similar property or services are sold.

(aa) Causing coercion and duress as the result of the time and nature of a sales presentation.

(bb) Making a representation of fact or statement of fact material to the transaction such that a person reasonably believes the represented or suggested state of affairs to be other than it actually is.

(cc) Failing to reveal facts that are material to the transaction in light of representations of fact made in a positive manner.

(dd) Subject to subdivision (ee), representations by the manufacturer of a product or package that the product or package is 1 or more of the following:

(i) Except as provided in subparagraph (ii), recycled, recyclable, degradable, or is of a certain recycled content, in violation of guides for the use of environmental marketing claims, 16 CFR part 260.

(ii) For container holding devices regulated under part 163 of the natural resources and environmental protection act, 1994 PA 451, MCL 324.16301 to 324.16303, representations by a manufacturer that the container holding device is degradable contrary to the definition provided in that act.

(ee) Representing that a product or package is degradable, biodegradable, or photodegradable unless it can be substantiated by evidence that the product or package will completely decompose into elements found in nature within a reasonably short period of time after consumers use the product and dispose of the product or the package in a landfill or composting facility, as appropriate.

(ff) Offering a consumer a prize if in order to claim the prize the consumer is required to submit to a sales presentation, unless a written disclosure is given to the consumer at the time the consumer is notified of the prize and the written disclosure meets all of the following requirements:

(i) Is written or printed in a bold type that is not smaller than 10-point.

(ii) Fully describes the prize, including its cash value, won by the consumer.

(iii) Contains all the terms and conditions for claiming the prize, including a statement that the consumer is required to submit to a sales presentation.

(iv) Fully describes the product, real estate, investment, service, membership, or other item that is or will be offered for sale, including the price of the least expensive item and the most expensive item.

(gg) Violating 1971 PA 227, MCL 445.111 to 445.117, in connection with a home solicitation sale or telephone solicitation, including, but not limited to, having an independent courier service or other third party pick up a consumer's payment on a home solicitation sale during the period the consumer is entitled to cancel the sale.

(hh) Except as provided in subsection (3), requiring a consumer to disclose his or her social security number as a condition to selling or leasing goods or providing a service to the consumer, unless any of the following apply:

(i) The selling, leasing, providing, terms of payment, or transaction includes an application for or an extension of credit to the consumer.

(ii) The disclosure is required or authorized by applicable state or federal statute, rule, or regulation.

(iii) The disclosure is requested by a person to obtain a consumer report for a permissible purpose described in section 604 of the fair credit reporting act, 15 USC 1681b.

(iv) The disclosure is requested by a landlord, lessor, or property manager to obtain a background check of the individual in conjunction with the rent or leasing of real property.

(v) The disclosure is requested from an individual to effect, administer or enforce a specific telephonic or other electronic consumer transaction that is not made in person but is requested or authorized by the individual if it is to be used solely to confirm the identity of the individual through a fraud prevention service database. The consumer good or service shall still be provided to the consumer upon verification of his or her identity if he or she refuses to provide his or her social security number but provides other information or documentation that can be used by the person to verify his or her identity. The person may inform the consumer that verification through other means than use of the social security number may cause a delay in providing the service or good to the consumer.

(ii) If a credit card or debit card is used for payment in a consumer transaction, issuing or delivering a receipt to the consumer that displays any part of the expiration date of the card or more than the last 4 digits of the consumer's account number. This subdivision does not apply if the only receipt issued in a consumer transaction is a credit card or debit card receipt on which the account number or expiration date is handwritten, mechanically imprinted, or photocopied. This subdivision applies to any consumer transaction that occurs on or after March 1, 2005, except that if a credit or debit card receipt is printed in a consumer transaction by an electronic device, this subdivision applies to any consumer transaction that occurs using that device only after 1 of the following dates, as applicable:

(i) If the electronic device is placed in service after March 1, 2005, July 1, 2005 or the date the device is placed in service, whichever is later.

(ii) If the electronic device is in service on or before March 1, 2005, July 1, 2006.

References

Crandall, R., *Do Computer Purchasers Need Lemon Aid,* 4 N.C. J.L. & Tech. 307 (2003).

Lamis, A.P., *The New Age of Artificial Legal Reasoning as Relfected in the Judicial Treatment of the Mangnuson-Moss Act and the Federal Arbitration Act,* 15 Loy. Consumer L. Rev. 173 (2003).

Lloyd, D.G., *The Magnuson-Moss Warranty Act v. the Federal Arbitration Act: The Quintessential Chevron Case,* 16 Loy. Consumer L. Rev. 1 (2003).

Martin, J.S., *An Emerging Worldwide Standard for Protections of Consumers in the Sale of Goods: Did We Miss an Opportunity with Revised UCC Article 2?* 41 Tex. Int'l L.J. 223 (2006).

Warren, D.A., *Car Trouble: Some Help for the Uninformed Buyer,* 66 Ohio St. L.J. 441 (2005).

Part III

Contract Drafting

Chapter 16

Contract Drafting Suggestions and Techniques

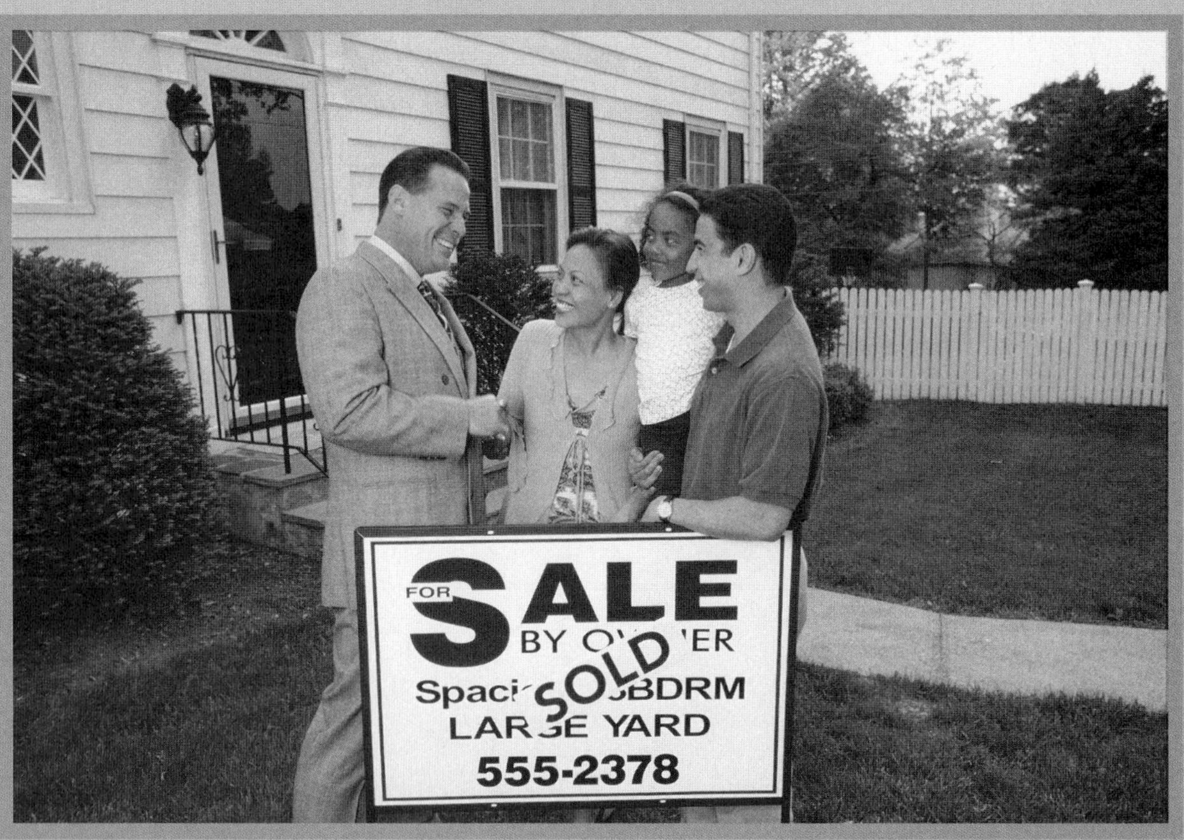

After reading this chapter you will be able to:

1. Explain why it is very important to say what you mean when you draft a contract.
2. Describe the three P's of contract drafting.
3. Discuss important clauses that should be considered when drafting any agreement.
4. Describe the steps necessary to establish a framework when drafting a contract.
5. Explain why Old English is frowned upon in modern contracts.
6. Identify examples of improper English that might be used in poorly drafted contracts.

Key Terms

Ambiguity
Conspicuous
Entire agreement clause
Integration clause
Legalese
Locus sigilli
Predict, provide, protect
Securities and Exchange Commission
Signature line
Testimonium

Drafting a contract is an art that requires skill and foresight. As we have seen throughout this text, ultimately a contract represents the will or intent of the parties. It represents the agreement involving private rights and private rules and formalizes the promotion of commerce and trade. The written form captures, like a snapshot, the essence of the parties' intent with an eye to the future. Good contract drafters know that in addition to establishing the who, what, when, where, why, and how of the agreement, embodying the agreement in writing can still be a game of chess requiring serious consideration of future issues between the parties. If there is ever a disagreement between the parties after a contract has been formed, the first thing likely to occur is that the parties run to the contract to see what it says about the issues or how to resolve the dispute. As such, the meaning of a particular word or phrase can have a huge effect on the relationship between the parties. In most cases, any ambiguities are construed against the offeror. It is important to remember principles learned throughout this text such as, "the offeror is the master of the offer" in Part I and the phrase "unless otherwise agreed" in Part II.

At the end of the day, a contract involves real people with real issues and concerns, and it is not just merely a piece of paper. That is why lawyers are paid to draft agreements and judges are elected or appointed to interpret them when necessary. The contract negotiation process does not have to be rigid, but it does often involve some sort of structured procedure. For example, the parties might reach a preliminary deal which then leads, possibly, to a letter of intent (LOI) which could lead to the swapping of forms and documents, modifications and adjustments, and ultimately the final product.[1] Though nothing in this chapter constitutes legal advice,

[1]Compare the merchant's "firm offer" of UCC §2-205.

its goal is to offer contract drafting suggestions and considerations when forming a contractual relationship. It is also important to consider how important contracts are to preserving business relationships or, unfortunately, destroying them.

PLAIN ENGLISH

When drafting a contract, it is important to use plain English.[2] This means one should avoid colloquial (slang) language and to try to avoid **legalese** (i.e., special lawyer language). On the other hand, it is no crime to use legalese, and some clients may prefer such language. In fact, the **Securities and Exchange Commission** (SEC) has a plain English rule. The SEC adopted rules in 1998 that require all securities registrants, including investment companies, to use plain English principles in writing the cover page, summary, and risk factors sections of prospectuses.[3] This is just an example of the recent trend to regard legalese as being anachronistic and arcane.

CONSUMER PROTECTION

While plain English rules are generally meant to promote contemporary language, it also serves another purpose: to protect consumers from language that most people cannot understand. States and the federal government, in some instances, protect consumers is by discounting or eliminating the use of fine print in certain contracts. In other cases, certain language may need to be bolded, capitalized, and even be a certain font size so that it is **conspicuous** and that attention can be drawn to it. This is quite common at the state level, involving health club contracts, leases, and real estate sales contracts.[4] Conspicuousness is also required, in many cases, with regard to waivers, disclaimers, and exculpatory clauses. For example, many states require that when a used car is sold a disclaimer of liability must state "AS IS" in boldface and capitalized font.

OLD ENGLISH

While using plain English is important, it is equally important to consider avoiding Old English. Terms such as *herein*, *whereas*, and *witnesseth* are still quite common in contracts as it is no crime to use these terms today. However, other terms

---

[2] I acknowledge that the use of English as an official language for commerce is a hotly debated topic in many cities, counties, and states in the United States presently. I am not making a statement on policy here but rather emphasizing the clarity aspect of any language between the parties rather than the use of colloquial or slang language.

[3] *See* SEC Rules 421(b) and (d).

[4] Arguably, consumer protection is a latent theme that flows throughout the UCC and is addressed both at the state and federal levels. One of the ways to address consumer protection concerns is to legislate rules related to in-home sales presentations which often involve high-pressure sales pitches and then allows a consumer to void such a contract which might involve the sale of a vacuum cleaner, magazines, water purifiers, encyclopedias, and so on within 72 hours (or three business days whichever is later often described as the "three-day rule"). Another way to address concerns is to have objective industrywide (as opposed to state regulation) certification standards or measures of quality such as ISO-9000 certified companies.

such as *hereinafter, heretofore*, and *hereinabove* are not only old English, but also can be confusing as well and should be avoided if possible. Additionally, using Latin expressions is generally frowned upon today in contracts though there is no doubt that recognition of the use of Latin in the study of law generally remains vital. For example, as mentioned earlier in this text, in many older contracts the phrase ***locus sigilli*** (abbreviated L.S.) was often used to establish where a seal or signature or just a mark was to be placed on the paper itself. Seals in the United States are now extinct except for certain publicly filed documents such as real estate deeds.[5] Phrases such as "Know all Men by these Presents" are so arcane that even most lawyers do not know what they mean and it can even be considered gender insensitive.

USE PROPER ENGLISH

It goes without saying that proper English grammar should be used in contracts. This means that the contract drafter should be cognizant of the difference between effect and affect, between their, there, they're, and principal and principle. Realize that the word "judgment" is properly spelled with only one letter "e."[6] One should pay careful attention to maintaining proper subject and verb agreement. For example, "the parties agrees" is improper and can speak volumes to a subsequent viewer of your contract (such as a judge) as to the training, attention, and consideration to detail by the contract drafter. Finally it is wise to avoid using he/she or s/he as that not only looks strange, but it also is quite impersonal. Instead, a person may be better served in a contract by either using their own name or by referring to them in a gender neutral ways such as a person, applicant, tenant, sponsor, individual, and so on.

AMBIGUITIES

The general rule is to avoid **ambiguity** in a contractual agreement. This is relevant especially if a court declares that a contract is void for vagueness due to blatant ambiguities. Good contract drafters will define their terms in the agreements so as to avoid ambiguities. On the other hand, sometimes being ambiguous is preferred and may actually be to your advantage as a contract drafter or to simply close a deal. For example, consider the role that requirements and output contracts play in the sale of goods in which the quantity element is missing. It is okay to create a price floor or ceiling in this instance even if the quantity element is otherwise vague. Remember to "say what you mean, and mean what you say." Also, the word "shall" means shall. It does not mean "may." Be consistent. When characterizing a party by a name, it is important to use that same name throughout the document. Finally, note that the connector and/or really means and *or* or.

---

[5]UCC 2-203 expressly rejects the seal requirement for a sale of goods.

[6]The word judgement is an acceptable British spelling. *See* http://www2.gsu.edu/~wwwesl/egw/jones/differences.htm.

APPEARANCE COUNTS

Make the contract appear nice and neatly organized as a matter of aesthetics. Do not abuse computer skills with bold, underline, italics, different fonts, sizes, and so on throughout the agreement. You are the artist, and the contract should be a work of art.

USE THE 3 P'S

Predict, provide, protect your client (could be yourself).[7] Predict what might happen, provide for it in the agreement, and protect you and your client. Also be sure to define the parties and the purpose of the agreement (i.e., intent). Dates, times, and addresses are vital. The date of the signing may be different than the effective date of the contract or the term of the agreement. This happens often in leases, for example. Anticipate that a court will review the entire document later. Yes, write for the parties, but also write with an eye toward litigation or ADR in which someone else (such as a court or arbitrator) might be called upon to interpret your contract.

THE INITIAL DRAFT

Starting from point zero is a waste of time. Consider the following when it comes time to prepare a document:

A. Use a model.
B. Use the form books.
C. Consult other contracts.
D. Realize that there is no perfect contract out there, but you need to pick the best from a variety of sources to suit your needs.
E. Utilize computer software and, of course, consider the role of the Internet in drafting and communicating with contracts.

DEVELOP A FRAMEWORK

It is important to consider the following items in order to establish a solid framework to move forward in creating a contract. Though the list is not exhaustive or complete, it should give the reader pause and can be a springboard for consideration of other possible issues as well.

1. Describe the agreement by giving it a title (e.g., "Endorsement Agreement").
2. Provide a shorthand way to identify the parties by giving them a consistent name ("Endorser"; "Company"; "Borrower"; "Buyer"; "Tenant").

[7]I was made aware of the three P's in law school and it is not my original idea. We utilized the text *Drafting Contracts* by law professor Scott J. Burnham (Michie Company, 1987), and I fully credit Professor Burnham's work with this concept.

3. Include a date that the agreement was signed and the date that the contract is effective.
4. Introduce the world to the agreement by signifying why the parties have entered into an agreement. This used to be the numerous *whereas* language found in contracts which was repeated over and over and over again. Using *whereas* is okay, but do not overdo it.
5. Introduce the world not only why, but also what the parties have agreed upon ("It is agreed that"; "The parties agree as follows"; "A and B hereby agree").
6. Establish the consideration element of the contract (the price of the promise).
7. Define terms if necessary to avoid ambiguities. For example, "reasonable efforts" and "best efforts" mean different things.
8. State the obligations of the parties (e.g., "shall," "agrees to," "will"). When stating obligations, always ask yourself what would happen if either party does not perform.
9. Consider conditions in contracts: precedent, concurrent, subsequent.
10. Include key clauses:

    A. *Force Majeure:* What happens if performance becomes impracticable because of an event beyond the offeror's control? What about acts of God, weather clauses or forces of nature?

    B. *Venue:* Where must the parties to a contract go if there is a dispute?

    C. *Law:* Whose law will apply in the event of a breach?

    D. *Merger:* Satisfies the parol evidence rule's concern that the contract represents the final agreement between the parties. (Sometimes referred to as an **integration clause**.) This is very important to avoid the later he said/she said. It is sometimes referred to as an **entire agreement clause**.

    E. *Assignment and Delegation:* Can rights and duties under the agreement be delegated and/or assigned? If so, how? Consider how third parties might influence the agreement and deal with it.

    F. *Modification:* How (if at all) can the agreement be modified? Must it be in writing first? It is okay to say that all modifications must be in writing and signed by both parties first.

    G. *Severability:* If a court refuses to enforce part of the agreement, will the rest of the agreement remain binding?

    H. *Exclusivity:* Consider issues related to trade secrets, no compete clauses (covenants not to compete), and so on.

    I. *Liquidated Damages:* Agree ahead of time what the damages will be for a breach of contract if, for example, there is a delay in performance.

    J. *Arbitration Clause:* Arbitration cannot normally be compelled without a provision so include it if that is what you want.

    K. *Attorneys Fees:* Who pays in the event of a breach? The common law rule is that each side pays their own fees if the case goes to litigation. (Consider the English rule versus American rule regarding payment of legal fees.)

L. *Disclaimer of Warranties:* Make sure they are conspicuous, particularly if they are Article 2 (sales) disclaimers.

M. *Time Is of the Essence:* Often makes dates and times found in a contract strictly liable (enforceable). It emphasizes to the parties and a court that the parties were concerned over time-related issues.

N. *Best Efforts:* A vague clause often used to create a subjective standard for which an employer or offeror might have the right to terminate an agreement if they feel the offeree (employee) is not giving their "all."

O. *Incorporation by Reference:* A paragraph that might refer to another document (or part of that document) not found in the contract itself. The parties can review it separately from this agreement.

P. *Termination:* One of the most important paragraphs in any agreement which should explain the rights and the steps that allow one to end an employment or business relationship.

Q. *ADR:* Though most contracts start out as a beneficial relationship between the parties, it is well known that over time attitudes and behaviors can change. Therefore the contract drafter should use exceptional care to ensure that policies and procedures are provided for in order to address situations and legal issues that might arise when something does go wrong. Good contract drafters protect their client in the event such a situation might occur. Consideration should be given to alternative forms of dispute resolution (ADR), including mediation and arbitration.

11. There should be a final paragraph uniting the contract often referred to as the closing or even ***testimonium***. The purpose of this concluding paragraph is to demonstrate that the parties assent to the contract without reservation or other conditions. The parties who sign must be the same as the ones recited in the caption. Remember the **signature line** for both parties, too, and use the word "by" to establish agency or authority such as when an employee signs the contract on behalf of the organization as a whole.

FINAL DRAFTING CONSIDERATIONS

1. Sign in blue ink (or any non-black) if possible. This allows the parties to easily determine the original document when photocopies are made.
2. Abbreviations are okay, but if in doubt, define them. Some common examples include:

   T/A = Trading As

   D/B/A = Doing Business As

   F/S/O = For the Services Of

   Re = Regarding.

3. Do not be cute—avoid humor.

4. Avoid contractions (don't; won't; can't) because that is too colloquial and unprofessional.
5. There is something to be said for brevity. Remember, "Say what you mean and mean what you say." Many contracts are way too long (and lawyers are paid accordingly).
6. If you can afford a lawyer, hire a lawyer to draft your contracts. While lawyers might be unnecessary in some cases, lawyers compete to get into law schools and sacrifice years of their life to be trained to see things that are not easily seen when it comes to contract drafting.
7. Print only on one side of the page. This might even be required under state law.
8. Number the pages for the benefit of all parties.
9. Give subparagraphs titles so that readers can easily locate the paragraphs for future reference.
10. Write out numbers in language as well ($100 is "one hundred dollars").
11. Take a deep breath, walk away, and look at it again later to see if it all makes sense.

CHAPTER SUMMARY

Drafting a contract does not need to be a Herculean effort. Utilizing all available resources is wise in order to memorialize the agreement between two or more parties. Drafting agreements in plain English is preferred and avoiding legalese is favored today. On the other hand, it is no crime to utilize older English language, and it might appear impressive and formal at times. Avoiding ambiguities is generally a wise choice and certainly the appearance of the contract may matter to the parties. Considering the three P's, consulting other agreements, and developing a framework should give any contract drafter a great start. While virtually anyone may prepare a contract, one must be careful not to give legal advice unless they are a licensed attorney.

Discussion and Review Questions

1. What are some of the qualities of a good contract drafter?
2. What is legalese and when should it be used (or not)?
3. When is Old English appropriate in a contract if at all?
4. When drafting a contract, is it every appropriate to be ambiguous?

Critical Thinking Exercises

1. When forming a contract, sometimes an issue arises in which there is information that you should ethically disclose but have no legal obligation to do so. Can you think of situations in which this might occur?
2. Victor plays basketball for a team in the National Basketball Association. As part of the standard player contract, Victor has to refrain from specific types of hazardous activities such as skydiving, hang gliding,

snow skiing, rock or mountain climbing, hiking, rappelling, and bungee jumping. Well, Victor hurts himself during the summer months while he is skateboarding. Can the league fine him for engaging in such off-season activity even though skateboarding was not specifically mentioned? *See* http://www.nbpa.com/cba_exhibits/exhibitA.php. *See also* http://www.msnbc.msn.com/id/17404736/.

3. A Michigan company in Detroit contracts with a company from Sarnia, Ontario (Canada). The contract is working fine until the Canadian company has to pay for the delivery of the goods. You see, while the Canadian company agreed to pay for delivery, the dollar amount listed did not differentiate between American or Canadian dollars (the American dollar is worth slightly more). The lawyers who drafted the agreement admit that this was an oversight. The American company wants payment in American currency, while the Canadian company insists it should be in Canadian currency. You are called in to mediate the situation. What options might you propose and why?

Online Research Exercises

1. Explore private (corporate) and public (city/county/state) policies related to utilizing plain English that are found on the Internet.
2. Consider how cities, counties, and some states have rallied to proclaim or legislate that English is the preferred language in certain types of acts and transactions.
3. Explore and compare professional sports contracts such as the NFL, NHL, MLB, and NBA. Note that standard player contracts are the by-product of the collective bargaining process. See if you can find special clauses such as "hazardous activity" clauses and the like found in professional sports contracts. For example, the National Basketball Association (NBA) *Uniform Player Contract* includes language in paragraph 12, *Other Athletic Activities,* which prohibits such activities: . . . (i) sky-diving, hang gliding, snow skiing, rock or mountain climbing (as distinguished from hiking), rappelling, and bungee jumping; (ii) any fighting, boxing, or wrestling; (iii) driving or riding on a motorcycle or moped; (iv) riding in or on any motorized vehicle in any kind of race or racing contest; (v) operating an aircraft of any kind; (vi) engaging in any other activity excluded or prohibited by or under any insurance policy which the Team procures against the injury, illness or disability to or of the Player, or death of the Player, for which the Player has received written notice from the Team prior to the execution of this Contract; or (vii) participating in any game or exhibition of basketball, football, baseball, hockey, lacrosse, or other team sport or competition. http://www.nbpa.com/cba_exhibits/exhibitA.php.
4. Visit the website for the International Organization for Standardization which establishes measures of quality in a variety of settings. http://www.iso.org/iso/en/ISOOnline.frontpage. Consider how these ISO standards could influence contract drafting especially in the manufacturing industry.
5. Consider how English only workplaces might have an impact on contracts or contract drafting. *See* http://www.usatoday.com/money/workplace/2007-05-06-english-only-usat_N.htm.
6. Some companies are attempting to offer their employees contracts (really waivers) which would allow employees to pursue consensual relationships while at the same time protecting the employer from a lawsuit in the event the office romance goes sour. These are sometimes referred to as "love contracts" and they have been gaining a lot of attention lately. Explore http://www.sfgate.com/cgi-bin/article.cgi?f=/c/a/2001/12/02/AW129618.DTL. *See also*

http://www.gutierrez-preciado.com/Hot_Topics/Office_Romance.htm.

7. Many feel that college coaching contracts in football, basketball and baseball have become an out of control arms race with no restraints (yet). What do you think? Visit http://www.usatoday.com/sports/college/football/2006-11-16-coaches-salaries-cover_x.htm. Consider that student-athletes (as a general rule) cannot be paid for their services as an athlete at anytime, but in the meantime their coaches are becoming multi-millionaires.

CASE APPLICATIONS

Case 1

Note the court's analysis involving the wording and drafting of a contractual agreement involving limitation of liability for an alarm system.

UNITED SERVS. AUTO. ASS'N v. ADT SEC. SERVS.

2006 Ky. App. LEXIS 284 (Ky. Ct. App. Sept. 8, 2006)

MILLER, Special Judge

United Services Automobile Association ("USAA"), Leslie Branch ("Branch") and Barbara Bennett ("Bennett"), husband and wife, bring this appeal from an order of the Fayette Circuit Court granting summary judgment for appellees, ADT Security Services, Inc. and ADT Security Services (South), Inc. (collectively "ADT"). For the reasons stated below, we affirm. We are to determine whether a limitation-of-liability clause in an alarm system contract is valid and enforceable under Kentucky law.

Branch and Bennett were insured by USAA under a homeowner's insurance policy. On March 1, 1997, the residence of Branch and Bennett located at 3217 Tates Creek Road, Lexington, Kentucky, was heavily damaged by an accidental fire. At the time of the fire, the residence was equipped with an ADT fire alarm system. ADT furnished and retained title to the system, charging an initial installation fee and a monthly fee for service and maintenance.

The contract, dated April 27, 1994, between Branch and Bennett and ADT contained a clause purporting to limit ADT's liability to $250.00 as liquidated damages in the event its equipment failed to function properly. It is undisputed that the system failed to alert the ADT monitoring service or the local fire department of the March 1 fire. An investigation of the fire determined that it was accidental and most likely caused by faulty wiring of the home, not the alarm system. Additionally, an examination of the alarm system was conducted to determine what might have caused its failure. It was determined that the most likely cause of the alarm system failure was a malfunction of the "microprocessor" inside the alarm monitor control panel.

USAA subsequently paid approximately $885,000 to Branch and Bennett under the terms of their insurance contract. On October 8, 1999, USAA brought a subrogation action, joined by Branch and Bennett, against ADT to recover their losses. In their complaint, appellants stated claims based upon breach of warranty, strict liability, and negligence. On May 9, 2005, the circuit court entered an order granting summary judgment to appellees. This appeal followed.

First, Appellants contend that the contract for alarm service was one of adhesion; perforce, the limitation of liability provision should be held for naught. We disagree.

Generally, a contract of adhesion is a standardized contract, which, imposed and drafted by the party of superior bargaining strength, relegates to the subscribing party only the opportunity to adhere to the contract or reject it. Here, Branch and Bennett were not presented with a "take-it-or-leave-it" proposal. Indeed, the contract provided that they could pay an additional amount in exchange for ADT assuming greater liability:

> IF THE CUSTOMER DESIRES ADT TO ASSUME A GREATER LIABILITY, ADT SHALL AMEND THIS AGREEMENT BY ATTACHING A RIDER SETTING FORTH THE AMOUNT OF ADDITIONAL LIABILITY AND THE ADDITIONAL AMOUNT PAYABLE BY THE CUSTOMER FOR THE ASSUMPTION BY ADT OF SUCH GREATER LIABILITY PROVIDED, HOWEVER THAT SUCH RIDER AND ADDITIONAL OBLIGATION SHALL IN NO WAY BE INTERPRETED TO HOLD ADT AS AN INSURER.

Branch and Bennett could have bargained with ADT for more favorable terms, but chose not to do so. Thus, we are of the opinion that the contract is not one of adhesion.

Next, Appellants argue that the limitation-of-liability provision should be rejected as unconscionable. We disagree. It is settled law that, absent fraud in the inducement, a written agreement duly executed by the party to be bound, who had an opportunity to read it, will be enforced according to its terms. A narrow exception to this rule is the doctrine of unconscionability. The doctrine is used by the courts to police the excesses of certain parties who abuse their right to contract freely. It is directed against one-sided, oppressive and unfairly surprising contracts, and not against the consequences per se of uneven bargaining power or even a simple old-fashioned bad bargain.

Here, the limitation-of-liability clause is not one-sided, oppressive nor unfairly surprising. It states:

> Limit of liability—it is understood that ADT is not an insurer, that insurance, if any shall be obtained by the customer and that the amounts payable to ADT hereunder are based upon the value of the services and the scope of liability as herein set forth and are unrelated to the value of the customer's premises. ADT makes no guaranty or warranty, including any implied warranty or merchantability or fitness that the system or services supplied, will avert or prevent occurrences or the consequences therefrom, which the system or service is designed to detect. It is impractical and extremely difficult to fix the actual damages, if any, which may proximately result from failure on the part of ADT to perform any of its obligations hereunder. The customer does not desire this contract to provide for full liability of ADT and agrees that ADT shall be exempt from liability for loss, damage, or injury due directly or indirectly to occurrences or consequences therefrom, which the service or system is designed to detect or avert; that if ADT should be found liable for loss, damage or injury due to a failure of service or equipment in any respect, its liability shall be limited to a sum equal to 10% of the annual service charge or $250, whichever is greater, as the agreed upon damages and not as a penalty, as the exclusive remedy, and that the provisions of this paragraph shall apply if loss, damage or injury irrespective of cause or origin, results directly or indirectly to person or property from performance or nonperformance of obligations imposed by this contract or from negligence, active or otherwise, of ADT, its agents or employees. . . .

The limitation-of-liability language is located on the back of the contract document. Branch signed the contract on the bottom front of the document. Directly to the left and above Branch's signature the contract states in all capital letters and bold print, "**ATTENTION IS DIRECTED TO THE LIMITED WARRANTY, LIMIT OF LIABILITY AND OTHER CONDITIONS ON REVERSE SIDE.**" We note that this language stands separate and apart from the rest of the paragraphs and is easily readable. Additionally, while the font size of the limitation-of-liability text on the back of the document is relatively small, it is not unreadable. The limitation-of-liability clause, being composed of approximately 350 words, is not unduly lengthy nor does it contain oppressive terms couched in vague or obscure language. Branch, a highly educated medical doctor, testified that he was given the opportunity to, and did, read the document before signing it. Appellants chose to forego their prerogative to impose additional liability upon ADT for failure of its service or equipment. Unconscionability determinations are fact specific and we address such claims on a case-by-case basis. Under these facts, we are of the opinion that the contract cannot properly be characterized as unconscionable.

Appellants also aver that the limitation-of-liability clause amounts to an unenforceable "penalty" rather than "liquidated damages." We disagree. A provision in a contract providing for liquidated damages will be enforced, provided it is in actuality liquidated damages and not a penalty. If such provision is in fact a penalty it will not be enforced and the injured party will be entitled to recover the actual damages suffered. Where, at the time of the execution of the contract, damages may be uncertain in character or amount, or difficult to reasonably ascertain, a provision for liquidated damages will be enforced, provided the amount agreed upon is not greatly disproportionate to the injury which might result.

Here, appellants and appellees both agreed that "if ADT should be found liable for loss, damage or injury due to a failure of service or equipment in any respect, its liability shall be limited to . . . $250 . . . as the agreed upon damages and not as a penalty" (emphasis added). At the time of the execution of the contract, appellees assumed a duty to install and monitor the alarm system in the appellant's home. The $24.00 per month fee appellants paid to appellees was based solely upon the cost of the monitoring service and not the value of the home or its contents. Damages based on a breach of the contract by the appellees would have been difficult, if not impossible, to ascertain because they did not contract to assume the duties of an insurer and did not know the value of the home, its contents, or the extent of any possible fire damage that might result. Additionally, the $250.00 limitation of liability amount represents nearly one year of monitoring fees and is reasonably proportionate to the damages expected from a breach of a $24.00 per month monitoring agreement. Accordingly, we hold that the $250.00 contemplated under the agreement is a proper measure of liquated damages and does not constitute an unenforceable penalty.

Appellants also contend that enforcing the limitation-of-liability clause would be contrary to Kentucky's public policy of allowing recovery for damages caused to persons or property. We disagree.

Appellants rely on Kentucky's Product Liability Act, *Kentucky Revised Statutes ("KRS") 411.300 et seq.*, for the proposition that they can recover from appellees for the "manufacture, sale, and/or installation of a defective product, namely the ADT alarm system." However, the clear import of the contract is that it is a contract for services only. ADT agreed to supply the fire alarm system, but by the clear terms of the contract, title to the control set remained with ADT. The alleged defective "product," the fire alarm system control set, remained the property of ADT. The contract obligated ADT only in the service and maintenance of the system.

We have held that "to prevail in an action based upon strict products liability, a plaintiff must establish: (1) that there is a 'product,' . . . which (5) results in physical harm to the ultimate user or consumer or his property." Thus, because this contract involves a contract for services, no cause of action can be maintained based on strict liability. Similarly, the Uniform Commercial Code is inapplicable as it applies only to contracts for the sale of goods and does not apply to a contract for services. See *KRS 355.2-201* and *KRS 355.2-105*. The Code affords no basis for an action for breach of warranty.

We now decide whether appellants can maintain an action for negligence. Under Kentucky law a party to a contract may agree to release another from liability for ordinary or gross negligence, but not for willful or wanton negligence or where contrary to public policy. Exceptions to this rule include:

> (1) Contracts for exemption from liability for a willful breach of a statutory duty; (2) contracts between master and servant relating to negligent injury of the servant in the course of his employment; and (3) contracts where one of the parties (such as a railroad) is charged with a duty of public service, and the bargain relates to negligence in the performance of its duty to the public.

Contracts exempting from liability for negligence are not favored and are strictly construed against the parties relying on them. The wording of the release must be "so clear and understandable that an ordinarily prudent and knowledgeable party to it will know what he or she is contracting away; it must be unmistakable."

In *Hargis*, our Supreme Court cited four alternative factors as determinative in upholding a pre-injury release: (1) it explicitly expresses an intention to exonerate by using the word "negligence"; or (2) it clearly and specifically indicates an intent to release a party from liability for a personal injury caused by that party's own conduct; or (3) protection against negligence is the only reasonable construction of the contract language; or (4) the hazard experienced was clearly within the contemplation of the provision. *Id.*

Here, there is no allegation that the appellees were guilty of willful or wanton negligence. Nor does the contract involve a statutory duty, master/servant relationship, or public service duty. Moreover, the wording of the limitation-of-liability clause is clear and easily understandable to an ordinarily prudent and knowledgeable person. It satisfies all of the alternative factors set out in *Hargis*. The clause explicitly expresses an intention to exonerate or limit ADT's liability by using the word "negligence"; it clearly and specifically indicates that liability is limited for injury caused by ADT's own conduct; protection of ADT against its own negligence is the only reasonable construction of the contract language; and, the hazard experienced, failure of the ADT alarm system, was clearly contemplated by the contract provision. Under these facts, the limitation-of-liability clause in the alarm system contract is controlling and properly enforceable.

Finally, there is a broad public policy of freedom of contract in Kentucky and permitting alarm companies to limit their liability does not leave consumers unprotected. Consumers are encouraged, and indeed are many times required, to purchase insurance to protect their property interests from fire and other hazards. Thus, we conclude that the limitation-of-liability provision in ADT's alarm service contract does not contravene public policy.

There appears to be no case under Kentucky law specifically deciding the issue of whether limitation-of-liability clauses in alarm service agreements are enforceable. However, other jurisdictions have faced the issue. The majority have determined that such clauses are valid and enforceable. We see no reason to depart from the majority rule. For the foregoing reasons the judgment of the Fayette Circuit Court is affirmed.

Case Questions

1. ADT had a liquidated damages clause that limited its liability up to what dollar amount?
2. Did the alarm system work correctly?
3. The insurance company sued ADT in what dollar amount to recover damages?
4. Was the alarm system contract one of adhesion?
5. Was there evidence of negligence in this case?

Case 2

In the following case, the Eleventh Circuit Court of Appeals strongly differentiated between litigation and arbitration, a form of alternative dispute resolution (ADR). What are the strengths and weaknesses of ADR?

B. L. HARBERT INT'L, L.L.C. v. HERCULES STEEL CO.

441 F.3D 905 (11TH CIR. 2006)

CARNES, Circuit Judge

The Federal Arbitration Act (FAA) liberally endorses and encourages arbitration as an alternative to litigation. The reasons for this strong, pro-arbitration policy are "to relieve congestion in the courts and to provide parties with an alternative method for dispute resolution that is speedier and less costly than litigation." The laudatory goals of the FAA will be achieved only to the extent that courts ensure arbitration is an alternative to litigation, not an additional layer in a protracted contest. If we permit parties who lose in arbitration to freely relitigate their cases in court, arbitration will do nothing to reduce congestion in the judicial system; dispute resolution will be slower instead of faster; and reaching a final decision will cost more instead of less. This case is a good example of the poor loser problem and it provides us with an opportunity to discuss a potential solution.

B. L. Harbert International, LLC, is a Delaware corporation based in Birmingham, Alabama, which makes money in large construction projects including some done for the government. Hercules Steel Company is a North Carolina corporation based in Fayetteville, North Carolina, that manufactures steel used in construction.

On August 25, 2000, the United States Army Corp of Engineers, Savannah District, awarded Harbert a contract to construct an office complex for the Special Operations Forces at Fort Bragg, North Carolina. Harbert, in turn, awarded Hercules a $1,197,000 steel fabrication and erection subcontract on September 21, 2000.

The subcontract between the parties includes a provision that disputes between them will be submitted to binding arbitration under the auspices of the American Arbitration Association, using the Construction Industry

Arbitration Rules. Later, the parties executed a separate Agreement to Arbitrate, which recognizes that the Federal Arbitration Act, *9 U.S.C. § 1*, would control arbitration proceedings.

The subcontract further provides that Harbert will issue a "Progress Schedule" for the project and will provide a copy to each subcontractor. It states that the subcontractor must perform all work "in accordance with Progress Schedule as prepared by [Harbert] and as it may be revised from time to time with the Subcontractor's input." The subcontract also provides that the subcontractor is liable for damages caused by its failure to complete its work within the time provided in the "Project Schedule." The terms "Progress Schedule" and "Project Schedule" are not defined.

Harbert's failure to define those terms might have gone unnoticed if it had created only one schedule for the project, but Harbert developed two, which it referred to as the 2000 and 3000 schedules. Harbert claims that it created the 3000 schedule to update the Corps of Engineers about the progress of the project, and the 2000 schedule to manage the work of its subcontractors, including Hercules. In any event, neither schedule is mentioned in the subcontract.

The dispute-generating problem is that the 2000 schedule contained earlier completion dates than the 3000 one. According to the 2000 schedule, Hercules was to begin work on March 5, 2001, and finish it by June 6, 2001. That did not happen. Hercules began work in April of 2001, and did not finish it until January of 2002. That completion of the work was, however, within the more lenient deadlines of the 3000 schedule.

Dissatisfied with the timeliness of Hercules' work, Harbert stopped making payments to Hercules and demanded that it pay delay damages exceeding the amount due Hercules on the subcontract. In response, on January 21, 2003, Hercules filed a demand for arbitration with the American Arbitration Association, seeking to recover the balance due on the subcontract, other damages, interest, and attorney's fees. Harbert counterclaimed for delay damages, acceleration costs, miscellaneous back charges, interest, and attorney's fees.

The arbitration proceedings took place on seven days in February and May 2004. As is customary in construction industry arbitrations, the parties decided not to have a court reporter take down the proceedings. We can, however, tell from the parties' briefs and statements during oral argument in this Court what their principal positions and arguments were in those proceedings.

We know that the main disagreement of the parties was about which of the two progress schedules that Harbert issued applied to Hercules. Hercules took the position that the only one that applied to it was the 3000 Schedule, whose deadlines it had met. The several arguments Hercules made in support of this position included one that the subcontract language was ambiguous because it referred to both a "Progress Schedule" and "Project Schedule," but did not define either term. Hercules argued that the subcontract provisions had to be interpreted in light of an implied element of reasonableness. It also argued that Harbert had abandoned the 2000 schedule thereby authorizing Hercules to perform in accordance with the 3000 Schedule. Additionally, Hercules presented evidence that it did not have notice of the 2000 Schedule at the time it began work on the project.

Harbert, on the other hand, contended that the subcontract language unambiguously gave it complete authority to set the schedule which would mean that Hercules was bound by the 2000 schedule. Harbert asserted that the 2000 schedule was the "Progress Schedule" referred to in the subcontract because it was the only schedule Harbert issued to all of its subcontractors.

After considering the parties' opposing arguments and a voluminous record, the arbitrator issued his "Award of Arbitrator" on September 8, 2004. That award denied Hercules' delay damages claim, denied all of Harbert's counterclaims, denied both parties' claims for attorney's fees, and awarded Hercules $369,775, representing the subcontract balance and the interest on that sum. Because the award, not counting interest, was nearly $100,000 less than the amount the parties had agreed was the subcontract balance, Hercules believed that the arbitrator had made a scrivener's or mathematical error. It submitted a request for clarification which pointed out the problem.

Harbert moved for clarification and modification of the award but on different grounds. Harbert's motion pointed out that the award did not contain the specificity the parties had agreed they needed, and it requested that the arbitrator modify it to provide "enough discussion" on each of the six "Issues for Decision" that had been identified by the parties to enable them to understand the result and the arbitrator's reasons for granting or denying any specific item of damages. The first of those six issues was: "What was the schedule to which Hercules was bound under its subcontract with Harbert?"

On October 18, 2004, the arbitrator issued his "Disposition for Application of Modification/Clarification of the Award," a decision document which corrected the scrivener's error by increasing the award from $369,775 to $469,775. The document also revealed the arbitrator's findings on the six issues, stating in answer to the first one that Hercules was contractually bound to the more generous "project schedule submitted to the Corps of Engineers which was used to build the project [the 3000 schedule] . . . not the sixteen week schedule unilaterally set by Harbert [the 2000 schedule]." The arbitrator stated in answer to another of the six issues that Harbert was not entitled to any damages because "the delay and acceleration damages are necessarily dependent on the claimed project schedule which has been found not applicable."

On November 18, 2004, Harbert filed in the district court a motion to vacate the arbitration award, contending that the arbitrator's rationale reflected a manifest disregard of the applicable law. Hercules opposed Harbert's motion with one of its own, asking the court to confirm the award pursuant to *9 U.S.C. § 9*.

On February 7, 2005, the district court entered an order denying Harbert's motion to vacate the award and granting Hercules' motion to confirm it. While there was no transcript of the arbitration hearing, the district court had before it the pre-and post-hearing briefs that both parties had submitted to the arbitrator, and an affidavit from Harbert's lead attorney during the arbitration proceeding. (A copy of that affidavit is not in the record on appeal, and Harbert has made no effort to inform us of its contents.)

The district court interpreted the arbitrator's award and his disposition of Harbert's post-award motion as concluding that the reason Hercules' conduct did not breach the subcontract is that it was bound by the 3000 schedule not the 2000 schedule. The court noted that the arbitrator had before him evidence of the 2000 schedule and some evidence that it had been sent to Hercules before the subcontract was signed. Finding no evidence of manifest disregard for the law, the court on that basis distinguished this case from *Montes v. Shearson Lehman Bros., Inc., 128 F.3d 1456, 1461 (11th Cir. 1997)*. As a result, the court entered judgment enforcing the arbitration award.

Unhappy with the district court's judgment, as it had been with the arbitrator's decision, Harbert filed a notice of appeal and a motion for stay of the judgment pending appeal. The district court granted the stay, and we now decide the appeal.

Judicial review of commercial arbitration awards is narrowly limited under the Federal Arbitration Act. See *9 U.S.C. § 10-11*. The FAA presumes the confirmation of arbitration awards, and federal courts should defer to an arbitrator's decision whenever possible, *Robbins v. Day, 954 F.2d 679, 682 (11th Cir. 1992)*. The FAA sets out four narrow bases for vacating an award, none of which are even remotely applicable in this case.

In addition to those four statutory grounds for vacatur, we have said that there are three non-statutory grounds. An award may be vacated if it is arbitrary and capricious, or if the award was made in manifest disregard for the law, *Montes, 128 F.3d at 1464*.

Harbert's challenge to the arbitrator's award rests solely on its contention that the arbitrator acted in manifest disregard of the law. This ground for vacating an arbitration award requires clear evidence that the arbitrator was "conscious of the law and deliberately ignore[d] it." A showing that the arbitrator merely misinterpreted, misstated, or misapplied the law is insufficient. *Id. at 1461-62*. We review de novo the district court's legal conclusions on this issue.

This Court first adopted manifest disregard for the law as a basis for challenging an arbitration award in the Montes case. *128 F.3d at 1461*. It remains the only case in which we have ever found the exceptional circumstances that satisfy the exacting requirements of this exception.

The Montes litigation arose out of a dispute between an employer and employee about overtime pay. See *Montes, 128 F.3d at 1458*. The controlling law, the Fair Labor Standards Act, was against the employer's position, and during the arbitration proceedings its attorney repeatedly urged the arbitrators to disregard the requirements of the Act and rule for the employer on the basis of equitable considerations. *Id. at 1459*. He told the arbitrators that: "you as an arbitrator are not guided strictly to follow case law precedent . . . you can also do what's fair and just and equitable and that is what [my client] is asking you to do in this case." Id. Instead of contending that the law could be applied favorably to his client's position, the attorney argued the arbitrators that "in this case this law is not right," and "the law says one thing. What equity demands and requires and is saying is another." *Id.* He explicitly asked the arbitrators not to follow the law. *Id.* ("Thus, as I said in my Answer, as I said before in my Opening, and I now ask you in my Closing, not to follow the FLSA if you determine that she's not an exempt employee.")

The arbitrators in Montes found in favor of the employer, and in their award they repeated the plea of the employer's attorney that they disregard the law. There was nothing in the transcript of the proceedings or the award itself to indicate that the arbitrators had not heeded that plea, and the evidence and law did not support the award. *Id. at 1461–62*.

In holding that the arbitrators had acted in manifest disregard of the law in Montes, we disavowed any notion that an arbitrator's decision "can be reviewed on the basis that its conclusion or reasoning is legally erroneous." *Id. at 1461*; accord *id. at 1460* ("This does not mean that arbitrators can be reversed for errors or misinterpretations of law."). And we emphasized the rare nature of the circumstances in that case. *Id. at 1461–62*.

While *Montes* shows the exception, the rule is shown in every other case where we have decided if the arbitration loser had established manifest disregard of the law. In all of those other cases the loser in arbitration was the loser in our decision.

The facts of this case do not come within shouting distance of the Montes exception. This is a typical contractual dispute in which the parties disagree about the meaning of terms of their agreement. There are arguments to be made on both sides of the contractual interpretation issue, and they were made to the arbitrator before being made to the district court and then to us. Even if we were convinced that we would have decided this contractual dispute differently, that would not be nearly enough to set aside the award. See *Peebles, 431 F.3d at 1326* ("[A] litigant arguing that an arbitrator acted in manifest disregard of the law must show something more than a misinterpretation, misstatement, or misapplication of the law."); *Brown, 211 F.3d at 1223* ("Arbitration awards will not be reversed due to an erroneous interpretation of law by the arbitrator."); *Montes, 128 F.3d at 1461* ("An arbitration board that incorrectly interprets the law has not manifestly disregarded it. It has simply made a legal mistake.").

Harbert's argument that the arbitration award clearly contradicts an express term of the contract is simply another way of saying that the arbitrator clearly erred, and even a showing of a clear error on part of the arbitrator is not enough. The arbitration loser must establish more than that in order to have the award set aside, the more being that the arbitrator actually recognized a clear rule of law and deliberately chose to ignore it. *Peebles, 431 F.3d at 1326* ("A manifest disregard for the law involves a conscious and deliberate decision to ignore the applicable law."); *id. at 1327* ("At most, the arbitration panel may have misunderstood the effect and weight to be given to cases cited by the parties. On the record before us, we cannot find proof that the arbitrators recognized a clear rule of law and chose to ignore it. Therefore, we cannot find that the arbitrators acted in manifest disregard for the law."); *Univ. Commons, 304 F.3d at 1338* ("We cannot find proof that the arbitrators recognized a clear rule of law and, furthermore, chose to ignore it. Therefore, we cannot find that the arbitrators acted in manifest disregard for the law . . ."); *Brown, 211 F.3d at 1223* ("Brown argues that the arbitrator applied the wrong legal test in assessing his retaliation claim, but does not assert that this alleged error was intentional or that the arbitrator made a conscious decision not to follow the appropriate legal standard. Even if the arbitrator applied the wrong standard, which we need not decide, no manifest disregard for the law has been shown, and Brown's argument fails.").

Harbert's unconvincing position to the contrary has two legs, neither of which will support it. One is Harbert's insistence that the contract is part of the law the arbitrator must apply, so that any misapplication of the contract is a misapplication of the law. The contract is not part of the applicable law, but the agreement of the parties to which the law is applied. In any event, as we have already explained, errors of law are not enough to justify setting aside an arbitration award.

The other leg of Harbert's position is dicta from our University Commons opinion. In that case a developer and construction company arbitrated their dispute over the company's alleged failure to meet its contractual deadlines. *304 F.3d at 1333–34*. The arbitrators found in favor of the developer, awarding it lost rental income for a particular time period even though the project had been completed before that period began. See *id. at 1336–37*. The construction company argued that was error which established the arbitrators had acted in manifest disregard for the law and on that basis the company moved to set aside the award. *Id.*

The district court instead entered an order confirming the arbitrators' award, and we refused to reverse its order on the ground that the arbitrators had acted in manifest disregard of the law. *Univ. Commons, 304 F.3d at 1345* (vacating the district court's order and remanding for findings with respect to another ground). In doing so, we emphasized that there was no showing in the record of the arbitrators' thinking other than the award itself. *Id. at 1337*. We explained that we could not ascertain from the "bare-bones statement of the award" what principle of law the arbitrators allegedly chose to ignore. *Id.* Because there was no transcript of the proceedings, we could not examine the arbitrators' questions or remarks for possible evidence of their legal rationale. *Id.* There also did not appear to be any clear rule of law that the arbitrators might have broken. *Id. at 1338*. We reiterated in University Commons the holding of our decisions that "to manifestly disregard the law, one must be conscious of the law and deliberately ignore it." *Id. at 1337* (quoting *Brown, 211 F.3d at 1223* (alteration in original)). The arbitration loser having failed to establish a manifest disregard for the law, we rejected that attack on the award, holding: "We cannot find proof that the arbitrators recognized a clear rule of law and, furthermore, chose to ignore it. Therefore, we cannot find the arbitrators acted in manifest disregard of the law." *Id. at 1338*.

Faced with that result and reasoning in University Commons, Harbert focuses on a sentence of dicta from the opinion in that case: "Theoretically, we suppose, the arbitrators' approach to the award of damages could be in disregard of the law altogether, if it differed from the provisions of the contract." See *id. at 1338 n. 7*. This one sentence of speculative dicta in one footnote of one opinion cannot plausibly be construed as setting out a rule of law—that misinterpretation of a contract may constitute a manifest disregard of the law. That is especially true since such a rule would be contrary not only to the holding and express rationale of University Commons, but also to the settled Eleventh Circuit precedent which governed that decision. Under the well-established law of this circuit, which we have already discussed, if we believe that the arbitrator's approach differed from the provisions of the contract, at most that only establishes the arbitrator erred, which is not enough to conclude there was a manifest disregard of the law. See *Montes, 128 F.3d at 1461*.

There is no evidence that the attorney for Hercules urged the arbitrator to disregard the law, and Harbert does not even suggest that happened. There is no evidence that the arbitrator decided the dispute on the basis of anything other than his best judgment—whether right or wrong—of how the law applies to the facts of the case. There is, in short, no evidence that the arbitrator manifestly disregarded the law. The only manifest disregard of the law evident in this case is Harbert's refusal to accept the law of this circuit which narrowly circumscribes judicial review of arbitration awards. By attacking the arbitration award in this case Harbert has shown at best an indifference to the law of our circuit governing the subject. Harbert's refusal to accept that there is no basis in the law for attacking the award has come at a cost to the party with whom Harbert entered into the arbitration agreement and to the judicial system.

In litigating this case without good basis through the district court and now through this Court, Harbert has deprived Hercules and the judicial system itself of the principal benefits of arbitration. Instead of costing less, the resolution of this dispute has cost more than it would have had there been no arbitration agreement. Instead of being decided sooner, it has taken longer than it would have to decide the matter without arbitration. Instead of being resolved outside the courts, this dispute has required the time and effort of the district court and this Court.

When a party who loses an arbitration award assumes a never-say-die attitude and drags the dispute through the court system without an objectively reasonable belief it will prevail, the promise of arbitration is broken. Arbitration's allure is dependent upon the arbitrator being the last decision maker in all but the most unusual cases. The more cases there are, like this one, in which the arbitrator is only the first stop along the way, the less arbitration there will be. If arbitration is to be a meaningful alternative to litigation, the parties must be able to trust that the arbitrator's decision will be honored sooner instead of later.

Courts cannot prevent parties from trying to convert arbitration losses into court Victoriaies, but it may be that we can and should insist that if a party on the short end of an arbitration award attacks that award in court without any real legal basis for doing so, that party should pay sanctions. A realistic threat of sanctions may discourage baseless litigation over arbitration awards and help fulfill the purposes of the pro-arbitration policy contained in the FAA. It is an idea worth considering.

We have considered ordering Harbert and its counsel to show cause why sanctions should not be imposed in this case, but have decided against doing so. That decision is the product of the combined force of three reasons, which we list in reverse order of weight. First, there is speculative dicta in the University Commons opinion that provided Harbert with a little cover for its actions, although this factor alone does not carry much weight. The rule that prior panel precedent trumps later decisions, to say nothing of later dicta, is so well known and well established that lawyers and their clients should be held responsible for knowing that rule and acting accordingly. Second, Hercules did not move for sanctions against Harbert in either the district court or in this Court. While we can raise and consider the issue of sanctions on our own, after giving the parties notice and an opportunity to be heard, the lack of interest in sanctions shown by the party to whom any monetary sanctions would be paid is a factor to consider.

Third, and most importantly, when Harbert took its arbitration loss into the district court and then pursued this appeal, it did not have the benefit of the notice and warning this opinion provides. The notice it provides, hopefully to even the least astute reader, is that this Court is exasperated by those who attempt to salvage arbitration losses through litigation that has no sound basis in the law applicable to arbitration awards. The warning this opinion provides is that in order to further the purposes of the FAA and to protect arbitration as a remedy we are ready, willing, and able to consider imposing sanctions in appropriate cases. While Harbert and its counsel did not have the benefit of this notice and warning, those who pursue similar litigation positions in the future will. AFFIRMED.

Case Questions

1. Why do you think that such strong language was used in this case by the court?
2. What does *vacatur* mean in the context of arbitration?
3. What can be learned from this decision related to a contract drafter's perspective?

Exercise

Using all that you know now, review the following simple personal appearance contract for a triathlete. Using this model, create another simple appearance contract between you and the celebrity of your choice for a backyard party!

PERSONAL APPEARANCE CONTRACT

AGREEMENT made this the _____ day of _________________200 _____, by and between Triathlete (hereinafter referred to as "Triathlete"), and _____________________________ (referred to as "Club").

IN CONSIDERATION of the mutual promises herein contained, and for other good valuable consideration, the parties hereto agree as follows:

1. Material Terms and Conditions. The Club hereby engages the Triathlete to perform the terms and conditions herein set forth including those that may be contained in an Addendum attached, which is hereby made part of the contract. Material Terms include:

A. PLACE (S) OF APPEARANCE: ______________________________

B. DATE (S) OF APPEARANCE: ______________________________

C. NUMBER OF APPEARANCES: ______________________________

D. STARTING TIME OF APPEARANCE (S): ______________________________

E. LENGTH OF EACH APPEARANCE/INTERMISSION: ______________________________

F. FULL (i.e., grand total) PRICE AGREED UPON: ______________________________

2. Deposit. A deposit of $___________________ shall be paid by Club to "Triathlete c/o Triathlete's Agent" and mailed to ___________________, Mount Pleasant, Michigan, 48858, upon signing of the contract by the Club. Thereafter, $ ______________________ shall be mailed or hand delivered to Triathlete prior to the engagement. All payments shall be paid in the form of cash, check, or money order.

3. Conditions Precedent. This agreement shall not be effective until signed by both parties and until all deposits are received. Additional, the **CLUB SHALL PROVIDE AT ITS SOLE EXPENSE THE FOLLOWING FOR TRIATHLETE:**

(Details expressed next to each item or attached to this Agreement)

a. Transportation: ____

b. Airline Tickets: ____

c. Hotel or Other Accommodations: ______________________________

Such conditions precedent shall be communicated to Triathlete or his/her agent prior to travel and shall include all tickets and an outline of the logistics plan.

4. Club's Own Expenses. Club agrees to furnish at its own expense on the date and at the time of each Appearance herein all that is reasonable and necessary for the proper presentation of each appearance, including, but not limited to, a suitable gym, theater, hall, or auditorium, and with a public address system or acoustics in good working condition. Club, at its own expense, will obtain all necessary licenses, permits and other permissions for such engagement and shall solely pay any taxes, if required.

5. Personal Services. It is expressly understood and agreed that Triathlete's Agent is acting hereunder solely in the capacity of agent of Triathlete, Triathlete's Agent is not a party to this personal services contract and shall not be liable or responsible in any way for the omissions of Triathlete, nor for any failure by Triathlete to adequately perform or comply with any term or condition hereof.

6. Creativity. Triathlete shall have the sole and exclusive control over the production, presentation, and appearance of the entertainment unit in connection with each appearance hereunder, including the sole right to designate and change any other performing personnel if at all.

7. Promotion. Club agrees to use his best efforts to promote and advertise this appearance and is solely responsible for such costs. Additionally, Triathlete agrees that Club may use Triathlete name, pictures, photographs, and other likeness in connection with advertising and publicizing the Appearances (s), but use shall not be used without prior approval of Triathlete. Club's right to use Triathlete's name ends upon the performance of this agreement or the termination of this agreement.

8. Recording. No portion of any Appearance hereunder may be recorded, filmed taped, or reproduced in any form whatsoever unless Triathlete's prior written consent is obtained. No interviews will be arranged without Triathlete's prior approval.

9. Force Majeure. Triathlete's obligations hereunder are subject to detention or prevention by sickness, inability to perform, accident, failure or delay of means of transportation, acts of God, riots, strikes, labor difficulties, epidemics, any act of any public authority or any other cause, similar or dissimilar, beyond Triathlete's control. In the event of illness, strike, act of God, governmental regulation of other force major occurrence, Triathlete is unable or is prevented from performing the appearance any part thereof, Club shall be reimbursed for any deposit previously received in toto, sent by mail within a reasonable amount of time of such inability to perform.

10. Cancellation by Triathlete. Club agrees that Triathlete may cancel the Appearance hereunder for any reason without liability by giving the Club written notice thereof at least two weeks, or fourteen days prior to the commencement date of the appearance. Club shall be fully reimbursed for any deposit previously received, sent by mail within a reasonable amount of time of such cancellation.

11. Cancellation by Club. In the event Club fails to make promptly, at the times provided herein, any payment due Triathlete hereunder, or cancels or postpones any appearance hereunder for any reason, Club shall be deemed to have substantially and materially breached this agreement, relieving Triathlete, of all obligations hereunder. In the event of any material breach, termination or cancellation by Club, all deposits in Triathlete's possession shall be retained by Triathlete for Triathlete's won account and benefit. Each of the terms and conditions hereof is of the essence of this agreement and necessary for Triathlete's full appearance hereunder.

12. Notices. All notices required hereunder shall be given in writing at the addresses set forth above. This agreement may not be changed, modified or assigned. This agreement shall be constructed in accordance with the laws of this State of Michigan. Any claims arising out of this agreement must first be submitted to mediation. If no agreement can be reached, then all litigation must take place in the state of Triathlete's residence. Nothing contained in this agreement shall be construed to constitute the parties as a partnership or joint venture, and Triathlete shall not be liable in whole of in part of any obligation that may be incurred by Club in carrying out any of the provisions hereof, or otherwise.

13. Execution. The person executing this agreement on Club's behalf hereby warrants his/her authority to do so, and such person hereby personally assumes liability for Club's obligations hereunder.

IN WITNESS WHEREOF, the parties agree that this is the sole and exclusive representation of the agreement between the parties and no prior oral or written agreement shall be valid or admissible to contradict the terms of this agreement.

______________________	______________________
Club	Triathlete
______________________	______________________
Mailing Address	Mailing Address
______________________	______________________
Date	Date

ADDENDUM OF ADDITIONAL TERMS TO PERSONAL APPEARANCE AGREEMENT

The following terms and conditions serve as a legally binding addendum to this Agreement:

CLINIC THEME: SWIM, BIKE, RUN

____

____

____

____

______________________	______________________
Club	Triathlete
______________________	______________________
Date	Date

References

Adams, K.A., A MANUAL OF STYLE FOR CONTRACT DRAFTING (American Bar Ass'n, 2004).

Browder, D., *Liquidated Damages in Montana*, 67 Mont. L. Rev. 361 (2006).

Burnham, S.J., DRAFTING CONTRACTS (The Michie Co., 1987).

Fox, C.M., WORKING WITH CONTRACTS: WHAT LAW SCHOOL DOESN'T TEACH YOU (PLI Press, 2002).

Haggard, T.R., CONTRACT LAW FROM A DRAFTING PERSPECTIVE-AN INTRODUCTION TO CONTRACT DRAFTING FOR LAW STUDENTS (West Group, 2003).

Lewis, C.C., The *Contract Drafting Process: Integrating Contract Drafting in a Simulated Law Practice*, 11 Clinical L.Rev. 241 (2005).

Lloyd, R.M., *Making Contracts Relevant: Thirteen Lessons for the First-Year Contracts Course*, 36 Ariz. St. L.J. 257 (2004).

Tollen, D. W., *Three Lessons About Entertainment & Sports Technology Contracting*, 24 Ent. & Sports Law. 4, 6–7 (2007).

GLOSSARY

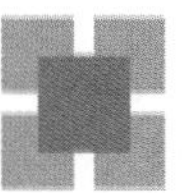

Acceptance An element of a contract in which the offeree expresses the intent to be bound by the offeror's offer. When involving the sale of goods, it occurs when the buyer (or lessee) signifies by words or conduct that the goods that were delivered either conform to the contract or are not rejected even though there is a nonconforming delivery.

Access contract An agreement that allows a user to access a private online database, usually for a fee.

Accord and satisfaction A way to describe the settling of a dispute—often contract related—in which a debtor and creditor or offeror and offeree agree to different terms than what was formerly agreed upon in the original agreement.

Account party One of the parties to a letter of credit. Usually the customer of the bank (known as the issuer) who is lending the money to a third party (the beneficiary).

Adequate assurance of performance Phrase used to describe when a party to a contract demands in writing that the contract will not be breached. Usually occurs when one party has a legitimate cause for concern that the other party will not perform as agreed.

Adhesion Term used to describe when a contract is offered on a "take-it-or-leave-it" basis. Often described as an unconscionable contract, it is used as a defense when a party claims that that really was no meeting of the minds since they had no real bargained-for exchange.

ADR clause Clause found in modern contracts in which the parties agree that if there is a dispute they will resort to an alternative form of dispute resolution such as arbitration or mediation rather than litigation.

Advertisements Technically an invitation to negotiate and not an offer in contract law unless specific or to a particularly described customer.

Agreements to agree Phrase often used in a preliminary negotiation of a contract which has no legal effect under contract law principles.

Airbill A bill of lading in which goods are being delivered via airplane rather than train, ship, or truck.

Ambiguity Term used to describe when a contract word or term is vague and might have to be interpreted by a court at a late date.

American Law Institute Founded in 1923, this private organization is made up of lawyers, judges and legal scholars who unite to make the law better or more consistent. Participated in the drafting and amended versions of the Uniform Commercial Code.

Anticipatory repudiation When a party to a contract asserts that they will not perform as agreed upon.

Antitrust Category of law in which monopolistic behavior is found to be illegal and which has unreasonable restraints of trade.

Article 2 Major article of the UCC which governs the sale of goods. Article 2A governs the lease of goods.

Assignee The party to whom a contract right has been transferred or assigned.

Assignment When contractual rights are transferred to another.

Assignor The party who transfers some legal or contractual right.

AS IS Disclaimer conspicuously found on goods in which the seller is disclaiming some sort of state of quality or characteristics of the goods.

Attribution The term used in electronic business transactions referring to the procedures that may be used to ensure that the person sending an electronic record is the same person whose e-signature accompanies the record. This is often the user name/password that is used to access a Web site.

AUCC Acronym for the Amended (i.e. revised) Uniform Commercial Code (2003).

Auction The formal process of selling goods in which bidders compete for the right to own the goods based upon their offers. There are various types of auctions, including those with reserve, without reserve, silent auctions, and Dutch auctions.

Automatic stay Term used in bankruptcy law in which the trustee in bankruptcy tells all creditors to stay away from the debtor during the process of settling a bankruptcy estate.

Bailee One who receives possession of a good and is responsible for it though they do not obtain title to it.

Bailment The transfer of goods to a bailee—without transferring title or deed—and with the expectation that the goods will be returned to the bailor.

Bailor One who transfers possession of a good—but not title—to a bailee.

Bankruptcy Federal law designed to give debtors a fresh start under a formal legal process.

BAPCPA The most recent federal modification to the Bankruptcy Code. Effective in 2005, the Bankruptcy Abuse Prevention and Consumer Protection Act of 2005 makes it more difficult for consumers to file for bankruptcy protection when it is apparent that some measure of debts can be repaid to creditors.

Bargained-for exchange An exchange between parties (whether oral or written) that ultimately leads to an enforceable agreement.

Beneficiary Sometimes referred to as a third-party beneficiary, it is a nonparty to a contract who either was intended to benefit from the agreement (i.e., an intended beneficiary) or merely benefited incidentally to the arrangement (an incidental beneficiary).

Benefit of the bargain Phrase used to describe whether a party to a contract actually received what they had bargained for in a contract.

Bilateral contract When a promise is made by one party to a contract to another for a return promise. An exchange of promises.

Bill of lading A document involving the sale of goods which displays the contents of the delivery during a shipment. Sometimes referred to as an airbill or even warehouse receipt. It is not a title to the goods themselves.

Black-letter law Term used to describe common law contracts. It is a way to describe the centuries-old process of judicial decisions that have helped to shape contract law as one of the most consistent and predictable areas of the law.

Boilerplate When a contract is on a preprinted form which is often produced in mass quantities.

Breach When a party does not live up to their original promise or obligation in a contract.

CIF or C&F (cost, insurance, freight) Way to describe who is financially responsible for the cost of insurance or freight during a shipment contract.

COD "Cash on delivery." It means that a buyer must pay for goods when they are delivered, usually in cash. The buyer has no right to inspect the goods prior to paying for them.

Cancel at anytime Clause in a contract that can create problems for courts because it allows the buyer or seller to terminate a contract for any reason. Issues might remain, however, in poorly drafted contracts as to whether a party should receive some compensation for the efforts under *quantum meruit* or no compensation at all.

Capacity The ability to enter into a contract from a legal point of view.

Carrier One who delivers goods from the seller to the buyer. It is sometimes referred to as a shipper.

Caveat emptor Latin for "let the buyer beware."

Caveat vendor Latin for "let the seller beware."

Charitable subscription An enforceable promise or pledge made to a charity, religious group, or other private organization.

CISG The United Nations Convention on Contracts for the International Sale of Goods. Acronym for the international version of the Uniform Commercial Code.

Click-on agreement An online contract in which the user must click on I AGREE or I DECLINE before proceeding on the Web site or with the software.

Collective bargaining agreement Often abbreviated as CBA, it represents to contract between management and labor unions in a wide variety of contexts.

Commercial impracticability Nonperformance of a contract is temporarily excused for an extreme or unexpected condition or occurrence such as a weather issue which delays the shipment of goods.

Common law Judge-made law. Sometimes referred to as precedent.

Compensatory damages Damages sought to compensate the plaintiff for out-of-pocket costs when a breach of contract has occurred.

Condition A provision in a contract that provides that if a certain event occurs, then the parties may exercise, suspend, or terminate their rights in some way.

Condition concurrent The simultaneous performance of duties by the parties of a contract.

Condition precedent A condition in a contract that must be met before another party's obligation arises.

Condition subsequent A condition in a contract that if it occurs, would then discharge or excuse another party's obligation to perform.

Conforming goods Goods that are delivered and conform to the buyer's order.

Consequential damages Foreseeable damages that naturally arise as a result of a breach of contract.

Consideration The price of a promise. It is something that has legal value and is given in exchange for a return promise.

Consignee An agent in a consignment relationship or the one to whom goods are delivered to be sold.

Consignment An arrangement in which a consignor delivers goods to an agent (the consignee) to find a buyer for a sale. The consignee then receives a fee or commission for the sale.

Consignor The seller in a consignment relationship or the one who delivers goods to a consignee (agent) to be sold to a buyer.

Conspicuous Term in various areas of contract law—including warranties—in which statements must be clearly bold, visible, and in some cases of certain size font.

Contra proferentem Latin expression which means that if an ambiguity is created in a contract, the words will be construed against the drafter if necessary.

Contract A legally binding agreement between two or more parties.

Counteroffer In the process of forming a contract, a response by the offeree who modifies a term of the offeror and counters in a form of role reversal. The offeree now becomes the offeror and the original offeror becomes the offeree and so on.

Cover When a buyer seeks to buy or lease substitute goods due to the seller's failure to provide the goods properly, in accordance with the terms of the agreement or in a timely fashion.

Creditors Those who are owed money or other things of legal value by debtors.

Cure When the seller has the right or opportunity to repair or replace a defective good or shipment of goods.

Cybernotary A legally recognized certification authority similar to a notary public but in cyberspace.

Damages Monetary compensation for a breach of a contract. When involving the sale of goods, it represents the difference between the contract price and the market price (plus incidentals in some cases).

Debtor One who owes a debt to the creditor.

Defects A way to describe a nonconforming good.

Defense A means of avoiding a contractual responsibility. The three major contract defenses are fraud, duress, and mutual mistake.

De Havilland law Entertainment industry personal services law in California which mandates that a studio may not "own" an individual's rights for more than seven years.

Delegation When a party to a contract transfers responsibility (i.e., duties) to another but is still legally responsible for any nonperformance as opposed to an outright assignment.

Delegator One who remains ultimately responsible for the transfer of a responsibility to a delegee. A delegator might also be known as a delegor or delegant.

Delegee The person to whom a contractual duty is delegated.

Delivery The process of shipping goods from point A to point B.

Delivery ex-ship The process of unloading goods from one ship to another.

Destination contract A contract that requires that the seller deliver goods to either the buyer's place of business or to another specific geographic location as stipulated in the contract. Seller assumes the risk of loss until the goods reach that location.

Detrimental reliance Synonym for promissory estoppel. It means that one party relies on the promise of another—to their legal detriment—and is justified in doing so.

Disaffirm The act of rescinding a contract usually by a minor. However, the minor must still place the adult in at least the same or better position prior to entering into the agreement. Sometimes referred to as disaffirmance.

Discharge When the parties to a contract have fulfilled or terminated their obligations and the contract is complete. In bankruptcy law, when the trustee in bankruptcy relieves the debtor of a specific obligation.

Disclaimer Also known as a waiver, release, or exculpatory clause. A statement in a contract or in an offer which relieves a party from responsibility of some sort.

Duress A defense to a contract. A party claims that they had no real bargained-for exchange in that they were presented a contract that they could not refuse out of a threat or perceived threat.

Dutch auction An auction in which the auctioneer starts at a high number and works their way down to an acceptable offer by a bidder.

Duty of cooperation One of the major themes of contract law. Parties have a legal duty to work with each other and in good faith.

Electronic signature An electronic sound, symbol,or process (such as a PIN number) to verify that an individual is who they say they are.

Emancipated minor A person under the age of 18 who has been legally removed from the responsibility of their parents or guardian. They often, then, have the same rights as an adult even if they have not yet reached the age of the majority.

End-user Someone who has been granted the right to use software based upon a license.

Entire agreement clause Also known as a merger clause. It is a clause placed at the end of an agreement which states that any prior oral or written statements are null and void and that the written contract represents the full agreement between the parties.

E-SIGN Electronic Signatures in Global and National Commerce Act enacted in 2000 to promote commerce over the Internet. It essentially stands for the idea that a contract that is electronically signed may not be denied its legal effect. It is superseded by a state that enacts UETA.

Estimates Usually not considered offers under contract law principles but still must be made in good faith.

Exculpatory clause See also Disclaimer. It relieves a party from a legal obligation or responsibility.

Executed A completed contract, also known as a "fully executed" contract. In some industries it refers to the fact that both parties have actually only signed the contract.

Executory A contract that has yet to be completed or fully performed.

Existing goods Those goods that exist at the time of sale and can be identified.

Express contract An agreement that is expressed either orally or in writing.

Extended warranty A warranty that a consumer purchases from either the manufacturer or a third party (such as a retail store) which extends the length of time of the manufacturer's original warranty.

FAS (free alongside) A shipping delivery term which describes the transfer of risk of loss when one ship pulls up next to the other.

Firm offer An offer made by a merchant that is irrevocable for at least some period of time.

FOB (free on board) Expression that is associated with some geographic location at which point risk of loss transfers to the buyer.

FOB destination point An expression in a sales contract in which the seller is responsible for the risk of loss of goods up until the goods reach a particular destination.

FOB shipping point An expression in a sales contract in which the buyer is responsible for the risk of loss once the goods are loaded onto the carrier.

Formal (contract) A contract that requires some sort of special form, method, or procedure.

Forum selection clause A clause in a contract in which the parties agree to the actual state, county, or courthouse where all claims must be heard if there is subsequent litigation.

Fraud The intentional deception of fact or value by another. Also known as misrepresentation or intentional misrepresentation.

Freedom of contract Contract law principle which holds that parties may come to any legally binding agreement that suits their needs.

Frustration of purpose A contract law doctrine that excuses the performance of a party due to subsequent circumstances which may make the contract irrelevant or even impossible.

Full warranty An unlimited warranty for the repair or replacement of product defects during the warranty period. *See* Magnuson-Moss Warranty Act.

Fungible goods Goods such as oil, wheat, and wine and referenced by the Uniform Commercial Code since they could deteriorate over time.

Future goods Goods not yet in existence at the time of sale. Often referenced as crops which have yet to grow or unborn animals.

General damages Damages that naturally flow as a result of a tort or breach of contract.

Good faith One of the major themes of contract law. When dealing with the sale of goods, it means honesty in fact as to the particular conduct or transaction.

Goods Tangible, moveable things that can be identified at the time of a sale.

Guarantor One who promises to pay a debt if a party to the contract fails to do so. Also referred to as a surety.

Hazardous activity clause Popular clause in contracts—especially sports contracts—in which one of the parties to the agreement must refrain from indoor or outdoor activities that increase the likelihood of a personal injury.

Hybrid sale A sale of both goods and services.

Identification of goods The process under a sales contract specifying which goods actually fall under the contract itself and differentiate themselves from other goods.

Illusory promise A contract that fails to be a legally binding agreement since it lacks consideration. Sometimes referred to as a *nudum pactum* or "naked agreement."

Implied contract An agreement that has been inferred by a contract based upon the conduct of the parties rather than express statements.

Implied-in-fact An obligation that can be implied by a court based upon the particular circumstances between the parties themselves.

Implied-in-law Also known as a *quasi*-contract, an obligation imposed by a court to avoid injustice or to prevent unjust enrichment.

Implied warranty An unwritten promise or guarantee that accompanies the sale of a good.

Implied warranty of fitness for a particular purpose A particular warranty under the UCC which states that a seller will be responsible for supplying a buyer (or consumer) with goods that meet the particular needs of the buyer since the latter is relying on the seller's skill, expertise, and judgment at hand.

Implied warranty of merchantability A particular warranty under the UCC which implies that sold (or leased) goods are fit for the ordinary purposes for which they are to be used. In the event they are not fit, the seller has the right to repair or replace them.

Impossibility of performance The nonperformance of a contract obligation is excused or discharged based upon objective circumstances such as the law changes which makes the agreement illegal or if the subject matter of the contract is destroyed prior to delivery.

Impracticability of performance Temporary suspension or delay of a contract performance due to an unforeseen circumstance such as a weather delay.

Incidental beneficiary A third party to a contractual agreement who was not originally intended to benefit from a contract between two other parties and therefore cannot enforce the agreement if it fails to be executed by the parties.

Incorporation by reference A phrase in contract drafting which allows the parties to refer to a document outside the contract itself.

INCOTERMS Acronym for International Commercial Terms. First published in 1936, it represents the definitions for international trade terms by the International Chamber of Commerce (ICC) in France.

Informal (contract) An agreement that is legally binding even though there was no formal process of establishing it.

Installment contract A contract that requires or allows goods to be delivered in separate lots over time.

Insurable interest An expression that means that party may purchase insurance on goods or a transaction since the party has something to lose financially.

Integration clause Also known as a merger clause or entire agreement clause, it states that all prior oral or written statements are null and void and that the contract represents the full and entire agreement between the parties.

Intended beneficiary A third party to a contractual agreement who was intended to benefit from a contract between two other parties such as the beneficiary of a life insurance policy.

Issuer One of the parties to a letter of credit, usually the bank.

Legalese A term used to describe words used by lawyers when drafting contracts or other documents.

Legality One of the major elements of a contract which establishes that all contracts must be legal otherwise they are void.

Lemon laws A way to describe consumer protection laws—particularly with the sale of motor vehicles—which grant a consumer the right to a complete refund in the event that the goods need the same repair after three or four attempts at the same issue.

Letter of credit A written document in which a bank either promises to pay a third party in the event they do not pay, or a statement by the bank that a seller or buyer has certain assets on-hand and is "good" in terms of credit history.

Letter of intent Sometimes abbreviated LOI and often described as a Memorandum of Understanding, it is a curious phrase used in contract law which demonstrates that at least one of the parties is serious as to their intent of forming a legally binding agreement.

License The right to use another's intellectual property under a set of conditions.

Licensee The one who purchases or accepts the terms and conditions of use of the seller's intellectual property such as software.

Licensing The process of granting the right to use intellectual property (such as software) between a buyer (licensee) and seller (licensor).

Licensor One who grants another the right to use their intellectual property (such as software).

Lien A claim by a creditor on property for the payment of a debt or other obligation.

Lifetime warranty A warranty on the lifetime of a product. Can be problematic for courts or others if the warranty does not specify which "life" the warranty covers.

Limited warranty A warranty on a product by a seller or manufacturer for a specified period of time. Terms must be explained in clear language under the Magnuson-Moss Warranty Act.

Liquidated damages Agreed-upon damages, for example, when parties agree ahead of time what the "penalty" would be for a delay of delivery or completion of performance. Disfavored by many courts but usually enforceable nonetheless.

Liquidation The process of selling the assets of a business that is going out of business or one that has filed bankruptcy under Chapter 7 of the Bankruptcy Code.

Locus Sigilli Latin for "place of the seal." Often abbreviated L.S., it is still found in many real estate, banking, and insurance documents though it has no real effect in modern contract law. It was formerly used to represent where an individual's signature or shield was to be placed. Analogous to the shield or stamp of the modern notary public.

Lost profits Claims made by the nonbreaching party in a contractual relationship that but for the breach, the nonbreaching party would have earned these profits from subsequent sales. Must be proven with hard (as opposed to circumstantial) evidence.

Lucid interval Phrase used to describe when an otherwise incapacitated or mentally ill person actually knew and appreciated the fact that they were entering into a contractual obligation and therefore the agreement should (arguably) be enforced by a court since there was a "meeting of the minds."

Magnuson-Moss Warranty Act Federal law from 1975 which mandates that if a manufacturer wishes to disclaim the quality or performance capability of its goods then it must do so in a conspicuous way which is clear to the consumer.

Mailbox rule Rule that states that an acceptance of a contract is effective and thereby creates a legally binding contract once the acceptance is dispatched (i.e., dropped in the mailbox). Not as important today as it used to be and good contract drafters can avoid this rule altogether.

Malum in se Latin for "evil in itself." Contracts are *malum in se* (and therefore illegal) if they are morally wrong in any sense such as an agreement to commit murder.

Malum prohibitum Latin for a "prohibited evil." Contracts are *malum prohibitum* if a state or federal legislature proclaims that certain types of acts are unacceptable though not necessarily morally wrong. An example would be usury laws in which the state establishes that certain agreements are void if the rate of interest charged exceeds the maximum state limits.

Mass-market license A widely marketed electronic contract which is offered with boilerplate language for users to click on and is the same for all customers.

Material breach A substantial breach that occurs when a party renders performance considered to be inferior.

Merchant One who is considered to be regularly involved in the sale of goods and is held to a higher standard of care than nonmerchants.

Merger clause Also known as an entire agreement or integration clause, it is often found at the end of a contract and states that all prior oral or written statements are null and void and that this written agreement represents the entire relationship between the parties.

Minors Those who have not yet reached the age of the majority, usually 18 years old. Minors may enter into contracts but also hold a special privilege in that they can undo their agreements as long as they put the other party in no worse position they were in prior to the execution of the contract.

Misrepresentation *See* Fraud.

Mitigation of damages Legal principle that holds when there is a breach of contract (or even a tort) a party has a duty to make matters no worse than they already might be.

NCCUSL The National Conference of Commissioners on Uniform State Laws is responsible for drafting numerous model acts, including the UCC, for states to adopt so that there are more uniform laws throughout the United States. Compare ALI.

Necessaries Term used to describe food, clothing, and shelter.

Negligence The failure to act as a reasonable person. Usually associated with tort law.

Negligent misrepresentation Similar to fraud, it is when a seller knew (or should have known) about the nature, characteristic, or quality of a product when selling it but took no steps to ascertain the truth.

No-compete clauses Also known as covenants not to compete, these are clauses used in contracts which generally prevent a party or former employee from leaving the contractual relationship and competing with the previous party for goods or services. Generally disfavored by courts but will be enforced if reasonable in time, scope, and geography.

Nonconforming goods Goods that do not comply with an order.

Novation An agreement between the parties to a contract to discharge one or more of the obligations and thereby create a new contract.

Nudum pactum Latin for "naked agreement." Also known as an illusory promise or one that simply is unenforceable though it may sound good.

Objective theory of contracts Contract law principle that the intent of the parties is to be judged by the reasonable person standard and not the subjective standard of the parties themselves.

Offer The manifestation of the willingness to be bound to an agreement.

Offeree One who receives an offer.

Offeror One who makes an offer to an offeree.

Oral contracts Verbal agreements, that is, those not made in writing.

Output contract A special type of enforceable contract in which the buyers tells the seller that they will buy all the goods that the seller produces within reason.

Pacta sunt servanda Latin for "agreements must be served." It means that the goal of courts should be to enforce contracts and not to avoid them when possible.

Parol evidence rule Rule of evidence which says if a written agreement is complete and final, that any prior oral or written statements that contradict the terms of the agreement should not be admissible in evidence.

Partnering agreement An agreement between two or more parties online as to the terms of their contractual arrangement.

Past consideration Expression used to describe that obligations in the past cannot count for the consideration element of a current or future contract. Prior acts will not support the new agreement.

Perfect tender rule Common law contract principle which holds that when a seller delivers goods to a buyer the goods must mirror exactly what was ordered. However, this rule has been largely abolished by the UCC since there are so many exceptions to it and sellers have the right to "cure."

Personal services contract A nontransferable contract in which unique talents, abilities, or skills are contracted for thereby rendering a delegation or assignment null and void. Often occurs in sports, artistic, or entertainment related contracts.

Plain meaning rule Unless otherwise stated or defined in a contract, courts will interpret words and phrases in their ordinary meanings.

Pledge An enforceable promise made to a charitable organization such as a college or university or religious organization.

Preexisting duty rule Contract law principle that a promise lacks consideration if it is based upon a previous act or an already-existing obligation.

Preferential transfer A transfer of money or assets just prior to filing a bankruptcy petition that can be undone by the trustee as being unfair to the other creditors.

Preliminary negotiation A nonbinding exchange between parties which does not create a legally binding agreement.

Privity of contract Contract law principle which held that a consumer or purchaser of goods could only pursue remedies against a retailer—as opposed to a manufacturer, wholesaler, or distributor—since this is the only "person" that the buyer had privity of contract with. This principle is generally not accepted as a limitation of remedies for consumers today.

Promissory estoppel An equitable doctrine also known as detrimental reliance which prevents the withdrawal of an offeror's offer if it was reasonably foreseeable that the offeree would rely on the promise to their legal detriment.

Puffery Statements of opinion as part of the sales process. Also known as puffing language.

Punitive Damages Not available in breach of contract actions but available in tort law. Also known as exemplary damages, it is designed to punish the misconduct of the defendant or use them as an example for others not to follow.

Quantum meruit Latin for "as much as he (or she) deserved." In an implied contract situation, a court can calculate damages so that one party is not unjustly enriched by the goods or services of another. Often awarded as "reasonable" value of the goods or services provided using a fair market value analysis.

***Quasi*-contract** An implied contract to prevent unjust enrichment. Thus, a contract that is implied in law.

Ratification The imposition by the law after a minor turns the age of the majority which binds the minor to the agreement even though they held, as a minor, the right to void a contract prior to turning the age of the majority. When not dealing with minor, it is an after the fact acknowledgment by a party in which they agree to be bound by the terms of the contract or even though they did not originally grant permission to be bound.

Recipient One of who receives the delivery of goods from a shipper or carrier.

Rescission The act of canceling a contract either by one or more parties, assuming they have the legal right to do so. An action to undo a contract if there has been a material breach or of there was fraud, duress or mutual mistake.

Record The Amended UCC (AUCC) uses the term record rather than "writing" to reflect the age of modern commercial transactions electronically.

Reformation An equitable doctrine that permits the court to rewrite a contract for equitable purposes.

Rejection The outright denial of acceptance of an offeror's offer.

Release *See* Waiver.

Remedy The means or method for which a legal right is enforced.

Requirements contract Special type of contract in which a buyer tells a seller that they will buy all they need. There is a missing quantity element, but as long as it is in good faith it will still be enforced under contract law and the UCC. *See* Output contract.

Restitution The act of returning goods to the other party. It is an equitable remedy to restore a person to the position they were in had there been no contract at all or if there was no breach.

Revocation The withdrawal of an offer by the offeror before it is accepted by the offeree.

Reward offer A special type of offer that is usually made to the public at large and is enforced by courts as a matter of public policy. States differ on enforceability if one did not know of the existence of the reward offer in the first place.

Rider An addendum to a contract.

Risk of loss Principle under the UCC that establishes who is financially responsible if goods are damaged during transit.

Rules of construction Established contract law principles which assist in determining how to read a contract when there is a term missing or terms conflict with each other.

Sabbath laws Laws that prohibits certain activities usually on Sundays. Some states refer to these as blue laws. Often refers to the sale of alcoholic beverages or automobiles.

Sale Under the UCC, the passing of title from a seller to a buyer for a price.

Sale on approval A special type of sale in which the sale is not complete until the buyer accepts the goods after a trial basis of some sort.

Sale or return A special type of sale in which a buyer may actually return the goods to the seller if they are not sold or resold within a specific time frame. Usually buyers are then given credit of some sort with the seller.

Shipment contract A contract that requires the seller to ship the goods to the buyer via a carrier and the buyer assumes the risk of loss once the goods are loaded onto the carrier.

Shrink-wrap agreement When goods are shipped by a carrier, they often come with the contract terms wrapped in shrink-wrap on the outside of the box. The e-commerce analogy is a click-wrap or browse-wrap agreement.

Signature dynamics The signing of a contract or receipt of goods by using a stylus and signing on an electronic display.

Signature line The place on a contract where the parties sign their name.

Silent auction A type of auction in which either bids are made in writing on a piece of paper or electronically so that all the bidders can see each other's bids, or a way to describe an auction in which bids are "blind" in that they are dropped into a box or bin and the sale then goes to the highest bidder.

Special damages Contract damages that are unique to the special circumstance in an agreement between the parties and that flow naturally from the breach such as lost profits if they can be proven with reasonable certainty.

Specific performance A court order (injunction) requiring someone to perform. Not favored in personal services contracts, specific performance is an acceptable remedy if, for example, one party unjustifiably refuses to follow through with a promise to purchase real estate.

Statement of fact An affirmative statement of quality or characteristics which becomes part of the basis of the bargain of a contract. It is to be distinguished from a statement of opinion which is not enforceable.

Statement of intention Also known as an agreement to agree, it is an unenforceable statement made by an alleged party to a contract as to what they might (or might not) do.

Statement of opinion An unenforceable and nonbinding statement often made by seller's as part of the art of selling goods or services. Often referred to as puffing language.

Statute of frauds Principle that evolved from England which stands for the proposition that certain types of contracts must be in writing if a party seeks to enforce the agreement in court. It allows a court to dismiss a claim if the contract is not in writing in those specific instances.

Statute of limitations The amount of time one has to bring a lawsuit for breach of contract. A matter of state law but anywhere from three to five years in most cases from the date of the breach.

Substantially impair Phrase under the UCC in which a buyer may reject the entire contract if a series of installments of nonconforming goods substantially impairs the contract as a whole.

Surety Similar to a guarantor, one who promises to answer (i.e., "pay") for the debts of another in the event the party to a contract fails to pay.

Termination by operation of law Expression used to describe when a party to a contract is no longer obligated to perform, such as when a contract is discharged in bankruptcy.

Testimonium: Latin word which exemplifies the final statements made by the contract drafter.

Third party A person who may (or may not) be entitled to enforce obligations under a contract.

Title The legal right of ownership. Under the UCC, title is established by identification of the goods, risk of loss, and insurable interest.

Trustee The person in charge of a bankruptcy estate after the petitioner files for bankruptcy under federal law.

UCITA Uniform Computer Information Transaction Act which was only adopted by two states and was touted as being not friendly to consumers and purchasers of software.

UETA The Uniform Electronic Transactions Act (of 1999) adopted by almost all of the states and put forth by the NCCUSL.

Unclean hands doctrine Contract law doctrine which states that if you go to court for judicial relief that you must not be partially to blame for the breach.

Unconscionable Term used to describe a contract whose terms would "shock" the consciousness of a reasonably minded person. Often used to describe contracts of adhesion or when considering whether charged interest rates are excessive.

Undue influence Where one party to a contract takes advantage of another's mental, physical, or emotional weakness and uses that vulnerability to their contractual advantage in a way that conveys the lack of free will when entering into the contract.

Uniform Commercial Code (UCC) A model act governing the sale of goods and a host of other commercial situations adopted by all states—including Louisiana. Originally drafted in the 1950s to address interstate commerce issues and various inconsistent state laws.

Unilateral alteration Usually an unacceptable modification of a contract by one party.

Unilateral contract A promise for an act. Acceptance of an offer is made by performing what was expected, not by merely making the promise to perform (i.e., a bilateral contract).

Unjust enrichment Term used to describe that it would be unfair in that particular instance not to imply some sort of legal obligation on the part of a party who received a benefit conveyed by another.

Usury State laws that dictate that certain rates of interest are excessive and thereby render a contract invalid due to illegality.

Valid A term used to describe the vast majority of contracts. A legally binding agreement which has all the elements necessary for contract formation.

Void A contract is illegal or nonbinding from its inception due to one of various factors including, possibly, illegality.

Voidable A voidable contract is one that allows a party to a contract to undo the agreement (or a part of the agreement) upon the occurrence of a certain condition.

Void for vagueness An expression used by courts to describe when a contract term, paragraph, or the entire contract itself is invalid due to blatant ambiguity.

Waiver Also known as a release, disclaimer, or exculpatory clause. It is the express relinquishment of a legal right.

Warehouse receipt A form of bill of lading which states who was responsible for delivering and picking up goods that are stored in a warehouse.

Warranty The assurance by a seller or manufacturer that the goods meet certain standards of quality.

Warranty of title A statement by a seller that they indeed are the true owner of the goods. It is often implied in the sale of consumer goods.

Without reserve An auction that does not give the seller the right to refuse to sell to the highest bidder. Sometimes referred to an absolute auction.

With reserve An auction that gives the seller the right to refuse to sell to the highest bidder, especially if a minimum level of bid is not met.

INDEX

A

B

C

D

E

F

G

H

I

N

O

Q

R

S

T

U

V

W

Y

Z